P9-CLY-966

THE NATIONAL INSTITUTE OF
ECONOMIC AND SOCIAL RESEARCH

Economic and Social Studies
XXIX

THE DIFFUSION OF NEW INDUSTRIAL PROCESSES: AN INTERNATIONAL STUDY

The National Institute of Economic and Social Research is an independent, non-profitmaking body, founded in 1938. It has as its aim the promotion of realistic research, particularly in the field of economics. It conducts research by its own research staff and in cooperation with the universities and other academic bodies. The results of the work done under the Institute's auspices are published in several series, and a list of its publications up to the present time will be found at the end of this volume.

THE
DIFFUSION OF NEW
INDUSTRIAL PROCESSES

AN INTERNATIONAL STUDY

EDITED BY

L. NABSETH and G. F. RAY

CAMBRIDGE UNIVERSITY PRESS

Published by the Syndics of the Cambridge University Press
Bentley House, 200 Euston Road, London NW1 2DB
American Branch: 32 East 57th Street, New York, N.Y. 10022

Library of Congress Catalogue Card Number: 73–88309

ISBN: 0 521 20430 5

First published 1974

Printed in Great Britain at
The University Press
Aberdeen

To
the Memory of
ALFRED H. CONRAD

CONTENTS

vii

8   THE APPLICATION OF GIBBERELLIC ACID IN
    MALTING   215
    by G. F. Ray

    Gibberellic acid   215
    The malting industry   216
    Innovation and adoption   217
    The inquiry and its findings   221
       Legal regulations   221
       Information   222
       Profitability   224
       Investment   225
       The 'bandwagon' effect   225
       Management attitudes   226
       Size of firms   227
    Intra-firm diffusion   228
    Summary and conclusions   230

9   CONTINUOUS CASTING OF STEEL   232
    by W. Schenk

    Introduction   232
    The continuous casting of steel   232
    Historical development   234
       Austria   234
       France   235
       Italy   235
       Sweden   235
       United Kingdom   236

PREFACE

This book is the joint work of a number of research institutes in several countries.

The initiative for the inquiry came early in 1967 when the National Institute of Economic and Social Research, London, invited a number of other economic research institutes in Europe to participate in a joint study. The invitation was accepted by the IFO-Institut für Wirtschaftsforschung, Munich, the Istituto Nazionale per lo Studio della Congiuntura, Rome, the Industriens Utredningsinstitut, Stockholm, the Österreichisches Institut für Wirtschaftsforschung, Vienna, and the Bureau d'Information et de Prévisions Economiques, Paris. The French institute, after taking an active part in the first stage of the inquiry, was unable to continue in the second. On the other hand, the National Bureau of Economic Research, New York, joined the group for the second stage in 1969. From the inception of the project to completion of the manuscript of the present volume took six years altogether, of which two were taken by the first stage and four by the second; for most of this time work was going on in six or seven countries.

The group wishes to make a number of acknowledgements. First, thanks are due to those who financed the project. A grant from the Ford Foundation covered the costs of the meetings of the group as well as providing a contribution to national costs. The remainder of the national costs was covered by grants from HM Treasury in Britain, and from the Bank of Sweden Tercentenary Fund and the Norrland Foundation in Sweden; their generous assistance is gratefully acknowledged. In the other countries the national expenses were met from the general funds of the institutes concerned.

Secondly, we are most grateful to Mr G. D. N. Worswick who took the Chair at our meetings. With the assistance of Mr G. F. Ray who acted as Secretary, he alternately encouraged and exhorted us to sort out difficulties, to resolve points of difference and to produce drafts on schedule, or at any rate not too far behind. The appearance of this book owes much to his patience and persistence. In addition, the authors of the individual chapters have benefited greatly from his wisdom and experience.

The group is also grateful to Mrs K. Jones, the Secretary of the National Institute of Economic and Social Research for administering the Ford Foundation grant so efficiently that she was able to finance an extra – and very necessary – final meeting. Mrs Jones has also been responsible for arranging the publication of this book. Miss G. I. Little of the National Institute prepared the text for the printer and Miss F. Ware compiled the index.

In the course of the group's work, a large number of companies, trade associations, and individual experts were consulted; without their active cooperation the material on which our report is largely based could never have been collected. Our sincere gratitude is due to them.

Finally, we wish to acknowledge the work of all the researchers and other staff members of the participating institutes who in one way or another contributed, in addition to those who have actually signed particular chapters of this book.

December 1972   LARS NABSETH
                                             Industriens Utredningsinstitut,
                                             Stockholm

                                             GEORGE F. RAY
                                             National Institute of
                                             Economic and Social Research,
                                             London

PARTICIPATING INSTITUTES AND THEIR ABBREVIATIONS

Bureau d'Information et de Prévisions Économiques, Paris	BIPE[1]
IFO-Institut für Wirtschaftsforschung, Munich	IFO
Istituto Nazionale per lo Studio della Congiuntura, Rome	ISCO
Industriens Utredningsinstitut, Stockholm	IUI
National Bureau of Economic Research, Inc., New York	NBER[2]
National Institute of Economic and Social Research, London	NIESR
Österreichisches Institut für Wirtschaftsforschung, Vienna	OIW

[1] Participated for the first two years (1967–9) only.
[2] Joined the group only in 1969.

SYMBOLS USED IN THE TABLES

— = nil or negligible
.. = not available
n.a. = not applicable

INTRODUCTION

By G. F. Ray, NIESR

THE ADVANCE OF TECHNOLOGY

It has become commonplace to talk of the advance of technology. Jet aircraft, nuclear power, colour television and the ballpoint pen have become familiar features of life. None of them was heard of 30 years ago. Less familiar but equally important are the radical changes in industrial processes and methods of production; these too have developed out of all recognition.

The interest of economists in the advance of technology stems from the study of the process of economic growth. Many of the best known attempts to analyse economic growth in general terms have been made in the United States. Schmookler suggested that the growth of the national product of the United States in the 70-year period ending in 1938 was due in equal parts to the growth of physical resources and to the growth of efficiency in using these resources – especially the growth of labour productivity.[1] Abramovitz and Kuznets supported this view,[2] which found its greatest champions in Solow and Kendrick.[3] According to them, from about 1900 to 1920 technical progress (as Solow called it) or productivity advance (Kendrick's expression) contributed 1 per cent a year to the rise in United States national output, and between 1920 and 1950 this contribution increased to 2 per cent a year. Solow added that no more than an eighth of the growth of output per head could be attributed to increased capital input, and the remaining seven-eighths should be ascribed to technical progress. This conclusion corresponded with the findings of Abramovitz and was independently supported by Hogan, according to whom some 90 per cent of the growth of productivity in the non-farming sector of the United States was due to technical change.[4] The most recent and perhaps the most ambitious

[1] J. Schmookler, 'The changing efficiency of the American economy, 1869–1938', *Review of Economics and Statistics*, vol. 34, August 1952, pp. 214–31.

[2] M. Abramovitz, 'Resources and output trends in the United States since 1870', *American Economic Association Papers and Proceedings*, vol. 46, May 1956, pp. 5–23; S. Kuznets, *National Product since 1869*, New York, NBER, 1946.

[3] R. M. Solow, 'Technical change and the aggregate production function', *Review of Economics and Statistics*, vol. 39, August 1957, pp. 312–20; J. W. Kendrick, *Productivity Trends in the United States*, Princeton (NJ), University Press, 1961.

[4] W. P. Hogan, 'Technical progress and production functions', *Review of Economics and Statistics*, vol. 40, November 1958, pp. 407–11.

attempt at calculations of this kind was made by Denison, who allocated the overall growth of the national income of the United States and of a large number of other industrial countries to a number of causes ranging from the different age–sex structure of the population, education and the age of capital to economies of scale.[1]

Empirical studies have tried to test the hypothesis that technological change has accelerated since the war,[2] to measure its direct and indirect effects through the creation of external economies,[3] to specify whether it is capital-saving, labour-saving, or neutral,[4] and to evaluate its impact on possible factor shifts.[5] These attempts have not been restricted to the United States. For example, Oppenländer concluded that some 60 per cent of the growth of the German economy during the 20 years following World War II was probably due to technological advance.[6]

These estimates have mostly been based on one of several methods of estimating production functions. Contributions to economic growth by quantifiable factors – labour and capital – were estimated, and the residual between actual growth and the amount which could be imputed to these factors was treated as the joint contribution of technological progress, improved management methods and all other unquantifiable factors. Several scholars were, however, not satisfied with this 'residual' approach for a variety of reasons. Some, such as Jorgenson and Griliches, questioned the very existence of the residual, arguing that it virtually disappeared if quantities of input were measured correctly.[7] Others did not question the existence of the residual, but argued that it merely indicated the extent of ignorance,[8] or else suggested that besides technological change there were a host of other factors not easily

[1] E. F. Denison assisted by J. P. Poullier, *Why Growth Rates Differ: postwar experience in nine Western countries*, Washington (DC), The Brookings Institution, 1967.

[2] J. W. Kendrick and R. Sato, 'Factor prices, productivity and growth', *American Economic Review*, vol. 53, December 1963, pp. 974–1003; R. Nelson, 'Aggregate production functions and medium-range growth projections', *American Economic Review*, vol. 54, September 1964, pp. 575–606.

[3] E. F. Denison, *The Sources of Economic Growth in the United States and the Alternatives before us*, New York, Committee for Economic Development, 1962.

[4] Solow, 'Technical change and the aggregate production function'; B. F. Massell, 'Investment, innovation and growth', *Econometrica*, vol. 30, April 1962, pp. 239–52; W. E. G. Salter, *Productivity and Technical Change*, Cambridge University Press, 1960.

[5] M. J. Beckmann and R. Sato, 'Aggregate production functions and types of technical progress: a statistical analysis', *American Economic Review*, vol. 59, March 1969, pp. 88–101; B. F. Massell, 'A disaggregated view of technological change', *Journal of Political Economy*, vol. 69, December 1961, pp. 547–57.

[6] K. H. Oppenländer, 'Investitionen und technischer Fortschritt', paper read to the 9th CIRET Conference in Madrid, 1969.

[7] D. W. Jorgenson and Z. Griliches, 'The explanation of productivity change', *Review of Economic Studies*, vol. 34, July 1967, pp. 249–83.

[8] For example, T. Balogh and P. Streeten, 'The coefficient of ignorance', *Bulletin of the Oxford University Institute of Economics and Statistics*, vol. 25, May 1963, pp. 99–107.

quantifiable, such as learning by doing, superior skills acquired by practice, and differences in the technical 'dynamism' of managements, which could equally well account for a growth of output per unit of input.[1]

Whether quantifiable or not, there cannot be any doubt that advance in scientific knowledge (know-why) and progress in its technological application (know-how) have added very appreciably to economic performance. However, even allowing a considerable role in economic growth to technological advance, the pace of this progress is itself influenced by the many other factors which affect national performance in every country, ranging from differences in the educational system to differences in taxation. While such differences might lend themselves to sociological, anthropological or psychological analyses, they do not easily respond to econometric investigation.

There are also studies, though not so many, which have investigated the problem on another level. They attempt a more direct analysis of the actual process of technological advance, and are concerned not simply with trying to quantify its contribution to economic growth, but with understanding more about the process itself. The difficulty is that these 'micro' studies have to be based on company data, which are always difficult to come by, with the further impediment that any results must usually be published in such a way that information about individual companies is not disclosed. Indeed, this dual difficulty with the data is probably the main reason why such reports and monographs are scarce compared with the more theoretical 'macro' studies. Those studies which do exist, attempt – amongst other things – to relate the inter-firm rate of diffusion of a particular innovation to its profitability defined in terms of opportunity cost,[2] and to specific economic or managerial variables, such as size of firm, market structure, or the age of managers.[3] Perhaps Schumpeter's hypothesis of a positive correlation between a firm's size and technological leadership has been the object of the most intensive investigation; the policy implications of a conclusion on this point are obvious.[4]

[1] N. Kaldor, *Essays on Economic Stability and Growth*, London, Duckworth, 1960; also his paper written jointly with J. A. Mirrlees, 'A new model of economic growth', *Review of Economic Studies*, vol. 29, June 1962, pp. 174–92.

[2] Z. Griliches, 'Hybrid corn: an exploration in the economics of technological change', *Econometrica*, vol. 25, October 1957, pp. 501–22.

[3] E. Mansfield, *Industrial Research and Technological Innovation – an econometric analysis*, New York, Cowles Foundation, 1967; also, by the same author, *The Economics of Technological Change*, New York, Norton, 1968.

[4] Ibid., see also OECD, *Gaps in Technology. General Report*, Paris, 1968. A comprehensive survey of the literature on technical progress is given in C. Kennedy and A. P. Thirlwall, 'Technical progress: a survey', *Economic Journal*, vol. 82, March 1972, pp. 11–72.

DIFFUSION AND TECHNOLOGICAL PROGRESS

The diffusion of a new process or product is one stage in the complex sequence of technological change. Basically, there are three main phases. First, there is research and development, leading to the new idea or invention, usually in the form of a technically feasible prototype. Secondly, the invention is developed and modified so as to make it commercially superior in certain respects, culminating in the first application or innovation – that is an economically feasible prototype. Thirdly, the recognition of the innovation as a more efficient technology results in its further application within the same firm and its introduction to other firms in the industry – that is its diffusion.

Even after innovation has taken place and the diffusion process has started, the technique is still liable to be modified further, often as a result of experience gained in actual commercial operation. These further modifications are aimed at reducing or eliminating faults or disadvantages arising in application, widening the scope of production for which the process is economically feasible, and increasing further the relative advantages of the new process over the technique it superseded. Thus, the successive stages often overlap and the lines of demarcation between them are blurred. Not infrequently further development amounts to a new invention, so that the sequence becomes invention, innovation, invention, innovation.[1]

Taking into account this variation on the three phases, the speed of technological advance in the economy can be said to be determined in a simplified way by:

(a) the frequency with which inventions occur;

(b) the rapidity with which they are brought to fruition in the form of innovation with commercial superiority established;

(c) the amount of activity involved in successfully modifying new techniques after innovation;

(d) the speed at which diffusion of new techniques takes place.

These four factors have been set out in order of increasing importance, the last being the most decisive. Furthermore, they not only determine the speed of technological progress, but also, largely, the rate of economic growth, provided we hold, as do most of the studies mentioned

---

[1] In our case studies there are many examples of this sequence, for example the development from the more primitive to the present form of continuous casting, the perfection of the LD basic oxygen process which enabled it to make steel from pig iron of high phosphorous content, the widening product range of float glass, etc.

earlier, that the pace of technological advance is the largest single contributor to economic growth.[1]

That economic growth would be accelerated by technological progress, which itself would be stimulated by a faster flow of innovations, seems too obvious to warrant discussion.[2] It might seem equally obvious that economic growth will also be faster the more rapid the diffusion of innovations. But here it is necessary to tread a little more warily. If we postulate that new technical knowledge (in the form of inventions) comes like manna from heaven at a uniform rate, and is immediately available in all countries, then the fact that diffusion is faster in one country than another will not affect its long-run *rate* of growth; all that will happen is that the country with faster diffusion will reach any given *level* of output at an earlier date. This apparently surprising result applies only to 'steady state' conditions. If there is a temporary speeding up of the flow of inventions, or if the productivity-raising effect of inventions becomes greater, then, during a transitional period, the country with the more rapid diffusion will also grow at a faster rate, and will continue to do so until the country with the slower diffusion has completed the process of absorbing the new batch of innovations. If there were to be permanent acceleration in the flow of inventions (or in the extent of productivity increase from individual inventions) then the growth *rate* would be permanently higher in the country with more rapid diffusion.[3]

If, in a country, the rate of diffusion had been rather slow for some time, and it then speeded up in all or most industries, that country could for a while grow faster than others where there had been no such change. The scope for such transitional increases in the growth rate, or for the kind mentioned earlier where there is a temporary acceleration in the flow of inventions, depends on how long it takes in the various countries to absorb any new innovation completely. One of the most striking observations in the studies reported here is that quite frequently

[1] There is another difference between diffusion and the first three, or at least the first two, factors above: whereas the latter may take place, at least to some extent, outside the company or the country and can be taken over from 'abroad', diffusion must be indigenous.

[2] It might be said that there is the possibility of 'technological' unemployment, but whether or not genuine technological unemployment occurred in the days of laissez faire, it can hardly exist for more than short periods at most in advanced countries in which the government plays a positive role in the management of demand.

[3] This speculation is of course highly simplified. It assumes that all other things remain equal, which they seldom do. It does not take into account international specialisation, which may promote or hamper the application of innovations (or, vice versa, the latter may influence specialisation). In some cases innovations may be applied too early, that is diffusion may be too rapid, so that overcoming the teething troubles may inhibit overall economic growth. Again, in other cases concentration on a few selected innovations in areas where a country has some particular advantage might yield better results in terms of overall economic growth than the diffusion of a larger number of innovations in a wider area.

the diffusion process may last for many decades; there is thus plenty of scope in practice for temporarily falling behind or catching up in the rate of growth of industrial output per head. Moreover, we have assumed so far that all countries have, and continue to maintain, all the industries in which inventions occur, but this is to take no account of competition in international trade. An industry which fails to adopt techniques found successful elsewhere may find itself losing export markets and, increasingly, its home market, which is penetrated by the products of overseas firms using the new methods.

When we designed the original project, we intended to study as much the effects of different rates of diffusion as their causes, but it is rarely possible to carry out empirical research exactly as originally planned, and in the event we have devoted much more attention to the factors explaining different rates of diffusion than to the study of the impact of those different rates upon economic performance. But we came across little evidence to make us question the view that faster diffusion is associated with better economic performance measured by such indicators as the growth of output.

NEW TECHNOLOGY AND THE INDIVIDUAL FIRM

Diffusion of a new technique takes place as individual firms introduce it, as a rule by installing equipment embodying it. However, the point at which this equipment is installed is usually the ultimate, or penultimate, stage of a long process of response to the technique. The first stage is when the first information about the technique enters the firm (chart 1.1). Then, more and more facts come in about the advantages and limitations of the technique from various sources – suppliers, competitors, trade and research associations, or indeed the company's own research and development work. Soon the awareness stage is reached; information about the technique is plentiful, although not always consistent. After a certain time, the accumulated information leads to a more systematic evaluation, especially if the firm is in any case planning a re-equipment programme. A study is set in train to assess the value of the new technique, allowing for the firm's special circumstances; this is the stage of consideration. If the decision is to install the technique, adoption takes place, and then the new technique comes into actual operation. Adoptions at micro-level add up to diffusion at macro-level.

Information about a technique spreads through various channels and not all firms hear about it simultaneously. In the course of our inquiry we paid special attention in some cases to the diffusion of information, the best documented example being that of special presses in paper-making (chapter 4).[1]

The time between information (awareness) and consideration may also vary with the circumstances of the individual company – its interest

Chart 1.1. *The internal process of diffusion within a firm*

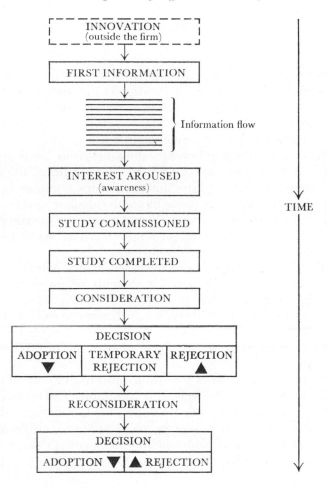

in innovation in general and its operating conditions in particular. This stage is essentially influenced by the same factors as the decision for or against the adoption of the new technique. The more alert the management, the shorter the time taken in consideration.

[1] One can, in fact, speak of the diffusion of information (cf. chapter 4) as well as of the diffusion of adoption; but when the word 'diffusion' appears on its own in this study, it always means diffusion of adoption.

The time between consideration and adoption of any particular technique is the time required for planning and erecting new buildings, purchasing and installing the equipment, reorganising the workflow, and so on, and it might be expected to be roughly the same for all firms. But there is little to support this hypothesis, and it was thought useful to check whether or not any significant differences could be found, not only between countries but also between firms in the same country.[1]

MEASURES OF DIFFUSION

There are a number of ways in which the diffusion of a technique at any particular time can be measured: the proportion of companies or plants in the industry which use it, or the share of output, capacity, or employment of labour which it accounts for in relation to the industry's total output, capacity, or employment.

The first, the number of companies who have applied the new technique, only measures diffusion among firms, the others measure diffusion both among firms and within firms, though in different ways. The first measure is an easier figure to calculate, but for many purposes other measures are needed. For example, in assessing the impact of diffusion of the new technique on productivity, the proportion of output it accounts for is the decisive factor.

Often the denominator in this fraction (the potential area of application of the new technique) is difficult or impossible to define un-ambiguously. In some cases a new technique may be successfully applied to a whole industry, whose limits are easy to define, but there are also many techniques which are only suitable for application, at least in their early stages, to a certain type of production within an industry. Then it is necessary to decide whether to take as the relevant total production that of the whole industry, or only of that part of the industry for which the technique is suitable. The former is chosen more often, because it is frequently impossible to determine the actual range of the technique at any given point of time, or because the effect of subsequent modifications and improvements to the technique on the range of its application cannot be foreseen.

THE PATTERN OF THE DIFFUSION PROCESS

In the literature on the diffusion process, there is considerable agreement about the time pattern of the diffusion which may be expected following the first introduction of a new technique (or innovation). This agreement holds good between highly heterogeneous new tech-

[1] The case of float glass (chapter 7) illustrates this point.

niques in widely varying environmental contexts, and for new processes and new products alike. The cumulative pattern of adopters of a new technique, or the cumulative proportion of activity accounted for, usually conforms quite closely to a cumulative normal distribution function or some similar rising sigmoid (S-shaped) curve, for example, an asymmetrical skewed-logistic or Gompertz type of curve.

It is not difficult to pick out a number of influences which might lead to a sigmoid curve. Considering first the opening phase, where we are looking at a process of adoption which is initially slow but begins to accelerate:

(1) There are usually a few firms willing, and even anxious (having some special compelling reason), to be among the earliest to try out new techniques, which may initially involve considerable uncertainty and risk.

(2) If a few pioneer firms overcome the teething troubles of a new technique, they substantially reduce the risk in the eyes of those who have yet to adopt it.

(3) Good reports of a new technique from entrepreneurs already using it may carry considerably more weight with the large majority of firms than reports in the press or publicity by suppliers.

(4) Modifications to the new technique in the early stages of commercial application may substantially increase the potential range of production to which it can be applied, as well as increasing the superiority of the new method over existing methods in the feasible range of application.

(5) There may be a bunching of the new adoptions as part of a cyclical mechanism of the Schumpeterian type.[1]

(6) Other factors may also work in the same direction, for example, the age of existing technology to be replaced by the new one.

These factors are all consistent with an acceleration in the diffusion process following a slow beginning. After a time, however, other factors may slow down the process:

(7) It may transpire that there are areas of production in which the new technique is, after all, not very suitable; probably the most promising areas will have been exploited first.

(8) The very success of the new technique in its early stages may stimulate some firms to improve their existing methods of production for fear of being driven out of the industry, or for other reasons.

[1] J. A. Schumpeter, *Business Cycles*, vol. 1, 1st ed., New York and London, McGraw-Hill, 1939.

The factors (1) to (8) have been put forward as suggestions why some kind of sigmoid curve of diffusion might be expected. It is possible to formulate more exact and explicit models of imitative behaviour which would generate mathematically various kinds of sigmoid curve.

The diffusion pattern of new techniques may be of interest for many purposes: for instance, forecasting the changes in technology, in sales of new equipment, in investment trends, in manpower projections, and in skill requirements and retraining. Attempts to fit curves which demonstrate or explain the diffusion paths of some of the innovations studied are presented in this book. However, it is not possible to do this in all cases, since many of the new techniques considered (unlike the majority of those studied in previous research in this field) are relatively recent arrivals on the industrial scene, and their diffusion is still incomplete.

It seems that in the early stages inter-firm diffusion usually predominates, and often it takes this form exclusively for some time after the innovation. In most cases though, firms which have already introduced the new technique will eventually want to build new capacity embodying it; this may be the result of a need for additional capacity to expand production, to replace existing capacity, or to use the proven advantages of the new technique more fully. Later, therefore, the diffusion of a new technique, particularly one which has already achieved a high rate of inter-firm diffusion, is usually characterised by high levels of internal or intra-firm diffusion. This aspect also received attention in the course of our inquiry.

THE INQUIRY

The work of the group of institutes started by looking for a quantifiable link between technological progress and economic growth. Previous studies had pursued similar aims but they usually employed production functions at the macro-level, leaving a residual which was treated as a measure of technical advance. Our aim was to study technological advance at the micro-level, and for this purpose the diffusion process seemed the most promising line of investigation. Diffusion studies offered some scope for quantification; despite a certain amount of empirical investigation,[1] this is still a largely under-researched area.

The group decided to study the diffusion of new industrial processes, because less is known about this than about the diffusion of new

[1] Salter, *Productivity and Technical Change*; Griliches, 'Hybrid corn'; Mansfield, *Industrial Research and Technological Innovation* and *The Economics of Technological Change* (a pioneer in this area but his works were restricted to the relatively homogenous United States market); and more recently L. Wohlin, *Forest-based Industries: structural change and growth potential*, Stockholm, IUI, 1970, especially ch. 8 and 9.

products, and the aims of the investigation became clearer after several discussions. These were:

(a) to assess the scope and extent of the diffusion of selected new processes in the countries covered and to establish the international differences in the level and speed of their diffusion;

(b) to study the factors which affect the speed of diffusion;

(c) to make some attempt to account for the differences between countries.

The inquiry was conceived as an exercise in two stages. The first pilot stage aimed at assessing the speed of diffusion of selected processes – more precisely, the date of introduction in each country, the time-path, and the level achieved by about 1968. In addition, a large amount of ancillary material was collected which paved the way for the second stage, in which the determinants of diffusion in the different countries were investigated more deeply.

For a study of this nature, parallel investigations in each country of a common set of new technologies were required. The group's main interest was in diffusion, but some examination of the invention and innovation phases, as well as the processes of production, was also necessary. Ten new processes introduced in the last 15–20 years (in nine different industries) were selected for the pilot inquiry.[1] They were the basic oxygen process and continuous casting in steelmaking, special presses in paper-making, numerically controlled machine tools in metalworking, shuttleless looms in the weaving of cotton and man-made fibres, float glass in glassmaking, gibberellic acid in malting and brewing, tunnel kilns in brick-making, new plate marking and cutting methods in shipbuilding, and automatic transfer lines in the production of car engines. All these processes except the last two were analysed in greater depth in the second stage of the inquiry.

Ten processes are too few to represent industry as a whole, but the sample is reasonably well balanced in a number of respects. It includes processes which require small and large capital investment; industries which produce consumer, investment and intermediate goods; products whose share of output exported ranges from considerable to negligible; and industrial categories with varying proportions of large firms. Furthermore, all the processes selected are important in their respective fields.

We did not set out to select processes which could lay claim to some

---

[1] At the outset the problem was thought to be one of choosing from among a large number of possible alternatives. In actual fact, however, the scientists and technologists approached found it quite difficult to give us examples of major new technologies lending themselves to this kind of investigation.

kind of undisputed technological 'supremacy'. It is known, for example, that advanced research is being conducted on steelmaking by direct reduction. It is possible, though not at all certain, that this new process will replace the basic oxygen process. The situation may be similar for some other of the selected processes. The selection had to be restricted to processes in actual use, otherwise the diffusion could not have been measured. Even so, there were difficulties about two points. First, some of the processes selected are still being developed; and secondly, many of them are not necessarily the only candidates for the replacement of older techniques – there may be alternative technologies. Relatively clear-cut cases – such as Diesel traction replacing steam traction – are exceptional; technological advance is usually more complex.

The preliminary results of the pilot stage of the inquiry were published in an interim report[1] and the main findings are summarised in chapter 2 of this book. The method of inquiry differed considerably between the two stages. Questionnaires agreed internationally formed the basis of the studies in both instances, but in the pilot stage these were sent to companies by mail and supplemented where necessary by telephone calls (only in exceptional cases by personal approaches); in the second stage (the main inquiry) personal interviews played the most important part. In both stages additional information was obtained from technical and industrial experts, as well as from 'central' sources such as trade associations and technical or industrial research institutes.

The quality of the resulting data is uneven, particularly in the coverage of industries in the different countries. In some countries and some industries companies were more cooperative than elsewhere. We have therefore made a special point of supplying a careful description of the sample used for investigating the diffusion of each technique and of the circle of respondent companies in each case – that is, the statistical base of the analysis and the findings.

The various factors which might conceivably influence the incidence of innovation and the speed of its diffusion add up to a formidable list. Among the most important which were investigated were:

(1) *Technical applicability:* the new process may not be applicable, for technical reasons, to the whole range of a company's or a country's productive operations. Diffusion might be confined within some 'technically feasible' maximum or a 'technological ceiling', which could be only a fraction of total production, although often this is difficult to calculate unambiguously.

[1] This was written on behalf of the group by G. F. Ray and was published in the *National Institute Economic Review*, no. 48, May 1969, pp. 40–83. It was also published in the original English version by IUI (Smatryck Nr. 46, Stockholm, 1969) and in German by OIW (*Die Ausbreitung neuer Technologien*, Vienna, 1969) and also by IFO (*Die Verbreitung neuer Technologien*, Berlin and Munich, Duncker and Humblot, 1970).

(2) *Profitability:* it was assumed that the economic advantages which make the new process profitable relative to alternative, more conventional, technologies would help to explain its diffusion. This, however, is not an easy concept to define, let alone measure. Factor costs varying between countries, the age and the technical standard of the existing equipment, the product-mix and many other considerations can influence profitability calculations.

(3) *Finance:* lack of financial resources might delay the diffusion of new processes, even when their profitability has been established.

(4) *Size, structure and organisation:* large companies may, for a number of economic, technological, or other reasons, behave differently from medium-sized or small firms; the organisation and structure of the industry as well as of the companies (for example, their foreign associations, or the vertical or horizontal integration of companies within a holding company) can also have a marked effect on diffusion, and may be particularly important in explaining international differences. High concentration, or a monopoly position, may create conditions which can influence innovation or diffusion either way.

(5) *Other factors,* such as research and development activity, access to information, the labour market (availability of certain skills), licensing policy, the market situation and, more precisely, the growth of demand for the product as well as the competitive position with special regard to import competition, all illustrate the wide range of factors which could contribute to explaining differences in the speed of diffusion.

(6) *Management attitudes:* these are, unfortunately, the most difficult to assess or quantify,[1] but, nevertheless, they may be as important as economic factors in influencing the rate of adoption of new methods. Attempts have been made by the authors of some of the chapters to quantify management attitudes (especially in chapter 6).

In more general terms, it was believed that the application of new technologies is heavily influenced by the specific situation of each individual company. The multiplicity of factors is such that for each company the situation is unique: there is some factor, or some combination of factors, which operates for that company and for no others. Further, many of the factors are not quantifiable. They cannot on those grounds be rejected from the analysis, but they are difficult to handle in an exercise which aims at generalisations.

[1] Mansfield, *The Economics of Technological Change*; E. M. Rogers, *Diffusion of Innovations*, 1st ed., New York, Free Press of Glencoe, 1962.

In the course of the research we attempted to collect a large amount of information along the above lines. Our experience highlights very clearly the great variation in the scope of industrial, financial and other information available from published or public sources in different countries. Certain data which were easily accessible in one country were not available at all in another, and some of the companies interviewed even regarded them as vital secrets. Great efforts were made to eradicate inconsistencies in the basic information, and while some success was achieved, perfect comparability could not always be ensured. The difficulty arose not only from differences in national statistical series and in the attitudes of the companies and other bodies which were co-operating in the research, but also from varying interpretations of accounting and economic concepts. Despite great efforts to standardise both data and concepts by the authors of the various chapters and by the editors, we cannot claim that all such differences have been eliminated. Nevertheless, those that remain are unlikely to invalidate the general statements made in the book, or to affect the findings in any fundamental way. It also has to be borne in mind that, apart from certain information concerning the steel processes, statistical information on these subjects, and even the basic data on the diffusion of the techniques, has so far (with the exception of our interim report) been completely lacking.

The nature of this study may be more readily understood if the group's method of work is described briefly. To keep the research as far as possible on a similar footing in each country and on each subject, it was necessary to meet regularly – on average three times a year – during the period of the inquiry. At the earlier meetings much effort was devoted to reaching a single research design which could be applied to all of the technologies; that is to say it was hoped to enumerate a set of common questions which would be analysed in the same way and thus permit, in principle, generalisations concerning diffusion of technology.

After several efforts this approach had to be abandoned. On closer inspection, different technologies suggested differences in the range of questions most likely to throw light upon the process of diffusion. Moreover, the research design had to be tailored to the information which was likely to be available in the participating countries, and this differed from one technology to another. Consequently a different strategy was ultimately adopted, whereby the responsibility for preparing the initial design for each technology was assigned to one of the institutes, all the other institutes agreeing to act as data collectors under the orders, as it were, of the institute in charge. Thus each institute found itself responsible for directing the research for one technology (exceptionally NIESR was assigned three), but each was also responsible for collecting data in its own country concerning all technologies. The research designs proposed by the institutes for the technologies for which they were responsible were submitted to the group, discussed and agreed. In every case questionnaires to be addressed to companies, and in some cases two types of questionnaire, were discussed in great detail at successive meetings.

Once the general plan was agreed, each institute collected the facts from its own country. The institute responsible for the project drafted an analysis of the data collected (which were coded to ensure strict confidentiality) and these drafts were discussed at subsequent meetings of the group. The final responsibility for the chapters in this book concerning each technology rests with the institute which drafted it, and with the author or authors who signed it. Nevertheless, at each stage of the work, written and verbal comments were made by other members of the group. The responsibility for this introduction and for the concluding chapter rests, however, with the editors appointed by the group, although, again, the group has seen and discussed these chapters in draft.

Our method of analysis presupposed that the diffusion of new technology could be accounted for rationally. More than this, we tried wherever we could to measure the influence of different factors. In some cases econometric analysis was feasible. Nevertheless, differences in the nature of the processes and, equally important, differences in the amount of material available, made us fall back in many cases on qualitative rather than quantitative statements. We have adapted the analysis to the nature of the problem and the quality of the data rather than insisting that a particular methodology, for example the use of econometric techniques, should be followed at all costs. We recognise, of course, that this catholic approach to the research design makes comparison of the results of the different analyses rather more difficult. On the other hand, we think this approach makes the best use of data which are rare and difficult to obtain even for one country, let alone on a comparable basis for a number of countries. Moreover, this method had one positive advantage: it enabled us to bring out more of the factors which are likely to influence diffusion in different types of situation than would be the case if we had pursued a standard methodology.

CHAPTER 2

SUMMARY OF THE INTERIM REPORT

By G. F. Ray, NIESR[1]

THE SIGNIFICANCE OF DIFFERENCES BETWEEN COUNTRIES

It is convenient to start a summing up of the case studies of the ten processes chosen for the first stage of the inquiry (see page 11 above) by tracing the penetration of each of them through the six countries from the date of their first introduction in one of the countries to the latest convenient year (table 2.1).

It appeared that on average the widest diffusion had been achieved in Sweden, with the United Kingdom in second place (section IV of the table). The same two countries led, though in the reverse order, in terms of average speed of introduction of the ten new processes (section II). But Austria and Germany tended to be the quickest to reach a substantial measure of diffusion (section III). The question arises whether the differences are significant or merely the result of having taken a small sample of techniques.

On the assumption that the sample is random, analysis of variance showed in fact that the difference between average timelags in introduction could have arisen by chance sampling fluctuations; it provided no evidence that any country tends to lead the others in introducing new techniques. (It is, however, important to stress that the extreme date, 1902, for the introduction of tunnel kilns in the United Kingdom, was excluded. Including this, the United Kingdom's leadership became statistically significant.)

At the time we had not got sufficient data to specify the properties of the diffusion curves which represent the shares of output produced by each new technique in each country. Mansfield advocated the use of a logistic (symmetrically sigmoid) curve; the results of our study did not provide convincing evidence for accepting this unconditionally and it was believed that there was probably a good case for using another type of sigmoid curve. At this stage, however, the simplest assumption was made (admittedly because of the lack of data proving anything else) – namely that the diffusion curves were linear. Neither the curves for individual processes nor their aggregation provided any strong contradiction of this assumption.

[1] Published originally as 'The diffusion of new technology' in the *National Institute Economic Review*, no. 48, May 1969. France was included in that stage of the inquiry.

Table 2.1. *Diffusion of the ten selected processes*

	Austria	France	Italy	Sweden	United Kingdom	West Germany
I. *Year of introduction*						
NC machine tools	1963	1957	1960	1958	1955	1962
Special presses	1966	1965	1965	1963	1964	1965
Tunnel kilns	1957	1949	1951	1948	1902[a]	1959
Basic oxygen steel	1952	1956	1964	1956	1960	1957
Float glass	—	1966	1965	—	1958	1966
Gibberellic acid	—	1966	—	1959	1959	—
Continuous casting	1952	1960	1958	1963	1960	1954
Shuttleless looms	1961	1953/4	1960	1957	1958	1954
Plate cutting methods	—	1960	1962	1950	1950	1953
Automatic transfer lines	—	1947	1950	1955	1947	1954
II. *Timelag after pioneer* (years)						
NC machine tools	8	2	5	3	—	7
Special presses	3	2	2	—	1	2
Tunnel kilns	9	1	3	—	n.a.	11
Basic oxygen steel	—	4	12	4	8	5
Float glass	n.a.	8	7	n.a.	—	8
Gibberellic acid	n.a.	7	n.a.	—	—	n.a.
Continuous casting	—	8	6	11	8	2
Shuttleless looms	7	—	6	3	4	1
Plate cutting methods	n.a.	10	12	—	—	3
Automatic transfer lines	n.a.	—	3	8	—	7
III. *Time for process to produce indicated percentage of output* (years)						
Special presses (*10*)	1	2	..	2	3	2
Tunnel kilns (*10*)	4	12	10	8	n.a.	2
Basic oxygen steel (*20*)	2	12	2	9	5	8
Gibberellic acid (*50*)	n.a.	..	n.a.	3	4	n.a.
Continuous casting (*1*)	10	..	7	3	6	9
Shuttleless looms (*2*)	..	..	3	9	6	6
Automatic transfer lines (*30*)	n.a.	..	15	2	10	1
IV. *Diffusion by 1966*[b] (percentages)						
NC machine tools	..	0·081	0·036	..	0·088	0·035
Special presses[c]	35	25[d]	4	52	24	15
Tunnel kilns	58	31	45	59	12	48
Basic oxygen steel[e]	67	17	27	33	28	32
Float glass	—	7	6	—	25	6
Gibberellic acid[c]	—	..	—	48	70	—
Continuous casting	1·2	0·6	2·0	2·2	1·6	2·4
Shuttleless looms[e]	5·0[d]	8·5[d]	3·0	2·4	8·0	9·5
Plate cutting methods	—	68	48	80	36	66
Automatic transfer lines[e]	—	..	39	97	52	81

SOURCE: inquiry.

[a] Omitted from sections II and III as extreme.

[b] As a proportion of national output, except for NC machine tools (proportion of tools) and tunnel kilns, shuttleless looms, plate cutting methods, automatic transfer lines (proportion of respondents' total output).

[c] By 1968.　　　[d] Estimated.　　　[e] By 1967.

The slope of the linear diffusion relation (that is the speed of diffusion) may be measured in several ways; the measure applied here (section III of table 2.1) was the number of years taken in each country to reach z per cent of an industry's output produced by means of each new technique. The level of z was varied between techniques since these were of different vintages and at different stages of development. Information on this measure of diffusion was available for seven of the ten techniques only (and even so it was incomplete since the basic data could not be assessed for each country). Scatter diagrams were prepared

Chart 2.1. *Relations between introduction and speed of diffusion (five processes)*

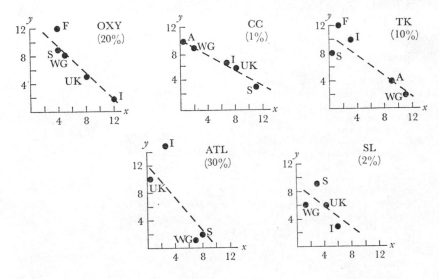

SOURCE: table 2.1.

Note: The regression equations are (omitting Austria for oxygen steel and the United Kingdom for tunnel kilns):

Oxygen steel (OXY): $y = 14.14 - 1.051x$; $R^2 = 0.886$, S.E. $= \pm 0.217$
Continuous casting (CC): $y = 10.27 - 0.606x$; $R^2 = 0.970$, S.E. $= \pm 0.062$
Tunnel kilns (TK): $y = 10.81 - 0.725x$; $R^2 = 0.796$, S.E. $= \pm 0.220$
Automatic transfer lines (ATL): $y = 13.37 - 1.415x$; $R^2 = 0.612$, S.E. $= \pm 0.796$
Shuttleless looms (SL): $y = 8.42 - 0.692x$; $R^2 = 0.346$, S.E. $= \pm 0.673$

where y = number of years to reach indicated percentage of output by the new process and x = timelag in years since introduction in the first country.

for each of these techniques with speed of diffusion plotted against the timelag in introduction. However, gibberellic acid was introduced at much the same time in Sweden and in the United Kingdom, and for special presses the speed of diffusion seemed to be independent of the timelag (or the technique may have been too recent for the speed to be accurately measured). For the other five processes (chart 2.1) the scatters indicated a *negative* correlation between the speed of diffusion and the timelag, but for each one of them the number of observations was quite small. The data for these five techniques (oxygen steel, continuous casting, tunnel kilns, shuttleless looms and automatic transfer lines) were therefore pooled (chart 2.2) and again the speed of diffusion was regressed on the timelag.

Chart 2.2. *Aggregate relation between introduction and speed of diffusion*

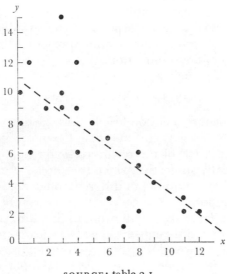

SOURCE: table 2.1.
Note: The five processes for which separate details are given in chart 2.1 are here aggregated into the regression equation

$$y = 10.766 - 0.764x; \quad R^2 = 0.560, \text{ S.E.} = \pm 0.148$$

The analysis of the pooled data also suggested a fairly marked negative relationship between the speed of diffusion and the timelag in introduction: in countries which are pioneers, diffusion tends to be *slower*. This result is consistent with the hypothesis that the pioneer faces all sorts of teething troubles – new problems associated with the new technique – which are likely to be solved, partly and gradually, by the time others adopt it. It is therefore not necessarily desirable to be the first to introduce a new technique.

This suggestion should be treated with caution. It could explain only part of the differences between countries and, even among the relatively few processes investigated, there were two which actually implied the opposite – that the pioneer's diffusion was the fastest. But special circumstances affected both cases. Special presses probably spread faster in Sweden than elsewhere because the paper industry is more important there than in any of the other countries. And float glass is quite exceptional because of the pioneer's world licence, the very special structure of the industry, and the important fact that in this case most of the teething troubles were probably ironed out by the inventor company before commercial introduction.[1]

Finally, and perhaps this is the main moral, the case studies revealed many special factors of varying importance which had to be taken into consideration when comparing diffusion rates between countries (or even companies). It is probably not justifiable to make such comparisons without analysing all aspects of the situation in the various countries and allowing for their possible impact on the introduction or speed of diffusion of any innovation.

CHARACTERISTICS OF INDIVIDUAL PROCESSES

It may be convenient to mention briefly those factors which, in the light of this pilot study, appear to have had the most significant influence on the diffusion of each of the techniques investigated. A selection of this type is naturally subjective, since the spread of new techniques is the outcome of a large number of different, often conflicting influences. The three most important and general were probably the advantage of the new process in terms of overall profitability, the attitude of management to the adoption of new techniques, and access to capital, though other considerations proved weighty in individual cases. The diffusion of each of the new techniques was of course also influenced by a long list of supplementary factors, but in general the importance of each of the latter appeared relatively minor.

In the case of oxygen steelmaking, limiting factors seemed to be at work on both the input and the output sides (the availability of hot metal and the special qualities of steel); another important aspect was the stock of still high-performance productive equipment of earlier vintage. Continuous casting has, for a long time, been hampered by technical problems; it seemed in its earlier stages to have suited small plants rather than large ones, where the maintenance of the internal balance of works, often disturbed by the introduction of this new technique, caused bigger problems. No such dominating influence emerged in the case of special presses for making paper and board, apart from their unsuitability in a relatively small section of the industry.

[1] This may indeed be an important aspect; some new techniques were obviously put on the market with the new equipment in a relatively underdeveloped state, and the many initial problems continued to hamper diffusion even after considerable development and improvement.

Numerical control of metalworking machine tools was probably most affected by the nature of the work to be performed – hence the rapid adoption in the aerospace industry. High servicing requirements, such as programming, might have acted as a deterrent.

Early teething troubles influenced the diffusion of shuttleless looms for some time; their advantages vary with the product-mix and their wider application appeared heavily dependent on the judgement of industrialists as to the future of the market, of their own competitive position, and of weaving as a technology. This case demonstrated another important point: that it is difficult to take two steps at once on the technological ladder – it is very expensive to introduce these new looms in weaving sheds which have not been kept in line with the previous stages of advance in the industry.

Float glass was an unqualified success: it made all previous techniques of producing certain grades of flat glass obsolete and has, by further development, been extended to a very wide area of glassmaking. The unique international structure of this industry (and to some extent, the existing traditional equipment) may have somewhat restrained its diffusion.

The tunnel kiln is not equally well suited to different qualities of clay and to the various types of bricks and other final products; thus, differences in the building habits and traditions in the various countries and areas played some part in its dissemination. It may also require higher management standards than some smaller producers can afford.

The case of gibberellic acid in malting provides a good example of how existing laws and regulations may affect the adoption of new techniques.

THE INFLUENCE OF COMPANY STRUCTURE

The pilot study provided no definite evidence that large companies have always been in the forefront of technical progress in the sense of being leaders in innovation and the adoption of new techniques. The leading role which they often play in research and development, their generally more sophisticated managerial set-up, and their easier access to new capital are likely to give them a lead over smaller firms; some of the case studies did indeed point to the outstanding part played by large companies, but in other cases it was the opposite way round.

Irrespective of size, any of a large number of tangible factors may make a new technique profitable and desirable in one company (or in one country) but not in another. The least tangible factor is, however, likely to have the greatest impact on the application of new techniques – the attitude of management.

CHAPTER 3

NUMERICALLY CONTROLLED MACHINE TOOLS

By A. Gebhardt and O. Hatzold, IFO

INTRODUCTION

The technique of numerical control differs in one important point from the other case studies in this book. In all the other cases the product being produced by the new technique can be precisely defined (for example, the float process produces flat glass, the paper press paper, the oxygen process steel). Machine tools, however, whether numerically controlled or not, generally produce certain parts or components of extremely heterogeneous and often very complex final products, and operate over the entire field of metalworking.[1] Accordingly, the diffusion of numerical control is not restricted to specific branches of engineering. This makes the measurement of the level and the speed of diffusion difficult, and the difficulties become even greater when it comes to international comparisons, or to the factors influencing this diffusion. The wide range of application of machine tools, and the almost infinite number and heterogeneous character of their products, further multiply the possible situations and the number of factors to be taken into account.

Metalworking machine tools are not the exclusive area of application of numerical control; it can be adapted to many industrial processes. But even in this relatively limited field the potential of the technique is enormous. Equally wide ranging is the variety of problems which surround the diffusion of numerical control in engineering alone.

This means that the results of the analysis presented in this chapter are perhaps less definitive than in some of the other case studies. Within the scope of the study the investigation had to be limited to a relatively narrow area in the wide field of engineering, which in most countries covered in the study accounts for about a third of total industrial production. However, it is believed that the findings of even this restricted survey will contribute to understanding the diffusion process of new techniques that can be applied as widely and generally as numerical control.

The design of this inquiry benefited considerably from the IFO-

---

[1] Machine tools are used in other areas as well, for making wood, plastic, and other products, but this study is restricted to metalworking.

Institut's previous experience with the problems of numerical control,[1] which has also been drawn upon in the present report. The inadequacies of the quantitative inquiry in the individual countries could thus be offset to some extent. However, the earlier experience of the authors was mainly based on conditions in Germany, and is not necessarily transferable to other countries.

The first section contains a short description of the technology, the application of a diffusion theory to the specific circumstances of numerically controlled machines, and a statement of the objects of the survey. Later sections demonstrate the level and speed of diffusion in the countries covered, analyse the explanatory factors and, finally, make an attempt to sum up the results. The concluding section attempts to classify the most essential factors as they affect the diffusion of numerically controlled machines, and to assess their importance for individual countries.

THE TECHNOLOGY

The operation of numerical control

Numerical control is a procedure for the automation of variable work phases on machine tools. It is based on the input of numerical (that is digital) data into a machine whose action is controlled by the instructions transmitted, all the operations necessary for the execution of the machine's function being prescribed. These items of information are transmitted (in the programming office) on to the information medium, normally a punched tape, and an electronic adapter attached to the machine, the 'numeric', conveys them as control commands to the machine. (Numerical control is identical with electronic control.)

Normally three types of control are distinguished: positioning, straight-line cutting, and contouring. In positioning control the machine is adjusted to a certain position (a reference point fixed by two co-ordinates) prior to the machining operation; the processing of the workpiece then actually begins. During the adjustment to the next reference point the tool remains idle. In practice this type of control is applied mainly to drilling and punching machines. In straight-line cutting, the machine will do any operation on the workpiece as long as it is

[1] O. Hatzold and K. Schworm, *Research and Economic Growth. Diffusion of numerical machine control and effects of the application of synthetics in the Federal Republic of Germany*, Munich, IFO, 1967; O. Hatzold, *The Effect of the Introduction of Numerically Controlled Machine Tools on Plant Level Issues in the Federal Republic of Germany. Report on six case studies*, Munich, IFO, 1967; A. Gebhardt, *NC Machine Tools. Handicaps and promotion of their diffusion in the Federal Republic of Germany*, Munich, IFO, 1969; M. Breitenacher, W. Mentzel, and K. Ch. Röthlingshöfer, *The Influence of Research and Development on the Foreign Trade of the Federal Republic of Germany. Statistical analysis and case studies*, Munich, IFO, 1970.

moved in a straight line between two points of reference; this is mainly suitable for uncomplicated milling and lathe work. Contouring control follows the same principle, but here the workpiece can be machined in any direction, in lines and surfaces with curvatures in two and three dimensions.

The machining operations of a numerically controlled machine are fully automatic and can be varied by just changing the information medium. Thus, the technology allows the automatic production of single pieces and small series, and introduces automation into areas which hitherto have been the exclusive realm of hand-operated machines. Mechanically controlled automatic machines have of course been economically employed for a long time – but for large-scale production only, mainly because any change in their production programme, once set, is time-consuming, cumbersome and costly. Numerical control makes this a quick and simple operation, and extends automation right down to one-off pieces.

Compared with hand-operated machines, numerically controlled ones cost more initially, and require programming which is an additional expense; their application therefore does not always and necessarily lower production costs. Only under special conditions are they economically suitable for the production of single parts and small batches. Conversely, the conventional mechanical automatic machine, of which the purchase price is usually lower and the processing periods often shorter, can compete with numerical control if uniform pieces are to be machined in medium and large quantities. The numerically controlled machine thus occupies an intermediate position between the hand-operated machine and the automatic machine for mass production, yet it is not possible to fix precise boundaries between them. Furthermore, apart from continuous technological improvement, the limitations to the application of numerical control are constantly changing with basic conditions, for example increasing wages which continually modify the economics of automatic machines and act as a further incentive to their employment.

The advantages

Replacement of hand-operated conventional machines by numerically controlled machines will yield all the advantages that are generally obtained by conversion to automated production. Compared to automatic machines with adjustable mechanical control, numerically controlled machines have the advantage of greater flexibility. In detail, the following are the advantages of the technique:

(1) *Savings in manpower:* in appropriate applications, numerically controlled machine tools are significantly more efficient than

conventional machines. One numerically controlled drilling machine can replace approximately three conventional machines; one numerically controlled milling machine, two to three traditional machines; one processing centre may, for example, do the work of two drilling machines, one milling machine and one boring mill. Reduced manpower requirements result, of course, in lower labour costs.

(2) *Savings in machining time:* numerically controlled machines require no fixtures, curves, or stencils, so that the idle periods (in which the machine is fixed, and the workpiece clamped and measured in preparation for the actual working cycle) are greatly reduced. The more often batches of an identical workpiece are produced at different times the greater is the advantage. Further, the actual machining operation on numerically controlled machines frequently requires less time than on conventional machines. The resulting cost reductions are often substantial. In addition, the two types of time saving make it possible to use the numerically controlled machines more intensively.

(3) *Savings on tools and accessories:* the uniformity of automatic processes prolongs the life of tools and accessories; this is another source of cost reduction.

(4) *Quality improvement:* automatic positioning and control generally allow greater precision. In repeated production, deviations from the workpiece originally manufactured are impossible.

(5) *Reduction of rejects and waste:* errors and measuring faults by the operating personnel are eliminated; there are no signs of fatigue or transmission errors with automatic machines. This reduces rejects and waste practically to nil. The uniform processing and the elimination of operational errors save wear and tear as well.

(6) *Reduced stockholding:* due to the greater flexibility of production, reduced stockpiling of parts and components, as well as of finished products, becomes possible.

(7) *Other advantages* are that numerically controlled machines make the automatically controlled production of complicated pieces economically possible (previously nothing but hand-operations could be considered); they also enable firms to vary their basic models more widely or more frequently if customers want it.

Chart 3.1 indicates the ratings of the various advantages given by the firms questioned in the countries covered by this study.

Chart 3.1. *Advantages of numerically controlled machines*

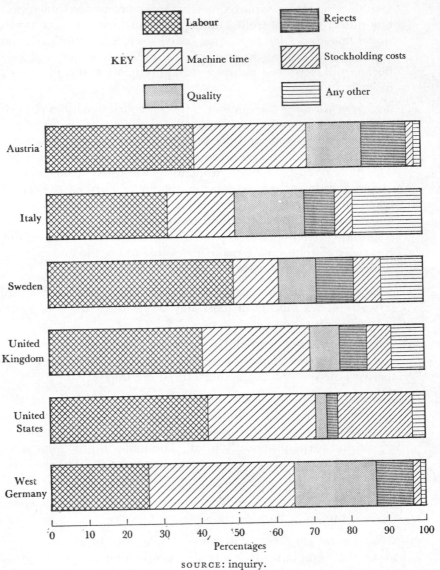

SOURCE: inquiry.

Note: From firms' lists of the three most important advantages, the first was valued at 3 points, the second at 2 and the third at 1. The points were then totalled for each advantage and expressed as percentages of the points for all advantages in that country.

A theory of diffusion and numerical control

Although the different phases of the innovation–diffusion process have been dealt with in chapter 1 of this book, it is convenient to come back to the underlying theory in order to demonstrate the development of this technique.

Whilst accepting the statements in chapter 1, we approach the question of technological advance, the innovation–diffusion process, somewhat differently and subdivide it into the two main stages of creation and diffusion. The first extends from the basic research and the development of a new technology (the phase of techno-scientific development), through the production of a marketable prototype and the world's first application, to the first application in the country to be examined (the phase of marketable development). The second (diffusion) stage comprises the subsequent applications until a degree of saturation is attained (the expansion phase) and the following phase of stagnation, which includes the gradual disappearance of the technology.

Each of these four phases can be subdivided again into two phases of impulse origination and impulse reception. Impulse origination offers the chance of advancing the innovation, while impulse reception represents the reaction of the economy. The innovation process of numerical control can thus be divided into eight:

(1) Basic scientific knowledge pointed to the feasibility of a new technique (techno-scientific findings). The idea of numerically controlled machines was probably triggered off by the electronic fire-control developed in the United States for air defence during World War II.

(2) This idea led to the conception and testing of a technical means of controlling machine tools to produce highly complex aircraft parts with greater precision, cheaper and faster (a technically feasible prototype). Development work in the United States was begun in 1947 on a cooperative basis by the universities, the Air Force and the aircraft industry; faster progress was made when the Air Force financed an extensive research project carried out by the Massachusetts Institute of Technology. The first development work in Europe started in Great Britain in 1950, followed by Germany and France in about 1955.

(3) Further developments led to a practicable technology (a marketable prototype). In 1952 the first numerically controlled machine applicable to industrial purposes was presented to the public.

(4) Completion of the marketable prototype was soon followed by the first application of the new technology in industry, in 1955 in the United States and 1956 in Britain.

(5) Experience gained concerning the performance and the advantages of the new technique, as well as the initial positive results, led to its application on a gradually increasing scale.

This was the take-off stage of diffusion, with the perception of the new technology.

(6) With further decisions to introduce the new technique, diffusion reached its expansion phase. Numerical control in all industrial countries is currently in this phase of mass application.

(7) Once the new technology has entirely displaced more traditional processes, expansion will come to an end. This is the saturation phase, which may be advanced if an even more modern technique emerges. In the case of numerical control we still are very far from this.

(8) Also we are far from the last phase, obsolescence, in which the technique gradually disappears.

The diffusion process takes place in phases (5) to (7), with emphasis on the expansion phase (6). This survey concentrates on the expansion phase.

THE OBJECTS OF THIS STUDY

A whole host of different factors influence the process of diffusion and determine its speed. If we conceive the diffusion of a new technology to be the resultant (vector sum) in a multi-dimensional space where the various influencing factors operate, the impact of these factors on the resulting diffusion can be illustrated by the force and direction of the various impulses in this space. However, an attempt to apply this model-like image numerically in a practical context meets virtually unsur-mountable difficulties. They are of two types: first, some influences cannot be quantified at all, and secondly, because of the variety of influences and the relatively small number of observations, there is no chance of testing such a model econometrically, in a truly scientific manner.

We had, therefore, to dispense with a demonstration of the vectors and of their exact position in space, and to restrict our attempts from the beginning to a less scientifically pretentious method: to identify at least the strongest promoting or hampering factors, to analyse them, and to classify them according to their estimated importance. Our main source of information was the inquiry, which was conducted on a uniform basis in six countries. In the first stage these included France but not the United States, and in the second stage the United States but not France.

THE INQUIRY

Although we started with a brief analysis of the diffusion of numerically controlled machines in general, the study in depth of the expansion and the factors influencing it could not embrace the whole of the engineering industries; to make the investigation manageable, specific sub-areas had to be chosen. A production programme of small or medium batches offers the best basis for the economic employment of numerically controlled machines; consequently the makers of pumps, turning machines, turbines, and printing machines were selected. Since these products are not made exclusively in large batches, their producers could reasonably employ numerically controlled machines. The selection was intended to reduce the heterogeneous field of the whole metal-working industry to a more uniform sector and to ensure that the firms examined would, as far as possible, have comparable structures and

Table 3.1. *Sizes of sample firms*

Numbers of firms

	Austria	Italy	Sweden	United Kingdom	United States	West Germany
Firms with						
1–499 employees	1	7	17	12	2	1
500–1499 employees	6	10	9	9	6	11
1500–4999 employees	2	3	3	11	3	12
5000 employees and over	—	1	2	4	2	8
All sizes	9	21	31	36	13	32

SOURCE: inquiry.

production programmes, these being among the most important conditions for the employment of numerically controlled machines. This procedure has the effect, of course, of omitting other important branches of the engineering industry which are eminently suited to the technology, such as the aerospace industry.

Two further points deserve special mention. First, numerically controlled machines produce different parts and components which may often be used for very dissimilar finished products. Secondly, nearly all companies in the inquiry were multi-product enterprises, which could not isolate workpieces for the selected finished products from those for other finished products. As a rule, therefore, their statements concerning the employment of numerically controlled machines covered their entire production programme, consisting in many cases not of our selected products alone but of others as well. For these two main reasons this study could not demonstrate the different characteristics of firms making different products.

Most tables and statistics concern the responding companies making the four selected products, but wherever possible national data have also been included. The results of the survey are based on written and oral inquiries made of 142 firms in 1969. Table 3.1 shows the sizes of the sample firms in each country. It can be seen, for example, that in Germany it was almost entirely larger firms that participated, whereas in Sweden they were mostly smaller.

Compared with the national stocks of numerically controlled machines, the representation also is different by country. Table 3.2 shows the number of firms using numerical control in 1969, their stock of such machines, and the latter as a percentage of the total national stock of numerically controlled machines.

Table 3.2. *Coverage of the samples*

	Austria	Italy	Sweden	United Kingdom	United States	West Germany
Firms using numerical control[a]	7	7	16	29	10	25
NC machines[b]						
In national industries	75	500	330	2,700	18,000	1,450
In respondent firms	31	36	127	170	214	205
Coverage (%)	*41*	*7*	*39*	*6*	*1*	*14*

SOURCES: inquiry; national data; IFO estimates.

[a] Among the sample companies.   [b] In 1969.

The four selected products are such a small part of the long list of those in the making of which numerical control might be used that the coverage, as related to national totals, also seems rather narrow. However, the replies and arguments put forward by the firms with regard to the various questions were sufficiently uniform (and characteristic of the situation in their particular countries, known from other surveys) for the information collected about the factors influencing diffusion to be considered representative. This is supported by the fact that the growth of the stock of numerically controlled machines in our sample corresponded well with the national trends as illustrated in table 3.3.

Nearly every firm investigated had different experiences, collected special knowledge, and offered interesting opinions and judgements, far beyond the information requested by our questionnaires. On the other hand, many questions were not answered by a number of firms who, apart from some fundamental data, had difficulty in supplying exact figures in answer to detailed questions. The nature of the technique itself often prevented accurate answers to questions about the characteristics of this new method. In other cases, the volume of work required to answer questions of a statistical nature made companies –

especially larger firms – reluctant to cooperate fully. This was the case, for example, with questions concerning investment and finance, resulting in so many gaps in the answers that an analysis of the entire complex of financing could not be carried out within the scope of the survey.

Table 3.3. *National stocks of numerically controlled machines*

Numbers of machines

	Austria	Italy	Sweden	United Kingdom	United States	West Germany
1966	4	110	109	1,000	..	450
1967	..	150	220	1,500	12,000	730
1968	..	400	269	2,100	..	1,030
1969	75	500	330	2,700	18,000	1,450
1970	115	..	400	3,200	20,000	1,930

SOURCES: inquiry; IFO estimates.

THE DIFFUSION OF NUMERICALLY CONTROLLED MACHINES

We interpret the word 'diffusion' in two senses. The level of diffusion, the standard attained, is a stock concept; whilst the speed of diffusion is a flow concept, reflecting the time required between two levels of diffusion.

The level of diffusion

The diffusion of numerically controlled machines is difficult to measure since it is impossible to delimit the area in which this new technology can displace the existing one. From a purely technical standpoint all machine tools could be replaced by numerically controlled ones; from an economic standpoint, however, this is not the case. For certain purposes, such as small-scale production, existing hand-operated machines are more efficient, whereas for a very large output fully automated machines are better. The area in which numerical control can be used with economic advantage lies somewhere in between, but the upper and lower limits do not lend themselves to generally applicable definition. For this reason we have to confine ourselves to an approximate indication of the degree of diffusion.

The growing number of numerically controlled machines installed provides an initial illustration of the level of diffusion in recent years in the various countries (table 3.3); figures such as the number of numerically controlled machines for every thousand employees, or for each plant, provide further indications (table 3.4). In 1967, compared with about 12,000 numerically controlled machines in the United States, the European countries were lagging considerably, especially Italy and Austria, where the introduction of numerical control started relatively late. Table 3.4 shows that in 1969 also the level of diffusion was highest relatively in the United States; in Europe the highest national levels were reached in Sweden and in Britain.

Table 3.4. *Levels of diffusion, end-1969*

Numbers of machines

	Austria	Italy	Sweden	United Kingdom	United States	West Germany
NC machines per thousand employees						
In national industries	0·1	0·1	0·4	0·3	0·9	0·2
In sample firms	3·5	3·9	2·5	3·2	9·6	1·1
NC machines per sample firm	4·4	5·1	8·5	6·0	21·4	8·2

SOURCE: inquiry.

However, these figures only give an approximation to the diffusion of numerically controlled machines. The best measure would be the share of the existing adoption in the total potential adoption of the technology. While this cannot be calculated exactly, one method of approximation might be to express the degree of diffusion as the percentage share of the new technology in all the procedures and means of production employed for the same purpose – in the case of numerical control in all machine tools. Hence the degree of diffusion may be expressed by the ratio of numerically controlled machines to all machine tools. This is shown for the responding firms in table 3.5, which indicates that in three-quarters of these firms the actual proportion of numerically controlled machines was below 5 per cent.

The level of diffusion can also be measured by relating numerically controlled production to total comparable production. Changes in capacity, which as a rule result from the employment of more efficient machines, are also reflected in this comparison. Data from some German firms alone are available for such a comparison. These are shown in table 3.6 and indicate that:

(a) the more valuable pieces tend to be produced on numerically controlled machines;

Table 3.5. *Numerically controlled machines as a proportion of all machine tools*[a]

	Austria	Italy	Sweden	United Kingdom	West Germany	All countries[b]	
	(numbers of firms)						%
NC share of machines							
0–1·9%	2	2	1	5	6	16	31
2–4·9%	2	5	6	5	5	23	45
5–9·9%	—	—	3	2	4	9	18
10% and over	1	—	1	—	1	3	6
All firms responding	5	7	11	12	16[c]	51	100

SOURCE: inquiry.

[a] Includes hand-operated and automatic machines, but only those for which numerically controlled machines could be substituted.

[b] Excludes the United States for which no data are available.

[c] Includes 11 producers of NC machines, for whom numerical control has special advantages.

(b) already by 1969 the production technically feasible by numerical control was three to four times what it actually was;

(c) these firms believed that, allowing for further development, numerical control would, within the next few years, account for half of their production.

Reports from American firms indicate that there the share by value of parts produced amounted to 5 per cent in 1964 and by 1968 had increased to about 15 per cent, already twice as high as in Germany. In the years 1969–70 some American firms increased this share further and reached the level which the German firms considered the maximum at the time of the survey. The figures in table 3.6 reveal that, with increasing use of numerical control, the gap between the shares by

Table 3.6. *Pieces worked by numerical control, West Germany*

	By number of pieces	By value of pieces
		Percentages
NC share in total production		
Actual 1969	4	7
Technically feasible 1969	15	25
Feasible in near future[a]	40	50

SOURCE: inquiry.

[a] Taking into account foreseeable technical and economic developments.

number of workpieces and by value tends to narrow; this makes it likely that with increasing diffusion it will become economic to produce less complicated and expensive parts on numerically controlled machines.

A classification of the stock of numerically controlled machines by size of the users, as in table 3.7, shows that the number of numerically controlled machines installed per firm rises, but the number per

Table 3.7. *Numerically controlled machines by size of firm*[a]

Numbers of machines

	Austria	Italy	Sweden	United Kingdom	United States	West Germany	All countries
Per company							
1– 499 employees	—	2·5	1·5	2·6	—	—	2·9
500–1499 employees	5·8	7·7	5·8	3·9	9·5	4·5	5·8
1500–4999 employees	2·5	4·0	11·0	6·9	27·0	8·6	8·6
5000 employees and over	—	—	32·5	13·8	51·5	11·4	20·2
Per thousand employees							
1– 499 employees	—	10·8	8·3	8·3	—	—	10·6
500–1499 employees	7·7	9·0	7·5	6·0	12·1	5·5	7·2
1500–4999 employees	0·9	1·3	—	3·2	—	4·0	3·7
5000 employees and over	—	—	1·7	1·9	8·5	0·5	1·2
Averages							
Per company	4·4	5·1	8·5	6·0	21·4	8·2	8·5
Per thousand employees	3·5	3·9	2·5	3·2	9·6	1·1	2·3

SOURCE: inquiry.
[a] In the sample firms.

thousand employees declines, with increasing size of firm. The reason for this may well be that, in contrast to smaller firms, the production programme of larger companies consists of longer runs of production, for which the economic applicability of numerically controlled machines is limited. This also indirectly reflects the fact that numerical control is best suited to the automatic production of smaller batches or one-off pieces.

The speed of diffusion

Since it is difficult to quantify with certainty the degree of diffusion, owing to the vagueness of the area of potential application, statements concerning the speed of diffusion are subject to considerable restrictions. Nevertheless, the development of the entire stock of numerically

Table 3.8. *First installations of numerically controlled machines*[a]

	Austria	Italy	Sweden	United Kingdom	United States	West Germany	All countries
Proportions of firms using NC				(percentages)			
1960	—	—	—	8	36	—	6
1962	—	—	6	20	82	42	27
1965	25	43	24	76	91	84	62
1969	75	100	77	92	100	96	90
1970	100	100	100	100	100	100	100
Firms responding	*8*	*7*	*17*	*25*	*11*	*26*	*94*

SOURCE: inquiry.

[a] In the sample firms.

controlled machines in the individual countries and in the firms studied, and the relationship between the date of first information about this technique and its introduction, provide a basis for approaching the subject. Changes between 1966 and 1970 in the stock of numerically controlled machines differed considerably in the countries studied, as indicated by table 3.3. Whilst the stock doubled in the United States and

Table 3.9. *Growth of the stock of numerically controlled machines*[a]

	Firms with less than 1000 employees				Firms with 1000 employees and over			
	Sweden	United Kingdom	West Germany	All countries[b]	Sweden	United Kingdom	West Germany	All countries[b]
Machines employed								
1961 and earlier	—	—	1	1	—	3	5	8
1962	—	—	2	2	1	3	9	13
1963	—	—	3	5	4	6	20	30
1964	1	—	9	13	7	14	38	60
1965	2	3	9	20	39	27	54	121
1966	7	4	16	35	44	39	91	175
1967	19	11	20	65	57	44	127	231
1968	37	15	25	107	69	57	167	301
1969	49	19	31	153	76	59	230	378
Firms responding	*11*	*7*	*5*	*33*	*3*	*5*	*20*	*32*

SOURCE: inquiry.

[a] In the sample firms.
[b] Includes Austria and Italy, but excludes the United States.

trebled in Britain, it increased four-fold in Sweden and Germany, and six-fold in Italy. In Austria, the small number of machines at the outset increased thirty-fold. In view of the levels of diffusion in table 3.4, it is evident that the increase in the stock of numerically controlled machines is proportionally less the greater the level of diffusion already achieved. This is in accordance with general experience on the speed of diffusion of new technologies. At the same time the differences between countries in the level of diffusion tend to decline.

Chart 3.2. *Growth of the stock of numerically controlled machines used by the sample firms*

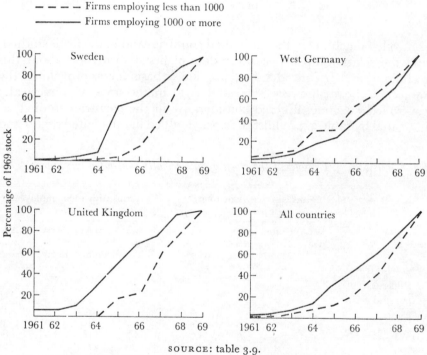

KEY

– – – – Firms employing less than 1000

————— Firms employing 1000 or more

SOURCE: table 3.9.

Note: 'All countries' includes Austria and Italy, but excludes the United States.

Table 3.8 shows the levels of diffusion reached (measured by numbers of firms) in various years. It confirms that the diffusion process of the technique had its origin in the United States, which was followed by Britain with a slight timelag. Diffusion in Germany and Sweden followed somewhat later, whilst Italy and Austria were the laggards.

The growth of the stock of numerically controlled machines in the

Chart 3.3. *The decision gap*

KEY

——— Firms with information about numerical control
– – – Firms using numerical control

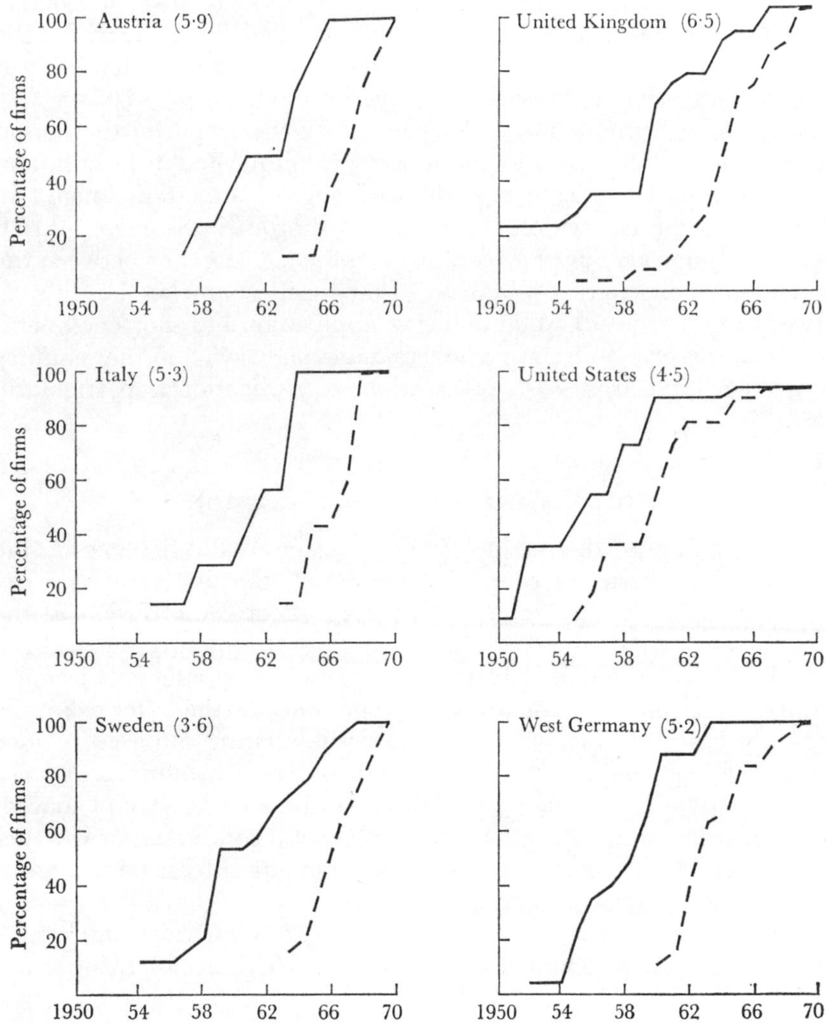

SOURCE: inquiry.

Note: Average gap in years between first information and first use of numerically controlled machines shown in brackets for each country.

sample firms is shown in absolute numbers in table 3.9 and as percentages of the 1969 stock in chart 3.2. These indicate that the intra-firm diffusion generally began earlier in large firms than in small firms. Germany is an exception; here small firms (including a number of manufacturers of numerically controlled machines) began to employ numerical control quite early. The above suggestion, that the stock of machines increases more slowly the greater the level of diffusion already reached, is confirmed by these data. In the period 1966–9 the stock of machines in small firms of all countries increased five-fold, whilst the larger initial stock in large firms only doubled. The same tendency is clear from the separate Swedish and British data.

The date of introduction is determined by the length of the period between the initial recognition of the new technique and its installation. Company reports indicate that this perception phase was longest in Britain, with an average of 6.5 years, and shortest in Sweden with an average of 3.6 years (chart 3.3). However, the convergence between the curves shown in chart 3.3 indicates that in all countries the interval between the first information and first application has shortened. This is particularly pronounced in Sweden and explains why in that country the average time from first information to application is particularly short.[1]

FACTORS INFLUENCING DIFFUSION

When searching for the reasons for the international differences in the diffusion of numerically controlled machines, the first step is to determine tentatively the factors which may affect the diffusion in the countries concerned; the second is an attempt to quantify them. A list of the influences amounts in fact to setting out our hypotheses, although at this stage it did not seem advisable to go much farther – for example, to group them into factors promoting or hampering diffusion – since the same factor could work both ways in different conditions. An important distinction, however, was whether the factors were of macro-economic origin and nature, arising from general conditions, or whether they had a micro-economic character which might differ from enterprise to enterprise.

Our basic hypothesis was that the diffusion of numerical control was a rational process, governed and determined by the following main factors:

[1] In interpreting these data it must be taken into account that it was impossible to confirm that the dates given by the firms for first information were in fact the dates from which first information was taken into consideration in policy decisions (it may have been the first information of which the respondent was aware). In addition, only answers from firms already employing numerically controlled machines were used.

(1) Generally, at *macro-economic level:* the comparative level of labour costs; the labour market; general conditions for investment; the attitude of economic powers outside management (trade unions and government); access to information generally (which may be different at the micro-economic level); the industrial structure of the country, which of course mainly influences national diffusion.

(2) Specifically, at *micro-economic level:* the pattern of the production programme; the organisation of the flow of information (of the right kind) to and within the company; the attitude to innovations; the ease or difficulty of introducing the technique (for example, organisational changes required); finance; the age of the existing machine tool stock; and a whole host of other factors which are generally of minor importance but could be of paramount significance to an individual company.

General factors: macro-economics

The diffusion of any new technology has quite dissimilar prerequisites in the different countries; these can be of a natural, social, political, economic or even accidental character. In the case of numerically controlled machines a whole list of important factors contribute to this heterogeneity in the countries studied.

Numerical control aims at the automation of frequently changing work cycles. It substitutes machine power for manpower, that is capital for labour. An important element is therefore the relation between the costs of these two factors of production. Generally, in a country with a high wage level the automation of any production process is more economic than in a low-wage country.[1] A comparison of the wage level in the six countries studied and the diffusion of numerical control achieved by 1969 supports this general hypothesis. The results of this analysis are shown in chart 3.4 in the dual form of a scatter diagram and a regression equation indicating a very strong positive correlation between the level of labour costs and the level of diffusion attained.[2]

[1] It is recognised that the causal relationship is unclear; the order can be reversed by saying that it is high-productivity machinery which enables the employer to pay high wages. Whilst the latter may be the case in very general terms, it is still believed that in the specific case of numerical control the relationship is the one described in the text (i.e. high wages favouring diffusion), because wage levels are given and numerical control has to be accommodated within the existing macro-economic conditions, which are unlikely to have been affected yet by this new technique. No doubt there may be cases, probably in isolation, in which managements consider that high-performance machinery – as one factor among many – may enable them to pay higher wages (e.g. for securing highly skilled labour), but these are unlikely to affect inter-country wage differences in any major way.

[2] The wage level indicators in chart 3.4 include an allowance for differences in the purchasing power of the various currencies, and they refer to total hourly labour costs, including all taxes, social charges and benefits. Purchasing power parities were used because

We may therefore conclude that our hypothesis is supported: leaving other influences aside, the high labour costs in the United States offered the most favourable environment for attaining a high level of diffusion of numerical control, and the conditions were relatively least favourable in those countries where wages were the lowest – Austria and Italy.

Chart 3.4. *The relation between labour costs and the diffusion of numerical control, 1969*

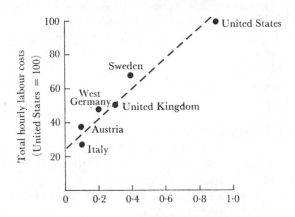

SOURCE: Statistisches Bundesamt; US Bureau of Labor; table 3.4.

Note: The regression equation is $y = -0.2775+0.0111x$; $R^2 = 0.927$, S.E. $= \pm 0.0016$, where x is the labour cost indicator (Austria, 38; Italy, 27; Sweden, 69; United Kingdom, 50; United States, 100; West Germany, 46) and y is the level of diffusion.

Our investigation of the connection between other conditions in the labour market and diffusion resulted in less satisfactory answers. It is generally believed that overall shortage of manpower promotes automation, hence it should promote the diffusion of numerically controlled machine tools, but on the basis of this inquiry no such clear relationship could be established. Indeed the analysis of company reports illustrates the complexity of this question; they show that decisions concerning changes in production techniques are very often influenced not by the shortage or abundance of labour in general, but by the local availability or lack of specific skilled labour. There were reports from Britain and

the question under consideration is affected more by the national wage level in the various countries than by differences in wage costs which may influence the performance in international trade. Similar calculations were made using the same total labour costs converted at the official exchange rates (i.e. without purchasing power adjustment), as well as using hourly earnings converted in the same manner; the regression results were in all cases very similar.

Germany saying that the installation of numerically controlled machines was seriously hampered because specialist workers with the required qualifications were not available, although in general the operative skills required for numerically controlled machines are inferior to those for traditional machine tools. However, in the case of other companies elsewhere in Germany, there was no lack of highly skilled (and highly paid) operatives and, if anything, the semi-skilled workers were in short supply.[1] The situation is further complicated by the fact that the introduction of numerical control also required operatives specialised other than in metalworking (for example, programmers) whose availability may be different from that of metalworkers even within the same region. We conclude that the influence of the labour market on diffusion may be specific to each company, depending largely on local conditions of labour supply.

General conditions for investment play an essential role in the diffusion of new techniques. In countries where the rate of self-financing is high, or where firms have easy access to outside financing, the transition to capital-intensive production is, in principle, easier. There is no doubt that companies in the United States, and to some extent Swedish firms too, are in a more favourable position than those elsewhere. Of course, the access to external capital and the possibility of internal financing may vary from company to company. The responses obtained in the course of the inquiry clearly underlined the importance of financing but did not enable us to analyse this aspect econometrically.

The automation process in the United States is strongly opposed by the trade unions. Cases could be found of active resistance to increasing automation, often delaying its implementation, for example, by means of wage agreements. An additional hindrance there (and to some extent also in Britain) was the fact that a numerically controlled machine consists of two major elements of a basically different nature; in some cases, according to company reports, two different unions have jurisdiction over the machine tool and over the electronic control, one of them insisting that the numeric is serviced and repaired by an electrician, and the other that the machine tool itself is serviced by an engineer.

In continental European countries no comparable situation seems to have arisen. In Germany the unions even sponsored the promotion of numerical control by, among other things, the early organisation of programmer courses. (However, this positive attitude might have been due to the virtually permanent over-employment in this country.)

---

[1] In Germany numerically controlled machines often replaced mechanically controlled automatic or semi-automatic machines which generally require lesser skills than hand-operated ones; this replacement would not result in any large savings in labour costs but in greater flexibility of the machinery.

Several British firms reported isolated difficulties with the unions but more serious conflict was not encountered.

The attitude of the government can have a far-reaching influence on speeding up and widening the diffusion of a new technology. The government in the United States played a very positive part in stimulating the risk-free development of numerically controlled machines, which was of great benefit to their general introduction on the market. In Britain, the diffusion of numerical control was advanced by a special government programme: the National Research Development Corporation administered a guarantee fund which rendered the experimental employment of numerically controlled machines practically free of risk.[1] Although this relieved the entrepreneur of the risk of a wrong investment in an innovation, the practical effects to date of this government sponsorship should not be overestimated; only about two-fifths of the British firms reported that government assistance had influenced their decision in favour of numerically controlled machines and, for the others, the influence of this scheme, or of the government otherwise, on their decisions concerning numerically controlled machines was negligible.

In the other countries no effects either promoting or hampering, could be assessed for government measures. In Germany there were many complaints that the efforts of the producers to obtain a higher rate of depreciation for tax purposes (such as that on data processing equipment) remained unsuccessful. Firms would also have expected government agencies in general to disseminate more information about this new technology, and in particular to eliminate possible misunderstandings and obscurities.

Although one would assume that information concerning an important innovation of the nature of numerical control would spread rapidly and almost simultaneously across international frontiers and within national industries, the inquiry provided powerful evidence in the opposite direction. It appeared that the first information reached firms in the various countries at different times; chart 3.5 indicates that these differences were very considerable. British companies received their first information on the technique significantly earlier than others in Europe, though they too were lagging behind American firms. This phenomenon could not be fully accounted for, but it seems likely to be connected with the significance of the British aerospace industry, where numerically controlled machines can be, and actually have been, em-

---

[1] The purchaser paid the full price, but was guaranteed the right to return the machine to the supplier within 24 months in the event that he could not employ it to his full advantage; in this case he was refunded a sum previously fixed by NRDC. The supplier could then sell the machine again to someone else.

ployed with great advantage. Otherwise it was not possible to identify any specific national differences in the main sources of information, whether technical journals, conferences, exhibitions or producers of the machines.

Chart 3.5. *First information on numerically controlled machines*

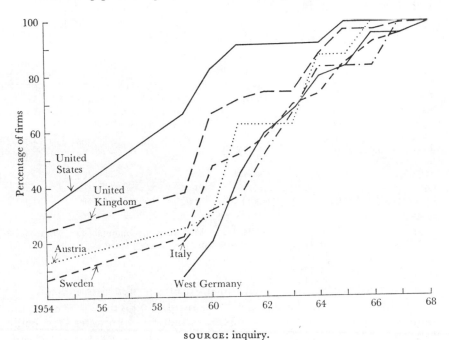

SOURCE: inquiry.
Note: The rapid increase in 1960 was due to the Machine Tool Exhibition in Paris in 1959

Among other things, the economics of numerically controlled machines depend on the production programme, more precisely the batch-size and how often production of the same piece is repeated. This – and therefore the applicability of numerical control – is different in the various branches of the engineering industry even within the same country, let alone internationally. The different structure of the engineering industries in the various countries may therefore account to some extent for the different levels and speeds of the diffusion of numerical control. The largest user of the technique is the aerospace industry, which has a considerable influence in some countries (the United States, Britain and Sweden), but is much smaller or practically negligible in others (Germany and Austria).[1] This is indicated in table

[1] Numerical control is particularly well suited to the complicated metalwork and to the special materials (light alloys) used in this industry.

3.10, which probably underestimates the impact of aircraft (and other aerospace) manufacture on the diffusion of numerical control.[1] Mechanical and electrical engineering are other branches in which a relatively large number of numerically controlled machines are used.[2] Structural differences – mainly the part played by the aerospace industry – can help to explain the lower level of diffusion in Germany and elsewhere than in the United States, Britain and Sweden.

Table 3.10. *Distribution of numerically controlled machine tools in the major industries*

Percentages

	Austria	Sweden	United Kingdom	United States	West Germany
Mechanical engineering	70·0	17·1	56·0	49·1	65·4
Electrical engineering	} 30·0	{ 40·9	12·0	12·0	7·5
Motor vehicles		—	3·0	1·3	10·7
Aerospace	—	18·1	25·0	18·2	1·8
Others	—	23·9	4·0	19·4	14·6
Total	100·0	100·0	100·0	100·0	100·0

SOURCES: OIW estimates; Verein Deutscher Werkzeugmaschinenfabriken, Frankfurt; OECD, *NC Machine Tools. Their introduction in the engineering industries*, Paris, 1970. *Note:* No data available for Italy.

Similar differences of a structural nature may stem from the impact of the size of the market on the method of production. It can easily happen that in one country mass production dominates a specific branch, while in another, because of the smaller market, similar products in the same branch of industry are being made in much smaller quantities, with more consideration given to individual requirements. Hence the production programme, a decisive precondition for the economic employment of numerical control in any enterprise, may also explain differences in diffusion. In the United States, for example, one-

[1] This is because the first- and second-line suppliers of aircraft companies are classified elsewhere. It was estimated in the interim report that, if these suppliers in various branches of the engineering industry are also considered, the aircraft and allied industries probably accounted for half of the British stock of numerically controlled machines. A supplementary survey conducted in Britain supports this: the study covered 42 firms which employed 262 numerically controlled machines in 1966 and 848 in 1970. Over the period 1966–70 the share of machines installed by aircraft and allied companies rose from 49 to 63 per cent; in 1970 an average of 4·4 numerically controlled machines per thousand employees was installed in these firms compared with only 2.3 in the other companies covered by this random survey.

[2] These, together with road vehicles, purchased 89 per cent of the numerically controlled machine tools sold by German producers on their home market in the period 1957–69. Mechanical engineering purchased 69 per cent, road motor vehicles 12 per cent, and electrical engineering 8 per cent.

off pieces or small batches are often produced by specialised suppliers, *quasi* sub-contractors. Production of this specific type of product is therefore concentrated with these specialists, who can thereby apply numerical control to operations for which otherwise the purchase of a numerically controlled machine would not be justified. This has contributed to the diffusion of the technique in the United States.

Specific factors at company and plant level: micro-economics

From the purely technological point of view there are practically no limitations to the employment of numerically controlled machines. All workpieces processed by hand-operated or conventional automatic machines can also be produced by numerical control, but their production would not be economic outside a rather narrow range. Even if general economic conditions favour the employment of numerically controlled machines, their economic use is decisively determined at plant level by the production programme. The number of identical pieces in the 'most economic batch', as well as the frequency with which this batch is produced, determines the type of machine which can be most economically employed.

If a relatively unsophisticated part is needed only once, production by a hand-operated, simple machine tool will generally be the most economic. In such a case production time is relatively long and labour costs accordingly high, but the capital cost of the machine is low and the programming cost, which would be required on a numerically controlled machine, is avoided altogether. The high capital cost of a numerically controlled machine would probably not pay off even if production of such a piece was repeated; hence hand-operated machines remain the answer. Numerical control has no advantages, at least at present, unless the piece requires highly complex operations.

At the other end of the scale, for large quantities, mechanical automatic machines are the most economic, either individually, or geared to each other in a system for simultaneous or consecutive operations. They mass-produce pieces quickly, but the changeover to making other products is time-consuming and costly (or indeed in some cases impossible). Long production runs of the same piece are the key to the economics of traditional automatic machines and, if the quantities are large enough, the capital cost per piece will be less than it would be for production by numerical control. For mass production the relatively inflexible automatic machines with changeable control are therefore more economic than the much more flexible numerically controlled machines.

The area remaining for economic application of numerically controlled machines is therefore in the range of small and medium-sized batches. Naturally the quantities where numerical control is most economic are quite different from workpiece to workpiece and from machine to machine. In very general terms, the technique is most favourable within the range of 5 to 50 pieces. The more complicated the piece to be produced, and the more frequently the same programme is repeated, the more advantageous is numerical control. For a large quantity which has to be broken down into many small batches (to save storage for instance), numerical control can be very economic.

Chart 3.6. *Minimum production costs on various machines in relation to batch-size and number of orders*

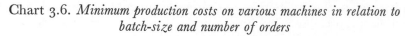

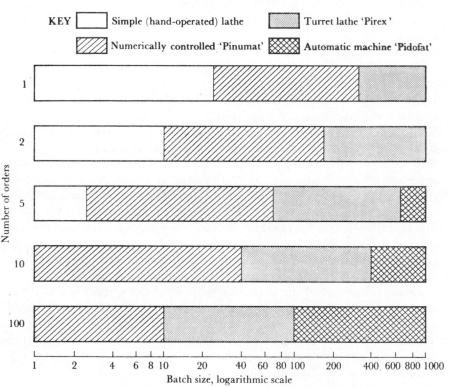

SOURCE: Pittler AG, Langen, West Germany.
Note: All based on costs for machining a bevel gear.

Chart 3.6 demonstrates the influence of the batch-size and of the frequency of repetition on the economics of the choice of machine by one particular firm. Four different turning machines are compared: a simple hand-operated lathe, a hand-operated turret capstan lathe with a pre-set gear (a semi-automated ' Pirex ' machine), a double-spindle automatic chuck lathe and electro-hydraulic cam gear (a changeable fully automatic mechanically controlled ' Pidofat ' machine) and a simple numerically controlled turning machine (' Pinumat').[1]

For producing a batch of up to 25 pieces in one single operation the hand-operated machine works most economically and is followed by the numerically controlled machine in the relatively wide range of 25 to 300 pieces, while the semi-automatic machine incurs the lowest costs per piece in quantities from 300 upwards. If the whole quantity required is broken down into five batches, the numerically controlled machine becomes the most economic from a batch-size of two upwards and remains so to a batch-size of 70; beyond this number and up to a total quantity of 3,500 the conventional semi-automatic machine, and for larger quantities the fully automatic machine, would have to be used. If the batch production had to be repeated about a hundred times, even for one-off production (a batch-size of one) the employment of a hand-operated machine would no longer pay off; the advantageous application of a numerically controlled machine would be reduced to a maximum batch-size of ten, and from a batch-size of 100 the fully automatic machine would be the most economic.

A similar cost schedule for other types of machine tools, such as drilling and milling machines, would of course be different, but the example will suffice to show how manifold the variation can be and how many alternative possibilities there are in terms of machine economics. It demonstrates just how difficult it is for an enterprise to decide whether numerically controlled machines are economic at all, and if so where within their whole range of operations, especially since this comparison would have to be made for every single workpiece produced and for all types of machines. Of course, now and then there are clear-cut cases, where the advantages of numerical control are so obvious that no doubts about its economics arise (an example would be the one-off production of a perforated disc with 1,000 holes, arranged in a uniform but highly precise manner). However, these cases are rare. The diffusion of numerically controlled machines is therefore decisively determined by two factors: the efforts made by firms to assess the

---

[1] The prices of these machines, including accessories, are DM 30,000, DM 63,000 DM 122,000 and DM 178,000, respectively. The cost per workpiece consists of preparatory costs divided by the foreseeable number of orders, plus costs of order repetition divided by batch-size, plus direct production costs. Preparatory costs include the programming or the cutting of stencils; order repetition costs are for the exchange of the tape or the changeover of the machine; direct production costs are those arising exclusively from the production of each piece in the batch, such as wages, energy consumption, machine depreciation, and other direct expenses. Costs which remain uniform for all machines were not considered, for example preparation of detailed drawings or the cost of materials. The costing reflects conditions in Germany in mid-1970.

possible range of economic employment of numerical control within their operations, and the extent to which their individual production programme is suited to numerical control (in other words, the proportion of their production accounted for by the range in which the technique is economic).

Table 3.11. *Unit costs of production on numerically controlled machines*

	Workpiece and operation	Batch-size	Ratio to costs on hand-operated machines
		(no. of pieces)	(percentages)
Austria	Leading wheel turning	50	21[a]
	Gland turning	50	55[a]
Italy	Tube/plate drilling	3	49
	Box drilling	15	69
	Cover turning	20	57
	Turbine shaft turning	10	50
	Lever drilling/milling	20	70
	Printing cylinder milling	10–40	83
Sweden	Turning	8	70
		12	75
	Cutting	5	40
United Kingdom	Drilling	50	50
	Turn and screw	12	30
		12	62
		30	56
	Turn profile	64	40
		20	35
West Germany	Box drilling	10	80
	Gearbox drilling	1	64
	Spindle box drilling	4	78
	Bush turning	5	70
	Box drilling/milling	40	37
	Turning	5	75

SOURCE: inquiry.
[a] Based on machining time only.

Table 3.11 illustrates some concrete examples of the cost savings achieved by a numerically controlled machine compared with a conventional machine. The complex problems connected with the economics of numerical control and machine choice make it impossible to examine this question in general terms; the above will, more than anything else, prove that the situation of the individual company – indeed, of the individual plant – is of paramount importance.

In order to obtain an indication of whether opportunities exist for the economic employment of numerical control, information was collected concerning the quantities typically required of the selected final products,[1] since in general there is a crude relation between the quantity of the final product and of its component parts. In table 3.12 the shares in total output of these quantities are shown. If they are compared with the number of numerically controlled machines per thousand employees in the sample firms shown in table 3.4, it suggests a loose correlation between the level of diffusion of numerically controlled machines by country and the medium range of quantities produced (about 2 to 50).

Table 3.12. *Production structures of the sample firms*

Series	No. of pieces	Austria	Italy	Sweden	United Kingdom	United States	West Germany
		(percentages)					
One-off pieces	*1*	38	73	39	31	6	53
Very small	*2–10*	19	10	39	29	22	30
Medium	*11–50*	19	15	11	15	38	14
Large/medium	*51–100*	11	1	4	6	10	1
Long	*101–1000*	12 }	1	7	11 {	23 }	2
Mass production	*1000+*	1			8	1	
Total output		100	100	100	100	100	100

SOURCE: inquiry.

Batch-sizes differ significantly from plant to plant. Table 3.13 gives an indication of the variety of batch-sizes in some of the companies using numerical control (not all of them were in a position to give us information, and not all respondents could answer all the questions concerning batch-sizes). These data suggest that the majority of these users concentrate on small and medium-sized batches. The inquiry could not provide clear evidence of whether this was their initial situation which induced them to install numerically controlled machines in the first place, or whether it was the effect of the machines that their production programme now takes this shape. There must have been forces working both ways, but the balance is likely to lie with the first; probably an initial reliance on small and medium-sized batches was the incentive which made them decide in favour of numerical control.

Firms in which no numerically controlled machines have yet been employed, especially in Germany, gave us the impression that this was due in some degree to lack of adequate information on the technology. Most German non-users gave an unsuitable production programme as the reason for the absence of numerically controlled machines (32 out

[1] Turbines, turning-machines (lathes), printing machines and pumps.

of 52 firms questioned), but there were several among them whose programme (for example making batches of 10 to 15) appeared to suit numerical control well, and yet they replied that these were 'too small series' or even that they had 'no large series'.

Another example, also from Germany, deserves mention here. In a firm, which by size, products and customers corresponded well to another firm with numerous numerically controlled machines, the

Table 3.13. *Batch-sizes in firms using numerical control*

Percentages

	Austria	Italy	Sweden	United Kingdom	United States	West Germany
Smallest batch						
1	50	—	50	41	80	78
2–10	50	80	40	50	20	22
11+	—	20	10	9	—	—
Most frequent batch						
1–10	60	17	40	31	60	58
11–50	40	83	30	63	40	37
51+	—	—	30	6	—	5
Largest batch						
1–20	60	—	20	15	—	25
21–100	40	100	40	55	100	69
101+	—	—	40	30	—	6
Firms responding	*6*	*6*	*10*	*22*	*5*	*19*

SOURCE: inquiry.

reason given for the non-employment of numerically controlled machines was that they were too expensive; on average they would have cost twice as much as conventional machines, and if the board allocated DM 1,000,000 for equipment, they could not double it just to introduce numerical control. The question of whether any comparative cost calculations had been made was answered in the negative. Possibly such a comparison would have turned out favourably for numerically controlled machines, since their higher price is more than balanced in appropriate applications by increased efficiency and capacity; this is just what makes a numerically controlled machine more economic than a conventional one. Such examples make us believe that insufficient information has been hampering the diffusion of numerical control in Germany, and the situation may well be similar in other European countries.

Management attitudes towards technological innovations play an important role in the diffusion process. Firms were asked in the inquiry to classify themselves into three categories: those introducing innovations as soon as possible, those who prefer to wait and see until more is known about the new technique (and possibly the teething troubles have been overcome), and those with no specific policy in these matters. The obvious dangers of asking such a question must be recognised, and some caution is advised against accepting the answers at their face value, without discounting, for example, the attraction for each company of classifying itself in the first category.

Table 3.14. *Attitudes to innovations among the sample firms*

Numbers of firms

	Austria	Italy	Sweden	United Kingdom	United States	West Germany
Introduction as soon as possible	2	11	2	13	—	19
Wait and see	6	3	23	13	7	2
No specific attitude	1	—	4	8	1	4

SOURCE: inquiry.

The results shown in table 3.14 are inconclusive. They indicate remarkable differences in the various countries. Thus, nearly all Swedish firms reported a hesitant attitude, while in Italy and Germany introduction of innovations as rapidly as possible was reported as the predominant policy. The results do not help to explain differences in diffusion; there does not seem to be any correspondence between them and any measure of the relative diffusion of numerical control. If anything, the two move in opposite directions.[1]

Management attitudes are notoriously difficult to specify and measure, but despite the above unsuccessful attempt at quantification, on the basis of the particular situation in each of the responding companies, it can be said with considerable certainty that the attitude of the management is one of the most important factors affecting the extent and speed of the diffusion process.

Radical organisational changes may be – and usually are – connected with the introduction of numerical control; therefore the management must be prepared to accept high risks. Apart from the possible need to install a programming office (and thus move an essential preparatory function further away from the workshop), reorganisation of the

[1] Similarly, a question relating to the age of management also failed to reveal any correlation with the diffusion of numerically controlled machines.

production process itself may be required, and the same applies to the holding and control of stocks, the wage system, and so on. Large firms may find it easier to take such risks. Should the introduction of numerical control fail, this may have more serious consequences in a small firm than in a large organisation. The need to introduce programming is an especially strong psychological barrier for many smaller firms, although all that is needed may often be relatively simple programming, not necessarily entailing the use of electronic data processing equipment.[1] Indeed, no correlation was found between the use of electronic data processing and the introduction of numerical control.

Numerically controlled machines are of course more expensive themselves – quite apart from ancillary outlays – than comparable conventional machines. It is virtually impossible to be accurate about the price differential, since this depends largely on the type of machine and on specific conditions, but in all cases it is substantial. Therefore, even if in the course of their operation they pay off their excess cost rapidly, numerically controlled machines require considerable capital investment. The decision to install them therefore often depends, as does all investment, on the access to capital. Ability to raise finance varied widely between the respondent companies and its impact on this – as on any other new technique – is obvious. Larger companies generally find it easier to finance investment, and the capital needed to install the first numerically controlled machines (as well as for the subsequent internal diffusion) is usually a smaller part of total investment in a large firm than in a small one.

This leads us to the question of the size of the firm. The bulk of numerically controlled machines in the countries studied are installed in large and medium-size companies, but we also found a fair number of smaller firms using them – some small firms were among the early adopters. Actually, smaller firms are often more suited to numerically controlled machines because they usually produce smaller batches than large firms. Our analysis also showed (table 3.7) that the level of diffusion per thousand employees declines with increasing size of firm. But smaller firms may face insurmountable financial difficulties, since the price of a single numerically controlled machine may be higher than their total average investment in a year.[2]

Due to their higher capital costs, numerically controlled machines should be operated in at least two shifts; this may create obstacles in

[1] Certain producers of electronic control offer short training courses in writing the programmes for numerically controlled machines.

[2] In reply to the inquiry, firms reported the following average purchase prices over the period 1960–9 for numerically controlled drilling–milling machines: DM 332,000 in Germany, Kr. 1,025,000 in Sweden, and Sch. 1,642,000 in Austria.

countries where workers are less prepared to work several shifts. This is the case for example, in Germany, but in the United States no difficulties in this respect appear to have arisen.

A machine stock of high average age offers good opportunities for the adoption of numerically controlled machines. An old machine is usually replaced by one of the latest technical standard and securing the most economic use of capital – the highest return. Furthermore, it is probable that if the machine stock is older than average, new machines will be purchased in greater number. (A definite statistical correlation between the age of the machine stock and the number of numerically controlled machines could not, however, be established.)

Occasionally a few firms said that the too rapid technical development of the control features was considered an obstacle to the purchase of numerically controlled machines. These firms prefer to wait until the development of the controls 'settles down' and they can obtain equipment of the new type already free of teething troubles.

As compared with the United States, the hesitant promotion and the slow diffusion of numerically controlled machines in continental countries, such as Germany, might have been caused by, among other things, the different approach to the development of controls. In the United States, development of the entire technology originated in the automatic machining of highly complicated missile and aircraft parts. The result of this was contouring control, and only later was attention devoted to solving simpler problems by means of less complex positioning and straight-line cutting controls. The case in Britain was similar. In Germany, however, the producers of controls started at the simplest end, the positioning control, and expanded their programme later to straight-line cutting and contouring. Numerically controlled machines for complicated functions had therefore to be imported into Germany in the initial stage of diffusion and this might have hampered the diffusion process, at least psychologically. Since in some of the important metalworking machine tools, for example turning machines, contouring is the most frequently used form of numerical control, the numerically controlled variety of such machines did not become popular before the end of the 1960s.[1]

Although it is generally the economies of numerically controlled machines which induce companies to adopt them, in the course of our

[1] This is well demonstrated by the annual production figures of German machine tool makers: production of numerically controlled machine tools was very small until about 1965, when it started accelerating quickly; the share of numerically controlled machines with contouring control rose from practically nil in 1965 to almost 50 per cent in 1969. Of the six most important types of machine tools, German production in 1965 was 162 machines, of which eight had contouring control; in 1969, output rose to 537 machines, including 249 with the contouring control.

inquiry we came across cases in which the concept of economies was interpreted more widely and pure cost saving was overshadowed by other factors. Thus some (especially British) firms reported that at the time of their introduction they had no clear notion of the economies of the numerically controlled machines but had installed these machines in order to adapt production to customers' demands, to save production time and to guarantee delivery dates. One British firm even stated that in those years exports had become increasingly important and this forced them to adapt quickly to the changed market situation abroad and improve their competitive position vis-à-vis mainly American and German suppliers; they considered numerical control the right means of achieving this.

Observations

It is obvious that because of the abundance of factors influencing the diffusion of numerically controlled machines, no list of these can claim to be complete. Their diversity is such that although we believe that our initial hypotheses, as well as our report, cover the most important factors, not even this can be guaranteed. There may be other influences, perhaps just as important as some of those studied. This is due especially to two facts: first, that diffusion at the plant or company level is largely determined by the particular situation, specific to the plant or company; and second, that the decisive factors influencing the diffusion of numerically controlled machines at the national level (partly due to the diversity of the conditions in the large number of individual plants) cannot be determined directly, but only by examining the correlation between hypothetical influences and the actual diffusion.

Considerable attention was devoted to the testing of such correlations,[1] but, probably owing to the insufficient data, no valid scientific conclusions could be drawn which would stand up to the usual tests of statistical significance. In view of the special nature of numerical control, the impossibility of identifying a 'product', the difficulties inherent in machine-by-machine cost comparisons of innumerable jobs and in the large variety of possible alternatives, this is perhaps not surprising. What must be emphasised is that in view of all this, a weak

[1] A large number of econometric experiments were done to estimate correlations: among others, the time (year) of the introduction of the first numerically controlled machine and the level of diffusion by companies was related to the year of first information, research and development expenditure, export share, employment size, output growth, age of the machine stock, share in the production programme of the batch-size most suited to numerical control, etc. In some cases the results were weak, in others somewhat more encouraging, providing some support for our statements. For the totals (i.e. companies from all countries pooled) the best value of R^2 was 0·35 and in most cases remained under 0·2; for companies in the individual countries some results were better, but these were based on a smaller number of observations and were accordingly less reliable.

correlation or the lack of its statistical evidence cannot *dis*prove our basic hypotheses. Our findings and statements are often more qualitative than quantitative, for the above reasons. Nevertheless, we believe them to be valid.

The objects of this survey were to analyse the diffusion of numerically controlled machine tools in the six countries, to make an attempt to explain the reasons for the differences found, and to investigate the factors affecting the adoption of numerical control.

By the end of 1969 the highest level of diffusion was reached in the United States, followed by Sweden and Britain. Germany was somewhat behind these countries, though considerably ahead of Austria and Italy. In no country – including even the United States – was the diffusion of numerical control at the time of the inquiry beyond the early stages of expansion and, on the company level too, most users of numerical control were still very far from utilising this technique to anywhere near its maximum potential.

A very large number of factors influence the diffusion of numerical control. At company or plant level it is probably the production programme which decisively determines the applicability of this technique; it is in the production of small and medium-sized batches (apart from highly complex individual pieces) that it offers the greatest advantages. Many other factors may be at work, most of them specific to the plant, and varying from the local labour situation, through the age of the machine tool stock, to the firm's access to capital and the attitude of the management to innovations.

On the national level, relative labour costs are probably the most important factor and show a positive correlation with the level of diffusion of numerical control. This relationship would explain why the United States was so much ahead of all other countries (partly due also to the early start of diffusion in America) and why the level of diffusion lagged behind in Italy and Austria at the time of the inquiry.

Another important factor which accounts for a considerable part of the differences between diffusion levels in various countries is the structure of industry. The most important sector is the aerospace industry, the presence or absence of which in the national industrial set-up widens or narrows the area of application of numerical control.

Our investigation could not quantify the large number of factors which may influence diffusion. At the company level, the possible alternative production programmes are very numerous – apart of course from many other aspects – and this made mathematical formulation impossible. On the national level, however, an attempt was

Table 3·15. *Factors affecting the diffusion of numerically controlled machines*

	Weight	Austria Value	Austria Score	Italy Value	Italy Score	Sweden Value	Sweden Score	United Kingdom Value	United Kingdom Score	United States Value	United States Score	West Germany Value	West Germany Score
Wage level	40	+1	40	—	—	+3	120	+2	80	+5	200	+2	80
Importance of aerospace industry	10	—	—	+1	10	+1	10	+4	40	+5	50	+1	10
Quality of information system	10	+2	20	—	—	+4	40	+4	40	+5	50	+2	20
Investment financing possibilities	10	—	—	—	—	+4	40	+3	30	+5	50	+1	10
Management attitudes	5	—	—	—	—	+3	15	+2	10	+5	25	+1	5
Condition of the market	5	+1	5	+1	5	+3	15	+4	20	+3	15	+5	25
Trade union attitudes	5	—	—	—	—	—	—	-2	-10	-4	-20	+1	5
Technical factors	5	—	—	+1	5	+2	10	+3	15	+5	25	+1	5
Labour market conditions	5	—	—	+1	5	+5	25	+2	10	—	—	+4	20
Other relevant factors	5	+2	10	+3	15	+3	15	+5	25	+5	25	+5	25
Total	100		75		40		290		260		420		205

SOURCE: IFO estimates.

Note: For explanation see text.

made to present those factors which we believe to be most noteworthy in a form reflecting their significance in the various countries. This is shown in table 3.15, where the ten probably most essential factors are listed to explain differences in the actual diffusion in the various countries. These factors were selected in accordance with the findings of this inquiry and our talks (and those of other institutes in other countries) with companies and experts; on these talks too we based the weighting of the individual factors. Using a scale ranging from $+5$ to -5, each factor was given a 'valuation', which when multiplied by the weight gave a score for each factor. There is, however, one factor – the batch-size determined by the production programme – which could not be included here; although this is of great importance at plant level, it cannot be evaluated at national level.

The pronounced correlation between the level of diffusion of numerically controlled machines in the countries covered by the investigation and labour costs indicates the prominence of this factor.[1] The higher the labour costs the more favourable are conditions for the adoption and rapid diffusion of the technique. Factors of medium weight include the importance of the aerospace industry, the quality of the information system concerning numerical control, and possibilities of investment financing, including promotional support by governments. All other factors were assumed to have relatively limited importance for the explanation of differences in diffusion, although most of them embrace a whole series of individual aspects. Thus the influence of any country's own research and development effort in the area of numerical control, the state of the machine tool industry and its technological and sales efforts, and the level of computer and programming technology belong to the technical factors. These and similar considerations were taken into account in the allocation of valuation figures to the different countries, largely based on the findings and statements in the earlier sections.

From the total of the scores for ten factors for each country a rank order is obtained which corresponds to the actual degree of diffusion. Obviously this scheme is arbitrary to a certain extent, and the score of each factor should not be taken as in any way precise. However, it is believed that the results truly reflect the importance of the main influences at the national level.

---

[1] For Italy it was assumed that the wage level neither promotes the introduction of numerically controlled machines nor hampers their diffusion. The valuation figures for the other countries reflect the rank order of the level of their labour costs.

CHAPTER 4

SPECIAL PRESSES IN PAPER-MAKING

By S. Håkanson, IUI

SPECIAL PRESSES

The function of a paper machine is to form a paper sheet by removing water from a web, which is a dispersion of fibres in water. The machine consists of a wire section, a press section and a drier, all of which cooperate in reducing the water content. Any improvement in the effectiveness of a section means that the machine can be run faster, so that output is increased.

There are different kinds of paper machines. Fourdrinier machines have several cylinders for drying, whilst Yankee machines have only one big one. Combined machines have a few small and one large cylinder. There are also specialised machines, for instance for making tissue or board.

The web is carried by a woollen felt through the nip of two rollers, where it is subjected to pressure. Two to five presses may be used depending on the quality of the paper. Early presses were solid and the water had to travel laterally in the felt, either escaping ahead of the nip and running down in front of the lower roller, or passing back through the felt. By making the bottom roller hollow and providing it with a perforated shell, water could be extracted into this roller by means of a vacuum. This was the 'suction press', introduced about 1925 and at that time considered a vast improvement. The water could now travel perpendicularly through the sheet and the felt, although some lateral movement remained because of the solid areas of the roller between the perforations. Nevertheless, the water removal capacity increased considerably and the suction press became widely used all over the world.

As paper machines grew bigger and speeds increased, the disadvantages of the suction press became more evident. The vacuum equipment was costly to install and had a high power consumption; cleaning the holes in the roller increased maintenance costs. In spite of these disadvantages it was about 30 years before a new pressing technique was developed.

The early development of special presses centered around attempts to improve the suction press. About 1956 Dr Otto Brauns and Mr Lars Jordansson, at the central laboratories of the Association of Swedish Paper Mills, conceived the idea of placing, beneath the felt, fabric which travelled in a separate loop around the bottom roller. The interstices of a plastic fabric, or the perforations in a rubber mat, held the water which had drained perpendicularly through the sheet and the felt during the passage through the nip; afterwards the water could be removed as convenient. Patents were applied for in Sweden in 1957 and in the United States, Canada, Germany, France and England in 1958.

The original idea was to use a rubber belt, but this did not function well. The Mead Corporation in Chillicothe, Ohio, in cooperation with the Huyck Felt Mills, then developed a woven fabric for use as the belt. The first commercial installation of this new press, called a fabric press, was made in December 1961 by the Mead Corporation; the second followed in October 1962 by the same company. In January 1963 the first fabric press in Europe was installed in a medium-sized Swedish paper mill.

A few years later the Beloit Corporation of Wisconsin presented the 'Venta-Nip' press, with cavities in the roller instead of a fabric. This was first installed in the United States in 1963, and in Europe in 1964 by a small British company. This has become the most widely used special press; more than 500 have been installed in the United States.

To simplify the fabric press and reduce costs, Swedish inventors suggested shrinking the fabric on to a solid or suction press, and the first 'shrink-fabric' press was introduced in Sweden in early 1965. Meanwhile another version of the vented press was developed in the United States by Black-Clawson of New York. This 'high-intensity' press, with a small vented roller between two large solid rollers, produces a higher specific pressure. It was first used commercially in 1966.

The general advantages of special presses over suction presses are:

(a) more efficient water removal, which allows the paper machine to be run faster with increased production capacity;

(b) no shadow marking;

(c) no crushing of the sheets by too high a pressure;

(d) lower capital costs in a new installation;

(e) reduced running costs, since there is no drilling or cleaning out of holes, elimination of vacuum equipment avoids high power costs, and steam consumption is reduced since the paper web is drier when it leaves the press section.

THE DIFFUSION MODEL

The analysis of diffusion

Most new industrial techniques are embodied in new capital equipment. Productivity can improve in existing plants and with existing equipment, but in a capital-intensive industry such as paper, the larger part of technical development probably involves capital expenditure.[1] 'Gross investment' states Salter, 'is the vehicle of new techniques, and the rate of such investment determines how rapidly new techniques are brought into general use and are effective in raising productivity.'[2]

Special presses are a capital-embodied technical development, and their diffusion is likely to be closely linked to investment, either in new paper machines or in modernisation of existing machines. These alternatives will be analysed separately in this chapter, since the incentives to install special presses differ considerably in the two cases.

New machines including special presses are installed as the best-practice technique at the moment of installation;[3] the presses represent only a very small fraction of the total investment cost and the decision on whether to put in a new machine can be influenced very little by the particular press chosen. The diffusion of special presses in this case is a function of the capacity increase in the paper industry and the replacement of paper machines.

When modernising existing paper machines, however, the investment decision is more directly linked with the choice of presses, so that these calculations are affected by the relative advantages of the new technique. In this chapter our main concern will be with this case, because it involves a direct and uncomplicated decision on technique. Furthermore, most special presses were installed in existing paper machines.

The diffusion of innovations can be studied at different levels of aggregation. One can start with national data and try to explain differences in diffusion between countries. The residuals then have to be explained by other factors, such as differences between individual firms. Alternatively one can start at the company level, aiming to explain differences in diffusion between firms, and then aggregate the data to the national level, so that differences between countries can be analysed. We adopted the second approach because data for special presses on a national basis were scarce, because five or six countries are too small a sample for statistical analyses and tests, and because the data were often not representative of the national paper industries. Our first objective therefore was to analyse the behaviour of individual companies.

A company or a group of companies consists of a hierarchy: the planning unit is often the widest concept covering the whole group; both a parent company and its subsidiaries are legal units; below that there are plants, which in turn consist of different technical units. We

---

[1] Wohlin, *Forest-based Industries*, p. 155.
[2] Salter, *Productivity and Technical Change*, p. 65.
[3] Ibid., for a further definition and discussion of the concept of best-practice techniques.

were primarily interested in decision units, and we chose legal companies as the level to be approached, partly because information on them is most readily available. This meant that subsidiaries were considered as independent, but not plants.

The decision process within a firm leads to the innovation being either accepted or rejected by the company; this process comprises a chain of events, starting when the first information is received. We were not able to study details of the decision process within the company, but limited ourselves to an observation of company behaviour from the outside, which means that we were mainly concerned with what decisions were taken and when.

Several stages in the process can be distinguished. Rogers defines five of them – awareness, interest, evaluation, trial, and adoption.[1] Many of these stages are ambiguous and difficult to measure, so we concentrated mainly on the first and the last – awareness and adoption. (We also tried to define an evaluation stage, but found it too difficult.)

The decision process as a whole might be regarded as the dependent variable to be explained in a general diffusion model, but, to keep the analysis manageable, we took only one stage – adoption – and focused our main attention on the actual use of new techniques. This variable, however, may well impinge on previous stages of the process, such as the point of time when a company receives the first information. If there is a relation between this date and the date of adoption, then the latter becomes an intermediate variable, and the former can be regarded as determining the adoption.

The timing and the character of the decision is dependent upon a number of independent variables, which we grouped into three categories – innovation, company and institutional variables. Innovation variables are directly related to the characteristics of the innovation as they are perceived by the individual company; Rogers defines five, of which relative advantage is of the greatest interest and significance in our model.[2] It is the degree to which an innovation is superior to ideas it supersedes,[3] and it can be measured in terms of profitability. Company variables consist of resource and attitude variables: the former reflect, at a given point of time, the financial and economic resources of the company, its facilities for obtaining information about new techniques and its ability to evaluate such information; the latter measure the general disposition of the company towards new techniques, innovations and technical advance in general. Institutional variables reflect the impact of the company's environment on the diffusion process, for example, legal regulations, or the activities of trade and research

---

[1] Rogers, *Diffusion of Innovations*, pp. 81ff.
[2] Ibid., ch. 5.   [3] Ibid., p. 124.

organisations. These may well be constant within countries, but are a possible source of inter-country differences.

Formulation of the variables

The dependent variable is defined as the date of first commercial introduction of special presses in a company or plant, or on a paper machine. This variable, T, is given by the month of adoption, starting with $T = 1$ in January 1963, the date the first special press was installed in the companies in the samples (in Sweden).

The relative advantage of a new technique is most naturally measured in terms of profitability. Our hypothesis states that, other things being equal, the length of time a firm waits to install a special press is inversely related to the profitability of the installation.[1] If we apply traditional economic theory strictly, the installation will be decided upon when profitability exceeds a certain level.[2] The risk that has to be taken into account is probably highest in early phases of diffusion, and decreases as experience and knowledge is accumulated. Our hypothesis takes this risk into account more effectively than would the use of a fixed break-even level.

The calculation of profitability is an important and difficult problem. We need a variable comparable between companies, that is, for each of them calculated in the same way and based on the same assumptions, which rules out any calculations performed by the companies them-selves. Furthermore, several respondents did not explicitly make such calculations, or did so only in the context of actual or potential instal-lations and not for other machines. Hence, we had to find an approxima-tion for the profitability of special presses.

One of the most important features of special presses is the extent to which they increase capacity. Discussions with machine manufacturers led to the conclusion that this is mainly a function of the age of the paper machines, so that we assumed a capacity increase of between 4 and 10 per cent, depending on age. Our next assumption was that the extra output could be sold at unchanged prices. The saving from special presses would then be the product of the capacity increase and the difference between the paper price and the variable costs, which mainly consist of pulp costs with a small addition for energy and steam. This saving is of course related to the capacity of the machine with special presses.

The investment cost was estimated on the basis of discussions with paper press manufacturers. It is an approximate function of the width

---

[1] See Mansfield, *Industrial Research and Technological Innovation*, p. 157.
[2] This level may differ between companies and will depend on, among other things, other investment opportunities and the availability of finance.

and the age of the paper machine; the wider and the older the machine, the more expensive special presses are to install. The estimated investment cost (which varied between \$20,000 and \$100,000) divided by the annual savings gave a pay-off period, which we used as an indicator of profitability:

$$P = \frac{I}{aQ\left(\mathcal{Z}_{pa} - 1 \cdot 05 \mathcal{Z}_{pu} - V\right)}$$

where P = pay-off period in years,

I = investment cost, a function of width and age (estimated from a nomogram),

a = percentage capacity increase, a function of age,

Q = annual capacity of the paper machine in 1966,

$\mathcal{Z}_{pa}$ = price per ton of paper,

$\mathcal{Z}_{pu}$ = price per ton of pulp,[1]

and V = other variable costs, such as energy and steam, equal to about \$10 per ton.

This formula has three provisos. First, it refers only to the installation of special presses in existing paper machines, which means rebuilding in the case of solid or suction presses; it is not applicable to new paper machines, in which the installation of special presses is cheaper than suction presses, and, since running costs are also lower, the pay-off period would be negative. Secondly, the formula is primarily based on fabric presses. Since we were not concerned with why a company chose a particular special press, we assumed that this pay-off calculation could be used at least to rank the machines according to profitability. No significant differences in profitability between different types were found. Thirdly, these calculations are hypothetical, in the sense that they do not depend on whether special presses really have been installed or not. Thus, we could calculate pay-off periods for paper machines without special presses.

The integration of a plant (pulp and paper) may slightly increase the profitability of special presses, mainly because of lower pulp costs (these effects were taken account of to some extent in the pulp prices used). There may be other factors making special presses advantageous, for instance, quality improvements, but they are very difficult to measure. Furthermore, discussions with companies indicated that quality improvement is less important than increased capacity.

Apart from the innovation variables, summarily represented by the pay-off period, a number of company variables were used. At various interviews company executives mentioned lack of financial resources as

[1] About 1·05 tons of pulp is required to manufacture 1 ton of paper.

an important reason for not installing an innovation despite its apparent profitability. One indicator of the availability to a company of financial resources is the ratio of self-finance, that is cash flow[1] as a proportion of total investment. A high ratio was assumed to make the company more willing to invest, especially in more risky projects such as those involving new techniques. In order to reduce the impact of annual variations, cash flow was measured as an average over the four years 1962-5, which, in most countries, just preceded the introduction of special presses. Total investment was measured as an annual average over the eight years 1960-7 to reduce the impact of business cycle fluctuations.

Facilities for collecting information may well be related to the company's international relations, for instance, foreign interests in it, subsidiaries abroad, and the export share of turnover. The exchange of know-how through formal agreements is more directly a part of this information flow between companies and countries. Membership of the industry research organisation can provide valuable information through exchanges with colleagues.[2] It is difficult to find a simple operational measure of these facilities, but at least a part of the conceptual variable can be covered by using various indicators.

When information has been received about a new technique, a company has to have the resources to analyse and survey its potentialities. These resources also had to be estimated by proxy variables. We assumed that the ability to analyse technical information was in some way related to the existence of research and development activity in the company, although the research department itself might not be directly involved.

From interviews with a number of executives, we realised that the attitudes of a company towards new techniques often has a decisive influence on the timing of the introduction. The problem was how to measure these attitudes. Answers to direct questions to company managers may indicate the actual behaviour of the firm, or only official dogma. To check the answers about special presses, we asked if firms were using, intended to use, had tested, and were interested or not interested in four other innovations – wet suction boxes, foils, synthetic forming fabrics and process control.

Mansfield tested the growth rate of a company as an explanation for the diffusion of innovations.[3] The overall growth of output in the paper industry can be separated into two parts: the first is extra capacity in new paper machines installed, which will be analysed

---

[1] Net profits after tax, inclusive of depreciation and deposits but excluding dividends.

[2] Our selection of variables is influenced to a certain extent by C. F. Carter and B. R. Williams, *Industry and Technical Progress: factors governing the speed of application of science*, London, Oxford University Press, 1957.

[3] Mansfield, *Industrial Research and Technological Innovation*, p. 165.

separately (see page 60 above); the other is the increased output of existing machines, largely due to technical improvements. This growth on existing machines ('net growth') can be used as an approximate measure of the general interest of the company in technical improvements.

We also tried to analyse two other variables – the profit trend and company size – both of which are related to several categories of our independent variables. A favourable profit development not only creates financial resources in a company, but is also a measure of a general managerial ability, which might be correlated with a willingness to try innovations.

Instead of using company size explicitly in our model, we tried to define a set of variables which reflect more directly the characteristics of a company often approximated by size – financial resources, facilities for external contacts and profitability of the innovation. In our econometric approach, however, we used company size as a proxy for a number of other variables. As a measure of size the number of employees was preferred to output, although this meant disregarding differences in labour productivity between companies and countries.

The variables and their definitions were as follows:

(1) *Dependent variable*

   T = month of introduction of first special press (January 1963 = 1).

(2) *Innovation variable*

   P = pay-off period for a special press (inversely related to the profitability).[1]

(3) *Company variables*

   C = self-financing ratio: cash flow (annual average 1962–5) as a percentage of gross investment (annual average 1960–7);

   O = foreign connections – parent company or subsidiaries abroad;

   E = exports as percentage of total sales in 1966;

   K = know-how agreements with other companies;

   M = membership of the industry research organisation;

   R = research and development activity in the company.

(4) *Attitude variables*

   B = behaviour of the company, calculated for four other new techniques on paper machines (the maximum value is 16 – all four techniques used rather early – and the minimum value 0 – none of the techniques used);

---

[1] See formula on p. 63.

G = 'net growth' – index of the production on Fourdrinier and Combined machines in operation in both 1962 and 1968 (index for 1968 based on index for 1962 = 100).

(5) *Other variables*

F = gross profit as percentage of turnover (annual average 1960–7);

S = size of the company measured by the number of employees in 1966.

EMPIRICAL DATA

Most empirical data were obtained from companies in the six countries, who were approached by questionnaires, mainly distributed by mail, but in many cases answered at personal interviews. Additional information was provided by other sources, such as trade and research associations and published statistics.

Two questionnaires were used: one, for each machine, dealt mainly with innovation variables, and the other chiefly with company variables.[1] Data for institutional variables were obtained from trade associations and national statistics.

Only paper manufacturers with Fourdrinier or Combined machines were approached. Other machines, such as Yankee and Twin-wire, were considered generally unsuitable for special presses and so their users were excluded. Details of the samples and the national industries from which they were drawn are shown in table 4.1. It was very difficult to ascertain either the total number of companies with Fourdrinier and Combined machines or the total production on such machines. The numbers of companies (line 1) and total production (line 4) therefore also cover other types of machine. It was possible, however, to estimate the total number of Fourdrinier and Combined machines in each country; production figures for all types of machine therefore provide a basis for estimating production on Fourdrinier and Combined machines, even though their average output is larger than that of other machines. Fourdrinier and Combined machines predominate in the United Kingdom; they are also quite common in Austria, Germany and the United States, but less so in Italy and Sweden.

In Austria and Sweden almost the whole of the industry is covered by the sample of respondents. In the United Kingdom about half of the industry is covered, but in Germany, Italy and the United States it is a considerably lower proportion. To analyse how far the samples

[1] Data from companies were collected during autumn 1968 and spring 1969 in the European countries and during 1970 in the United States.

were representative, the average volumes of production for all companies in the industry and for those in the samples were compared. This showed that large companies were heavily over-represented in Germany, Italy and the United States, partly because, especially in Italy, there are many very small paper-making companies, which were deliberately omitted from the study. Sample companies in Austria and the United Kingdom were slightly smaller on average than in all the countries

Table 4.1. *National paper and board industries, 1966, and coverage of the samples*

	Austria	Italy	Sweden	United Kingdom	United States	West Germany
Number of companies						
In industry	21	586	47	50	400	226
In sample	16	29	31	23	17	12
Coverage (percentages)	*76*	*5*	*66*	*46*	*4*	*5*
Production (thousand tons)						
By industry	738	2,633	3,182	4,469	45,000	4,143
By sample companies	399	717	2,783	1,853	6,000[a]	1,229
Coverage (percentages)	*54*	*27*	*87*	*41*	*13*	*30*
Average production of a company (thousand tons)						
In industry	35	5	68	89	112	18
In sample	25	25	89	81	353	102
Machines						
All types	80–90	891[b]	280	310	2,500	493
Fourdrinier and Combined						
Total	60	432[b]	121	300	2,000	364
In sample	51	55	121	149	153	48
Coverage (percentages)	*85*	*13*	*100*	*50*	*8*	*13*

SOURCES: national data; inquiry.

[a] In 1968.   [b] In 1965.

covered, because some board production and production on Yankee and other non-special press machines was excluded. Nevertheless in Austria and the United Kingdom, as well as Sweden, the sample companies were reasonably representative as to size. The United States sample was quite small – 17 companies, out of which only four answered the full questionnaire, while 13 responded to a shortened version. The biases in the German, Italian and American samples, of course, affect comparisons with the other countries and, in the analysis of country

differences, attention will be mainly devoted to Austria, Sweden and
the United Kingdom.

The response rate differed considerably between the six countries. In
Austria, Sweden and the United Kingdom, the companies were quite
willing to reply, but in Germany, Italy and the United States less than
half responded. These figures are shown in table 4.2.

Table 4.2. *Respondents among the companies approached*

	Austria	Italy	Sweden	United Kingdom[a]	United States	West Germany
Approached	17	60	31	50	50	31
Replied	16	29	31	41	17	12
Coverage (percentages)	*94*	*48*	*100*	*82*	*34*	*39*

SOURCE: inquiry.

[a] Numbers of plants.

Coverage as shown in table 4.1 tells us nothing about the quality of
the answers. In fact, the response rate on individual questions was very
different. The chief problem was that some companies, mainly in the
United Kingdom, were reluctant to give production figures, so that
these had to be estimated. Questions about companies' economic and
financial status were almost never answered except in Sweden. Many
companies also had difficulty in answering questions about the resources devoted to research and development.

When translating conceptual variables into operational ones, one is
always concerned with the extent to which a variable really measures
what is intended. Unfortunately, our ability to test the validity of
variables was very limited, and we had to fall back on a verbal analysis
of the problem.

Profitability probably involves the most important validity problem
in this study. This variable is based on a number of simplifications and
assumptions, and yet it is important because it directly reflects traditional profit-maximising theory. We assumed, however, a reasonably
high validity because:

(a) the pay-off period incorporates empirical experience, not only
theoretical assumptions;

(b) profitability values obtained from companies showed a certain
agreement with our calculations;

(c) press manufacturers and paper-makers who were consulted in
general accepted our method of estimating profitability.

However, the pay-off period as defined should not be seen primarily as an objective concept, but more as a means of ranking different paper machines as to their suitability for special presses.

The fact that we limited ourselves to the observation of company behaviour from the outside emphasises the validity problem involved in the company variables, which to some extent are meant to illustrate characteristics of the company as an organisation. Here again, however, we found some support in our discussions with company representatives. Furthermore, our theory took account of previous researchers' studies of the different variables.[1]

THE DECISION PROCESS

First information

The companies investigated were asked when they first became aware of special presses and from what source they received that information. These are, doubtless, rather difficult questions to answer, but we have some reason to give weight to the answers. Very often the person we approached had had long experience in the company, as a technical supervisor or production engineer, and he was often able to trace back the first information to a certain event, for instance a visit to a research institution or another company.

The diffusion of information can be illustrated by curves showing the cumulative percentage of firms which had received the first information, as in chart 4.1. Five of the curves reach 100 per cent, indicating that no company in those countries was unaware of special presses at the time of our investigation.[2] However, it should be remembered that, while the Austrian, British and Swedish samples are representative of the national paper industries, the samples from Germany, Italy and the United States are biased, with large firms and also firms using special presses over-represented. These biases may affect the information curves.

The Swedish information curve is a few years ahead of the others. This might be because special presses were originally invented in Sweden, which facilitated the information flow. The difference was especially important during the early phase of diffusion; by 1960, two years before the first special press was in commercial use in Sweden, eleven Swedish firms had information about the technique, compared with only three in the United Kingdom and one each in Austria, Italy and the United States. The American information curve seems rather late, especially considering the amount of development work on special presses carried out in the United States.

---

[1] For instance, Carter and Williams, Mansfield, and Rogers.
[2] One company in Italy learned about them after the investigation started.

Chart 4.1. *Diffusion of first information on special presses*

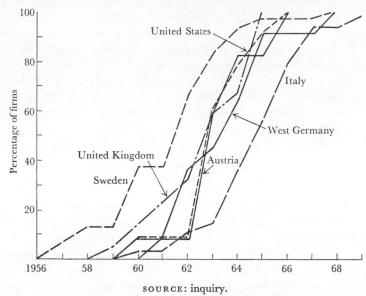

SOURCE: inquiry.

Note: Based on data from 12 firms in Austria, 29 in Italy, 30 in Sweden, 22 in the United Kingdom, 13 in the United States and 11 in West Germany.

Information about new processes might be expected to spread very rapidly in highly industrialised countries. The long interval – in Sweden 12 years – between the first and the last receipt of information is thus surprising. One should remember, however, that the technique is relatively small, not revolutionary and not a very common subject of discussion in trade journals. Moreover, by omitting the extreme 20 per cent of firms the time-span is practically halved, as shown in table 4.3, where it can also be seen that in Sweden, where the information spread earlier than in the other countries, the rate of diffusion was considerably slower even when the extremes are omitted.

Table 4.3. *Timelags between first and last receipts of information*

Years

	Austria	Italy	Sweden	United Kingdom	United States	West Germany
Total sample	6	10	12	8	7	8
80% of sample	3	4	6	5	3	4

SOURCE: inquiry.

When firms were asked to identify the source from which they received their first information about special presses, many had difficulty in identifying a single source and answered with two or three. Despite this duplication, we believe that the answers adequately reflect the relative importance of the various sources, as shown in table 4.4. The three groups shown are fairly distinct from each other, and within the groups the differences are smaller.

Table 4.4. *Sources of information: frequency in replies*

	In 50% of replies or more	Intermediate frequency	Very infrequent
Austria	Journals Manufacturers and licence-holders Congresses, fairs and conferences	—	Competitors Research institutions Customers
Italy	Journals Manufacturers and licence-holders	Congresses, fairs and conferences	Competitors Customers Research institutions
Sweden	Journals Manufacturers and licence-holders Research institutions	Congresses, fairs and conferences	Competitors Customers
United Kingdom	Journals Manufacturers and licence-holders	Congresses, fairs and conferences Competitors	Research institutions Customers
United States	Manufacturers and licence-holders Journals Congresses, fairs and conferences	Competitors	Research institutions Customers
West Germany	Journals Manufacturers and licence-holders Congresses, fairs and conferences	—	Competitors Customers Research institutions

SOURCE: inquiry.

The ranking pattern is very similar for the six countries. In Europe, technical journals are considered the most important source of information, followed by manufacturers and licence-holders; congresses, fairs and conferences came third. The American replies agree quite well with those from European countries, although the order of the first two sources is reversed: manufacturers of presses were far the most important source in the United States, and information spread through competing firms only to a limited extent. In five of the countries,

research institutions were unimportant as a source of information, but
not in Sweden, where such an institution played an important role –
naturally enough since the fabric press was invented at the central
laboratories of the Association of Swedish Paper Mills.

First adoption

The second stage studied in the decision process was the actual adoption
of special presses by individual firms. This will be analysed more
thoroughly in the next section. Here only the diffusion curves are

Chart 4.2. *Diffusion of first adoption of special presses*

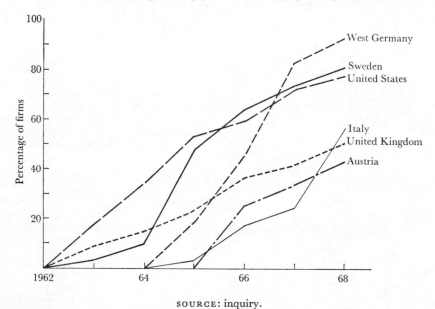

SOURCE: inquiry.
Note: Based on data from the same firms as chart 4.1, except for the United States, where
based on 17 firms.

shown (chart 4.2). Like the curves for information, the diffusion of
adoption started early in both Sweden and the United Kingdom, but
in the latter the subsequent increase was comparatively slow, taking five
years to reach about 40 per cent diffusion as compared with only two
to three years in the other European countries. The American adoption
curve is much earlier in relation to the curves of other countries than
the information curve, indicating that the period between information
and introduction was comparatively short in the United States. The
German, Italian and American adoption curves are probably affected
significantly by the biases in those samples.

The theoretical model, discussed above (pages 65–6), contains a set of independent variables which hypothetically determine the dependent variable, the date of adoption. This is, however, a simplified description of the causal relationships. Some of the independent variables do not influence the date of adoption directly. The information variables, for instance, are assumed to be at least a partial explanation of when a firm gets information on an innovation; subsequently,

Chart 4.3. *Diffusion of information and adoption compared*

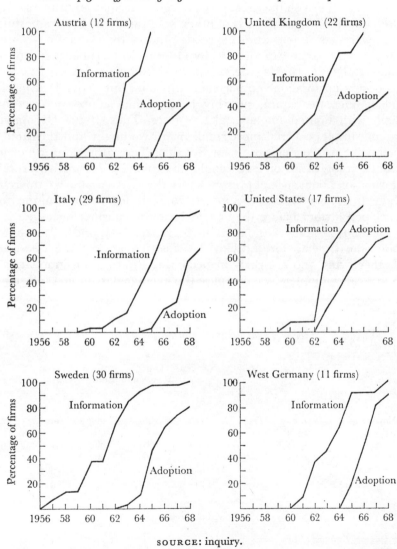

SOURCE: inquiry.

evaluation resources will presumably affect the date of consideration. The model thus implies that early information creates good conditions for early decision. Thus, a graphical illustration of the duration of the decision process within a firm might provide a basis for a preliminary discussion of different groups of variables.

Curves for the two stages of this decision process in each country are shown in chart 4.3. The patterns differ considerably: the Italian, German and Swedish curves seem, to some extent, to converge over time (adoption diffuses quicker than information), while the American, Austrian and British ones seem to diverge (information diffuses quicker than adoption). On the basis of other investigations, Rogers postulated that awareness (information) spreads quicker than adoption,[1] but our findings only partly support this hypothesis. In Germany, and to some extent Italy, the timelag decreases as diffusion increases. In Sweden this occurs up to about 50 per cent diffusion, but above that level the timelag increases again, possibly because late adopters were rather small, with limited managerial resources. Thus, if the German and Italian samples covered more small firms, we might find the same late divergence in their curves as for Sweden. The rather long timelag for Sweden at low diffusion levels could be explained if some firms received information about special presses before they were usable commercially. These firms would thus be forced to wait for the technique to be developed further before they could seriously consider installing it.

The above is, however, based on aggregate data, and tells us nothing about the timelag for individual firms. To answer the question of whether firms who are early in becoming aware of an innovation are also its early adopters, we compare the average date of first information

Table 4.5. *Average year of first information by categories[a] of adopters*

	Austria	Italy	Sweden	United Kingdom	United States	West Germany	All countries
Adopters							
Early	n.a.	n.a.	1961	1961	1963	n.a.	1962
Majority	1963	1964	1961	1963	1964	1963	1963
Late	1964	1965	1961	1962	1964	1965	1964
Non-adopters	1963	1966	1966	1963	1962	1965	1964
All categories	1964	1965	1962	1963	1964	1964	1963

SOURCE: inquiry.

[a] As defined on p. 76.

[1] Rogers, *Diffusion of Innovations*, p. 108.

for different categories of adopter (table 4.5).[1] We find only rather weak evidence that early information advances the date of adoption of an innovation. In Sweden, for instance, the average year of first information is the same for all three categories of adopter, although considerably later for non-adopters. In the other countries the differences between different categories are also quite small, which is consistent with findings by Rogers.[2]

INTER-FIRM DIFFUSION

We are concerned first with diffusion at the company level – that is how soon a company introduced its first special press for commercial use – and we begin by defining both the dependent variable and the profitability measure to be used in the analysis.

The dependent variable is the date a special press was first used by a company in any of its plants, that is the T-value. The pay-off period refers to that paper machine in each company which is most profitable (with the shortest pay-off period). The machine is not necessarily the one on which a special press was first installed; a company might do so on a machine with a longer pay-off period if, for instance, the most profitable machine was very large, so that trying a new technique on it involved a correspondingly large risk. The shortest pay-off period therefore represents the maximum return that the company could earn.

The diffusion of an innovation among companies can be measured by the total number of companies which have adopted it. Chart 4.2 demonstrated this measure in graphical form. In the United States, special presses diffused quite quickly after their introduction in 1961. In both Austria and Sweden almost half the companies were using the technique within three years, and in Sweden it took another two years to reach about 75 per cent diffusion. The Swedish curve seems to be S-shaped with the point of inflexion at 30–40 per cent. The British curve on the other hand is almost linear; it starts as early as the Swedish one, but after some years tends towards the Austrian curve, which starts three years later. The curves for the other three countries all reach quite a high level of diffusion, and all show quite a high rate of increase, but we must remember that those samples are not unbiased.

An exploratory approach

In this section we first analyse the impact of profitability and then discuss the effects of the company variables. The reason for this two-step analysis is that profitability is directly related to the specific innovation, whilst company variables only reflect the innovative activity and behaviour of the company in general. The traditional profit-maximising

---

[1] See definitions, p. 76.   [2] Rogers, *Diffusion of Innovations*, p. 108.

theory is represented by profitability, and the company variables are then used in an attempt to explain the residuals.

Since time (of adoption) is continuous, any classification into different adoption categories must involve an arbitrary element. As Rogers shows,[1] a wide variety of classifications have been used by different researchers. Rogers himself presents one which assumes that adopters are approximately normally distributed over time;[2] categories of

Table 4.6. *Sample companies by categories[a] of adopters*

	Austria	Italy	Sweden	United Kingdom	United States	West Germany
Adopters						
Early	—	—	5	2	6	—
Majority	4	4	15	6	4	4
Late	3	13	6	3	4	6
Non-adopters	9	10	5	12	3	2
All categories	16	27[b]	31	23	17	12

SOURCE: inquiry.

[a] As defined in the text below.

[b] Two sample companies omitted: they have machines installed after 1965.

adopters are defined by distance from the mean in multiples of the standard deviation. Although the Swedish observations seem to be roughly normally distributed, the number of companies in each sample is too small to make normality meaningful.

Instead we divided the companies into four categories on the basis of the Swedish distribution (table 4.6). The first three are distinguished by time limits rather arbitrarily chosen: 'early adopters' span a period of two and a half years, while the 'majority' group covers only one and a half years; 'late adopters' are those which installed special presses more than four years after their introduction.[3]

Our only, though complex, innovation variable is profitability, or more precisely the pay-off period. This is, however, only available for the European countries, not for the United States. The British, Italian and Swedish data in table 4.7 seem to support our profitability hypothesis: the pay-off period distinguishes well between adopters and non-adopters. The data from Austria and Germany are more confusing, but can be explained to some extent by the large impact of extreme values

[1] Ibid., ch. 6.   [2] Ibid., pp. 259ff.

[3] In subsequent tables the number of companies in different categories may not add up to the totals for various countries in table 4.6. This is due to lack of information on some variables. For the companies in table 4.6, data for some of the variables are available, but not necessarily all.

Table 4.7. *Average pay-off periods by categories of adopters*

Years

	Austria	Italy	Sweden	United Kingdom	West Germany	All countries
Adopters						
Early	n.a.	n.a.	0·5	0·2	n.a.	0·4
Majority	1·1[a]	0·7	0·5	0·6	1·4	0·7
Late	0·5	0·4	0·6	1·3	0·7	0·6
Non-adopters	0·6	3·2	3·0	2·4	0·1[b]	2·3

SOURCE: IUI estimates.

[a] 0·2 if one extreme value is omitted.   [b] Based on one observation only.

when the averages are based on so few observations. Closer examination shows that, in Sweden, a pay-off period of one year separates adopters from non-adopters almost completely, and this is also true for the rather unreliable Italian sample. No other country shows such a sharp separation, although a pay-off period of 18 months does fairly well for the United Kingdom in this respect. In the other countries, however, there appears to be no strong correlation between the pay-off period and the date of first adoption.

The first of the company variables is the self-financing ratio, but data on this were rather difficult to obtain in some countries, so that our analysis had to be limited to Sweden and the United Kingdom. For Sweden data are available for all except five companies, mainly small ones, and for the United Kingdom information is lacking only for ten smaller companies. The average self-financing ratio for different categories of adopters is shown in table 4.8.

Table 4.8. *Self-financing ratios[a] by categories of adopters,*
Sweden and the United Kingdom

Percentages

	Adopters			Non-adopters
	Early	Majority	Late	
Sweden	99	79	70	91[b]
United Kingdom		100		71

SOURCE: IUI estimates.

[a] As defined on p. 65.   [b] Based on four companies only.

For Sweden the average ratio is highest for the early adopters and decreases for later categories. The comparatively low profitability (long pay-off period) for the non-adopters explains why they have remained non-adopters in spite of available finance (a high self-financing ratio). British observations are few, but also give some support to our hypothesis that a high self-financing ratio favours the introduction of a new technique. The pay-off period is, however, also longer on average for non-adopters, which precludes any general statement about the causal relationship.

The information variables are meant to indicate the resources a company has for attracting and evaluating information about new techniques. We analysed the impact of these variables on the timing of the introduction of special presses by calculating the percentage of companies in each category of adopters with foreign connections (parent company or subsidiaries abroad), with know-how agreements, with membership in the industry research organisation, and with research and development activities within the company; we also calculated the average share of exports in total sales. The results of this analysis are shown in table 4.9. With few observations in some of the categories, the deviation around the mean becomes large; some tendencies can, however, be noted.

We postulated relatively high values for all variables in the early adopter categories and correspondingly low figures for non-adopters. There is such a tendency, although somewhat weak for some variables, in Sweden and the United Kingdom, but in other countries the picture is more mixed. We can also see that the difference between early adopters and the majority group is small; the line is more evident between the first two and the last two categories.

The difference between adopters and non-adopters is relatively clear in regard to foreign connections (except for Austria) and to know-how agreements (except for the United States). There are large differences between the countries in respect of membership of research organisations: in Sweden, the United Kingdom and the United States almost all companies are members, but this is not so in the other three countries. This variable is probably more suitable for explaining differences in diffusion between countries, and the same can be said of the share of exports; Austria and Sweden are large exporters of paper compared to the other four countries. As to research and development, American companies are more often engaged in such activities than the companies in the other countries.

Foreign integration consists of two elements – either the company has foreign subsidiaries, or it is itself a subsidiary of a foreign company. The assumption is that in both cases the ability to obtain technical information

Table 4.9. *Information variables[a] by categories of adopters*

	Number of companies	Proportion of companies with				Average exports/ total sales (E)
		Foreign connections[b] (O)	Know-how agreements (K)	Research organisation membership (M)	R & D activities (R)	
		(percentages)				
Austria						
Adopters: Majority	4	—	25	50	50	—
Late	3	33	37	67	67	38
Non-adopters	10	70	10	30	10	34
Total	17	47	24	41	29	35
Italy						
Adopters: Majority	4	50	—	75	50	4
Late	13	—	23	46	23	4
Non-adopters	10	10	10	50	30	2
Total	27	11	15	52	30	3
Sweden						
Adopters: Early	5	20	40	100	60	67
Majority	15	20	33	100	56	62
Late	6	18	18	100	18	59
Non-adopters	5	—	—	80	40	31
Total	31	16	28	97	56	57
United Kingdom						
Adopters: Early	2	50	50	100	100	13
Majority	6	50	67	100	100	8
Late	3	33	—	100	—	2
Non-adopters	12	8	17	67	42	1
Total	23	26	30	83	57	4
United States						
Adopters: Early	6	..	40	80	100	3
Majority	4	..	25	100	100	25
Late	4	..	50	100	75	24
Non-adopters	3	..	40	100	100	2
Total	17	..	40	93	94	15
West Germany						
Adopters: Majority	4	25	25	75	25	2
Late	6	50	33	50	50	3
Non-adopters	2	—	—	—	100	4
Total	12	33	25	50	50	3
		(O_p) (O_s)				
All countries						
Adopters: Early	13	43 —	42	92	85	37
Majority	37	18 9	32	89	64	31
Late	35	16 3	29	69	35	18
Non-adopters	42	3 21	13	55	39	15
Total	127	14 11	26	72	50	22

SOURCE: inquiry.

[a] See definitions on p. 65.

[b] For all countries divided into O_p = parent company of foreign subsidiaries; and O_s = subsidiary of foreign parent company.

would increase, but the combined variable gives hardly any support to this assumption. If it is split into two variables: O_p = parent company of foreign subsidiaries, and O_s = subsidiary of a foreign company, we find that the Austrian and Italian figures refer to O_s, while the Swedish and British figures refer to O_p. In Austria seven out of ten non-adopters, but only one of seven adopters, are subsidiaries of foreign companies; in the United Kingdom five out of eleven adopters, but only one of twelve non-adopters, have subsidiaries in other countries. Thus it seems there is a positive correlation between the introduction of special presses and the existence of foreign subsidiaries, but a negative correlation with having a parent company abroad.

Pooling of data from all countries provides a larger number of observations. These results are more consistent with our hypotheses and assumptions than the results for the individual countries, possibly because the pooling takes into consideration structural differences between countries.

The attitudes of a company's managers and technicians are alleged to have a decisive influence on the introduction of new techniques. Attitudes affect the evaluation of risk and uncertainty and, thus, the management's perception of the relative advantage of a new technique; they also affect the amount of effort devoted to a search for information.

We asked companies explicitly about their attitudes towards new techniques, but the answers were difficult to interpret. A direct measure of the actual behaviour of the companies with respect to new techniques was given by the variable which measured their behaviour regarding four other new techniques on paper machines.[1] We estimated the correlation between it and their stated attitudes: in both Austria and Germany correlation coefficients were negative; in Italy and Sweden they were positive but rather low; only in the United Kingdom was there a comparatively high positive coefficient ($R^2 = 0.40$). From this we concluded that the stated attitudes of the companies were a somewhat unreliable measure of their actual attitudes.

In Sweden and the United Kingdom the variables measuring company attitudes were checked by another method. An industry expert in each country ranked the companies by their innovative capacity. Both the correlations between expert opinion and actual behaviour were considerably better than the correlations with the companies' stated attitudes. This supports our conclusion that our measure of behaviour is more reliable than the stated attitudes; its average values for different categories of adopters are shown in table 4.10.

These results give some support to the hypothesis of a positive relationship between company attitudes (measured by B) and the early

[1] B, see p. 65.

Table 4.10. *Company attitudes to four other new techniques[a] by categories of adopters*

	Austria	Italy	Sweden	United Kingdom	United States[b]	West Germany	All countries
Adopters							
Early	n.a.	n.a.	10	12	12	n.a.	10
Majority	5	9	9	12	..	8	9
Late	4	8	6	8	10	7	7
Non-adopters	5	4	2	9	8	5	6
All categories	5	7	8	10	10	7	7

SOURCE: inquiry.
[a] Average value of B (maximum 16) as defined on p. 65.
[b] American values based on five companies only.

introduction of special presses. As with the information variables, the differences between the early adopters and the majority are relatively small. The main division is between the majority and the late adopters, at least for Sweden, the United Kingdom and the United States. The large differences between countries in the average values of B may partly be explained by differences in the samples; where large companies are over-represented, B may be higher than its value for the whole national industry.

The other variable assumed to indicate a favourable attitude towards innovations was the growth of output from paper machines which were in operation in both 1962 and 1968. These output increases on individual machines would have been caused mainly by technical improvements.

Table 4.11. *Growth in machine productivity[a] by categories of adopters*

Indices for 1968, 1962 = 100

	Austria	Italy	Sweden	United Kingdom	United States	West Germany	All European countries
Adopters							
Early	n.a.	n.a.	134	145	(161)	n.a.	137
Majority	166	122	141	124	(123)	132	137
Late	130	134	128	109	(143)	156	134
Non-adopters	134	128	113	134	(111)	99	127
All categories	140	129	133	128	(135)	138	133

SOURCE: inquiry.
[a] Average values of G as defined on p. 66, except for United States, where figures refer to total output and thus include machines built or taken out of production during 1962–8.

They are shown for different categories of adopters in table 4.11. Although output on individual machines increased over the six-year period between 30 and 40 per cent, which is 4 to 5 per cent a year, the figures give only weak support to our hypothesis; in the column for all countries, later categories show only slight decreases. The averages over all categories for the different countries are, however, surprisingly close to each other.

Neither the profit rate nor the size of companies fit explicitly into our model as independent variables. The former, defined as the average annual gross profit 1960–7 as a percentage of turnover, is available only for most Swedish companies and for some British ones. Averages for the different categories are shown in table 4.12, where it appears that non-adopters had considerably lower profits than adopters, the figures for Sweden and the United Kingdom being remarkably similar.

Table 4.12. *Profit rates[a] by categories of adopters,*
Sweden and the United Kingdom

Percentages

	Adopters			Non-adopters	All categories
	Early	Majority	Late		
Sweden	13·2	13·1	13·5	10·5	12·8
United Kingdom	13·5	13·0		11·7	12·7

SOURCE: inquiry.
[a] Average values of F as defined on p. 66.

The impact of company size on the adoption of special presses is not through size itself as an independent variable, but because several other variables, for instance, the pay-off period and the company variables expressing resources, appear to be related to size. In the debate about technological progress, interest has frequently focused upon the extent to which large companies are more innovative than small ones. Thus, it is interesting to examine directly the relation between company size and the adoption of special presses.

In table 4.13 the average size of companies in different categories of adopters is shown using two measures. The number of employees illustrates the size of the company as an organisation, and may thus be related to the resource variables; the volume of production is more likely to be related to the profitability variable. The number of employees is evidently correlated with the date of adopting special presses, at least in Sweden and the United Kingdom. The largest differences occur between the first two and the last two categories, as with the information variables. In Austria, Germany and Italy we find that late adopters are generally larger than the majority, whilst non-adopters, except in Germany, are the smallest. British early adopters are large partly because many of them are company groups, which we were not

Table 4.13. *Average company size by categories of adopters*

	Adopters			Non-adopters	All categories
	Early	Majority	Late		
Austria					
Employees	n.a.	886	1002	721[a]	821
Output (000 tons)	n.a.	61	47	20[a]	36
Italy					
Employees	n.a.	386	667	174	298
Output (000 tons)	n.a.	32	21	18	20
Sweden					
Employees	1430	1189	620	252	966
Output (000 tons)	72	133	67	13	91
United Kingdom					
Employees	4958	3688	731	628	1816
Output (000 tons)	300	147	37	17	81
United States					
Employees	2558[b]	1617	2440[c]	1793[d]	2127
Output (000 tons)	569[b]	497	273[c]	86[d]	416
West Germany					
Employees	n.a.	377	1726	1132	1177
Output (000 tons)	n.a.	44	162	71	107
All countries					
Employees	2485	1421	922	554	1094
Output (000 tons)	317	145	80	23	105

SOURCE: inquiry.

[a] Based on eight companies only.   [c] Based on three companies only.
[b] Based on five companies only.   [d] Based on two companies only.

able to separate into individual companies. Output seems to have an even higher explanatory value for the date of introduction; in four countries the averages decrease for later categories. However, in Germany the late adopters and in Sweden the majority have considerably higher output than earlier adopters.[1] The pooled observations at the bottom of the table support the view that there is a definite correlation between company size and date of adoption.

[1] Swedish early adopters were manufacturers of higher quality paper, requiring relatively more labour.

An econometric approach

By testing some of our hypotheses in an econometric model, we can compare our results with those of Mansfield in his study of the inter-firm diffusion of 14 innovations in four industries in the United States.[1]

The dependent variable – the date of first introduction of special presses by a company – is of course only available for those companies that have introduced the technique. In order to include non-users in our calculations we assigned them fictitious T-values, taking early 1975 as a hypothetical date for those companies. (The T-values were re-calculated in terms of the number of quarters from the first quarter of 1963 instead of the number of months from January 1963.) As there were relatively few observations the number of independent variables had to be limited; we selected four – the profitability variable (P), company size (S) as a proxy for many other variables, the date (year) of first information (I) as a proxy for information resources, and actual behaviour (B) from among the attitude variables.

We had data on all these variables for 103 companies – 11 each in Austria and Germany, 27 in Italy, 31 in Sweden and 23 in the United Kingdom. Estimations were made on data for Italy, Sweden, the United Kingdom and all five countries together. Data for Germany and Austria were not used separately because of the small number of observations.

Mansfield used a model with a multiplicative relationship between the variables. His argument for this form was that 'the effect on T of each of the exogenous variables is likely to depend on the level of the other. For example, differences in firm size would be expected to have less effect if an innovation is extremely profitable than if it is less so'.[2] The model can be written:

$$T = A' . P^{a_1} . S^{a_2} . B^{a_3} . I^{a_4} . \epsilon'_a$$

which can be transformed into an additive form,

$$\log T = A + a_1 \log P + a_2 \log S + a_3 \log B + a_4 \log I + \epsilon_a$$

where A is a constant, $a_1 \ldots a_4$ are regression coefficients and ϵ_a is a random error. As the pay-off period is inversely related to the profitability of the investment, the sign of a_1 as well as the sign of a_4 is expected to be positive, while the signs of a_2 and a_3 should be negative.

The estimates of the coefficients are shown in table 4.14. The results for Sweden provide some evidence of the effect of P, S and B on the timing of the introduction of special presses – the coefficients are generally significant at the 90 per cent level; I appears less important. For the

---

[1] Mansfield, *Industrial Research and Technological Innovation*, ch. 8.
[2] Ibid., p. 158.

British observations the coefficients of P and S are both significant at the 95 per cent level, but both B and I are of more limited importance; what is surprising is the sign of the coefficient for B. The Italian results are less good: the significance of the coefficient of P is lower than in

Table 4.14. *The influence of four selected variables on the date of adoption of special presses by a company*

	Constant	Coefficients of				R^2
		P	S	B	I	
Italy	3·41	0·110				0·101
($n = 27$)		(1·67)				
	4·12	0·046	−0·147			0·189
		(0·61)	(1·62)			
	4·65	0·022	−0·087	−0·49		0·400
		(0·33)	(1·06)	(2·84)		
	4·33	0·021	−0·084	−0·48	0·11	0·400
		(0·31)	(0·95)	(2·60)	(0·12)	
Sweden	3·00	0·468				0·401
($n = 31$)		(4·41)				
	5·10	0·311	−0·339			0·520
		(2·74)	(2·64)			
	4·76	0·258	−0·202	−0·33		0·568
		(2·27)	(1·37)	(1·73)		
	3·72	0·229	−0·190	−0·32	0·38	0·576
		(1·87)	(1·27)	(1·68)	(0·71)	
United Kingdom	3·24	0·501				0·369
($n = 23$)		(3·50)				
	5·44	0·356	−0·333			0·570
		(2·74)	(3·06)			
	4·91	0·404	−0·358	0·32		0·588
		(2·86)	(3·17)	(0·89)		
	2·11	0·404	−0·339	0·52	0·88	0·601
		(2·83)	(2·91)	(1·17)	(0·79)	
All countries	3·20	0·244				0·156
($n = 103$)		(4·32)				
	4·48	0·165	−0·215			0·270
		(2·93)	(3·95)			
	4·63	0·151	−0·181	−0·20		0·296
		(2·70)	(3·21)	(1·90)		
	1·43	0·145	−0·112	−0·15	1·05	0·353
		(2·68)	(1·89)	(1·51)	(2·95)	

SOURCE: IUI estimates.

Notes: (i) A stepwise multiple regression computed by the program BMD 02R.
(ii) Numbers in brackets are t-ratios, for which critical values are 2·00 at 95%, 1·70 at 90%.
(iii) See pp. 65–6 for full definitions of the independent variables.

Sweden and the United Kingdom, while the significance of B seems higher. The results for all countries together substantiate the importance of the variables. R^2 is, however, considerably lower, which is quite natural, because the pooling has introduced country differences which have not been taken into account in the model. In some cases these 'pooling effects' may improve the coefficient and its significance, but this improvement often only indicates institutional differences between the countries other than those connected with the explicit variables.

We also tried estimations with an additive model, but their explanatory values were lower than for the multiplicative formulation.

In his model Mansfield also used profitability and the size of the firm as variables. His estimates of the coefficient of P differed considerably between various innovations, so that a comparison with our results would be meaningless. The effect of company size is, however, easier to compare: Mansfield estimated the coefficient of S at -0.4 in a model with only P and S as independent variables;[1] our results of about -0.33 (for both Sweden and the United Kingdom) are slightly lower.

In conclusion, it seems that profitability and the size of firm had significant effects on the introduction of special presses, which is consistent with the findings of our exploratory approach. Actual company attitudes and the date of first information also had some explanatory value. Our results as regards profitability and size agree quite well with Mansfield. We were, however, also able to estimate the parameters for different countries or groups of countries, which Mansfield could not do, and found that the pooling of observations might increase the explanatory value of a variable compared with an estimation for one country only. Hence, inter-country models also need variables for country differences. This will be discussed further below.

DIFFUSION WITHIN COMPANIES

Hitherto we have been concerned only with companies' first adoption of special presses. Diffusion within companies can be regarded as a further stage in the diffusion process.

The numbers of companies, plants and paper machines (Fourdrinier and Combined) in the six countries are shown in table 4.15. In Austria and Italy most firms have only one plant; in the other European countries the average ratio is higher, almost two in Germany and the United Kingdom. The number of paper machines per plant is lowest in Italy, less than two, and highest in the United Kingdom, almost four on average. The higher these ratios are, the more interesting will be the breakdown of the aggregated company data, because there are more

[1] Ibid., p. 161.

observations. We have no data on individual plants in the United States.

The curves in chart 4.4 show the diffusion in the five European countries of companies, plants and paper machines using special presses. Diffusion at plant level is lower in all countries than at company level, indicating that firms first use the new technique in one of their plants and later apply it to machines in other plants, which is, of course, just what we would expect. The same can be said about the diffusion at the machine level compared with the plant level.

Table 4.15. *Plants and paper machines[a] in the sample companies*

	Austria	Italy	Sweden	United Kingdom	United States	West Germany
Companies	16	29	31	23	17	12
Plants	19	33	43	41	..	23
Machines	51	55	110	147	163	50

SOURCE: inquiry.
[a] Fourdrinier and Combined machines.

Diffusion at plant level

We chose legal companies as the level to be approached, so that plants are not treated as separate units. However, they often have considerable independence in the replacement and modernisation of their productive equipment, at least as regards initiatives and proposals. Since the plant is a more homogeneous unit than the company, a brief analysis of diffusion at plant level is worth making, if only to compare with our findings above concerning diffusion at company level.

The diffusion curves at the plant level in chart 4.4 tell us very little about the date at which a company introduces special presses in other plants within the company after its initial adoption of the technique. It is, however, possible to construct two other curves which are upper and lower limits for diffusion at plant level, given the diffusion at the company level. The lower (minimum) curve shows what the diffusion would have been if each company used special presses in one plant only; the upper (maximum) curve shows the diffusion if each company introduced special presses in all its plants at the time it first adopted the technique. The three curves for each country are shown in chart 4.5. At the beginning, actual diffusion and the minimum curve are identical, but after a few years some companies start to introduce the technique in a second and third plant, so that these curves start to deviate; the

Chart 4.4. *Diffusion of special presses at the levels of companies, plants and machines^a*

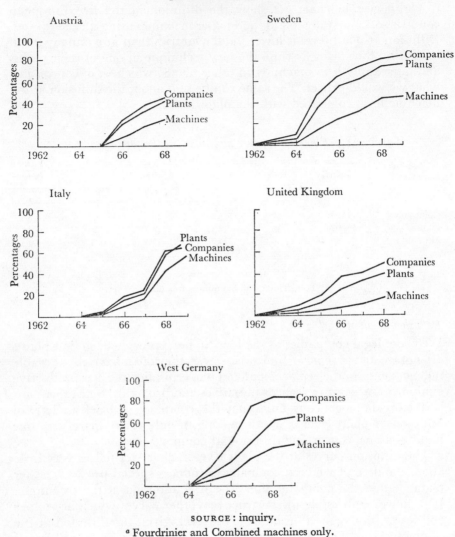

SOURCE: inquiry.

^a Fourdrinier and Combined machines only.

shadowed area between them illustrates the intra-firm diffusion of special presses. When the actual diffusion curve touches the maximum curve, as in Italy, this means that in all companies using them, special presses are installed in all plants.[1] The distance between the minimum

[1] In fact, in the Italian sample non-using plants within using firms seem to have been omitted.

Chart 4.5. *Maximum, actual and minimum diffusion of special presses at the plant level*

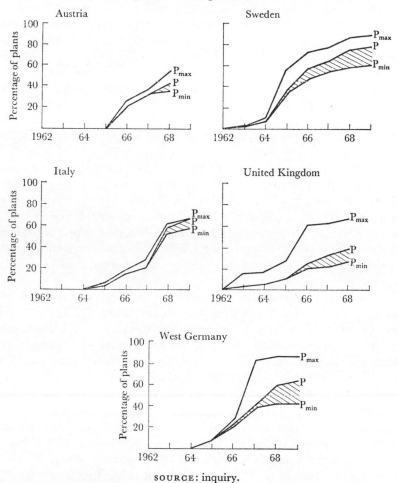

SOURCE: inquiry.

Note: P_{max} = percentage of all plants in firms using special presses.
P = percentage of plants actually using special presses.
P_{min} = percentage of plants if only one per firm was using special presses.

and maximum curves indicates the number of plants compared with the number of companies. In Austria and Italy this ratio is quite low, but considerably higher in Germany and the United Kingdom. It was two to three years after the first introduction of special presses in each country before the intra-firm diffusion to plants started, this period being shortest in Germany, and longest in Italy and the United Kingdom.

In principle it should be possible to reproduce our analysis of the impact of profitability and the 'company' variables (re-defined in terms of plants) upon diffusion among plants within a company. In practice we have suitable data for only eight multi-plant companies in Sweden and six in the United Kingdom, so that we report only the main findings of the analysis of these two sets of data.

We found that the diffusion of special presses was quicker in Sweden not only at the company level; once a Swedish company started to use special presses, it was also quicker than a British one to introduce them in other plants. Swedish firms to a greater extent than British firms introduced special presses in an order which supported our profitability hypothesis.

Considering plants as separate units and disregarding their connections with other plants, profitability seemed to have an explanatory value for the timing of the introduction of special presses. Average pay-off periods were shorter for early adopters in both Sweden and the United Kingdom, but, compared with Sweden, there are a considerable number of non-using plants in the United Kingdom with quite a short pay-off period. They constitute, at least from this point of view, a large group of potential users.

The influences of company variables agreed with our findings at the company level with one exception: in the United Kingdom, early adopters seem to be large firms, whilst at the plant level late adopters seem to be largest on average. This is an interesting finding because plants are more comparable than companies. Furthermore, we found no similar pattern in the Swedish data.

Diffusion at machine level

When a company has decided to install its first special press, on which paper machine will it do so? According to the profitability hypothesis it should be on the machine with the lowest pay-off value. Table 4.16 shows the numbers of multi-machine plants using special presses,[1] and the percentages of such plants where the first special press was introduced either on the most profitable machine, or on one of two most profitable machines.[2] While in Germany, Italy and Sweden at least 50 per cent of plants had their first special press installed on the machine with the shortest pay-off period, this proportion is considerably lower in Austria and the United Kingdom. In this comparison, however, we need again to recall the weakness of the German and Italian data.

The above considers only the first special press introduced in a plant. Can profitability differences between first and second installations

---

[1] Of course, only plants with more than two paper machines are of interest for this analysis.
[2] As measured by the length of the pay-off period.

Table 4.16. *First introduction of special presses at plant level and machine profitability*

| | Multi-machine plants using special presses | Plants where first special press installed | |
		On most profitable machine	On one of two most profitable machines
	(no. of plants)	(percentages)	
Austria	6	*33*	*83*
Italy	11	*64*	*100*
Sweden	23	*57*	*83*
United Kingdom	15	*33*	*67*
West Germany	8	*50*	*100*

SOURCE: inquiry.

explain at least a part of the timelag? Average pay-off periods for first and second installations in plants with at least two machines equipped with special presses are compared in table 4.17. As there are so few plants with at least two special presses in Austria and Germany, only results for Italy, Sweden and the United Kingdom are given. In Italy and Sweden the pay-off period is considerably lower for the first installation than for the second one; in the United Kingdom, however, machine profitability seems to have no effect on the order of the installations.

Finally, another difference between the Swedish and the British data is shown by chart 4.6. This groups all paper machines in the two countries according to their calculated pay-off value. The percentage of machines equipped with special presses was then calculated for each pay-off interval. In Sweden a high proportion of the machines with

Table 4.17. *Timelags between first and second installation and profitability, Italy, Sweden and the United Kingdom*

| | Special presses installed | | Average timelag | Average pay-off periods | |
	First	Second		First	Second
			(months)	(years)	
Italy	December 1967	October 1968	10	1·1	1·6
Sweden	June 1965	May 1967	23	1·1	1·6
United Kingdom	April 1965	March 1968	35	1·5	1·4

SOURCE: inquiry.

Chart 4.6. *Paper machines in each pay-off interval equipped with special presses, Sweden and the United Kingdom*

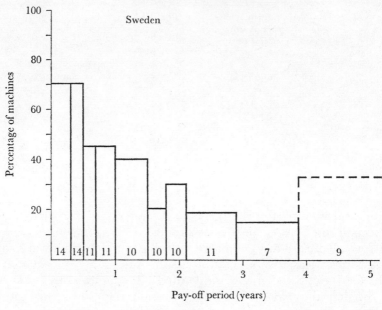

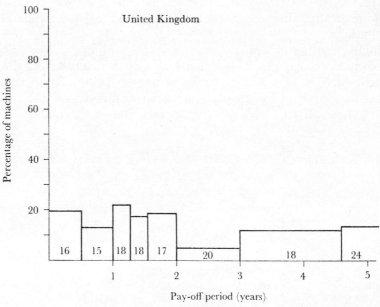

SOURCE: inquiry.
Note: Total number of machines in each interval shown at the bottom.

short pay-off periods has been equipped with special presses and as profitability decreases so does this proportion. For machines with a pay-off period of less than six months it is 70 per cent, whereas in the groups with a pay-off period of over two years it is only about 20 per cent. In the United Kingdom, however, the percentage does not appear to be related to the pay-off period and is about 20 per cent for all intervals.

AN INTER-COUNTRY COMPARISON

Although in previous sections we have, from time to time, commented on various averages for companies or plants in different countries, we have in the main been concerned with a model which was common to all or most countries. Now we shall look for explicit differences between countries and try to account for them.

Diffusion data already presented on numbers of companies, of plants and of machines using special presses can be drawn upon for national comparisons, and diffusion can also be measured in yet another way – in terms of the output of paper from machines with special presses. Whereas, in the other measures, companies, plants or machines are given equal weight, in this measure machines using special presses are weighted by their output. It is arguable that this provides a better measure of the economic importance of the new technique for inter-country comparisons.

On a volume basis the six countries exhibit substantial differences in diffusion, although all the curves are, of course, lower than on a company basis, because when a company introduces a special press on the first of several machines, the company is immediately given full weight but the volume curve takes account only of the output of that machine.

A summary of our findings on diffusion patterns, which brings together with this presentation by volume the earlier presentations in terms of companies, plants and machines, shows that the Swedish curve always starts first and stays in front. The curve for the United Kingdom starts nearly as early, but then lags behind, so that after a time British diffusion by some measures was lowest among the countries studied. Austria was generally a late starter. The samples for the other countries were too unrepresentative to justify drawing any strong conclusions.

A little more may be said about the rate of diffusion. We can distinguish three stages in the diffusion curves – introduction, growth and saturation. If the extremes are eliminated, we can estimate the annual average percentage rates of increase during the 'growth' stage and these are shown in table 4.18, which confirms the low rate of diffusion in the United Kingdom in comparison with the other countries. However, we also see that in Sweden, although diffusion started earlier, it was not notably fast. The figures also support the hypothesis that early starters are slow growers and vice versa. There are plausible reasons for this: information about the new technique is more easily available when it has reached a certain diffusion level in other countries; when the technique is accepted by some countries, non-users feel a stronger pressure to adopt it, also a higher security. These are of course the familiar *a priori* arguments for the sigmoid logistic diffusion curve, applied here on an international level.

Table 4.18. *Average annual rates of increase of diffusion during the growth stage*

Percentages

	Austria	Italy	Sweden	United Kingdom	United States	West Germany
Information	31	20	16	14	28	20
Production						
Inter-firm	14	17	21	10	13	20
Intra-firm	15	15	16	4	4	12

SOURCE: inquiry.

Some explanations of country differences

One reason for the differences in diffusion between countries is the extent to which new paper machines have been installed. As mentioned already, in new machines special presses are cheaper than suction presses both to install and to operate. Thus we would expect that, in accordance with the profitability hypothesis, almost all paper machines installed after the introduction of special presses would be equipped with them. The diffusion of special presses would thus be positively correlated with the rate at which countries have been installing new machines.

In the six samples, 18 new paper machines were installed from 1966 onwards,[1] of which 17 were equipped with special presses when installed. (One large newsprint machine only was built in Sweden in 1969 without special presses.) Italy[2] and Sweden installed six machines each, while the remaining six were installed in the other four countries. The relatively fast diffusion of special presses in Sweden and Italy is thus partly accounted for, as shown in chart 4.7.

[1] The date when special presses can be considered fully developed and accepted.

[2] In Italy a considerable amount of capital became available in the 1950s and early 1960s through the nationalisation of other industries. Quite a large proportion of this capital was reinvested in the paper industry, thus explaining the number of new paper machines.

Chart 4.7. *Total paper and board output on machines with special presses and on new machines*

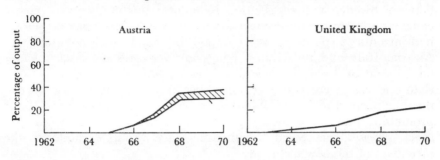

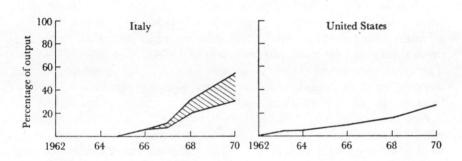

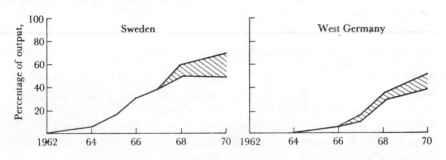

SOURCE: inquiry.

Notes: (i) Based on Fourdrinier and Combined machines only and new machines are defined as those installed in 1966 or later.

    (ii) Upper curve is output on machines with special presses, of which shaded area is output on new machines.

    (iii) Only one and two machines respectively were installed by the United Kingdom and United States sample firms since 1966 and no production data on them were available.

    (iv) The United States curve is based on estimates from manufacturers of presses. They might have taken a more conservative view than the European one in defining a 'special press'; hence the surprisingly low curve.

There are differences in the average length of the pay-off period between countries, and this might account for differences in diffusion between Sweden and the United Kingdom; but it is only a partial explanation. Almost all Swedish companies with a short pay-off period had introduced special presses by 1968, but many such companies in Austria, Italy and the United Kingdom were still non-users. About 60 per cent of Swedish paper machines with a pay-off period of less than one year were equipped with special presses, while the corresponding proportion in the United Kingdom was only 20 per cent. If our profitability index is a good measure of the true economic return on special presses, then Swedish companies have responded better to the incentives of the new technique.

This conclusion is based on the actual use of special presses in one year (1968). The impact of profitability on the timing of adoption is shown in table 4.7; the average pay-off period is lower for earlier adopters than for non-adopters.[1] The relation between declining profitability and later adoption is most obvious in the British sample. The econometric test (table 4.14) also provides clear evidence of the importance of profitability: its coefficient is highly significant for both Sweden and the United Kingdom.

Nevertheless we found that although, among British users, companies with the most favourable pay-off periods were also the earliest adopters, some companies with high profitability remained non-users. In Sweden some companies with quite long, but fully acceptable, pay-off periods were early adopters; there the main effect of profitability seems to have been to distinguish users from non-users.

Earlier we found (table 4.9) that both membership in research organisations and the share of exports in sales were probably more suitable for explaining differences between countries than between firms. In Austria, where diffusion was rather late, the first was relatively low; the second, it is true, was the second highest among the six countries, but this should be seen in connection with the variable for foreign integration, which tells us that Austrian companies tend to be subsidiaries of foreign (mainly German) ones, to which they export much of their production. The variable for behaviour was also low for Austria (table 4.10).

In Italy there is a connection between late diffusion and the low values of most company variables. This also holds for Germany, as although most German companies use special presses, they do so only to a limited extent. Although the level of diffusion in the United Kingdom is similar to that in Austria, the British company variables, except for share of exports, are generally as high as the Swedish ones,

[1] Except in Germany, and omitting the extreme value for Austria.

so that they do not explain the slower diffusion. In Sweden early diffusion corresponds with high average values on most company variables, and this holds also for the American sample.

Although our discussion of the variable for foreign connections implied that either subsidiaries or parent companies abroad played a minor role in the exchange of information, many companies said that they acquired information about special presses from foreign sources. This international flow of information can be studied in connection with the first use of special presses in the different countries. In chart

Chart 4.8. *Sources of information from abroad and years of first adoption*

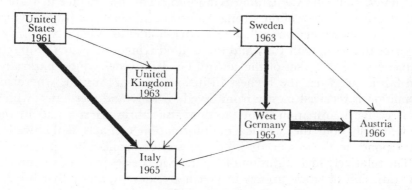

SOURCE: inquiry.
Note: The thickness of the lines between countries indicates the relative importance of the information flows.

4.8 the frequency with which foreign sources of information were reported is shown, with the year of first adoption in each country. We observe how, after 1961, experience from the United States spread to Europe. Sweden played an important role in the diffusion of information within Europe: it was the most common source of information for Germany, and German sources in turn were important for Austria, which adopted special presses slightly later. Italy was greatly influenced by American sources, though other countries were also important.

Different types of special presses
Chart 4.8 shows only direct information from one country to another. A closely related problem is how the different types of special presses have spread. The total diffusion figures for the countries can be split between four different types – the fabric press, the shrink-fabric press, the Venta-Nip press and the high-intensity press. These four differ in their country of origin. The fabric press and the shrink-fabric press are

primarily Swedish inventions, even though first tests on the former were carried out in the United States. The patents of both are in Swedish hands (except for fabric presses on the American market). Venta-Nip and high-intensity presses were developed in the United States and are sold under licence all over the world. Thus, special presses have spread over Europe from two directions – Sweden and the United States.

Although detailed data are not available for the United States, national estimates indicate that there some 70 per cent of all special presses, about 500, are of the Venta-Nip type; there are also about 200 shrink-fabric presses, 20 fabric presses, and only a few high-intensity presses. Venta-Nip presses are also the most common in Germany, Italy and the United Kingdom.[1] This dominance in Italy is not surprising in view of the strong American influence on Italian paper techniques shown in chart 4.8. The licence-holder for Venta-Nip presses has subsidiaries in both Italy and the United Kingdom, which probably influences the diffusion of the technique. In Sweden, quite naturally, the fabric press has the highest diffusion; also in Austria, where information is received mostly from Sweden. Italy and Germany, which also receive information from Sweden, use fabric presses, and in the United Kingdom the absence of information contacts with Sweden corresponds to the absence of fabric presses or shrink-fabric presses.

The relatively high diffusion of Venta-Nip presses in Sweden and the low diffusion of fabric presses in Germany, despite many Swedish information contacts (also the absence of Venta-Nip presses in Austria) cannot, however, be explained by the pattern of information flows. No very strong general conclusions can therefore be drawn, but the country of origin and the channels through which information on an innovation flows clearly exercise some influence on diffusion. This question has important policy implications both for individual companies and for countries as a whole. However, it needs a much more thorough examination than has been possible here.

Institutional variables

We suggested earlier that institutional variables, which characterise the environment of companies, might often be constant within countries, contributing mainly to inter-country comparisons. Some of the information sources just discussed can be looked at in this light, and we also collected data concerning industry research organisations. Such organisations did not in fact rank highest as a source of information; in most countries journals and congresses were mentioned more frequently. But in Sweden research organisations had a large impact on the diffusion

---

[1] The Beloit Corporation estimates that throughout the world the total number of Venta-Nip presses is about 800.

of special presses; both the fabric press and the shrink-fabric press were invented at the central laboratory owned by the Association of Swedish Paper Mills, to which 97 per cent of all companies belong. It appears, however, that such associations could not have played so important a part in other countries. In Britain it is true 83 per cent of firms in the sample were members of the industry research association and all non-members were medium or small firms not using special presses. None of the industrial experts consulted, however, thought that lack of

Chart 4.9. *Output with special presses of different grades of paper*

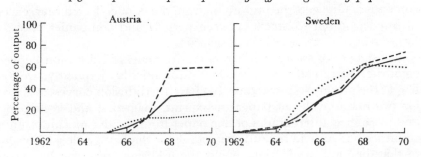

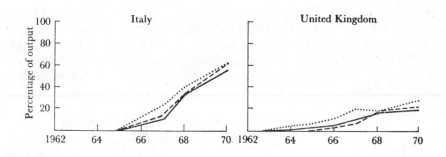

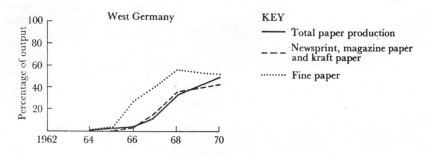

SOURCE: inquiry.
Note: No data available for the United States.

communication had been the reason for the relatively slow diffusion of special presses in the United Kingdom.

In Germany the tendency was more to follow technical developments abroad; only 50 per cent of companies in the sample were members of the research association. In Austria only 40 per cent of companies were members of the most important association. In Italy just over half the firms in the sample were members of research associations, and the Italian government gives some financial and research support to the paper industry. Almost all American firms are members of one research organisation or another, but most research is carried out by individual companies. One gets the impression from the data collected that, except in Sweden, direct contacts between persons and companies played a larger role than the research associations.

The impact of structural factors on differences in diffusion between countries has already been touched on implicitly. Explicitly, we look first at the production structure. In chart 4.9 diffusion curves are shown for two main grades of paper: newsprint, magazine and kraft paper, and more specialised grades of fine paper from smaller machines. In all countries but Austria the diffusion curve for the first grade is very close to that for total production, whilst the diffusion curve for the second grade is slightly above the total curve. In table 4.19 the average pay-off period for all machines in each grade is calculated. Other things being equal, we would expect the grade with the shorter pay-off period to have the faster diffusion. Comparing table 4.19 with chart 4.9 we find no significant relationship between profitability and diffusion. And, contrary to the hypothesis, for all countries except Italy the more profitable grade also shows the slower diffusion.

Table 4.19. *Average pay-off periods for machines making different grades of paper*

Years

	Austria	Italy	Sweden	United Kingdom	West Germany
Newsprint, magazine and kraft paper	2·7	1·1	0·9	1·8	1·3
Fine paper	1·8	0·5	1·4	2·5	5·4

SOURCE: inquiry.

We assumed in our profitability calculation that the extra paper which could be produced with special presses could be sold at unchanged prices. The extent to which this assumption is valid in different countries will depend on the demand for paper products in those countries. The development of demand indeed varied considerably in the decisive period 1963–9. Comparing domestic consumption in five of the countries, and demand in the whole OECD area for paper from Sweden (the paper exporter *par excellence*), the increases range from about 25 per cent in the United States and the United Kingdom to over 60 per cent in Italy, with German, Austrian and OECD consumption rising between 40 and 50 per cent. Thus, American and British paper manufacturers are likely to have been more doubtful of

Chart 4.10. *Output with special presses in companies of different sizes*

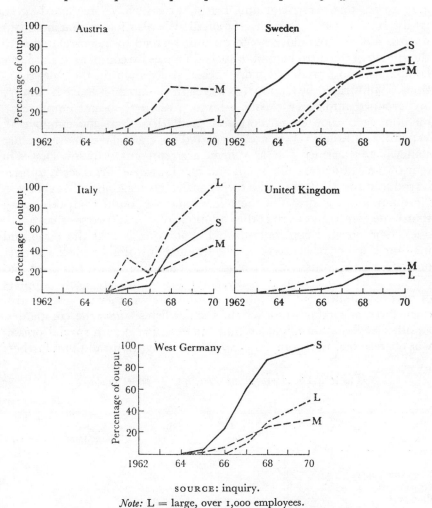

SOURCE: inquiry.

Note: L = large, over 1,000 employees.
   M = medium, 300–1,000 employees.
   S = small, under 300 employees.

selling the additional paper produced than, for instance, Swedish manufacturers. The high rate of increase of Italian consumption reflects the rapid rise of national product in Italy, and indeed a relatively large number of new paper machines was installed there (see page 94). Another factor that has probably favoured the Swedish paper industry most is the establishment of EFTA, which opened for Sweden new tariff-free markets, of which Britain was the most important. This meant that additional buyers have been easier to find for Swedish firms and more difficult for British firms.

The size of companies is another aspect of industrial structure. Table 4.13 shows that American and British firms are on average largest, whilst Italian firms are relatively small. We also found that both our measures of size (employees and output) seemed to be correlated with the timing of the introduction of special presses by companies. But large companies also introduced more special presses within their organisations, as illustrated by chart 4.10, where the companies in each country are grouped into three classes – large (over a thousand employees), medium (300–1000 employees) and small (less than 300 employees). When the diffusion curves are calculated for each class, the results are somewhat surprising. The large firms are represented by low curves in four of the countries, while small and medium-sized firms seem to have introduced special presses on a larger scale. This is especially evident in Germany and Sweden. On the other hand we found from table 4.13 that large companies were earlier adopters of special presses than small ones. One possible explanation of this paradox is that the large and medium-sized firms classed as early adopters introduced special presses on only a few plants and machines, in comparison with the later and often smaller firms. That is to say, large firms might be early adopters of new techniques, but it is more questionable whether they also introduce the new methods quicker than small firms *within* the companies. Another explanation might be that the experience with special presses was often so bad that companies were unwilling to install them further;

Table 4.20. *Average annual output of paper machines*

Thousand tons

	Austria	Italy	Sweden	United Kingdom	West Germany
Newsprint	28	..	77	40	29
Magazine paper	8	29	29	24	37
Kraft paper	10	8	39	14	14
Fine paper	10	20	9	6	9

SOURCE: inquiry.

this would have a greater effect on the diffusion figures for large companies. In fact, however, very few such difficulties were reported.

The size of paper machines is directly related to the profitability calculation. Table 4.20 shows the average size of the machines for both countries and different grades of paper: Swedish machines were largest on average; with one exception, newsprint machines were the largest and fine paper machines the smallest.

Table 4.21. *Average years when paper machines were installed*

	Austria	Italy	Sweden	United Kingdom	West Germany
Newsprint	1944	..	1945	1939	1948
Magazine paper	1896	1952	1921	1930	1934
Kraft paper	1925	1953	1946	1941	1932
Fine paper	1928	1959	1937	1923	1914

SOURCE: inquiry.

Table 4.21 shows the average year of installation for machines for different grades. British machines are considerably older than Swedish ones; Italian machines are all quite new – several companies there went into the paper industry on a large scale in the early 1960s and many new machines were installed. This explains both why Italian fine paper machines are larger than in other countries, and why Italian pay-off periods are so short. Austrian paper machines are on average the oldest, followed by German ones in at least two categories.

SUMMARY

Special presses have become fairly well established during a relatively short period in all the six countries studied. Levels and rates of diffusion, however, differ considerably. In Sweden and the United States, where the innovations took place, diffusion started a few years earlier than elsewhere. Diffusion has, however, been faster in Sweden, a fact which cannot be explained by the growth of total paper production. In both countries production increased by about 20 per cent between 1963 and 1966.

It was not possible to compare the average profitability of special presses in the two countries, but since the average American paper machine is larger,[1] there is no reason to believe that the profitability was lower in the United States. We found, however, that consumption

[1] 18 tons compared with 11 tons (see table 4.1).

on the American market increased much slower than in the markets open to the Swedish industry. Moreover, Sweden definitely gained from the creation of a large tariff-free market within EFTA.

Special presses were first used in the United Kingdom almost as early as in Sweden, but diffusion was much slower. The following have been suggested as possible reasons:

(a) average profitability is lower in the United Kingdom;

(b) consumption in Britain increased much more slowly than in the OECD as a whole;

(c) foreign competition increased considerably in Britain;

(d) investment in new paper-making capacity was lower in the United Kingdom.

The analysis showed that, even where profitability was the same, special presses have been installed by Swedish companies much more frequently than by British ones. This may be explained partly by a less encouraging competitive situation and slower economic development generally in Britain than in Sweden.

In the other European countries the diffusion of special presses started later and increased only moderately. The industrial structure – small companies and small machines – naturally affected profitability. The strong Nordic competition was restrained to some extent by tariffs (though not in Austria which is a member of EFTA). Investment in new paper machines was small or moderate in Austria and Germany, but quite large in Italy, which explains a great deal of the more rapid diffusion there of special presses. Overall economic development and rapidly increasing paper consumption also favoured development in Italy. Lower profitability in Austria, Germany, Italy and the United Kingdom is also due to production structure. Sweden produces large quantities of bulk grades or expensive high qualities, while more traditional grades are produced on smaller machines in the other countries.

The degree of integration of a plant can also affect profitability; the Swedish paper industry is largely integrated, with pulp and paper produced in one line. Most paper mills in the other European countries are non-integrated, which increases production costs and thus decreases the profitability of special presses. Again, this might contribute to the explanation of the faster Swedish diffusion.

Finally, there is an interaction between management attitudes and the industrial structure in the various countries in which it is difficult to distinguish cause and effect. Nevertheless, the study led us to believe that attitude patterns and industrial traditions have played an important role in the diffusion of this new technique.

CHAPTER 5

TUNNEL KILNS IN BRICK-MAKING

By L. A. Lacci, ISCO,
S. W. Davies and R. J. Smith, NIESR

BRICK-MAKING AND THE TUNNEL KILN

Clay building bricks are made by shaping the raw material, clay or some allied substance such as shale or marl, into blocks and hardening them by fire. The main stages of production are the quarrying of clay, the shaping (and if necessary drying) of raw bricks, and finally their burning. The subject of this study is the last of these stages – the burning of bricks. The preceding stages were not studied in detail,[1] but they are relevant to this investigation in two respects: first, the chemical composition of the raw material may have important implications for the method of firing and hence for the type of kiln used; and secondly, the efficient layout of the whole plant and the modernity of its equipment is to a large extent a precondition for building an up-to-date kiln, since modernising one phase of an otherwise obsolete production process is obviously uneconomic.

There are many types of brick (common and facing bricks, solid and hollow, glazed or otherwise treated); some require special handling in the course of burning. Kilns are either intermittent or continuous. In the intermittent kiln the fire is extinguished while the kiln is loaded with raw dry bricks and unloaded after burning; nowadays this is no longer in widespread use, except for burning special bricks, with a high value which offsets the excessive production costs. (These arise mainly from the higher fuel requirements of intermittent firing.) The bulk of brick production comes from continuous kilns, of which there are many variations on two basic types. In both burning can go on continuously, stopped only for kiln maintenance, often no more than once a year; in one the bricks to be burnt are stationary and the fire moves, whereas in the other, the tunnel kiln, the fire is stationary and the product moves through it.

The first patent for a continuous kiln was granted to Yordt in Denmark in 1840. This was a kiln of the tunnel type. Although the model proposed was improved elsewhere, the techniques of construction then available did not permit the building of kilns large enough to be

[1] Non-clay building bricks, such as sand-lime or concrete bricks, are also excluded because they do not require firing.

profitable in producing solid bricks, the type most commonly used at that time. Moreover, the control of the process (temperature, burning time, the speed of the waggonettes carrying the bricks) required instruments which were then either not available or insufficiently developed. Consequently the adoption of tunnel kilns had to be deferred; they were actually introduced first in other clay industries, such as china and pottery, which require smaller kilns and in which the higher value of the product balanced the higher investment costs. These costs included the more sophisticated and expensive mechanisms and instruments which had by then been developed.

Very soon, however, another kind of continuous kiln was adopted in the brick industry; it was patented in Germany by Hoffmann and Licht in 1858, and modified by Hoffmann in 1865 to the form which has been retained practically unchanged up to the present time. The Hoffmann kiln consists of a series of chambers, originally disposed in a circle, and later in two parallel rows connected by semi-circular or rectangular ends to form a complete circuit. Each chamber has a door opening to the outside of the kiln, through which burned bricks are unloaded and raw dry bricks introduced. The fire is kindled in one chamber, or two contiguous chambers, and when the bricks there have been burnt it is 'moved' to the adjacent chambers, thus continuing along the circuit. The raw bricks are preheated by hot air from the chambers under firing, whilst the burnt bricks are cooled by fresh air forced through the stacks.

In the course of the hundred years and more of its evolution, the Hoffmann kiln has undergone several modifications, aimed mainly at improving the circulation of air and easing the loading and unloading. (Apart from being very labour-intensive and costly, these are also the most exacting operations in terms of working conditions.) Earlier versions embodying such modifications were the transverse arch kiln and the zig-zag kiln.

For many decades, this process of burning bricks by moving the fire in continuous kilns was unsurpassed. Such kilns can use any kind of solid, liquid or gaseous fuel and are very flexible, switching from one kind of product to another by merely changing the firing time in the various chambers. But the process has several disadvantages. First, working conditions are adverse; the kiln operatives have to remove thousands of heavy bricks from very hot chambers which still retain a temperature of 50°C or more. Secondly, the moving fire alternately heats and cools the chambers with fluctuations of 900°–1,000°C in their temperature; this causes enormous heat losses and raises fuel costs, as well as wearing out the kiln's structures and involving frequent and costly maintenance. Thirdly, since a huge building such as a Hoffmann kiln is difficult to insulate perfectly, the moving fire may crack the walls and, by drying the kiln floor, the fire as it moves round can cause subsidence in the foundations.

The tunnel kiln eliminates or reduces these disadvantages. It consists of a straight tunnel, usually rectangular in cross section and up to 130 metres in length. The fire remains stationary in the central part of the kiln, while the bricks on special waggonettes travel through continuously at a uniform speed, which varies with the kind of brick. The tunnel is divided into three sections. The central one, about a quarter of the kiln's length, is the firing zone. In the first section the dry raw bricks are preheated by the hot air coming from the firing zone, while in the last zone they are cooled by the injection of fresh air.

The basic principle underlying the two continuous processes is the same: either the fire moves and the material is stationary, or vice versa. But the simple inversion of the process has several very important consequences. The stationary firing zone of the tunnel kiln can be insulated much better than the whole Hoffmann kiln, and because the fire is permanent, there is no alternate heating and cooling of the structure, which results in great savings in fuel and maintenance costs. In addition, the bricks are loaded and unloaded outside the kiln in less adverse conditions. However, the tunnel kiln too has its disadvantages: for a start, the investment cost is higher than for a Hoffmann kiln of equal capacity; secondly, the waggonettes require expensive maintenance; thirdly, whereas in the Hoffmann kiln the process is mostly controlled by visual inspection, in the tunnel kiln it is totally mechanised – the consequent automation and instrumentation of the tunnel kiln require special skills in the operatives and also more professional works management. Thus the adoption of tunnel kilns has gone hand in hand with a general improvement in the degree of mechanisation and automation of the whole productive process, and not just of the burning phase. Moreover, the automatic firing in the tunnel kiln requires a fuel which is easy to control; thus, oil and gas are more suitable than coal. The firing zone can only be inspected for maintenance when the firing is stopped and the tunnel kiln cooled, whereas the chambers of a Hoffmann kiln can be inspected and even cleaned during normal opening for reloading. Fuels with strong soot emission, such as coal, are therefore less suitable, and indeed very few tunnel kilns use coal. The diffusion of tunnel kilns is thus hampered in countries where coal is widely used, or cheaper and more easily available than oil and gas.

For similar reasons, the tunnel kiln is not used for the burning of bricks made of clay with a high carbon content,[1] since this makes fire

---

[1] Such as bricks made of coal slurry or 'fletton' bricks. Fletton bricks are made from a special type of clay ('lower Oxford') found only in the United Kingdom in a belt running

control difficult and vastly reduces the saving in energy costs, most of the firing fuel being included in the clay. In these circumstances the higher investment costs of a tunnel kiln cannot be recouped.

Practically any kind of clay bricks or blocks can be burnt in a tunnel kiln. But changing from one product to another usually requires re-setting the firing mechanism and adjusting the car speed, as well as totally emptying the kiln. All this is cumbersome and leads to a loss in capacity as against the more versatile Hoffmann kiln, which presents no such difficulties at changeovers and where, in fact, different products can be fired simultaneously. Thus, in countries where building customs call for a wide variety of bricks, the tunnel kiln starts with a handicap, although for mass production it offers undeniable advantages in terms of savings in production costs and easier working conditions.

In these circumstances many existing Hoffmann kilns have been modified to the tunnel type in the last two decades; this is particularly common among newer Hoffmann kilns, for kilns generally have a very long life during which, if properly maintained, they continue to produce bricks at a relatively stable cost. The traditional technology can be modified by cutting off the two semi-circular ends of the Hoffmann kiln and converting the two aisles into tunnels. Additional equipment is of course required, but at a cost of about a sixth of that of a new tunnel kiln; operating costs are reduced and the working conditions improved.[1] Although this conversion is a compromise solution which does not offer the full advantages of a proper tunnel kiln, it has found particular favour in Italy, where there are a fair number of firms with relatively new Hoffmann kilns.

THE INQUIRY

The basic method of collecting data was to send a standard question-naire to a sample of firms in each of the six countries concerned. To overcome problems of small sample size, a larger proportion of firms were approached in smaller countries. In the larger countries, in order to achieve a high coverage, more large firms were included; however, this does introduce an element of bias.

Not surprisingly, the best coverage (almost 100 per cent by output) was achieved in the smallest industry, Sweden. Similarly, in the United

across the Midlands and centred mainly in the Bedford–Peterborough area. Because its high carbon content provides most of the fuel needed, substantial economies in burning are possible; and its high moisture content means that no water needs to be added before the bricks are shaped, and the drying stage is totally dispensed with. Fletton and non-fletton bricks are virtually interchangeable in use.

[1] There are further developments of this idea: a 'multi-row' kiln has four or five tunnels alongside each other under one roof, with a great saving in floor space.

Kingdom, where there are few firms, coverage was very satisfactory. In the other countries, with perhaps the exception of Austria, the coverage was insufficient to allow firm conclusions, although the samples from Germany and Italy were fairly large.

Table 5.1. *Coverage of the samples*

	Austria	Italy	Sweden	United Kingdom	United States	West Germany
Firms, 1970						
In national industries[a]	130	841	50	130	484[b]	740[c]
Respondents to:						
Full questionnaire	9	37	35	23	6	56
Short questionnaire	11	—	—	62	5	—
Total coverage (%)	15·4	4·4	70·0	65·4	..	7·6
Output, 1969 (million bricks)						
National	911	6731[d]	267	6116	7806	4836
Of respondents to:						
Full questionnaire	315	958	260	4261	583	635
Short questionnaire	71	—	—	1010	309	—
Total coverage (%)	42·4	14·2	97·4	86·2	11·4	13·1

SOURCE: inquiry; UNECE, *Annual Bulletin of Housing and Building Statistics for Europe*.

[a] Estimates; in many cases the latest published figures are four or five years out of date.

[b] Number of establishments, 1967.

[c] Only 584 firms employing 10 or more.   [d] 1968.

Table 5.1 also shows that in all countries respondents tended to be the larger firms in the industry (in that coverage was much higher as measured by output than by numbers of firms).[1] For Italy and Austria this was quite significant, with the average output of the respondents over four times and twice the national averages. For the United Kingdom and Sweden, the divergence, while still noticeable, was smaller owing to the larger coverage. Furthermore, the information received is not completely comparable, as in the United Kingdom, Austria and the United States many firms only responded to a shorter questionnaire, having failed to answer the fuller standard questionnaire.

THE PRODUCTIVITY OF THE TUNNEL KILN

Before proceeding to examine the causes and impediments of diffusion it is useful to confirm, on the basis of the evidence from the inquiry,

[1] The figures for numbers of firms are very tentative and for the United States we have data only on numbers of establishments, of which there are of course more than numbers of enterprises.

some of the claims made for the tunnel kiln, in particular that it is more capital-intensive and productive than conventional kilns. This is done by comparing capital intensity and productivity in adopting firms before and after adoption.

The movements in factor shares between 1964 and 1969 for three groups of German and Italian firms are plotted in chart 5.1. It will be

Chart 5.1. *Movements of factor shares, 1964–9, among adopters and non-adopters, Italy and West Germany*

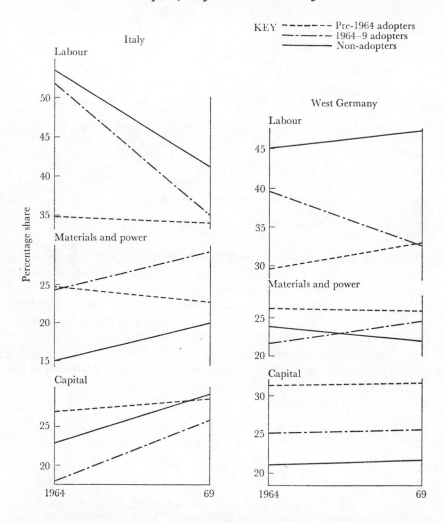

SOURCE: inquiry.

seen that, in the firms adopting during that period, the capital share changed only very little, the share of materials and fuel rose somewhat, whilst the most noticeable change was the big downward movement in the share of labour. There was little change in the components of output in the remaining groups of firms, apart from non-adopters in Italy; in this group the factor shares would appear to reflect the widespread adoption of the modified Hoffmann kiln, which appears from the chart to produce very similar, though weaker, effects on the structure – a fall in the labour share and rising shares of materials and capital. Thus tunnel kilns seem to be capital-intensive by the criterion of the capital–labour ratio, but not by capital–output. Certainly they are labour-saving. It can also be safely asserted that capital is used no less efficiently in the new process, for despite the fact that in all of the countries except Italy depreciation (and maintenance) costs were generally 5 to 10 percentage points higher for adopters than for non-adopters, kilns (like many other pieces of plant in most branches of industry with an economic life of more than 30 years) are conservatively depreciated over a shorter time-span. The result is that nominal depreciation, especially in the early years of installation, overstates quite considerably the actual wastage of capital in those years. Under these circumstances, the disparity in this item between users and non-users could be considered quite small and, from this point of view, real depreciation per unit of output may be as low (or even lower) for tunnel kilns as for their conventional counterparts, implying that 'real' capital is being used at least as efficiently.

There is another consideration which suggests more strongly that capital productivity increases with the introduction of tunnel kilns. The share of materials and power for firms which adopted between 1964 and 1969 shows a distinctly upward trend in both countries, while remaining relatively flat for the earlier adopters and the non-adopters. This is an important finding; normally there is little difference between conventional and tunnel kilns in the efficiency with which raw materials are used, so that the share of materials in output would be expected to remain more or less constant with the adoption of this new technology. Moreover, because of the improved heat utilisation of the tunnel kiln, one of its more important benefits, the share of power in output would, if anything, be expected to fall. The observed rise in the share of materials and power together can therefore only imply that the costs of other factors, including capital, show larger real falls, which indicates in particular that the tunnel kiln yields savings *overall*, and not just in one factor.

The analysis of the more straightforward case of labour productivity points to some remarkable changes. The German case, which is typical

5

of the other countries in this respect, is shown in chart 5.2.[1] The pattern
is obvious enough: in firms in which there is no adoption, productivity
climbs gradually (unless perhaps it suffers a slight setback, if, for instance there is a severe depression in the market); then, in the four-year
period in which adoption takes place, productivity rises massively;
finally, productivity growth settles down, although still with a tendency

Chart 5.2. *Productivity changes, 1960–9, among adopters and
non-adopters, West Germany*

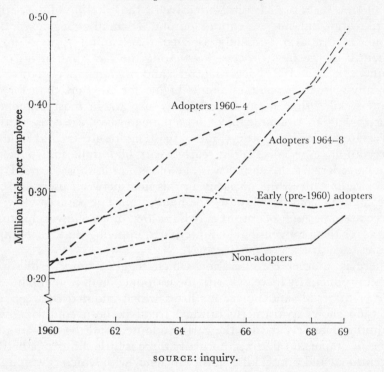

SOURCE: inquiry.

to be faster than before. There are variations: productivity growth in
periods of adoption may differ between groups, with later faster
adopters growing because their kilns are newer; or there may be a spurt
in productivity in a non-adopting period with the modification of conventional kilns to a tunnel basis (as with Hoffmann kilns in Italy); but
the basic theme is the same for almost all the countries.

[1] The German case is particularly clear-cut on labour productivity (more so than on
factor shares) because of the predominance of single-kiln firms in the German sample. The
existence of more than one kiln in a firm inevitably blunts the effects of replacing a single kiln
where data are given at firm rather than at kiln level. The general increases in 1968–9 were
due to high boom conditions in Germany.

TECHNICAL FACTORS IMPEDING DIFFUSION

In this section and the next, the diffusion of the tunnel kiln is examined in the sample of firms from each country. Although much of the ensuing analysis is based on the implied assumption that the sample data are indicative of diffusion within the respective national industries, it should be remembered that the samples are liable to bias for various reasons and to this extent they are unrepresentative of the national industries. The United States sample in particular may be heavily biased because of its especially low coverage, and as such it will be treated only very briefly.

Table 5.2. *Diffusion among the sample firms, 1969*

	Austria	Italy	Sweden	United Kingdom	United States	West Germany
Firms						
Total in sample	20	37	35	85	11	56
Tunnel kiln users	12	20	22	23	10	45
Percentage of users	*60*	*54*	*63*	*27*	*91*	*80*
Output (million bricks)						
Total by sample	385	958	260	5271	893	625
From tunnel kilns	331	465	202	494	771	488
Percentage from tunnel kilns	*86*	*49*	*78*	*9*	*86*	*78*

SOURCE: inquiry.

Table 5.2 summarises the stage that diffusion had reached by 1969 in the six countries. It appears that there is a significant difference between Austria, Germany, Sweden and the United States on the one hand, and the United Kingdom, and to a lesser extent Italy, on the other. However, as noted earlier, technical factors, both the types of clay burned and the types of brick produced, limit the application of the tunnel kiln. Differences in diffusion stemming from such differences between countries should be removed from the international comparison to concentrate on the effects of variables more relevant to an economic study. To do this, it is necessary to introduce two new concepts:

(1) The *technological ceiling*, which is defined for each country as the maximum output that could be produced in tunnel kilns, given the existing stage of their technical development and taking into account the size of clay deposits and of brickworks.[1]

[1] Establishments, that is, as opposed to enterprises.

Table 5.3. *Factors hindering adoption among partial adopters[a] and non-adopters*

Numbers of firms (in italics) and annual output (million bricks)

	Austria		Italy		Sweden		United Kingdom		United States		West Germany	
	Partial adopters	Non-adopters	Partial adopters	Non-adopters	Partial adopters	Non-adopters	Partial adopters	Non-adopters	Partial adopters	Non-adopters	Partial adopters	Non-adopters
High carbon clay							329	*13* 3220				*2* 8
Production too varied/tunnel kilns inflexible			14			*1* 4	14	*1* 18				*1* 6
Future uncertain (non-economic factors)							9				4	
Shortage of clay deposits								*4* 74				
Insufficient annual production		*3* 9				*6* 11		*26* 101				
Shortage of capital/high initial cost[b]		*3* 26	358	*4* 69		*4* 17	537	*3* 35		*1* 17	12	
Depressed demand						*1* 5		*1* 98				
Old kilns satisfactory							90	*1* 9	52			*1* 9
Building a tunnel kiln		*1* 4		*1* 15			84	*3* 30	12		11	*2* 15
No reason/other reasons	13	*1* 3		*2* 37	19	*4* 13	85	*62* 44	25		16	*11* 55
Totals	*2* 13	*8* 42	*13* 372	*7* 121	*2* 19	*13* 41	*16* 1148	3629	*5* 104	*1* 17	*5* 43	*17* 93
of which: potential adopters	*2* 13	*5* 33	*12* 358	*7* 121	*2* 19	*6* 26	*12* 796	*18* 216	*3* 89	*1* 17	*4* 39	*8* 79

SOURCE: inquiry.

[a] Among the partial adopters, numbers of firms for individual factors not shown for reasons of confidentiality.
[b] But with sufficient annual production.

(2) A *potential adopter*, which is defined as a firm, part at least of whose output could feasibly be produced in a tunnel kiln. The output within the technological ceiling thus consists of the output of potential adopters only.

The remainder of this chapter deals only with diffusion in respect to the technological ceiling in each country, that is only among potential adopters. In order to obtain rough measures of these two concepts for each country, we need to ascertain which of the non-adopters in 1969 could not use tunnel kilns for technical reasons, and to exclude these and their output from the totals. Similarly, we need to know whether it was technical or economic reasons that prevented partial adopters from adopting totally. Table 5.3 shows ten sets of important reasons for non-adoption given by non-users and partial users; we now examine these reasons to ascertain how far the tunnel kiln was technically applicable in each country.

In the United Kingdom the most usual reason for non-adoption is that the tunnel kiln is less efficient than cheaper kilns when the clay used is 'lower Oxford' or others with a high carbon content. This effectively rules out the large British fletton sector. The claims that the tunnel kiln is too inflexible (or production is too varied) result from its technical characteristics – automatic firing allows only one type of brick to be made at a time, whereas different clay products require different times, and perhaps temperatures, for firing; thus the time taken to reset the controls effectively reduces most of the advantages of the kiln. Firms citing shortage of clay were presumably implying that their deposits were too small to keep a tunnel kiln running long enough to recoup the initial outlay. The firms who were uncertain about the future due to non-economic factors would not, in our opinion, conceive of building any type of new kiln. Thus, all firms and output covered by any of the above reasons are unequivocally outside the technological ceiling.

A certain amount of judgement is needed for those firms claiming that they were too small to adopt, or that the initial capital outlay was beyond them. There is certainly a minimum level of output which is needed before a tunnel kiln is an economic possibility;[1] this is reckoned to be between 10 and 15 million bricks per year. However, many firms which already have tunnel kilns consider their capacity to be well below 10 million bricks. This may be because the modern tunnel kiln is larger and more sophisticated than the older versions. Working on this assumption, non-adopters having a present output very much below 10 million bricks could never cover the initial costs of a tunnel kiln, even assuming

---

[1] Otherwise the rate of return is so low that initial costs can only be covered far into the future.

116

Chart 5.3. *The demand for bricks, 1954–69*

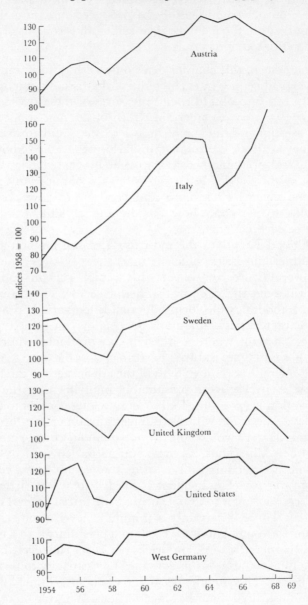

SOURCES: Department of the Environment, *Monthly Bulletin of Construction Statistics*, London, HMSO; UNECE, *Annual Bulletin of Housing and Building Statistics for Europe*.

Notes: (i) In the text, production data are treated as if they demonstrated brick demand. There is little or no international trade in bricks, and stock fluctuations though sometimes strong are usually short-lived, so that over 16 years production figures give a good reflection of movements in demand.

(ii) United Kingdom data are for non-fletton bricks only.

they managed to expand their market.[1] On the other hand, non-adopters citing the high initial costs of the kiln but producing at least 10 million bricks are taken to be potential adopters; in these cases we assume that their decision results either from lack of knowledge about the capabilities of the tunnel kiln, or from unnecessarily black expectations about future demand based on its depressed levels in most countries in 1969 (see chart 5.3). Similarly, 'depressed demand' does not seem to rule out adoption from a technical point of view, given that firms have a sufficiently high output; rather, it is a cyclical factor

Table 5.4. *Diffusion with respect to technological ceilings, 1969*

	Austria	Italy	Sweden	United Kingdom	United States	West Germany
Firms						
Potential adopters	17	37	28	41	11	53
Actual adopters	12	30	22	23	10	45
Diffusion (%)[a]	*71*	*81*	*79*	*56*	*90*	*85*
Output (million bricks)						
Technological ceiling	376	944	246	1506	878	606
From tunnel kilns	331	465	202	494	771	488
Diffusion (%)[a]	*88*	*49*	*83*	*33*	*88*	*81*

SOURCE: inquiry.

[a] Including those firms which were building or planning to build a tunnel kiln at the time of the inquiry, diffusion would be as follows by 1971:

Percentages

	Austria	Italy	United Kingdom	West Germany
By firms	*82*	*86*	*63*	*89*
By output	*89*	*51*	*40*	*83*

which changes from year to year. We do not consider 'old kilns satisfactory' to rule out adoption technically; this is again probably based on imperfect knowledge in most cases. Finally, firms which were building tunnel kilns at the time of the inquiry or who gave no reason for earlier non-adoption are assumed to be potential adopters, as are a remaining few which gave other (confidential) reasons.

Table 5.4 restates diffusion performance with respect to the technological ceilings. As compared with the unadjusted data in table 5.2, the only major change is in the performance of the United Kingdom

[1] This is often impossible anyway because of geographical limitations, etc.

(mainly due to the exclusion of the fletton sector), but it still has by far the lowest diffusion measured in terms of output. It is interesting to note that, at the time of the inquiry, there were rather more new tunnel kilns planned in the United Kingdom than in any of the other countries. This suggests that diffusion will continue in the United Kingdom through the 1970s, whereas in Austria, Sweden, and Germany it was apparently nearing completion by 1969. In Italy the majority of firms had adopted, but at the same time very many large firms were still using other kilns,[1] while in the United Kingdom, although more firms had adopted than had not, many, especially the large firms, had adopted only partially.

THE DIFFUSION PROCESS

The observed time-path

The information in table 5.4 should be seen in its proper context; it is only a 1969 snapshot of a continuous process, and just as important is the time-path by which that position had been attained. This is shown for the European countries (though not for the United States) in chart 5.4, in so far as it was possible to assess the values for the two relevant measures of diffusion: the proportion of potential adopters that had adopted by year t (measure A) and the proportion of output within the technological ceiling actually produced by tunnel kilns in year t (measure B).

Unfortunately, owing to gaps in the questionnaire answers, it is not possible to derive yearly series of these measures for all countries. In the Austrian sample, yearly data are only available for half the firms; the other half, respondents to the short questionnaire, only provided information for 1964 and 1969. The former may, however, be regarded as fairly representative of the total sample in these two years at least. For the United States we have data only for two years, in addition the sample is small and unrepresentative. For the United Kingdom we were unable to calculate satisfactorily the output from other kilns, which was needed to compute output with respect to the technological ceiling, but we have data on numbers of adopters. The deficiencies in the Italian data extend also to this series, but we have information for the years 1956, 1960, 1964, 1968 and 1969, which gives a good impression of the general shape of the curve. Only for Germany and Sweden are we able to present a full time series, based on samples of a reasonable size.

---

[1] The treatment of the modified Hoffmann kiln (see p. 108) is to some extent arbitrary and debatable. However, its output has been included within the technological ceiling, on the basis that it is a potential candidate for replacement by a tunnel kiln. At least two Italian companies use their modified Hoffmann kilns only to cope with periods of peak demand.

Chart 5.4. *The time-paths of diffusion*

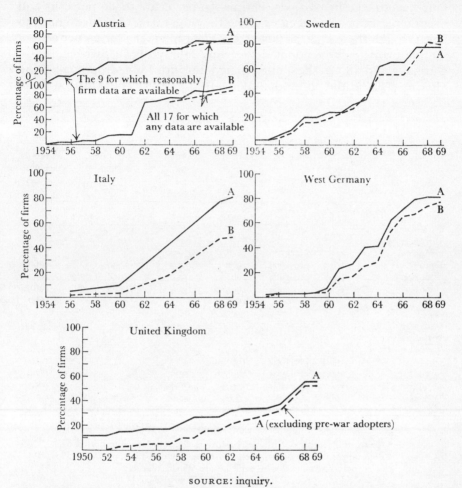

SOURCE: inquiry.

Note: Measure A gives the percentage of potential adopters who have adopted; measure B gives the percentage of output within the technological ceiling produced in tunnel kilns.

As is apparent from table 5.5, the United Kingdom had a substantial lead in the date of first introduction of the tunnel kiln, and five firms had adopted by 1939. On the basis that the earlier tunnel kilns are somewhat different from their post-war counterparts, we confine our analysis in the remainder of this section to the post-1945 diffusion. Here, the United Kingdom was second to adopt, two years after Italy, the other three European countries all following within two years.[1]

[1] One Swedish firm outside the sample in fact adopted as early as 1949.

For ease of exposition, we arbitrarily divide up the diffusion into four stages – the first 20 per cent, 20–50 per cent, 50–80 per cent and over 80 per cent – and then examine the time taken by each country to pass through these phases (table 5.5). The time taken for 20 per cent of sample firms to have adopted was only four years in Sweden, six in Germany and nine in the United Kingdom, with Italy, dropping behind after its early initial adoption, taking 10–13 years. The Austrian small

Table 5.5. *The time-paths of diffusion*

	Austria*a*		Italy	Sweden	United Kingdom*b*		West Germany
	A	B			C	D	
First adoption	1955		1951	1954	1902	1953	1955
Year when diffusion by firms reached:							
10%	1955	pre-1964	1960	1957	pre-1950	1958	1960
20%	1957	pre-1964	1961–4	1958	1958	1962	1961
50%	1963	1964	1965–8	1964	1968	1968	1965
80%	—	—	1969	—	—	—	1967
Year when diffusion by output reached:							
10%	1959	pre-1964	1961–4	1957	..	..	1961
20%	1962	pre-1964	1965–8	1960	..	..	1962
50%	1962	pre-1964	—	1964	..	..	1965
80%	1966	1965–9	—	1968	..	..	1969

SOURCE: inquiry.
a A = small sample of firms responding to the standard questionnaire;
  B = larger sample of firms responding to any questionnaire.
b C = including tunnel kilns built before World War II;
  D = excluding tunnel kilns built before World War II.

sample is more likely to be unrepresentative because of its size, but it is interesting to note that it was the quickest to reach 20 per cent diffusion (two firms out of nine), doing so within two years. (For the more reliable large sample, less than eight years was needed, although we cannot tell how long exactly.) In all countries for which both measures of diffusion were available, 20 per cent diffusion by firms was reached earlier than 20 per cent by output, suggesting either that early adopters were smaller firms, or that they were larger firms which adopted only partially at the outset. As we shall see later, a bit of both is the case.

The next phase of the diffusion process, up to 50 per cent, seems to have been completed quickest in Germany, in four years, whilst Sweden, the United Kingdom and perhaps Austria each needed six years; it is impossible to be certain about Italy, although it seems that it needed at least four years and probably slightly longer. The third phase was achieved in only two more years in Germany, while by 1969 Sweden was still slightly short of 80 per cent diffusion by firms, although it had achieved slightly more diffusion than Germany as measured by output. By 1969, Austria too had still to reach 80 per cent diffusion by firms, even though it was probably the first country to attain that level by output, while in Italy a very high diffusion by firms (over 80 per cent) was accompanied by an output diffusion of under 50 per cent, and the United Kingdom sample was lagging far behind using firms as a measure of diffusion.

In summary, Sweden and Austria were probably the fastest starters and at all times achieved rapid diffusion, although in Germany particularly, as well as in Italy on the measure by firms, diffusion was faster in the later stages, the latter after a very slow take-off. The United Kingdom was particularly slow at all stages. By 1969, Austria, Sweden and Germany were producing over four-fifths of their output within the technological ceiling in tunnel kilns, as against only half for Italy; four-fifths of potential adopters had adopted in Germany, Sweden and Italy, as compared with two-thirds in Austria and just over half in the United Kingdom.

A model of diffusion

The tunnel kiln is a lumpy capital investment, which yields, as already shown, large savings in labour costs and smaller savings in fuel costs, but requires a heavy initial outlay and often, for the vast majority of firms whose share of the market justifies only one tunnel kiln, the rebuilding of the whole brickworks. The reasoning that follows applies to such an innovation, not to innovations generally.[1]

In the perfect world of complete information about both the present and the future, of perfect capital markets and of profit-maximising entrepreneurs, diffusion should be instantaneous when the increase in profits ensuing from adoption yields a rate of return on the initial outlay (including, where necessary, the costs of shutting down an older plant) in excess of the rate of interest. However, in practice, the world is not 'perfect', so that there may be many reasons for non-instantaneous diffusion. In other words, for any firm i, y_i^* its subjective assessment of the rate of return to be gained from adoption, will not usually equal y_i the true rate of return to be gained, although one would expect the two

[1] Given the deficiencies of the diffusion data already acknowledged, there seems little point in elaborating a more sophisticated and sensitive diffusion model.

to be correlated. Similarly, r_i the critical rate against which y_i^* must be judged and the rate required before any investment will be made, will not be the ruling rate of interest, but rather some rate embodying the accepted norm in the industry, plus the risk premium used by the individual firm. Symbolically, investment by firm i will only take place at a given time if $y_i^* \geqslant r_i$ *and* if sufficient funds are available, whether from retained profits or the capital market.

At any point in time, given the unique existence of y_i^* and r_i for all firms, it follows that $y_i^* - r_i$ (the deficiency or excess of firms' subjective assessments from or over their required rate of return) must exist uniquely for all firms; hence, for any country, a uniquely defined distribution exists of values of $y_i^* - r_i$. The study of the diffusion process may thus be posed in terms of the shape of this distribution and its changes or movements over time.

Given the imperfect nature of the world, r will inevitably vary between firms and between countries. It can be expressed as some function of the norm in the industry – the relative importance within the corporate utility function of such things as increased profits, the 'quiet life', and aversion to risk-taking, as well as, of course, the cost of capital, which will be different for various types of firm because of imperfections in the capital market. In particular, it need not be strongly influenced by changes in the rate of interest. There seems to be little reason to expect the values of r_i to vary very much from year to year, although they may move gradually over time to the extent that entrepreneurs' opinions of what are reasonable rates of return may alter, as too may their risk premiums given a noticeable change in the underlying trend or stability of demand. If this is the case, it is likely to occur only gradually and over a period of time, and even then it need not be systematic. The average r ruling may vary between countries according to differences in attitudes to risk, the degree of competition, the level of demand and perhaps the current rate of interest.

The value of y_i^* will depend crucially on information and expectations, as well as on y_i. The last will obviously vary between firms and countries, due to differences in the age of the kilns to be replaced (or indeed whether the investment is to be for replacement or not), in the local or national cost and availability of the other factors of production (fuel and labour) and, between countries at least, in future developments in demand. Over time however, y_i will, broadly speaking, be stable, or rise slightly as refinements to the new technology occur. Rather, it is the entrepreneurs' assessments y_i^* which can be expected to change, and the most important single influence on y_i^* over time will surely be entrepreneurs' growing knowledge of the capabilities of the tunnel kiln. Again, it is worth distinguishing spatial and temporal differences. We would expect information to spread more rapidly and accurately in those national industries that are highly concentrated both geographically and industrially, and in those that are more technically dynamic, for example, with large research and development budgets and employing more highly qualified manpower. Information flows within a country over time will be dominated by the experience of the adopting firms; the more firms that adopt, the more information about the applicability of a new process will be available to non-adopters. In particular, firms whose neighbours and competitors adopt the tunnel kiln will have their attention drawn towards its possibilities and are likely to make a conscious assessment of it, possibly for the first time.[1] Expectations, too, vary over time and space; being most probably based on current or recent demand conditions, they vary over time with the building trade cycle, and between countries with differences in the underlying trends and extent of fluctuations in demand.

Although in what follows we assume that a non-negative value of $y^* - r$ invariably leads to a decision to adopt, this will only in fact occur if sufficient finance is available. Shortage of cash on hand in a firm is almost always the result of low profit levels over preceding years, often associated with depressed levels of demand, and hence production below capacity. It may be argued that it is always possible to raise capital on the equity market; but for many firms with unconvincing prospects, especially the smaller ones, this can only be done, if at all, at punitive cost. Of the 94 firms in our samples, almost half financed all their investments in the period 1965–9 from retained profits, and a further third financed over half their investments in this way. The stock exchange or other external sources of capital played a limited part indeed. Thus low profit levels, by depriving the firm of ready cash, could well act as a constraint on adoption and, when pervasive throughout the industry in times of depressed demand, would certainly be a drag on diffusion at the national level.

A TEST OF THE DIFFUSION MODEL

Theory only yields two measurable variables for time-series analysis applicable in this case. First, given that the distribution is normal and moves to the right at a constant rate, we would expect diffusion to have a cumulative normal curve. On this basis, we use the almost equivalent symmetrical logistic curve first introduced by Mansfield,[2] which, apart

---

[1] This is, of course, another expression of the 'bandwagon' theory, see p. 218.

[2] E. Mansfield, 'Technical change and the rate of imitation', *Econometrica*, vol. 29, October 1961, pp. 741–66.

from its attractive simplicity, appears also the most plausible. Chart 5.5 demonstrates the application of this type of curve to tunnel kilns, illustrating how 'movement to the right' is to be interpreted.[1] Secondly, the rate at which the distribution moves may well be a function of expected output and profits in the future, as well as of availability of finance, and, since both are assumed to be a function of present demand

Chart 5.5. *A possible distribution of firms with respect to their expectations[a] at the date of first adoption*

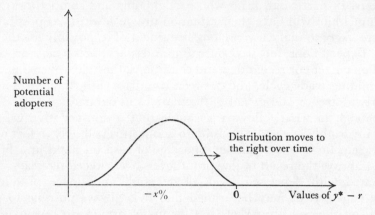

[a] As measured by $y*-r$ (see text). Values to the left of 0 are negative and to the right positive.

conditions, it is necessary to postulate that the movement to the right will accelerate or decelerate according to (say) the level of, or change in, brick demand, as measured by current production. To allow for the lag between the decision to invest and the date of actual first use, this variable was lagged by half-year periods.

The basic curve used by Mansfield is:

$$\frac{m}{n} = \frac{1}{1+\exp(-a-\beta t)}$$

where m is the number of firms which have adopted and n the total number of potential adopters. This function is modified to:

$$\frac{m}{n} = \frac{1}{1+\exp(-a-\beta t-\gamma x)} \tag{1}$$

where x represents demand conditions r half-years previously ($r = 0$, $1\ldots5$). As we have postulated that x will affect the speed at which the

[1] We assumed that the rate of this shift remains constant, although of course other formulations are possible, for example a shift that maintains a constant rate up to half-way and then slows down, generating the long-tailed Gompertz curve.

curve moves to the right and the curve itself is bell-shaped, then it would be expected that the nearer we get to the mid-point in diffusion (the peak of the normal curve) the greater the effect on diffusion of a given deviation of x from trend; once this peak is passed the marginal effect of x will diminish again. This is the effect of (1).

Unfortunately it was not possible to incorporate x in such a meaningful way when employing the normal distribution crudely as an independent variable. In this second type of regression, diffusion data were regressed against x and the normal distributions generated by inserting the means and standard errors of the actual data in the standard formulae. The marginal effect of x on diffusion was then constrained to be equal throughout the period.

These formulations were applied to the diffusion data measured as proportions of firms for the United Kingdom and Italy, and of both firms and output for Germany and Sweden. In order to dampen the random effects of possible misquoting of the year of introduction, or the rare inconsistencies in questionnaire replies, the data were transformed into two-year moving averages. The results of the tests, shown in table 5.6, provided firm corroboration of distribution and shift hypotheses for these series, but the effects of demand levels were slightly weaker, with the proxy variables not always significantly different from zero. Moreover, the average timelag between changes in demand and in the diffusion pattern appeared to differ somewhat between countries. Given that both the hypotheses relate to numbers of firms rather than output, it is not surprising that the series for firms show a better fit than output series from either the Swedish or the German samples.

Except in the case of Germany, the normal distribution curve in fact gave the neater fit, as measured both by the correlation coefficient, R^2, and the Durbin–Watson statistic (D.W.). The latter, which measures the covariance of successive residuals, was generally very low, especially where the demand variable was excluded. However, this is quite easily explained in this sort of case in terms of systematic cumulative movements in the residuals, which are partly attributable to the effects of the omitted demand variable, but are normally present to some extent anyway when one cumulative variable is regressed on another. Nevertheless, any elimination of autocorrelation, as reflected in an increase in D.W., is welcome; in this case the fall in autocorrelation using the normal distribution as an independent variable reflects especially that it is more flexible than the logistic curve as formulated here with one less parameter. Further, as a control test, the six observed cumulative diffusion patterns were regressed against a straight line. The results were very much what would have been hoped for where, as in the present case, a logistic or similarly inflected pattern is being postulated; D.W.

Table 5.6. *Least squares analysis of diffusion over time*

	Constant	Coefficient of		D.W.	R^2
		Time	Brick demand[a]		
Diffusion measured by firms					
Standard logistic form[b]					
Italy	−4·13	0·32		0·414	0·954
	(0·19)	(0·02)			
Sweden	−3·62	0·32		0·615	0·967
	(0·16)	(0·02)			
United Kingdom	−4·02	0·24		0·746	0·979
	(0·94)	(0·01)			
West Germany	−4·61	0·43		0·825	0·976
	(0·18)	(0·02)			
Modified logistic form[c]					
Italy	−5·69	0·24	0·021	0·891	0·978
	(0·42)	(0·03)	(0·005)		
Sweden	−3·74	0·32	0·007	0·564	0·969
	(0·50)	(0·02)	(0·008)		
United Kingdom	−5·32	0·24	0·012	0·860	0·983
	(0·68)	(0·01)	(0·006)		
West Germany	−7·64	0·43	0·025	1·397	0·989
	(0·96)	(0·01)	(0·007)		
Standard normal distribution[d]					
Italy	2·95	0·99		0·621	0·974
	(2·05)	(0·03)			
Sweden	1·81	0·97		0·917	0·982
	(1·64)	(0·03)			
United Kingdom	3·19	0·92		0·849	0·982
	(2·41)	(0·04)			
West Germany	−0·13	0·92		0·676	0·988
	(1·50)	(0·03)			
Modified normal distribution[e]					
Italy	−19·85	0·98	0·096	1·036	0·985
	(10·19)	(0·04)	(0·023)		
Sweden	−25·94	0·92	0·241	1·188	0·987
	(11·30)	(0·03)	(0·217)		
United Kingdom	−23·61	0·92	0·230	1·042	0·986
	(11·40)	(0·04)	(0·106)		
West Germany	−26·47	0·93	0·247	0·898	0·992
	(12·12)	(0·02)	(0·115)		
Linear form[f]					
Italy	−6·21	5·43		0·472	0·931
	(3·20)	(0·39)			
Sweden	−11·12	5·60		0·574	0·959
	(3·06)	(0·30)			
United Kingdom	−8·74	3·14		0·241	0·925
	(2·42)	(0·22)			
West Germany	−17·25	6·31		0·366	0·943
	(4·10)	(0·40)			

Table 5.6.—*continued*

	Constant	Coefficient of		D.W.	R²
		Time	Brick demand[a]		
Diffusion measured by output					
Standard logistic form[b]					
Sweden	−3·82	0·32		1·092	0·988
	(0·10)	(0·01)			
West Germany	−4·90	0·42		1·266	0·976
	(0·17)	(0·02)			
Modified logistic form[c]					
Sweden	−3·95	0·33	0·001	1·487	0·996
	(0·62)	(0·01)	(0·005)		
West Germany	−6·95	0·42	0·019	1·534	0·980
	(1·24)	(0·02)	(0·012)		
Standard normal distribution[d]					
Sweden	−0·03	0·96		1·229	0·993
	(1·02)	(0·02)			
West Germany	1·47	1·06		0·721	0·983
	(1·58)	(0·04)			
Modified normal distribution[e]					
Sweden	−28·43	0·93	0·130	1·487	0·996
	(10·96)	(0·02)	(0·084)		
West Germany	−29·81	1·03	0·184	0·923	0·985
	(13·42)	(0·04)	(0·139)		
Linear form[f]					
Sweden	−12·94	5·89		0·482	0·970
	(2·58)	(0·25)			
West Germany	−20·75	6·31		0·289	0·926
	(4·73)	(0·46)			

SOURCE: NIESR estimates.

[a] Lagged results, of which only the most significant are shown – one year ($r = 2$) for Italy and West Germany, and 18 months ($r = 3$) for Sweden and the United Kingdom.

[b] Estimated in the reduced form $\log [m/(n-m)] = a + \beta t$, where m is the number of firms which have adopted, and n the number of potential adopters.

[c] Estimated in the reduced form $\log [m/(n-m)] = a + \beta t + \gamma x_r$, where x is brick demand lagged r half-years.

[d] Estimated in the form $m/n = A + BN$, where N is a cumulative normal distribution generated from the means and standard errors of the actual data.

[e] Estimated in the form $m/n = A + BN + Cx_r$.

[f] Estimated in the form $m/n = a + bt$. The form $m/n = a + bt + cx_r$ was also tried, but the results are not reported as the coefficient of x_r was hardly ever significant.

[g] In these equations m and n are respectively the output produced by tunnel kilns and the technological ceiling.

Notes: (i) Figures in brackets are standard errors of the estimates.
(ii) The series for Italy relates to a larger sample of firms than the one used in the remainder of the chapter.

values were much lower in this test than in the equations featuring the logistic or normal pattern and the correlation coefficients also fell substantially.

The performance of the variable measuring demand for bricks varied widely between countries; unfortunately in almost all cases it was highly collinear with the shapes of the logistic curve and the normal distribution, so that there was some difficulty in distinguishing the influence of the two factors on the actual diffusion pattern.[1] Where both the factors were simultaneously significant a quite important result was achieved, and this occurred for the German, Italian and British series for diffusion measured by firms, but not for the Swedish. This variable was never significant in the German and Swedish output series, but, as mentioned above, the hypothesis relates to numbers of firms rather than levels of output.

Another interesting feature is the apparent variation between countries in the timelag which is that showing the greatest significance and contributing most to the correlation coefficient. For Italy and Germany, an easily rationalised one-year lag seems to apply, corresponding closely to an intuitive assessment of a gestation period for a new kiln (the total time required first to decide upon it and then actually to construct it). For the United Kingdom, however, a lag of 18 months produced the most satisfactory results, from which one may conclude that British firms were slower to react, or perhaps took longer to accumulate sufficient profits to finance the adoption. It is tempting to extend this result from the British sample to the Swedish, which also shows a lag of 18 months, but this is hazardous, given the low significance of this variable in the Swedish case.

INTER-COUNTRY DIFFERENCES

At this point it is worth taking stock of what conclusions can be drawn so far and stating the aims of the rest of the chapter. Undoubtedly, the logistic curve yields a fair description of the time-path of diffusion in the four countries studied. Further, the buoyancy of activity and expectations in the national industries can be seen to have exerted an important mitigating influence. But it must be admitted that the curve fitting exercises in the previous section do not supply a comprehensive explanation of inter-country and inter-firm differences in diffusion, and it is to these aspects that the remainder of this chapter is directed. First, we attempt to explain why there may have been differences between countries in values of r, y^* and y due to differences in demand conditions and the make-up of each national industry; secondly, still within the framework of these key parameters, the effect of characteristics at firm level is examined.

It is perhaps helpful, therefore, to restate the differences in diffusion

[1] For another view of this collinearity see below, p. 139.

performance that we are trying to explain. Sweden particularly, and probably Austria, have at all stages been among the leaders; although in both countries there are still a substantial number of non-adopters, they account for only a small part of total output. Germany, after a rather sluggish take-off, has adopted very fast, and was certainly quickest over the middle and later stages. In Italy, and most noticeably in the United Kingdom, even though initial adoption was very early, diffusion was extremely sluggish thereafter and, in terms of output particularly, is still at a low level. On the basis of the small sample from the United States, diffusion in that country appeared to be high in 1969.

One way to measure r at the national level would be to compute the average rate of return on existing capital and use this *ex post* concept as a proxy. This is unsatisfactory, however, as it presumes that entrepreneurs' *ex ante* assessments of new plant have been fulfilled in the past, and that in any case their yield criteria are constant over time. In fact no explicit measurement of the *ex ante* criteria for returns on new investment is really feasible short of asking a group of entrepreneurs, but we can to some extent examine factors likely to influence it.

Competitive pressures, for instance, might be expected from economic theory to have an inverse relationship with r. Only in the United Kingdom is production highly concentrated in the hands of a small number of companies; the three main enterprises accounted for about 57 per cent of national brick production in 1963.[1] In Austria, the seven largest plants accounted for 20 per cent of total value added in 1964, although one group now probably produces over 20 per cent of output. The one and only large group in Italy, scattered across the country, accounted for about 7.5 per cent of total output in 1968; whilst in the United States the three largest producers were responsible for only 20 per cent of total output. The degree of concentration in Germany is apparently even lower: in 1966, four companies out of a national total of 907 accounted for less than 19 per cent of total sales, while 720 with less than 50 employees were responsible for 42 per cent of total sales. In Sweden a remarkable increase in concentration has occurred in recent years under the pressure of a fall by one-third in both the number of enterprises and the volume of production; in 1964 the eight largest companies out of a national total of 88 were responsible for 27 per cent of total production, whilst in 1968 they accounted for 49 per cent.

The initial conclusion is, then, that only in the United Kingdom is there a significant deviation from the general pattern of many small companies with a sprinkling of medium-sized ones. This is, however, misleading, for one company (producing virtually all fletton bricks)

---

[1] This and other figures given in this section relate to the whole industries and not just the national samples.

accounts for over 40 per cent of British national production. Rather than reducing competition, the existence of this company, with its highly sophisticated transport system, has increased the competitive pressures on local non-fletton producers, not least because fletton bricks are now cheaper in areas where high transport costs had previously given local non-fletton producers a quasi-monopolistic position.[1] It would thus appear that in all the countries competition has probably been high, with the proviso that the high cost of brick transport everywhere but in the United Kingdom inevitably creates situations of local monopoly.

Table 5.7. *Uncertainty of demand for bricks, 1954–69*

	Austria	Italy	Sweden	United Kingdom	United States	West Germany
Mean annual growth rate[a] (%)	1·48[b]	6·28	−1·53[b]	−0·88	2·05	−0·60
Standard deviation of annual growth rate	6·41	9·42	9·22	9·06	9·69	5·92

SOURCES: UNECE, *Annual Bulletin of Housing*; Department of the Environment, *Monthly Bulletin of Construction Statistics*.
   [a] Based on numbers (not volume) of bricks.   [b] 1954–68.

A second factor which almost certainly affects the rate of return required on new investments is the degree of uncertainty in demand. Differences between countries in this factor have two aspects: first, uncertainty itself may exist in differing degrees, and secondly, entrepreneurs' reactions to uncertainty may also vary with their attitudes to risk. This second aspect leads, of course, into the obscure area of differences in national characteristics and quality of management.

As can be seen from chart 5.3, brick demand in all six countries was highly cyclical in the period 1954–69: in five countries three or four cycles can be discerned, whilst for Italy only two are apparent. In many cases, year to year changes were extremely large. The standard deviation of the yearly growth rate is used to assess variability of demand. In the extreme case where demand grows at the same rate each year, this standard deviation would be zero, while the more the growth rates vary (leading to greater uncertainty among entrepreneurs about the immediate future) the higher it will be.

Table 5.7 shows that the United Kingdom, the United States, Sweden and Italy have all had a similar variability in their brick demand, as

[1] For a fuller discussion see S. W. Davies, 'The clay brick industry and the tunnel kiln', *National Institute Economic Review*, no. 58, November 1971, particularly p. 62.

opposed to Austria and Germany, which have experienced considerably less fluctuation. Considered on its own, however, this variation is somewhat misleading, as it cannot distinguish uncertainty in a market that was nevertheless predominantly buoyant from uncertainty in a market that was static or declining. On the assumption that variation in demand around an upward trend is less likely to induce caution than the same degree of variation where demand is stable or falling in the longer term, variation in year to year changes in brick demand should be viewed alongside the underlying trend of demand over the period. For this we have to use the mean annual growth rate over the whole period as an indicator, there being no obvious single trend in any of the six industries during the 16 years.

Taking the two measures in table 5.7 together, it would seem that the Austrian industry experienced less than average uncertainty (a low standard deviation together with a rising trend in demand), whilst the British and Swedish industries experienced more than average uncertainty (high standard deviations and negative mean growth rates). The other three countries present less clear-cut pictures. The Italian industry, whilst obviously facing very uncertain demand conditions, was at least secure in the certainty that the underlying trend was strongly upward (except for one disastrous short-lived slump). The same is also true to a lesser extent for the American industry. In Germany, on the other hand, brick-makers probably faced conditions similar to Britain and Sweden, for, although the annual variation in Germany was relatively small, the market obviously contracted slightly over the period.

Given that the two coefficients provide a measure of uncertainty, the next question is what the reaction of entrepreneurs was and did their response per 'unit' of uncertainty vary. Direct evidence is of course unobtainable on this point, but from questions on sales and investment expenditure it was possible to compute for most of the sample firms an investment–output ratio for the period 1965–9. Grouping these ratios for the five European countries and comparing them with the growth of output for the sample firms in each country over the same period, we can gain some insight into the response of investment decisions to expectations and uncertainty in the various countries (table 5.8).

In each country except Italy this was a period of severe decline in demand at national level, yet all samples (or, more exactly, the sub-samples of those firms which provided investment data) show an overall increase in output. This discrepancy can be explained by the shutting down of a large number of less efficient firms as a consequence of the overall decline in demand; equally, however, it is quite conceivable that our samples are to some extent biased towards the more dynamic

Table 5.8. *Growth in output and investment, 1965–9*[a]

	Austria	Italy	Sweden	United Kingdom	West Germany
Mean annual growth in output[b] (%)	0·25	6·70	1·20	0·15	2·50
Investment–output ratio	8·41	17·97	16·53	10·90	19·16

SOURCE: inquiry.

[a] Sample firms only; excluding United States because of insufficient information.

[b] Measured by sales in numbers of bricks.

of the firms still in existence. At any event table 5.8 tells us very little. Assuming that higher growth can somehow be equated with more investment, the ordering reveals two discrepancies – the Austrians invested relatively less than the British and the Italians less than the Germans.

As suggested earlier, the expected rate of return on a tunnel kiln y^* may be supposed to be correlated, for any firm, with the actual rate y; although the determinants of y^* will be largely the same as those of y, the two will be unequal to the extent that entrepreneurs' assessments of the capabilities of the tunnel kiln are incorrect. In other words, although tunnel kiln adoption is likely nearly always to be beneficial, the extent of the benefits will vary between both firms and countries. At this stage, we confine the analysis of differences in benefits to the national level.

Table 5.9 shows the age distribution in 1955 of kilns in four of the country samples. Clearly, Austria had the most to gain from replacing old kilns, virtually all of the kilns there being built before World War I. In Germany, too, 60 per cent of kilns were built before 1914, and even

Table 5.9. *Age distribution of tunnel kilns, 1955*

	Austria	Sweden	United Kingdom	West Germany
Number of kilns built				
Pre-1914	23	13	..	29
1915–39	1	2	..	14
1940–55	2	5	..	6
Mean age in 1955 (years)	*52*	*38*	*18*	*38*

SOURCE: inquiry.

in Sweden, where there was a higher proportion of kilns built after World War II, 65 per cent of kilns were pre-1914. British kilns were substantially newer, perhaps due to the large inter-war boom in house-building and hence brick production. Pressures to replace less efficient old kilns must therefore have been weaker in the United Kingdom than in Sweden, Germany and, particularly, Austria.

A similar sort of conclusion can be drawn from an analysis of the supply, and presumably price, of fuels. The tunnel kiln is typically oil- or gas-fired, whilst the older types of continuous and intermittent kilns generally use coal. In the absence of historical data on relative fuel prices in the six countries, it seems fair to postulate that figures for the relative consumption of different fuels in the six countries reflect, to a large extent, differences in price and in availability.

Table 5.10. *Shares of solid and liquid fuels^a in total primary energy consumption*

Percentages

	1955		1965		1969	
	Solid	Liquid	Solid	Liquid	Solid	Liquid
Austria	65	28	40	51	29	64
Italy	33	56	13	81	10	86
Sweden	29	58	9	75	5	82
United Kingdom	86	14	66	32	56	43
United States	31	67	24	74	21	78
West Germany	92	7	59	40	46	53

SOURCE: United Nations Statistical Office, *World Energy Supplies* (various years).
^{a} Compared as million metric tonnes of coal equivalent.

In 1955, oil and gas were already being used very widely in the Swedish, American and Italian brick industries, as opposed to those of Germany, the United Kingdom and, to a lesser extent, Austria, which were still based heavily on coal and other solid fuels (table 5.10). If this reflects a relatively cheaper and more plentiful coal supply in the last three countries, the tunnel kiln would have been easier to adopt and would possibly have yielded greater savings in the early stages in the other countries. By the mid-1960s, however, while all six were using relatively more liquid fuels than previously, Germany, and particularly the United Kingdom, were still very dependent on solid fuels. Even in 1969, most of the United Kingdom's energy was derived from solid fuel, and Germany was only slightly less dependent on solid than on liquid fuels. These conclusions, of course rest on the assumption of a direct equivalence between the pattern of fuel consumption and the relative price and availability of liquid and solid fuels. To the extent that this is an over-simplification, they should be regarded as only tentative.

Table 5.11. *Anticipated and actual benefits from the adoption of tunnel kilns*

	Austria	Italy	Sweden	United Kingdom	United States	West Germany
Reasons for adoption						
Number of replies	7	30	19	11	7	36
Proportion of firms citing			(percentages)			
Labour savings	43	73	16	36	100	50
Better working conditions	57	30	26	18	—	28
Quality improvement	29	30	47	36	57	50
Increased capacity	29	17	42	—	14	22
Rationalisation of production	14	43	11	18	—	28
Other	14	33	21	36	—	31
Actual savings derived						
Number of replies	12	29	22	21	10	43
Proportion of firms reporting						
Labour savings[a]			(percentages)			
Important	83	93	23	76	90	82
Marginal	17	7	50	19	10	16
None	—	—	27	5	—	2
Fuel savings[a]						
Important	67	21	23	29	80	16
Marginal	25	41	27	48	20	58
None	8	38	50	23	—	26
Quality improvement[a]						
Important	67	52	77	38	90	67
Marginal	25	34	14	62	10	26
None	8	14	9	—	—	7
Maintenance savings[a]						
Important	42	17	32	28	60	28
Marginal	33	48	14	24	40	42
None	25	35	54	48	—	30

SOURCE: inquiry.

[a] These assessments are subjective, so that for fair comparison it is necessary to assume that entrepreneurs use the same yardstick; to the extent that they do not, the validity of the comparison may be weakened.

At this point it is worth looking at the reports from sample firms which have installed a tunnel kiln of both their reasons for adoption and their assessments of the gains accruing. This will confirm our previous conclusions and give further indirect impressions of inter-country differences in the conditions faced by individual brick-making firms.

As might be expected for the country with the oldest stock of kilns, among the European countries savings in maintenance were most commonly noted in Austria (table 5.11). In addition, a large proportion of the Austrian sample reported labour and fuel savings, and a larger proportion than elsewhere cited easier working conditions as a reason for adoption. Labour savings also figured high in Germany both as a reason for adoption, and as an actual benefit; fuel savings were less important, perhaps due to a natural abundance of coal (see table 5.10). In Italy, too, labour savings and easier working conditions were very important, while savings in fuel and kiln maintenance were much more marginal. Although also possessing a relatively old stock of capital in 1955, Swedish entrepreneurs regarded labour savings *ex ante* and *ex post* as less important than improvements in the quality of the output. In view of the age of the kiln stock and the fuel supply situation, it is not surprising that savings on fuel and kiln maintenance – both hoped for and actual – were lower in the United Kingdom. The major savings obtainable from a tunnel kiln are in labour costs, but from other points of view it is less beneficial in the United Kingdom than elsewhere. On the whole and ignoring differences in demand patterns, y the actual rate of return to be gained from adoption of a tunnel kiln, was probably highest in Austria and Italy, and then in Sweden and Germany together, and lowest in the United Kingdom. So far as we can tell it was probably high also in the United States.

Having examined the determinants of y, there remain the extra elements in y^* – ignorance of the capabilities of the tunnel kiln and lack of perfect foresight of future trends. It is possible that the former might vary between countries due to differences in the quality of information, but it is very difficult to be precise about this quality even at the present date, let alone over a number of years. Nevertheless, there are some factors which can be supposed to have influenced it – geographical and industrial concentration, membership of research associations, attitudes to research and development and so on – and we propose to examine how these vary between the countries.

Austria, for instance, while a small country with most of its brick industry concentrated in a relatively small area, has many small firms, with an average output in 1969 of seven million bricks. Only one firm in our sample was a member of a research association and only one carried out any research and development (although this expenditure was quite substantial in relation to the firm's sales). These factors account partially for the relatively late date of first adoption.

The German industry too is made up of hundreds of small brick firms, but in this case spread over a much larger geographical area. In 1969, the average output was 6.5 million bricks. Of the firms in our sample, 26 were members of the research association and as many as

29 of the 56 carried out research and development, although frequently not involving very large expenditure. A tentative conclusion is that the dispersion of the industry may have been a reason for the late start and slow early diffusion, but that a greater propensity to search for information may have more than made up for this at a later date.

Italy is very similar in having low concentration both geographically and by size of firm (average output in 1969 was eight million bricks) and, once again, this may well account for the extremely slow diffusion in the 1950s even after an early start. No information is available on membership of research associations, but 20 firms out of 37 were carrying on research and development.

In Sweden in 1969, despite a substantial increase in industrial concentration, particularly between 1964 and 1968, average output was still very low at five million bricks. It is a large country, but nearly all of the brick industry is situated in a very small area, near the major population centres. We have no information about membership of research associations, but only six of the 35 sample firms were undertaking any research and development. It seems unlikely that lack of information was ever a bar to diffusion, and this may well account for the Swedish lead in the earlier years and its good performance throughout, even with so many small firms.

Of all the countries, the United Kingdom had the highest concentration industrially and geographically, with the 1969 average output in the non-fletton sector as high as 28 million bricks. Seven of the 23 firms answering the long questionnaire (mainly larger firms) carried out research and development, most of these on quite a large scale. Virtually the whole of the non-fletton sector belongs to the research association. Given that the tunnel kiln has been installed in its various vintages throughout this century, it could reasonably be expected that information about the tunnel kiln would be most widespread in the United Kingdom.

Whilst geographically the United States industry is the most dispersed, the average size of firm is high at 16 million bricks. Of the six firms answering the long questionnaire, all were members of the research association and five were involved in research and development.

In considering the role of expectations as a determinant of y^*, the main question is whether or not demand conditions, which acted as a catalyst in the time-path of diffusion, accounted for any of the differentials between the different countries' performance. It has been seen that, over the period as a whole, uncertainty was rife in all countries to a varying degree, and that Germany, Sweden and the United Kingdom all faced declining demand; Italy was the one country in which output forged ahead almost continuously.

A breakdown can be made between adoption for replacement and to create new capacity by analysing adopters' output levels and numbers of kilns before and after adoption (table 5.12). Not surprisingly, only in Italy, where output grew at 6¼ per cent a year, did the number of kilns installed without a consequent closing down of an old one exceed 40 per cent, and in fact less than 20 per cent of kilns were installed solely as replacements. In Austria, the other country in which demand grew over the period as a whole (at 1½ per cent a year) figures for new capacity creation were second highest, and for replacement second

Table 5.12. *Purposes in building new tunnel kilns*[a]

Numbers of kilns[b]

	Austria	Italy	Sweden	United Kingdom	West Germany	Total
Creating new capacity without shutting down old kilns	2 (13)	9 (43)	— (—)	3 (10)	1 (2)	15 (12)
Replacing old kilns:						
And increasing capacity	9 (56)	8 (38)	14 (67)	5 (17)	18 (43)	54 (42)
Without increasing capacity	5 (31)	4 (19)	7 (33)	21 (73)	23 (55)	60 (46)
Uncertain: insufficient information on those built before 1956	6	11	3	16	4	40

SOURCE: inquiry.

[a] United States excluded due to insufficient data.
[b] Figures in brackets are percentages of all firms for which the purposes are known.

lowest. In Germany and the United Kingdom, the substantial majority of tunnel kilns were installed as replacements, which again is hardly surprising given the decline in demand in both countries. Sweden, where demand fell sharpest of all, appears to be an exception to this general pattern, for although no tunnel kiln was installed without dismantling an older one, two-thirds of new tunnel kilns yielded some increase in capacity. The explanation is that in that country firms had the highest death rate, so that the market for the surviving firms remained steady, and perhaps even grew for some of them. Table 5.12 demonstrates two points quite clearly: the brick industries faced with static or declining demand were concerned mainly with replacement of kilns; also, there is a strong correlation between the growth of national demand and the ratio of investment in new capacity to replacement.

When we come to examine the effects of trends in demand on

expectations and availability of finance, it is rather more meaningful to break the period 1954–69 down into the three discernible stages of diffusion. Taking the demand period 1955–8, which corresponds with the years 1957–60 in the diffusion process,[1] only in Austria did demand grow at all, and there (admittedly only on the basis of a small sample) by 1959 diffusion was highest by numbers of firms (table 5.5). On the other hand, in Germany and Italy, which both experienced heavily falling demand between 1955 and 1958, diffusion was slow. But the

Table 5.13. *Diffusion of tunnel kilns[a] and growth in output of bricks*

Percentages

	Austria	Italy	Sweden	United Kingdom	United States	West Germany
First period						
Output growth 1955–8[b]	1	−10	−20	−16	−17	−7
Diffusion increase 1957–60	11	3	13	11	..	4
Second period						
Output growth 1958–62[b]	23	42	33	7	6	17
Diffusion increase 1960–4	31	30	36	10	..	30
Third period						
Output growth 1962–6[b]	10	−12	−18	−5	20	−6
Diffusion increase 1964–8	16[c]	34	24	27	..	43

SOURCE: inquiry.

[a] The mean of the measures by firms and by output, except for the United Kingdom (by firms only).
[b] Totals over the period.   [c] Based on the large sample.

Swedish and British industries do not conform with this pattern; the former shows the largest decline in demand but also the best diffusion performance in the period on a compromise measure by firms and output (table 5.13); the latter also shows quite rapid diffusion in the face of falling demand.

For all countries, 1958–62 were years of comparatively fast growth of demand, in which expectations must have been buoyant and investment funds relatively abundant. Not surprisingly, the tunnel kiln diffused rapidly between 1960 and 1964 everywhere but the United Kingdom, which also showed the slowest growth.

The years between 1962 and 1966 saw fluctuations in demand in all countries, each one having at least one peak and one trough. Austria was the only European country to show a net growth over the period, yet, in the United Kingdom, Italy and Germany, 1964–8 constituted

[1] That is assuming a two-year lag between the decision to adopt and the first use of the new kiln, somewhat longer than the lags in table 5.6 to allow for possible distortions from the use of annual averages.

the years of fastest diffusion, and its slowing down in Austria and Sweden was attributable to the fact that both were nearing 100 per cent diffusion anyway. It is possible that, by this time, the tunnel kiln was seen throughout the industries as an unequivocally profitable proposition. Assuming that information had by then diffused almost completely, the role of expectations about future demand may have completely reversed itself, and poor expectations may have actually accelerated diffusion due to competitive pressures to cut costs. Overall, the similar diffusion performances of the four continental countries in the period

Table 5.14. *The influence of various factors on diffusion in each country*

	Austria	Italy	Sweden	United Kingdom	United States	West Germany
Factors determining r						
Concentration[a]	3	2	3	3	2	2
Uncertainty	$2\frac{1}{2}$	$2\frac{1}{2}$	1	1	2	2
Reaction to uncertainty	1	2	3	2	..	3
Factors determining y*						
Age of kilns	3	2	$2\frac{1}{2}$	1	..	$2\frac{1}{2}$
Fuel situation	2	3	3	1	2	1
Expected and actual savings	3	$2\frac{1}{2}$	1	2	3	2
Quality of information						
Geographical/historical effects	1	1	2	3	1	1
Industry's efforts	1	2	1	$2\frac{1}{2}$	3	2
Expectations and liquidity						
Capacity creation	2	3	2	1	..	1
Growth of demand						
1955–8	$\frac{2}{3}$	$\frac{1}{3}$	$\frac{1}{3}$	$\frac{1}{3}$	$\frac{1}{3}$	$\frac{1}{3}$
1958–62	1	1	1	$\frac{2}{3}$	$\frac{2}{3}$	1
1962–6	1	$\frac{1}{3}$	$\frac{1}{3}$	$\frac{1}{3}$	1	$\frac{1}{3}$
Total	$21\frac{1}{6}$	$21\frac{2}{3}$	$20\frac{1}{6}$	$17\frac{5}{6}$	15	$18\frac{1}{8}$
Average per factor	2·12	2·17	2·02	1·78	2·14	1·82

SOURCES: ISCO and NIESR estimates.

[a] Although in the text no significant differences were discerned, countries with a wide dispersion are awarded a mark of 2 to reflect the possibility of local monopolies, which may well adversely affect the later stages of diffusion. In the United Kingdom there are special circumstances, so that, although the industry is well dispersed, a mark of 3 is regarded as fair.

1960–4 (table 5.13) and the fact that between 1964 and 1968 diffusion was fastest in those countries which were farthest from 100 per cent diffusion in 1964, would suggest that liquidity problems and deficient expectations had less effect over the later stages of the diffusion process than the improved flow of information.

Having now considered all factors influencing r, y and y*, table 5.14

brings them together in order to ascertain the degree of explanation offered for differences in diffusion performance. A mark between 1 and 3 has been awarded for each factor, depending on how much it is likely to stimulate diffusion in that country.[1] For instance, Austria's 3 for concentration indicates the outcome most favourable to diffusion – on the other hand, Germany's 1 for fuel reflects the relatively inconducive supply situation there. Totalling all factors and giving each an equal weight,[2] the diffusion rankings appear to be: Italy, Austria, Sweden, Germany and last the United Kingdom. Referring back to table 5.4, which shows Germany leading in diffusion by firms in 1969, it is clear that the German rank should be much higher. This may be due to the arbitrary equal weighting; perhaps the factors on which the Germans score highest should be weighted more heavily. Perhaps, on the other hand, the exercise is more appropriate to an earlier stage of the diffusion process, say 1964, when the actual ordering of Austria, Sweden, Germany, Italy, and the United Kingdom was quite close to that indicated. At best the above procedure is impressionistic; it succeeds in drawing together the strands of the argument, but is also really an admission that there is no more systematic way in which these factors can be grouped to yield an overall explanation.

INTER-FIRM DIFFERENCES

In this section certain characteristics of individual firms are examined to see how far differences between adopters and non-adopters support the conclusions of the inter-country comparisons. The strongest influences on diffusion seemed to be firms' growth rates and the age of the existing kiln or kilns. Considerable regression work was carried out on the data, but in general the results were not encouraging enough to be reported, apart from the fact that the age of existing kilns was significant at the 95 per cent probability level.

We first investigated the diffusion pattern among firms of different size, on the grounds that the size of a firm may indicate its ability to acquire risk capital and may point to the rate at which risk is discounted within it; also, it is a common hypothesis that smaller firms are willing to take on risks that larger firms will not. The profiles of adopters and non-adopters are shown for Germany, Sweden and Italy in table 5.15, using production as a measure of the size.[3]

---

[1] We can only follow this procedure for the United States on those factors on which there is sufficient information. In view of this and the small size of sample, that country is excluded from the discussion below on rankings.

[2] Growth of demand in each sub-period is given a one-third weight only.

[3] For the United States and Austria there were too few firms to show a meaningful pattern, and in the United Kingdom there were too few adopting since 1956.

In Germany and Italy both small and large firms were adopters, with the smallest firms among the earliest in the field, thus confirming the hypothesis. The non-adopters in Germany were almost all medium-sized firms (also one large firm) and in Italy both medium and large. In Sweden some of the smallest and some of the largest firms were earliest in the field; the bulk of the later adopters were medium-sized firms, and the non-adopters mainly small firms, due to the tunnel kiln

Table 5.15. *Adopters and non-adopters:*[a] *size of firms*

Numbers of firms[b]

	Firms with annual production (million bricks)[c]						All firms
	0–2·5	2·5–5	5–10	10–15	15–20	20+	
Italy							
Early adopters	—	1	3	1	1	1	7
	(—)	(14)	(44)	(14)	(14)	(14)	(100)
Late adopters	—	1	3	2	1	2	9
	(—)	(11)	(34)	(22)	(11)	(22)	(100)
Non-adopters	—	—	2	1	1	2	6
	(—)	(—)	(33)	(17)	(17)	(33)	(100)
Sweden							
Early adopters	—	8	3	1	—	1	13
	(—)	(61)	(23)	(8)	(—)	(8)	(100)
Late adopters	1	—	4	—	—	—	5
	(20)	(—)	(80)	(—)	(—)	(—)	(100)
Non-adopters	6	8	5	—	—	—	19
	(32)	(42)	(26)	(—)	(—)	(—)	(100)
West Germany							
Early adopters	2	5	6	—	2	—	15
	(13)	(34)	(40)	(—)	(13)	(—)	(100)
Late adopters	1	4	10	4	4	—	23
	(4)	(17)	(44)	(17)	(17)	(—)	(100)
Non-adopters	—	3	6	—	—	1	10
	(—)	(30)	(60)	(—)	(—)	(10)	(100)

SOURCE: inquiry.

[a] Early adopters = pre-1964; late adopters = 1964–9; non-adopters are those who had not adopted by 1969.
[b] Percentages of all firms in that category given in brackets.
[c] Prior to adoption in the case of adopters.

being regarded as uneconomic for low levels of output. An impressionistic analysis of the United Kingdom data indicates a pattern broadly similar to the Swedish and for the same reasons. Splitting the adopters into full adopters (100 per cent of their production from tunnel kilns) and partial adopters, the largest firms in all the countries tend to

Table 5.16. *Adopters and non-adopters:*[a] *growth of firms*

Numbers of firms[b]

	Firms with annual growth rates (%)			All firms
	Negative	0–4	4+	
Italy				
Early adopters	—	1	5	6
	(—)	(17)	(83)	(100)
Late adopters	—	3	4	7
	(—)	(43)	(57)	(100)
Non-adopters	1	4	2	7
	(14)	(57)	(29)	(100)
Sweden				
Early adopters	—	4	7	11
	(—)	(36)	(64)	(100)
Late adopters	2	5	3	10
	(20)	(50)	(30)	(100)
Non-adopters	3	7	8	18
	(17)	(39)	(44)	(100)
West Germany				
Early adopters	2	4	8	14
	(14)	(29)	(57)	(100)
Late adopters	6	23	16	45
	(13)	(51)	(36)	(100)
Non-adopters	3	13	2	18
	(17)	(72)	(11)	(100)
All countries				
Early adopters	2	9	20	31
	(6)	(29)	(65)	(100)
Late adopters	8	31	23	62
	(13)	(50)	(37)	(100)
Non-adopters	7	24	12	43
	(16)	(56)	(28)	(100)

SOURCE: inquiry.

[a] Early adopters = pre-1964; late adopters = 1964–9; non-adopters are those who had not adopted by 1969.

[b] Percentages of firms in that category given in brackets.

be partial adopters, whereas almost all the smaller firms (and obviously those with a single kiln) are full adopters.

Fast growth at firm level, as at national level, might be considered conducive both to brighter expectations about the future and to building up financial reserves. The adopters of tunnel kilns had on average been growing faster prior to adoption than their non-adopting counterparts during the same period. This is shown in table 5.16 for all three countries for which sufficient data are available; it can also be seen that the earlier adopters as a group were growing faster just before their adoption than were the later adopters.

Differences between the availability of information to individual firms and the influence of these differences on the timing of diffusion at the national level were discussed earlier; an attempt was made to distinguish between the accessibility of information to users and to non-users as groups. In lieu of actual data on information channels, proxies

Table 5.17. *Adopters and non-adopters:[a] the average age of kilns*

	Average kiln[b] built				All firms	Firms with post-1915 kilns
	Pre-1900	1900–14	1915–39	Post-1939		
			(number of firms[c])			(%)
West Germany						
Early adopters	2	8	5	3	18	45
	(11)	(44)	(28)	(17)	(100)	
Late adopters	2	11	4	1	18	28
	(11)	(61)	(22)	(6)	(100)	
Non-adopters	2	1	5	2	10	70
	(20)	(10)	(50)	(20)	(100)	
All countries[d]						
Early adopters	4	11	7	4	26	42
	(15)	(43)	(27)	(15)	(100)	
Late adopters	4	15	5	4	28	32
	(14)	(54)	(18)	(14)	(100)	
Non-adopters	4	8	12	8	32	63
	(12)	(25)	(38)	(25)	(100)	

SOURCE: inquiry.

[a] Early adopters = pre-1964; late adopters = 1964–9; non-adopters are those who had not adopted by 1969.

[b] Includes all kilns, existing and replaced.

[c] Percentages of all firms in that category given in brackets.

[d] Excluding Italy and the United States.

had to be introduced, and the three proxies briefly considered were spending on research and development, association (financial or otherwise) with other companies, and membership of the industry research association. The pattern was, however, unclear: only in Sweden did noticeably higher proportions of users than of non-users possess these characteristics; there was a weak tendency in the same direction in the United Kingdom sample, but no discernible pattern in Germany.

A high labour–capital ratio may indicate a large local pool of labour which would discourage a capital-intensive innovation; but, at the same time, it may suggest an older kiln which is more likely to need replacing. An examination of the data on factor shares at firm level shows that neither influence is dominant. In the three countries, Germany, Italy and the United Kingdom, for which the 1964 factor shares were available for each firm, there was no significant difference between those firms which subsequently adopted and those which did not, and an estimate of the 1964 shares for Sweden from the 1969 figures suggests little difference there either.

Older kilns, besides being less efficient, are also likely to be in need of more frequent and costly maintenance. Company data seem to confirm the hypothesis that this dual incentive should generate a higher rate of innovation among operators of older kilns. We have reliable information concerning the age of the kilns of 46 firms in Germany, but only 40 in the Austrian, Swedish and United Kingdom samples together (table 5.17). This is not sufficient to investigate the situation in any of the latter countries separately, but the pooled data of the four countries strongly support the tendency indicated by the analysis of the German data, that non-adopters in the sample have newer kilns than adopters did prior to adoption. About two-thirds of the non-adopters had post-1915 kilns, but of both the early and later adopters in the sample some two-thirds of their kilns were originally built before World War I.

CONCLUSIONS

In this chapter, several major points seem to arise from the hypotheses advanced. To begin with, it has been established that the tunnel kiln is at least highly labour-saving compared with the conventional technology, and almost certainly also yields overall savings, despite a higher capital outlay and increased servicing costs.

It is essential to distinguish between technical and non-technical constraints on adoption. Given the wide diversity of types of clay and of bricks produced, not all firms may find the tunnel kiln applicable to their output for strictly technical reasons. Because of this, a 'technological ceiling' was constructed and attention was focused on those firms in the various national industries for which the tunnel kiln appeared to be a feasible proposition, and on the strictly economic influences affecting diffusion in those firms.

Many such economic factors have probably been influential; three, however, seem to stand out. First, there is the flow of information; its importance is amply demonstrated by the close correspondence of theoretical sigmoid curves to the observed diffusion patterns. Secondly, there is the optimism (or otherwise) with which entrepreneurs view the future, together with their ease of access to investment funds, both of which are to a large extent determined by demand conditions in the recent past, and are mitigating factors not only on the time pattern of diffusion at the national level, but also as major sources of inter-country and inter-firm differences in diffusion performance. Finally, again at both national and firm levels, an important part of the explanation of adoption may be traced to the age of the existing stock of conventional kilns.

CHAPTER 6

THE BASIC OXYGEN STEEL PROCESS

By J. R. Meyer, Harvard and NBER,
and G. Herregat, NBER[1]

STEELMAKING TECHNOLOGY AND THE HISTORY OF THE BASIC OXYGEN PROCESS

This chapter is concerned with the international diffusion of the basic oxygen process in steelmaking. Considerable controversy has occurred between outside analysts and industry spokesmen because of a fundamental discrepancy in the meaning given to the concept of technological changes that reduce costs. The outside analysts have thought mostly in terms of major, discontinuous innovations which displace old ways by new ones and are assumed to increase productivity considerably. Such innovations do occur from time to time. In the steel industry, however, engineers and businessmen are more prone to regard progress as a smooth, continuous process of improving the old ways by small changes. In the industry's view these evolutionary improvements can sometimes make an old technique competitive with a new, to the point even of delaying displacement by the new. To understand these possibilities, and thereby establish a basis for specifying an empirical model to analyse the diffusion of the process, a careful assessment of the underlying technology is helpful.

Steelmaking consists of refining pig iron by oxidation. Essentially pig iron contains iron and unwanted chemical elements, the most common of which are carbon, manganese, phosphorus, sulphur and silicon. All

[1] The National Bureau embarked on this study in 1968 under the direction of the late Professor Alfred H. Conrad. Although involved from inception, the two authors assumed responsibility for the study only after Alfred Conrad's untimely death. They acknowledge their debt to him for his exploratory work.

Most of the computations were done at the Yale Computer Center. We are grateful to Orin Hansen for his help in applying and considerably improving existing programmes used in this study. We have also benefited from the research assistance of Neville O. Beharie and Pamela Mash, who helped us to compile the data drawn from the questionnaires addressed to American firms in the steel and other industries. H. I. Forman drew the original charts. Vivian Batts, Teri Brilliante, Elizabeth Parshley, and Sydney Shulman shared the typing of the successive drafts of the manuscript.

Although initiated under the auspices of the National Bureau of Economic Research, this paper has not been submitted for approval to the National Bureau's Board of Directors and is not, therefore, an official Bureau publication. Accordingly, the authors are solely responsible for the statements made or views expressed herein.

of these elements must be removed, or at least drastically reduced, if steel is to be obtained. Sulphur is removed by adding lime to form a basic slag capable of combining with the phosphorus and sulphur. This reaction depends on the slag being sufficiently basic and on high temperature. The other unwanted elements are removed by adding controlled amounts of oxygen to the molten metal. The oxygen then combines with these elements and some of the iron to form oxides, which either leave the bath as gases or enter the slag.

By the time the steel is refined to the required specification, it usually contains between 0·05 and 0·10 per cent of dissolved oxygen, which has to be removed by subsequent treatment. If steel was left over-oxidised, then oxygen and carbon, for example, could react during ingot solidi-fication and cause blow-holes. Some deoxidant must therefore be added at the time of tapping to produce treatable rimming, semi-killed or killed steel from the 'wild' over-oxidised metal.

The first modern steelmaking process providing a large-scale, direct and relatively cheap method of refining pig iron into steel was developed independently by Henry Bessemer in England and William Kelly in the United States. The process was 'pneumatic', since it involved blowing air through molten pig iron contained in a bottom-blown vessel lined with acid refractories. This process could, however, only be used to refine low-phosphorus ores, such as those of Lorraine.

What is interesting for our purpose is that as early as 1856, the year in which he patented his invention, Bessemer had seen the possibility of using pure oxygen instead of air and he had even entertained the thought of introducing the gas through the top rather than the bottom of the vessel. In short, the design of the oxygen process was realised in essentials at a very early date. Application was, however, to be delayed for almost a century for two reasons. In the first place, pure oxygen was not available in commercial quantities or at an acceptable price; in the second, the increase in the oxygen content of the air-blast in the Bessemer converter was not technically feasible because of the damage done to the converter's tuyères and refractory lining.

However, the quality of the Bessemer steel was unsatisfactory for many purposes; its phosphorus content remained too high and, as soon as a new process appeared that took better care of the unwanted phosphorus, it had to dominate. Such a technique was the Siemens furnace, or open-hearth process, designed in 1880 with an acid brick construction. It was redesigned some eight years later with a lining of magnesite brick, which converted it into a basic process. In essence, the open-hearth process consists of passing burning fuel gas over the top of the materials (pig iron and ore in the Siemens furnace) so as to provide the heat required to purify the charge.

But while the Bessemer process in its later basic form requires pig iron with a phosphorus content of 2 per cent or more in order to maintain a temperature high enough to eliminate the phosphorus after oxidation of the carbon, the basic open-hearth process permits the use of iron of any phosphorus content up to 1 per cent, since it is able, due to the different temperature conditions, to eliminate the phosphorus before the carbon. This, of course, produces less phosphoric steel, but most of all it makes available the huge iron ore deposits of the United States, which could not otherwise be used because they have a phosphorus content too high for the acid Bessemer or acid open-hearth processes, but too low for the basic Bessemer converter.

This technology was further improved by the Martin brothers who, by substituting scrap for ore in the Siemens pig iron and ore process, found it possible to dilute the charge with steel scrap to such an extent that less oxidation was necessary. This improvement stimulated even wider adoption of the Siemens–Martin process and the displacement of the Bessemer converter wherever scrap was plentiful. And, of course, the expanding output of the industry generated quantities of scrap for recycling through open-hearth furnaces.

The development of the open-hearth process did not, however, stop interest and research in the use of oxygen for steelmaking. A series of patents were issued covering the application of oxygen. Indeed, the technical problems of producing high purity oxygen were solved by Carl Linde at the turn of the century by the process of liquefaction and distillation of air, but oxygen costs were still too high for steelmaking. It was only in the late 1920s that an efficient heat exchanger was developed which made tonnage production of oxygen possible at low cost.

As early as 1923, however, an advisory committee appointed by the United States Bureau of Mines recommended application of oxygen to the blast furnace smelting of iron ore whether by the Bessemer or the open-hearth process.[1] The first actual application of oxygen to the open-hearth process was apparently in a four-ton, oil-fired furnace at the Hammer and Sickle Steel Foundry in Moscow.[2]

In Germany, starting with articles stimulated by the report from the United States Bureau of Mines, attention was paid to using oxygen in the basic Bessemer converter, which was the major steel producing unit in that country. Considerable emphasis was put on this work when the need for greater production and for working with low grade ores of

[1] United States Bureau of Mines, *The Use of Oxygen or Oxygenated Air in Metallurgical and Allied Processes* by F. W. Davis, Washington (DC), 1923.

[2] B. M. Suslow, 'Oxygen enriched air in steel making', *Metal Progress*, vol. 26, September 1934, pp. 40–1.

domestic origin was deemed a matter of national survival. In 1930, the Maximilian Smelting Works at Rosenberg had installed an oxygen plant which was built by the German Linde Company and, by 1938, 95 per cent of all blows were made with air enriched to 27–31 per cent oxygen.[1]

However, the application of oxygen to the Bessemer converter continued to present problems. Oxygen, by producing higher temperatures, accelerated the destruction of the bottom of the furnace and the tuyères through which the gas was introduced. The blowing device was troublesome enough in a standard air-operated Bessemer converter; introduction of oxygen multiplied the difficulties and considerably shortened the life of the equipment.

During World War II the Germans built a large complex in Linz, consisting of modern blast furnaces, open-hearth and electric furnaces for steel conversion, and a nitrogen-producing plant that generated oxygen as a by-product. When, after the war, the Austrian government nationalised the plant, the plant engineers decided to take advantage of the existing oxygen production to carry out a systematic programme of studies. The fact that their steel furnaces were of the open-hearth instead of the basic Bessemer type turned out to be crucially important. An essential physical difference between the open-hearth furnace and the Bessemer converter is that in the former the fuel and air are burned over the top of the iron melt instead of being blown through the bottom of the furnace.

The Austrian experimenters at first simply blew oxygen into the space above the iron melt in an open-hearth furnace. They succeeded in accelerating the conversion of iron to steel, but the increased flame temperature destroyed the roof of the furnace and the regenerators for preheating air became clogged with dust. Next they tried feeding oxygen into an electric furnace; again the heat proved destructive, ruining the electrode holders. The Linz engineers then consulted Robert Dürrer who, with Heinrich Hellbruegge, was experimenting in Switzerland using oxygen in a two-ton Bessemer converter and in an electric furnace. Dürrer and Hellbruegge were injecting a jet of oxygen into the molten iron through a water-cooled lance placed just above the surface of the metal.

The first trials of this system, in experiments at Linz designed to follow Dürrer's instructions, failed. The heat destroyed the lance; the stream of oxygen blown deep into the melt caused damage to the bottom and other refractories of the vessel, and the treatment failed to remove

[1] W. Eilender and W. Roeser, 'Metallurgische Untersuchungen über das Arbeiten mit sauerstoffangereichertem Gebläsewind beim Thomasverfahren', *Stahl und Eisen*, vol. 59, September 1939, pp. 1057–67.

enough of the phosphorus impurity from the iron. The Linz engineers then abandoned the accepted practices of the time; they reduced the impact pressures of the oxygen jet by using a different nozzle and raising the lance further from the surface of the melt. This new concept worked well; the bottom of the vessel was undamaged, the lance survived, carbon monoxide gas generated by the burning of carbon in the iron stirred the melt, phosphorus was effectively removed, and the experiment produced steel of good quality. From the initial experiments in 1949 in a two-ton vessel, the Linz engineers went on to further tests with larger units, and in late 1952 they installed the system on a modest commercial scale, using vessels of 35-ton capacity. In 1953 a second plant of the same kind went into operation at Donawitz in the ironmaking district of Styria in Austria. The system has since been called the LD process, from the initials of the towns where the first two plants were installed.

The LD converter is a pear-shaped, tiltable vessel, which must be charged with hot metal; it therefore needs to be close to a blast furnace – oxygen converters cannot use cold charges as open-hearth furnaces can. Scrap is charged first, then the molten ore is poured in; the entire charging process takes less than four minutes.[1] The vessel is then returned to the upright position and the lance, a tube some fifty feet long and ten inches in diameter, is lowered through the mouth until its tip is four to eight feet above the metal bath. The lance is cooled by water circulating round it at the rate of about 400 gallons per minute so as to be able to withstand the furnace's heat. Oxygen of 99.5 per cent purity is then injected through the lance under a pressure of 150 pounds per square inch and at the rate of 10,000 cubic feet per minute. The resulting oxidation burns part of the iron and nearly all its carbon, silicon, manganese and phosphorus impurities, the oxides being absorbed by a slag formed by converter additives. The carbon is removed, since carbon monoxide burns as carbon dioxide when it mixes with the air on emerging from the mouth of the vessel. When the carbon has been consumed, the fire goes out, the refining process having taken only about 20 minutes.

Unlike an open-hearth furnace, the oxygen converter requires no fuel; it derives all the necessary heat from the original molten charge and the combustion of impurities by the injected oxygen. This feature modifies the composition of the charge; oxygen converters must operate with hot metal making up 70 to 75 per cent or more of the charge. This means a maximum of 30 per cent scrap, as opposed to the 'current' practice of 50 per cent in open-hearth and up to 90 per cent in electric furnaces. Originally, oxygen converters could accept no more than

[1] J. K. Stone, 'Oxygen in steelmaking', *Scientific American*, vol. 4, April 1968, pp. 24–31.

20 per cent scrap, but this percentage was increased in the early 1960s. In fact, oxygen converters, unlike the other processes, use scrap much less as a source of metallics than as a coolant for controlling temperature. This scrap ceiling, which may be at least partly overcome in time, constitutes a second important limitation in the oxygen process (as well as the required proximity of a blast furnace).

The 35-ton oxygen converter did not, on the other hand, mark the end of the development. Application was still limited to producing common-grade carbon steels and to processing hot iron with a relatively low phosphorus content (up to 0·4 per cent), which constituted still another limitation on the early applicability of the process. Research went on with the aim of widening the product-mix, particularly to include high-carbon and alloy steels, and making the process suitable for high-phosphorus ores.

For blowing high-phosphorus iron, two modifications were made to the original LD process. In the first, called the LD-Pompey process, lumpy lime is added to the bath during the blowing. In the second, called LD–AC or OLP, the metal is blown not with pure oxygen but with a stream of oxygen containing powdered lime. Both modifications allow for processing of ores with up to 2 per cent phosphorus.

Industry testimonies show, on the other hand, that the range of products of these processes was not widened before the early 1960s. For instance, Dilley and McBride, both of United States Steel, claim that when 'US Steel made its decision in 1962 to construct a two-vessel shop at the Duquesne shop, it was still not known whether such vessels would be capable of making high-carbon, silicon and alloy steels.'[1] They add that the decision was made to go ahead because 'five years of experimentation with its small-scale BOP facility at its South works led US Steel to believe that production of a wide range of products would be possible.'

Besides LD and its variants, two other oxygen processes have been independently developed. The Kaldo process has a rotating vessel whose speed can vary up to 30 revolutions a minute. Oxygen is not blown from the top but at a flat angle. Either high-phosphorus or low-phosphorus iron can be processed. A so-called Rotor process also uses a rotating vessel but with an opening at both ends. The speed of rotation is lower than that of the Kaldo furnace, originally only 0·5 revolutions a minute but now 5 revolutions a minute. Two streams of oxygen are used: one of high purity is blown through a lance underneath the bath surface to oxidise the impurities of the charge; another of lower purity is directed through a second lance on to the bath surface to assist the

[1] D. R. Dilley and D. McBride, 'Oxygen steelmaking – fact vs. folklore', *Iron and Steel Engineer*, vol. 45, October 1967, p. 13.

oxidation and burn the carbon monoxide. Here also, high- and low-phosphorus iron can be processed.[1]

Development of oxygen converters was paralleled by improvements in open-hearth practice. The decreasing cost of oxygen made possible its use for flame enrichment, which, as already noted, had been seriously contemplated for some time. Actually a British Iron and Steel Institute bibliography, published in 1959, lists some 82 papers from 1946 to 1959 dealing with the use of combustion oxygen and some 116 papers on the use of bath oxygen in open-hearth furnaces.[2] Essentially flame enrichment is achieved by an oxygen outlet under the fuel, which permits the mixing of oxygen and fuel to increase flame temperature and fuel firing rates.

Two other devices for using oxygen in open-hearth furnaces have also been developed (oxygen roof lancing and oxy-fuel lances). They both increase the bath's heat and therefore accelerate the refining process, since in open-hearth furnaces the speed of the process is mainly dependent on the rate at which heat can be supplied to the bath to melt the charge and reduce the iron dioxide. Normally, the rate of heat transfer from a flame to the bath through the slag is very low. However, when oxygen is injected, the heat generated by the direct oxidation is almost completely transferred to the bath, as compared with a maximum of 20 per cent efficiency of utilisation for the heat generated by conventional fuels burned over a bath of molten slag and iron.[3]

These other developments clearly raise the question of how to define technological progress in steelmaking. Innovation has not been limited to the basic oxygen converter. Open-hearth furnaces have been equipped with oxygen lances feeding the metal bath with up to 1,300 cubic feet of oxygen per ton of steel produced, as against 1,800 cubic feet per ton in LD converters.[4] Oxygen injection in open-hearth furnaces reduces the overall heating time to about eight hours from charge to tap, compared with ten hours in conventional open-hearth furnaces.[5] Oxygen converter operations, however, usually take less

[1] These processes have not, however, been very successful in terms of diffusion compared with the LD process. Only six commercial Kaldo installations exist (one in France, two in Sweden, two in the United Kingdom, and one in the United States) and only four Rotor plants seem to be actually operating (two in Germany, one in the United Kingdom, and one in South Africa). Nevertheless, to be complete, we have included, when relevant, these installations in the countries' oxygen converter capacity figures used in the statistical analyses.

[2] Iron and Steel Institute, *Oxygen in Steelmaking*, London, 1959.

[3] H. A. Parker and P. Schane, Jr, 'Use of oxygen lances and basic brick in open-hearth furnace roofs', paper prepared for presentation to the American Iron and Steel Institute, 25 May 1969, p. 28.

[4] Stone, 'Oxygen in steelmaking', p. 29.

[5] Data from 600 open-hearth heats made under comparable conditions in three United States Steel plants showed a saving in heating time of 10 to 25 per cent and a decrease in fuel consumption of 18 to 35 per cent when roof lances supplying 300 to 600 cubic feet of oxygen

than one hour. We thus have, on the one hand, a major technological breakthrough and, on the other, a continuous process of important parallel improvements to an existing technology. Understanding the diffusion rate of the newest technique therefore requires recognition of this double technological evolution.

DIFFUSION OF THE BASIC OXYGEN PROCESS

Chart 6.1 shows the share of basic oxygen production in total crude steel output since 1956 for most of the major steel producing countries of the world. To a first approximation the national diffusions could be

Chart 6.1. *Shares of basic oxygen steel in total crude steel output*

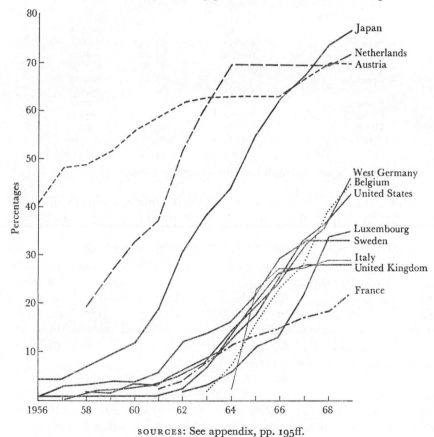

SOURCES: See appendix, pp. 195ff.

per ton were used. See United States Steel Corporation, *The Making, Shaping and Treating of Steel*, 8th ed., Pittsburgh, 1964, p. 488.

read as following reasonably well-behaved logistic curves. That observation, however, tells us little about the many dimensions of the diffusion process.

Two aspects of diffusion often considered of paramount importance are the speed of adoption and the share of the new technology. In order to combine these two aspects into one measure, we estimated the proportions of the total area below the curves, using Gini coefficients.[1] The

Table 6.1. *National diffusion coefficients, 1956–69*

	With 100% upper limit	With variable upper limit	
		Limit (%)	Coefficient
Austria	0·5442	80	0·6803
Belgium	0·1001	60	0·1669
France	0·0630	35	0·1800
Italy	0·0893	35	0·2553
Japan	0·2933	80	0·3666
Luxemburg	0·0734	40	0·1835
Netherlands	0·3642	80	0·4552
Sweden	0·1049	40	0·2623
United Kingdom	0·1022	35	0·2920
United States	0·1225	60	0·2042
West Germany	0·1273	60	0·2122

SOURCE: NBER estimates (see text and chart 6.1).

value of the area below each curve is not, of course, an index of *relative* positions; some unit of reference must be provided. Two assumptions were used to compute the relative positions: the first was that the best score for each country would have been to have had all its capacity installed in the new technique for the whole period; the alternative was to assign to each country (by intuition or knowledge, and admittedly somewhat arbitrarily) a particular upper limit assumed to be equal to the 'apparent' asymptote of its diffusion curve in 1969.[2] Diffusion coefficients calculated under these two different assumptions are presented in table 6.1. A similar exercise using a different diffusion period (1962–9) hardly affected the rankings.

These diffusion coefficients probably create a more meaningful ranking of national industries than a simple counting procedure, but their value is still more descriptive than explanatory. Among other deficiencies, any such measure of the basic oxygen share is necessarily

[1] C. Gini, *Variabilità e Mutabilità*, Bologna, Universita di Cagliari, 1912, part 2. For a description of our statistical procedure, see the appendix, pp. 198–9.

[2] It should be noted that some of the asymptotes we considered 'apparent' in 1969 have already, by 1972, been exceeded.

relative to total output and therefore tells us little about the absolute performance of a nation's industry, although any absolute measure also has limitations. Perhaps, though, the most obvious absolute measure for understanding diffusion of the process would be its total production by country, as presented in chart 6.2 for the years 1956–69. Even in

Chart 6.2. *Basic oxygen process production by countries, 1956–69*

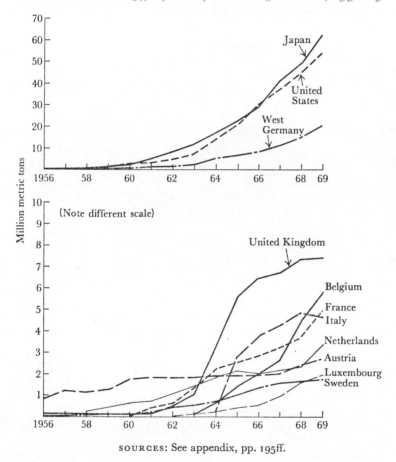

SOURCES: See appendix, pp. 195ff.

absolute terms diffusion to some extent follows a simple logistic pattern. However, chart 6.2 tells us nothing more than that a substantial expansion in the oxygen process occurred in countries that either had a very large steel industry at the beginning of the period or one that grew very rapidly during those years.

The behavioural or policy interpretations could depend crucially upon which of these two explanations dominated – rapid growth or a large national industry to start with. A crude answer to this question can be obtained by looking at time series of total steel output by countries during this period, as shown in chart 6.3. It is reasonably clear that the high absolute levels of total oxygen process capacity in the United States and the United Kingdom were mainly due to both nations possessing substantial steel industries at the beginning of the development period. In contrast, the Japanese involvement in the oxygen process was closely associated with a substantial expansion of

Chart 6.3. *Total steel output by countries, 1956–69*

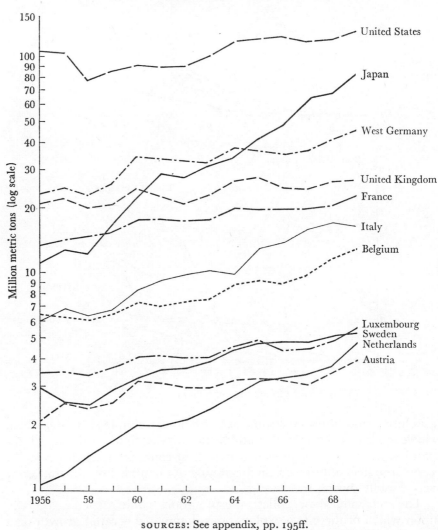

SOURCES: See appendix, pp. 195ff.

total output during the 1960s. On the other hand, Germany's substantial expansion in production by the oxygen process represented a
combination of the two circumstances, both a large steel industry at
the beginning of the period and some growth of the German industry
during the 1960s.

Table 6.2. *Ratios of changes in oxygen process capacity to changes in total
capacity plus changes in oxygen process capacity,*[a] *1959–69*

	Ratios
Austria	0.3736
Belgium	0.5405
France	0.3722
Italy	0.4293
Japan	0.5210
Netherlands	0.6124
Sweden	0.3569
United Kingdom	0.5496[b]
United States	0.8602[c]
West Germany	0.6101

SOURCES: OECD; UNECE; Kaiser Steel Corporation, *Linz-Donawitz Process Newsletter*
(various issues).

[a] These ratios can exceed 0.5 only if there is a net reduction in non-oxygen process capacity.

[b] 1968 total capacity because the 1969 figure is computed on a different basis not comparable with 1959.

[c] Total capacity derived from the Wharton index.

Another broad perspective on diffusion can be obtained by examining
the change in capacity in the oxygen process in relation to the change in
total steel capacity during the 1960s. Ratios of changes in ten major
steel producing countries for the period 1959–69 are shown in table 6.2.
A ratio near unity indicates that a country availed itself of virtually
every increase in capacity as a chance to introduce the oxygen process;
in contrast a ratio near zero would suggest that expansion of total
capacity was not used to any great extent as an occasion to extend
oxygen process capacity.

The figures in table 6.2 have some potentially surprising implications.
They suggest, for example, that the United States, the Netherlands and
West Germany were the most likely to introduce the oxygen process
whenever the opportunity presented itself. On the other hand, Japan,
which looks so aggressive by most diffusion measures whether relative
or absolute, seems to be only mildly aggressive in terms of this
'opportunity' ratio. France, however, which is hardly aggressive by any
of the previous relative or absolute measures, seems to be relatively
unaggressive by this opportunity measure as well.

Certain refinements could be made in these various gross diffusion measures, but none would alter the fact that they are still essentially more descriptive than explanatory. In essence, several major problems – mainly of defining the profitability of the process in the different national contexts – remain before these diffusion curves can be interpreted meaningfully.

THE COST ADVANTAGES OF THE BASIC OXYGEN PROCESS

Starting date

Perhaps the most obvious and difficult problem associated with defining the cost advantages of a process and thereby giving meaning to any simple diffusion curve is that of establishing the date at which a process has commercial applicability, that is an actual efficiency advantage over existing techniques. In addition, there is the question of the permissible scale of basic oxygen operations. It took three years for the Linz engineers to develop their small experimental converters into 35-ton commercial equipment, and there is no *a priori* reason to believe that further increases in scale did not require similar periods to implement the design. Keeping in mind, for example, that the whole Austrian steel industry's output is less than that of some plants in the United States and that until 1960 oxygen steel in Austria amounted only to about 50 per cent of that country's output, it becomes clear that international diffusion implied some size adaptations of the process itself. Furthermore, with the introduction of the oxygen process, blast furnace operations had to be timed with the increased number of heats at the steel shop, while casting lines and rolling mills had to be adjusted to the new feeding rhythm. It is not surprising, therefore, that the first adopters employed a size close to that of the innovator:[1] it was not until 1960, in the United States, that a 100-ton vessel went into operation, incontrovertibly establishing the actual size flexibility of the process.

Accordingly, any diffusion coefficient that indicated the countries' relative positions in terms of the date of first commercial application would, in fact, show a bias in favour of the countries or firms with operational conditions close to the innovator's own. Thus, such a diffusion coefficient for the oxygen process, at least prior to the early 1960s, should demonstrate a relatively high speed of adoption by countries experiencing the Austrian conditions – low-phosphorus ores, a limited range of product lines and small-scale operations.

[1] By the end of 1954, there were four plants throughout the world using oxygen converters: one in Canada with two 40-ton vessels, one in the United States with three 35-ton vessels, and two in Austria with five 30-ton vessels between them (see A. K. McAdams, 'Big steel: invention and innovation reconsidered', *Quarterly Journal of Economics*, vol. 81, August 1967, pp. 457–74).

However, it eventually became established that the oxygen process was more advantageous with large rather than small-scale operations, which makes it difficult to specify a 'structure' for investigating steel diffusion by econometric or statistical functions (since switching regression regimes would be involved). In order to avoid these difficulties, we have taken the position that 1961–2 constitutes the base period with respect to which differences in diffusion rates should be explained. We consider that by 1961 or 1962 all purely technological problems of adoption had more or less been solved, and that all countries and firms were facing a homogeneous technology, whose diffusion could then be explained by a set of independent variables with predictable and stable signs. The only major exception to this would be in the production of very highly specialised steels, as may have been the case in Sweden.

Cost-advantage analysis

Even if it were possible to estimate exactly the profitability of the different processes in each country – and needless to say, we do not have the necessary detailed statistical series – we would still be left with the question of the relevance of these highly aggregated figures. In fact, plant data would be best, since investments are made at the plant level within a specific technological environment. We shall therefore limit ourselves to specifying a set of variables measuring relative cost effects and the direction in which these might be expected to influence the decision to adopt.

A standard approach to comparative cost analyses for steel processes is to focus on relative capital costs. The comparison is, however, meaningful only in terms of installing or re-installing a given steel shop. When compared to a new open-hearth furnace, the capital cost of an oxygen converter is definitely lower; per ton of steel it is estimated at about half that of an open-hearth furnace.[1]

These estimates do not, however, take into account the capital cost of the blast furnace. Because oxygen converters can only operate with hot metal, the absence of a nearby blast furnace may tilt the cost advantage away from the oxygen process. This will definitely be so if electric furnaces are the alternative; since they can operate with a cold charge, their capital cost in some applications may be less than either oxygen converters or open-hearth furnaces. In fact, small, non-integrated firms usually opt for electric steelmaking, mainly on the basis of capital cost. This, in turn, suggests that plant size is a factor in

[1] UNECE, *Some Important Developments during 1953 in Iron and Steel Technology*, Geneva, 1954, pp. 13–15. A 1957 American estimate places the capital cost of the basic oxygen process at $15 a ton compared with about $40 for the open-hearth process (*Iron Age*, 12 December 1957, p. 87).

the choice between an oxygen converter and an electric furnace; that is, particularly after 1962, scale should be positively correlated with the capital cost advantages of basic oxygen capacity.

A frequent question in the 1960s, however, was not whether to install a new open-hearth furnace or a new oxygen converter, but whether to replace an old open-hearth furnace by oxygen or to improve the existing equipment. In other words, the problem is to find out whether or not production costs of the oxygen process are low enough compared with improved open-hearth furnaces to outweigh the additional capital cost of replacing an existing open-hearth furnace by an oxygen converter. Given that the decision is a replacement one, the choice then is usually between oxygen and electric steelmaking on the basis of total cost advantage. The comparison thus has essentially two dimensions: the total cost advantage when the existing (usually open-hearth) equipment has been fully depreciated, and the relative production costs, taking into account the particular technological constraints of each process. Because oxygen converters can only operate with a much lower percentage of scrap than other processes, relative production costs vary according to the relative metal prices.

Several estimates of these costs have been made, but they are inappropriate in the context, being based on metallic ratios closer to the constraints of the oxygen process than to the more flexible specifications of the other processes. One simple reason for this is that costs of the oxygen process cannot be defined for conditions beyond its technological capabilities. Such cost comparisons therefore necessarily present a biased image – particularly if the figures are extrapolated to conditions very different from those for which the studies were developed, for example, a situation of extreme scarcity of scrap as in Latin America.

A more representative cost comparison may be that made in a 1964 Battelle study.[1] Hypothetical plants in three sizes were defined for each of the three processes. Metal prices were assumed at reasonable current levels. The hot metal price was an estimated intra-firm value and was put at $39 a ton for small plants and $30 for large, which was considerably below the published price of cold pig iron ($60–$65). Scrap prices were fixed at $30 per ton for the grades used in open-hearth and oxygen converters, and $27 for those used in electric furnaces. The results clearly indicated the importance of the charge composition since the cost of metal amounted to between half and two-thirds of the total cost.

The electric furnace has a definite advantage over the oxygen con-

---

[1] See Battelle Memorial Institute, *Final Report on Technical and Economic Analysis of the Impact of Recent Developments in Steelmaking Practices on the Supplying Industries*, Columbus (Ohio), 1964.

verter when scrap is cheap relative to pig iron, or sometimes where very specialised steels are produced. One analyst of the steel industry claims in fact that 'the future is clearly with electric furnaces using super high-grade ore pellets or with direct reduction' of scrap or ore, since such plants cost a quarter as much to build and have operating cost savings running to about 18 per cent.[1] With respect to improved open-hearth and electric furnaces, the oxygen process is also deemed at a dis-advantage under American conditions by Battelle. The facts that no new open-hearth furnaces have been built in the United States recently and that large plants are not equipped with electric furnaces, lead to the conclusion that the Battelle estimates must be misleading (probably because their hot metal costs are too high). Nevertheless, one might tentatively conclude that with low scrap prices, electric furnaces have lower production costs than oxygen converters, especially in relatively small plants. In a large-scale operation, low scrap prices will partially offset the cost advantage of oxygen with respect to electric and existing open-hearth furnaces, but probably not completely. But whatever the scale effects, we should expect scrap availability to be negatively correlated with growth of the oxygen process.

Low scrap prices can, however, be an additional factor in reducing any potential advantage for oxygen over open-hearth furnaces, and where combined with fully depreciated open-hearth equipment, might even reverse the advantage patterns. Then it would be most favourable to keep and improve existing open-hearth furnaces instead of changing to oxygen – at least until the open-hearth capacity wore out. Indeed, these are the major points made by Dilley and McBride.[2] They argue, using reworked United Nations data, that when the 12 per cent capital charges are excluded from open-hearth total costs, oxygen steel becomes more expensive at all sizes, at least under American conditions. How-ever, they also show that, on their assumptions, the saving in total production costs of open-hearth over oxygen decreases from 3 per cent at 500,000-ton capacity to 1·1 per cent at 1,500,000-ton capacity. Thus, the cost advantage of the open-hearth process may diminish with scale so as to make replacement with oxygen rational, especially if expansion or scrapping of old capacity is considered.

To summarise, certain differences observed in diffusion rates of the oxygen process could be explained by differences in the objective circumstances of different producers, using the variables whose expected sign we have just specified.[3] The remaining unexplained variance might

[1] Andrew Bucharet, quoted in *Newsweek*, 23 January 1971, p. 60.
[2] 'Oxygen steelmaking – fact vs. folklore', pp. 17–19.
[3] We must meet at this point one frequent explanation of the so-called lagging behaviour of the United States steel industry in adopting the basic oxygen process. It has been argued that only *after* severe import competition had already taken place was the United States steel

then be treated as attributable to managerial or other less tangibly economic differences. Indeed, we shall return to this point again. First, however, we must define our models and indicate the character of the sample data available to us.

MODELS AND SAMPLES

Models

For the reasons just outlined, our initial emphasis will be upon explaining differences in diffusion rates, as far as we can, by straightforward appeal to economic considerations. To this end we shall assume that knowledge of steel technology is reasonably universal, and spreads rapidly and freely across international boundaries. Thus, to start, we shall assume that no national group of steel managers is much less well-informed about technological possibilities than any other. Of course, even if information is well dispersed, reaction to new technological possibilities may still vary widely because of differences in managerial aspirations, styles or other characteristics. We shall put these considerations aside for the moment and return to them later.

Given this initial emphasis on rationality, it would be expected that a major portion of observed differences in rates of diffusion of the oxygen process could be explained by differences in the objective environments within which managements operated. In particular, we would expect factor prices and market structures in various countries, for example relatively cheap scrap metal or expensive low-phosphorus ores, to influence the desirability of adopting the oxygen process. Similarly, if the price of electricity is moderate, plants are small and scrap easily

industry moved into replacing its open-hearth facilities by oxygen converters. But defining an 'export competition' variable presents enormous problems: for example, net export positions might hide different tariff and quota structures and non-tariff barriers such as the border taxes in EEC countries. Furthermore, United States net exports of steel products became negative only in 1958, remaining at around 2 million tons until 1964, and increasing to a maximum of about 8 million tons in 1966. Given a minimum construction lag of two years, the United States steel industry had already decided to produce 25 per cent of its output by the basic oxygen process by 1964, before import competition had really started to hurt. In fact, using a linear programming model of resource allocation, with a technology matrix representing the industry's input–output structure, C. S. Tsao and R. H. Day ('A process analysis model of the US steel industry', *Management Science*, vol. 17, June 1971, pp. B-588–B-608) found that, for the United States over the years 1955–68, the calculated steel output by the open-hearth and oxygen processes approximated very closely to the actual levels; in other words, that the actual decreases in open-hearth production and the actual increases in oxygen process production were almost 'optimal'. Only actual electric steel production was slightly below its computed 'optimal' path. Similarly, G. S. Maddala and P. T. Knight ('International diffusion of technical change: a case study of the oxygen steel making process', *Economic Journal*, vol. 77, September 1967, pp. 531–58) point out that, over the period 1956–64, the United States was a 'leader' in adopting the basic oxygen process, if a 'leader' is defined as any country where the ratio of increase in oxygen steel production to total steel production was greater than 50 per cent.

available, direct reduction may be competitive with *all* other processes. More generally, we would expect that large plants would favour adoption of the oxygen process, at least after 1962.

Beyond purely technical considerations, the rate of adoption may also depend upon the general rate of expansion of a firm or industry and the efficiency of the existing capital resources against which oxygen must compete.[1] The underlying logic of these presumptions is quite simple. One would expect that the more rapidly output is expanding and the older or less efficient the existing capacity, the stronger would be the ability and tendency to install a new technology such as oxygen steel. Ideally, of course, one would like to separate new investment to expand total output from investment to replace outmoded, inefficient or retired capacity. Similarly, one might like to separate capital expenditure on oxygen converters from other investments. Data limitations as well as conceptual difficulties, however, effectively rule this out.

To test these various hypotheses empirically we shall initially employ what one might call a two-stage recursive approach: the first stage will be an attempt to explain at least the broader or cruder outlines of the investment decision independently of the decision about the type of process, while the second stage will focus on the rate of adoption of the basic oxygen process given an established general investment or expansion rate. We shall see subsequently that it may not be possible to sustain this simplification; specifically, the investment rate may or may not be independent of adoption of the oxygen process. But we defer that complication for now.

The first stage will focus on testing fairly conventional and simple investment models. Given the limited data available, we concentrated specifically on investment functions of the following general type:

$$I_t = f(\text{CAPUT}_{t-i}, \text{CTO}_{t-i}, r_{t-i}, \Delta\text{PROD}_{t-i}, \text{KLR}_{t-i}, \text{LI}_{t-i})$$

where:

I_t = investment in year t;

CAPUT_{t-i} = capacity utilisation in year $t-i$;

CTO_{t-i} = cash throw-off in year $t-i$;

r_{t-i} = cost of capital in year $t-i$;

ΔPROD_{t-i} = change in output in year $t-i$;

KLR_{t-i} = ratio of implicit capital costs (implicit interest rate) to implicit wage costs in year $t-i$;

LI_{t-i} = labour intensity (as measured by the ratio of labour cost to sales) in year $t-i$.

[1] G. Terborgh, *Dynamic Equipment Policy*, New York, McGraw-Hill, 1949; Dilley and McBride, 'Oxygen steelmaking'.

The lags were determined by the crudest of empirical procedures – finding what fitted best.

Our investment function is a conventional capacity or accelerator–residual funds or profit type. The model is admittedly over-simplified, but it must be remembered that our primary objective is to explain the rate of adoption of the oxygen process; we are not particularly concerned with attempting to clarify the many conflicting arguments or to select from the many competing explanations about business investment behaviour. Rather, we simply wish to construct a reasonably plausible explanation of observed differences in investment rates for the particular national steel industries involved in this study. In general, and anticipating the formal empirical results, the capacity utilisation and cash throw-off variables seem sufficient to explain the broader outlines of steel industry investment behaviour; on the other hand, the capital cost and accelerator measures, perhaps because of their crudeness, do not seem to contribute much to such explanations. Indeed, because of the predominance of the capacity and cash throw-off variables, we shall report on those variables only in most of what follows.

For the second stage, that is the explanation of the rate of adoption of the oxygen process, a general functional representation of the hypotheses to be tested would be:

$$\text{BOPCAP}_t \text{ or } \Delta\text{BOPCAP}_t = f(I_{t-i}, \text{SCEXP}, \text{STPROD}_{t-i}, r_{t-i}, \text{PHOS}, \text{ELECPR},$$
$$\text{SMPLNS}, \text{KLR}_{t-i}, \text{LI}_{t-i}, \text{PDT}_{t-i})$$

where the variables are defined as follows:

BOPCAP = percentage of total capacity in basic oxygen process;

ΔBOPCAP_t = change in basic oxygen process capacity in tons in a given year, t;

I_{t-i} = investment in year $t-i$, or averaged over the same preceding period of years;

SCEXP = net scrap export position for a nation, defined at the national mean for the period of the study;

STPROD_{t-i} = steel production in year $t-i$;

r_{t-i} = cost of capital in year $t-i$;

PHOS = phosphorus content of the ore available;

ELECPR = proportion of total steel output in the same previous period $(t-i)$ accounted for by electric reduction (used as a measure of the relative attractiveness of electric reduction as a production technology in a given country);

SMPLNS = percentage of total plants producing less than 500,000 tons per year;

KLR_{t-i} = ratio of implicit capital costs (implicit interest rate) to implicit wage costs in year $t-i$;

LI_{t-i} = labour intensity, as measured by the ratio of labour costs to sales, in year $t-i$;

PDT_{t-i} = productivity in tons per year per employee in year $t-i$.

Many of the variables, in both the investment and diffusion functions, have been defined or can be constituted at different levels of aggregation. Some have been established on both a firm and a national basis, such as I, CAPUT, BOPCAP, CTO, STPROD, ΔPROD. Others – r, SCEXP, PHOS, ELECPR, SMPLNS – either make sense or are available only at the national level. The remainder – LI, PDT, KLR – have been used only with individual firm data. The interpretation of variables available on both a firm and a national basis could vary with the context. In general, though, the logic of including these various variables in the models should be reasonably clear from our previous discussion.

To anticipate again the empirical results, the variables for the investment rate, scrap exports, electric output and the capital to labour ratio seem to carry most of the burden when explaining diffusion. In fact, the results for the phosphorus content and capital cost are on the whole so perverse that they have not been reported in most of what follows. The failure of these variables may be as much a function of poor measurement as of anything more intrinsic; particularly this may be true of the variable for phosphorus content.

Samples

The empirical investigations of the diffusion functions were conducted at four different levels of aggregation. To begin with, our samples were based on two sets of annual observations – for the firm and for the national industry in a specific year. The years involved were mainly in the 1960s. The nations were those in the European Common Market (Belgium, France, Germany, Italy, Luxemburg, the Netherlands) plus Austria, Sweden, the United Kingdom, the United States and Japan, although the actual scope of the sample varied from one year to another. The firms were from these same countries excluding Japan. Indeed, some of the national aggregates were created from the individual firm data for the same countries.

Observations for national industries in a year were stratified into three different samples:

(a) annual cross sections wherein the observations were for different nations for one specific year;

(b) time series for one nation over the entire period of available observations (usually 1962–7);

(c) the pool created by merging all the observations from both the annual cross sections and the time series, thus creating what might be called a moving cross section.

The individual firm data were investigated mainly on the basis of an international cross section, using all-firm data for all countries in a given year as the basic sample. Finally, for testing cumulative diffusion the simple averages of both the relevant national industry and individual firm variables over the entire period were used, thus creating a cross section of average values for each firm or nation, roughly pertaining to the early and mid-1960s.

Of the 150 firms in eleven countries on which data were originally available, data limitations reduced our sample to 76 firms in eight countries. We were only able to retain two firms for the United Kingdom and had to exclude Italy and Luxemburg altogether for lack of a reported wage bill for any year, and Japanese firms because of different accounting and wage payment practices. Similarly, other firms in various countries had to be excluded for not reporting some crucial financial variable.

To keep the sample as large as possible, we constructed data in many instances when discontinuities appeared, and a missing observation for a particular year was often replaced by extrapolation. Such estimation was usually done on the basis of yearly rates of change of that variable derived from the continuous series for a country. More precise definitions can be found in the appendix.

Different arrangements can represent different ways of organising what is essentially the same data. One could argue, moreover, that strict statistical or econometric practice would demand that the various regressions by cross section, by year and by time series for a given nation should be tested for homogeneity before being incorporated into any larger sample or pool.[1] However, the small number of degrees of freedom in the time-series regressions limited the significance of the results of an exploratory covariance analysis, thus denying us the possibility of distinguishing between 'true' heterogeneity and simple data limitations.

MEASURING MANAGEMENT MOTIVATION

Techniques of analysis

As noted, it is often postulated that technological diffusion is related to management attitudes or motives. To test this would require some

[1] E. Kuh, 'The validity of cross-sectionally estimated behavior equations in time series applications', *Econometrica*, vol. 27, April 1959, pp. 197–214; G. Chow, 'Tests of equality between sets of coefficients in two linear regressions', *Econometrica*, vol. 28, July 1960, pp. 591–605; M. Nerlove and P. Balestra, 'Pooling cross section and time series data in the estimation of a dynamic model: the demand for natural gas', *Econometrica*, vol. 34, July 1966, pp. 585–612.

objective measure or identification of managerial attitudinal characteristics, say a scale or index. Ideally, the data should be generated by predesigned tests that reveal managerial objectives directly. Accordingly, as part of this study, questionnaires were drawn up and sent out to steel firms of the countries with a research institute involved in the project – Austria, Germany, Italy, Sweden, the United Kingdom and the United States. They included questions on staff mobility, on salary spread with respect to educational background, on research and development employment and expenditure, on lags between the decision to experiment, the pilot operation and the commercial application, and finally on attitudes towards risk. One of the questions relating to the lag aspect asked whether the timing of adoption of the basic oxygen process reflected what was considered to be company policy towards new techniques and called for illustration by the adoption history of other recent major improvements. The question on risk was asked in terms of preferences between situations involving different hypothetical pay-offs associated with different probabilities.

Answers to those questions could have been treated, among other ways, by scalogram analysis or Guttman scaling,[1] but the quality of answers to our questionnaire was inadequate for such analysis. For some countries we received no answers, or answers to differently phrased questions. For other countries sometimes only part of the questions were answered and the answer distribution was so random that no systematic treatment could be applied.

With no possibility of using the predesigned data, we were left to infer managerial profiles on the basis of published balance sheets and income statements. Our basic assumption was that managerial policy objectives are revealed by the juxtaposition of certain financial and productivity ratios normally or potentially under management control. These ratios or measures could, therefore, be looked upon as if they were scores obtained from psychometric tests and treated by factor analysis.[2]

The basic algebra of factor analysis is straightforward. Assume that a matrix of observations X_{ij} arises from a structure of the type

$$X_{ij} = \sum_{k=1}^{P} a_{ik} F_k + b_i U_i + c_i e_{ij}$$

[1] For two clear explanations of Guttman scaling, see A. L. Edwards, 'On Guttman scale analysis', *Educational Psychological Measurement*, vol. 8, 1948, pp. 313–18 and E. S. Bogardus, 'Racial distance changes in the United States during the past thirty years', *Sociology and Social Research*, vol. 43, November 1958, pp. 217–37.

[2] For a very first attempt to identify management profiles by factor analysis, see J. R. Meyer, 'An experiment in the measurement of business motivation', *Review of Economics and Statistics*, vol. 49, August 1967, pp. 304–18.

where F_k are factors influencing more than one X_i, U_i is a factor specific or unique to X_i and e_{ij} is an error term for the ith variable and the jth individual, while P is the number of factors. F, U and e are usually regarded as having unit variance; a, b, and c are weights to be determined from the data (the as are called factor weights). The object is to find Fs that can be interpreted by, or preferably are in agreement with, pre-specified hypotheses or types.

Factor analysis is thus based on the contention that observed relationships, or correlations between observed variables, are influenced by various determinants, some of which are shared by other variables. That part of a variable that is influenced by the shared determinants (the Fs) is usually called common, and the part that is influenced by idiosyncratic determinants (the Us) is usually called unique.

In many applications it may be assumed initially that the common factors are independent of one another[1] and can be found in descending order of importance, so that, for example, the first factor contributes the most to the generalised variance of the observed variables and is independent of (orthogonal to) all other factors. This so-called 'principal component' formulation reduces to finding, for each factor, the solution to a system of equations such as

$$R(A) = \lambda_1 \ldots \lambda_n(A)$$

where R is the correlation matrix, (A) is a matrix composed of the factor weights $a_1 \ldots a_i$ for each F_k and the vectors $\lambda_1 \ldots \lambda_n$ are the variances of the common factors. The descending importance of the factors follows the descending sizes of the latent roots.

Principal component analysis, in short, amounts to finding in descending order of importance, sequential linear combinations of variables which account for more of the variance in the data than any other linear combination. The first principal component, therefore, can be viewed as the single best summary of linear relationships exhibited in the data. The second component is then the second best (maximum variance) linear combination, subject to the constraint of being orthogonal to the first component. That is, the second component may be defined as the linear combination that accounts for the most variance in the data *after* the effect of the first component has been removed. Subsequent components can be extracted similarly until all the variance in the data is exhausted, at which point there would be as many components as variables.

In a 'classical' factor analysis it is postulated that certain unique factors exist (the Us) which cannot contribute to relationships among variables. It follows that the observed correlations must be the result of

[1] Though this need not always be so.

the correlated variables' sharing of the common determinants (the Fs). Since, by assumption, only part of the total variance can be explained, the common determinants will account for all the observed relations in the data but cannot be as many as the variables. That is, the number of Fs or common factors must be less than the number of variables. A basic difference between a strict principal component analysis and classical factor analysis is, therefore, that the main diagonals of the correlation matrix are replaced by communality estimates before factorisation is performed. In other words, while principal component analysis assumes unique variance, classical factor procedures do not and they insert estimates of (or guesses about) the communalities as the diagonals of the original correlation matrix.

In practice, and in keeping with the basic hypotheses of classical factor analysis, the factoring (extraction of principal components) is usually stopped before extracting all the components. Various rules or tests can and have been applied to determine when this should occur. For our present purposes very simple rules seemed sufficient. To start, we ran the analyses until either a communality of less than 5 per cent, or a minimum value of less than 0·05 was obtained for the latent root. After a bit of experience with the data (as explained below), we generally found that these limits were reached after only two or three components were extracted and, more important, only two components or factors generally seemed capable of interpretation; accordingly, we restricted most of our analyses to two factors only.

Obviously, we needed to define which relationships between variables we considered exemplified which common influences or motivational patterns. Towards that end, we drew on the results of previous studies to define several sets of interrelationships that might correspond to certain managerial profiles. These specifications, as shown in table 6.3, are restricted to variables that can be considered to be largely under the firm's control and thus to indicate intention. For example, looking at the third line of table 6.3, we postulated that a firm that would be self-satisfied or content with the *status quo*, would show a strong liquidity position, a policy of high dividend payments, and a very low level of debt. On the other hand, an expansionist profile would imply high depreciation and leverage (the firm would borrow to invest), while its net quick liquidity and dividend payments would be relatively low; also, for such firms productivity might be negatively weighted since the accent is on expanding rather than rationalising. A market-share orientation would be shown by high leverage and depreciation, a neutral productivity measure, and low dividend payments and liquidity. A 'senile' profile implied very high dividend payments and liquidity (say, at the expense of investment) and perhaps labour intensity, but leverage and depreciation would be low since little investment would have been planned. Finally, decadence was equated to accumulated senility: low liquidity and depreciation, and very high labour intensity due to lack of investment.

Table 6.3. *Sign patterns and rank orders of managerial profiles*

	Variables[a]					
	NQL	LI	LV	DP	PDT	DIVPAY
Original						
Expansionist	−	−	+	+	−	−
	(6)	(4)	(2)	(2)	(3)	(5)
Market-share	−	−	+	+	o	−
orientated	(5)	(6)	(1)	(2)	(3)	(4)
Contentment with	+	o	−	o	o	+
status quo (or	(2)	(4·5)	(6)	(3)	(4·5)	(1)
self-satisfaction)						
Senile	+	+	−	−	−	+
	(1)	(2)	(4·5)	(4·5)	(6)	(3)
Decadent	−	+	−	−	−	o
	(3·5)	(1)	(6)	(5)	(3·5)	(2)
Derived						
Aggressive[b]	−	−	+	+	o	−
	(5·5)	(5·5)	(1·5)	(1·5)	(5)	(4)
Non-aggressive[c]	+	+	−	−	−	+
	(2)	(2)	(5)	(5)	(5)	(2)
Grabowski–Mueller						
classifications						
Management	+	−	−	+	o	−
Stockholder	−	−	+	+	+	+

SOURCE: NBER estimates.

[a] Defined as follows:
   NQL (net quick liquidity) = (other current assets − short-term debt)/total assets
   LI (labour intensity) = (wages and salaries + statutory social contributions)/sales
   LV (leverage) = long-term debt/total assets
   DP (depreciation) = total depreciation/total assets
   PDT (productivity) = crude steel production/number of employees
   DIVPAY (dividend pay-out) = dividend payments/cash throw-off (CTO), where CTO = profit + depreciation − allocation for dividends.
[b] First two 'original' profiles combined.
[c] Remaining 'original' profiles.

Senility and decadence should not be understood as normative concepts. Meyer and Kuh found that there was a negative correlation between age of equipment and depreciation.[1] This empirical finding led them to reject the so-called 'echo-effect' theories of investment,

[1] J. R. Meyer and E. Kuh, *The Investment Decision*, Cambridge (Mass.), Harvard University Press, 1957, ch. 6.

according to which the older the existing capital stock the greater the investment demanded for replacement, and to suggest instead a 'senility effect' in the sense that firms which on average have older equipment will tend to keep it that way.

As one can see from table 6.3, we divided the managerial profiles into three groups – original, derived and Grabowski–Mueller classifications. The originals, as just described, were specified before doing any factor analyses. The derived patterns, in contrast, were modifications or syntheses of the originals suggested to us after we had proceeded with much of the analysis. In particular, we became convinced that our data and six variables would not permit anything but relatively gross identifications of two basic patterns, aggressive and non-aggressive. The final set of classifications, describing a dichotomy between management and stockholder orientated firms, suggested by H. Grabowski and D. Mueller,[1] was available to us only after we had completed our analyses; we included the Grabowski–Mueller classification scheme here primarily for purposes of comparison.

It should be noted that the Grabowski–Mueller approach to classifying managements' motivation is rather different from that implicit in ours. In essence, their approach assumes that managements behave reasonably rationally and consistently once one identifies their objectives. In contrast, we entertain the possibility that there may be some irregularity or irrationality (by conventional economic or efficiency standards) in observed management behaviour, so that some managements may behave very differently even when they believe themselves to be pursuing essentially the same objectives. We feel that it remains an open question which of these two approaches better describes reality. It may also be possible that firms can actually behave according to a given objective although they truly believe they are pursuing a different one. Furthermore, differences in the speed of response can be caused by different market structures that alter the profitability of a given investment, especially if the cost of finance is really influenced by sources of funds; for example, some firms might be identified as non-aggressive by our specifications, but their behaviour would not necessarily be irrational and might actually be quite rational in certain oligopolistic or similar situations.

The principal components

The first two principal components for each year of the period 1962–6 as derived from the individual firm data are shown in table 6.4. For 1962, 1963 and 1964 the first factor loads very heavily and negatively

[1] H. G. Grabowski and D. C. Mueller, 'Managerial and stockholder welfare models of firm expenditures', *Review of Economics and Statistics*, vol. 54, February 1972, pp. 9–24.

Table 6.4. *Principal components: factor loadings on financial and productivity ratios*

		Factors		Communality
		I	2	
1962				
NQL		−0·717	0·330	0·623
LI		−0·383	0·204	0·188
LV		0·312	0·699	0·586
DP		0·725	0·155	0·550
PDT		−0·266	0·752	0·636
DIVPAY		−0·840	−0·219	0·754
	Latent roots	2·060	1·277	3·337
1963				
NQL		−0·716	−0·464	0·727
LI		−0·172	0·347	0·150
LV		0·385	0·274	0·223
DP		0·526	−0·602	0·639
PDT		−0·266	−0·605	0·437
DIVPAY		−0·839	0·264	0·774
	Latent roots	1·742	1·209	2·951
1964				
NQL		−0·644	−0·490	0·655
LI		−0·294	0·576	0·419
LV		0·525	0·402	0·437
DP		0·496	−0·654	0·674
PDT		−0·131	−0·382	0·163
DIVPAY		−0·787	0·105	0·631
	Latent roots	1·660	1·318	2·978
1965				
NQL		−0·387	−0·449	0·351
LI		0·741	−0·240	0·607
LV		0·227	0·824	0·731
DP		−0·665	−0·116	0·456
PDT		−0·181	0·573	0·361
DIVPAY		0·587	−0·267	0·416
	Latent roots	1·571	1·351	2·922
1966				
NQL		−0·751	0·404	0·727
LI		0·540	0·433	0·479
LV		0·325	0·014	0·106
DP		−0·422	−0·644	0·593
PDT		−0·607	0·535	0·655
DIVPAY		0·220	0·536	0·336
	Latent roots	1·556	1·340	2·896

SOURCE: NBER estimates.
Note: For definitions of ratios see table 6.3.

on the dividend pay-out variable and net quick liquidity, and positively on depreciation and leverage. If we identify as zero any factor weight which when squared is less than $1/n$ (n being the number of variables), the productivity variable is generally neutral in the definition of the first factor; so is the labour intensity variable, although its weight is slightly on the negative side. Clearly, the first factor corresponds quite well, for these years, to our sign and rank pre-specifications of managerial aggressiveness. The only possible nonconformity is the labour intensity variable, which we would expect to be more clearly negative if the first component is associated with aggressiveness.

In contrast, for 1965 the first factor seems to correspond better to our passiveness than to our aggressiveness specifications. Although net quick liquidity has a negative sign, the first component loads very heavily and positively on labour intensity and dividend pay-out. Productivity and leverage have essentially zero weights, but depreciation is strongly negative.

In 1966, net quick liquidity is strongly negative but so are productivity and depreciation. Leverage and dividend pay-out have zero weights but labour intensity is positively weighted. Hence, the first component for 1966 does not correspond to our *a priori* specifications for aggressiveness, but neither does it correspond very well to the passiveness or contentment profiles.

The deviation of the 1965 and 1966 results from those for the preceding years may have been due in large measure to cyclical effects. In particular, image distortions can appear in our variables if either the numerator or the denominator reflect accidental variations rather than usual performances or goals. It may be significant, therefore, that the years 1965 and 1966 were, in general, poor for the nations and steel industries in our sample. In 1965, Germany, the United Kingdom and the Benelux countries introduced measures to control inflationary pressures or to bring their balances of payments into equilibrium. These were maintained or, in some cases, strengthened in 1966, with a consequent slowing in the demand for steel in these countries. Indeed, of our sample countries, only the United States, France and Italy were experiencing some expansion in these years. For the OECD countries in Europe, crude steel production fell by 2·3 per cent in 1966 compared with 1965, British steel production showing a 10 per cent fall. In the United States the increase was only 2 per cent. The ratio of steel production to capacity is not available for the United States, but for OECD countries in Europe it fell from a peak of 90 per cent in 1964 and an average of 87 per cent for the period 1961–4 to a low of 79 per cent in 1966. For the same countries, the ratio of apparent steel consumption to capacity fell from 81 per cent in 1964 to 71 per cent in

1966.[1] This may account for the highly negative loading on the productivity variable in 1966.

Some adverse price effects were also experienced in these years. Starting in 1965, home market prices in the European Economic Community were falling for most steel products. In fact, at the end of 1967, French, Italian, Belgian and Dutch companies adjusted the prices of many of their products on the lists filed with the Commission of the European Community either by lowering them or by introducing temporary rebates. German steel producers had already done so earlier in the year, on the occasion of a remodelling of the sales system for German iron and steel products. These reductions or rebates were primarily a way of bringing published prices more into line with those actually obtained in markets within the Community. Furthermore, export prices were already falling as a result of increased world competition and slackening of demand.[2] At any rate, with lower production levels and prices, any relative decrease in sales with respect to a less flexible wage bill would distort the measure of labour intensity.

Moreover, a decline in sales and prices could have a negative effect on cash throw-off. But a reduction in cash throw-off does not necessarily imply a parallel reduction in dividend payments. On the contrary, dividend payments might be kept as high as possible in recession years for a variety of reasons.[3] This, however, would push up the ratio of dividend payments to cash throw-off with consequent 'error' in the factor loading.

We therefore consider the years 1965-6 as abnormal for our purpose and unreliable evidence of stable policy objectives. Obviously, it would have been interesting to test for that stability for years after 1966, but unfortunately the data were not available at the time of the study.

If the first principal component corresponds remarkably well to the aggressiveness profile for the years 1962-4, the second factor presents a rather irregular image. For 1962, the only significant loadings relate to leverage and productivity, which would tend to show market-share orientation. However, for 1963 and 1964, the profiles correspond to some sort of decadence, with high labour intensity coupled with low

[1] OECD, *The Iron and Steel Industry in Europe* (various years).

[2] In fact, the low level of export prices led many analysts, at the time, to explain it by some general over-capacity. See for instance, *The Iron and Steel Industry in Europe*.

[3] S. P. Dobrovolsky, for instance, has shown that for the period 1922-42, the range of cyclical swings in dividends was much narrower than that shown by the net income series (*Corporate Income Retention 1915-1943*, New York, NBER, 1951, pp. 14-18). It is precisely because of that relative stability, which also occurred in later years, that J. Lintner could identify a dividend policy target ('Distribution of incomes of corporations among dividends, retained earnings and taxes', *American Economic Association Papers and Proceedings*, vol. 46, May 1956, pp. 97-113). For a more recent confirmation of much the same hypothesis see J. A. Brittain, *Corporate Dividend Policy*, Washington (DC), The Brookings Institution, 1966.

depreciation and low liquidity. In 1963, productivity loads negatively, but in 1964 its weight is zero. The dividend pay-out weights are also nil, as would be expected in a situation of decadence. For the years 1965 and 1966, the loadings once again seem to correspond more to accidental effects than to any true profiles.

A characteristic of the factorisation solution is that it is not unique. This element of indeterminacy allows for rotation of the original factors into transformed ones to approximate better to a 'simple structure', that is one that generates the expected clusters not previously observed in the initial orthogonal solution. To see if such simplifications could be achieved in our case, quartimax and varimax rotations were performed on the original principal components. Concordance with *a priori* specifications was, however, generally no better for these rotated factors than for the original principal components. Also, in order to measure the percentage of common variance, as opposed to total variance explained by the aggressiveness profile, we performed an image factorisation of the original correlation matrix. We found that about 50 per cent of the variations of the firms' financial and productivity ratios could be explained by their relative aggressiveness, the remaining variance being attributable to cross-sectional secondary characteristics and measurement errors.[1]

Having identified an aggressiveness dimension, we can now place each firm with respect to the sample mean of aggressiveness. By construction that mean is set equal to zero, so that passive firms will score negatively and aggressive ones positively. In order to remove any possible remaining year-to-year variation, we also averaged the principal component scores for the first or general factor over the three years 1962-4, these years being chosen for the cyclical reasons just given, that is they appeared to correspond to the simplest structure. (However, the application of Kendall's coefficient of concordance did not reveal any difference in the rankings under different plausible methods of estimation.)

The average scores in table 6.5 show that, on the basis of our definition, American firms seem less dynamic than their European competitors. This poses a problem since American firms also tend to be larger on average. In particular, one might wonder whether our *a priori* interpretation of the factorisation involves some bias in favour of a financial structure that would be more typical of small than of large firms. That is, does the emphasis on leverage, dividend pay-out ratios and depreciation in the interpretation of the factors indicate managerial

---

[1] For a more detailed analysis of the quartimax and varimax rotations and of the image factoring, see G. Herregat, 'Managerial profiles and investment patterns', Ph.D. dissertation, University of Louvain, 1972.

7

profiles that would only be applicable to small firms? A case could be made, for instance, that large firms tend to rely more on self-financing because of the very size of their internal cash flow, and would therefore be less leveraged and less aggressive than small firms. Similarly, since financial ratios may vary technically according to size (for example, by following a pattern of inventory optimisation), too much emphasis on them could possibly distort relative aggressiveness when firms of different

Table 6.5. *Average relative aggressiveness scores for firms,[a] 1962–4*

	Sample size	1962	1963	1964	Average, 1962–4
Austria	4	0·935	0·757	0·983	0·891
Benelux	4	0·079	0·447	0·347	0·291
France	12	1·012	0·939	0·936	0·962
Sweden	5	−0·185	−0·129	−0·164	−0·159
United Kingdom	2	−0·889	−1·526	−1·758	−1·391
United States	32	−0·762	−0·721	−0·672	−0·718
West Germany	17	0·641	0·695	0·550	0·628

SOURCE: NBER estimates.
[a] Scores on first principal component.

sizes were compared. However, application of the Kruskal–Wallis non-parametric one-way analysis of variance[1] yielded the tentative conclusion that the firms' aggressiveness scores were not affected by their size, thus clearing the way for at least some further experimental use of these aggressiveness scores in other applications. In short, even though they embody many obvious imperfections, these factor scores seem useful as preliminary quantifications of managerial profiles, particularly for the years 1962, 1963 and 1964. What remains to be determined is how much of the total variance in investment or in diffusion of the oxygen process these scores can explain.

EMPIRICAL RESULTS: INVESTMENT BEHAVIOUR

In our investment investigations the emphasis was on conventional cash throw-off (or profitability) and accelerator variables to explain observed investment behaviour. The simplest investment function is one

[1] W. H. Kruskal and W. A. Wallis, 'Use of ranks in one-criterion variance analysis', *Journal of the American Statistical Association*, vol. 47, 1952, pp. 583–621; W. H. Kruskal, 'A nonparametric test for the several sample problem', *Annals of Mathematical Statistics*, vol. 23, 1952, pp. 525–40.

Table 6.6. *Determinants of steel industry investment, national cross sections, 1961–6*

	Constant	CAPUT$_{t-2}$	CTO$_{t-2}$	R^2 Unadjusted	Adjusted
Absolute levels					
1961	2,360,297	−3,025·25 (2·39)		0·623	0·321
	−355,459	541·14 (0·37)	1·22 (3·14)	0·852	0·658
1962	2,199,120	−2,022·58 (2·16)		0·584	0·268
	−34,844	148·20 (0·19)	0·10 (4·15)	0·890	0·739
1963	2,617,649	−2,545·32 (2·63)		0·659	0·371
	−1,565,404	1,713·19 (2·16)	1·58 (6·34)	0·952	0·883
1964	3,198,618	−3,325·20 (1·86)		0·526	0·196
	845,683	983·10 (0·99)	1·71 (6·66)	0·943	0·862
1965	4,033,053	−4,332·87 (1·62)		0·476	0·141
	106,212	151·20 (0·24)	1·36 (14·32)	0·985	0·964
1966	1,565,641	−1,307·78 (0·42)		0·139	—
	569,858	−583·92 (1·15)	1·16 (18·08)	0·988	0·890
Deflated					
1961	−0·1241	0·225 (0·93)	1·09 (3·71)	0·819	
1962	0·0049	0·118 (0·63)	0·48 (2·46)	0·714	
1963	0·2706	0·448 (1·31)	0·25 (1·40)	0·485	
1964	0·2862	0·540 (1·56)	−0·36 (0·53)	0·489	
1965	0·0048	0·015 (0·12)	0·45 (1·92)	0·568	
1966	−0·4163	0·461 (2·13)	1·10 (3·28)	0·768	

SOURCES: See appendix, pp. 195ff.

Notes: (i) CAPUT = capacity utilisation index
 CTO = cash throw-off (in $ thousands)
 (see appendix for full definitions)
 (ii) Numbers in brackets are *t*-ratios.
 (iii) In deflated functions, investment (the dependent variable) and CTO are expressed as proportions of total assets.

that depends strictly on capacity utilisation and cash throw-off. The results obtained for such a function, using national cross sections for the years 1961–6, are shown in table 6.6. For these annual cross sections of national data only eleven observations were available, so that it was difficult to employ more than two explanatory variables at one time without encountering serious collinearity. To put the matter slightly differently, with so few observations it is difficult to extract useful information about the relationship of investment to more than two or three explanatory variables at one time; the historical experiments are just too limited to permit more.

The explanation of investment achieved by using only the capacity utilisation and cash throw-off variables unquestionably seemed better than for any other combination of two, or for that matter three, potential explanatory variables tested against the annual cross sections. The results for the different years also display reasonable consistency. Capacity utilisation was rather less helpful than we had anticipated; nevertheless, that variable usually has the right sign *after* the cash throw-off variable has been introduced into the equation and is at least moderately significant for the year 1963. With these two variables alone, the unadjusted R^2s are almost invariably substantial, explaining from 85 to 99 per cent of the total variation; even when adjusted for degrees of freedom they are quite substantial in most years.

The weakness of the capacity utilisation variable and the very high R^2s might be thought, *a priori*, to be due to the use of undeflated variables in the aggregate investment functions. The results of a size-deflated model are presented in the bottom half of table 6.6. In general, the R^2s are not very much lower than in the undeflated version and the capacity utilisation variable is not greatly strengthened.

The results for time series of individual nations, as shown in table 6.7, are much less consistent. Again though, cash throw-off tends to perform best. For at least three of the nations involved – Austria, Japan and Luxemburg – the results must be considered rather less than successful, though for Japan and Luxemburg the capacity utilisation variable does perform respectably or almost respectably. In general, the time-series results taken in conjunction with the annual cross sections tend to support the view that the steel industries of the world do behave as they often claim that they do; that is, by being highly sensitive to the availability of cash when making investment decisions.

The results from the pooled or combined samples, taken across all the cross sections and years, add nothing except further confirmation to this general proposition. These pooled results are shown at the bottom of table 6.7. In general, the cash throw-off variable is again dominant, with capacity utilisation a weak second.

Table 6.7. *Determinants of steel industry investment, national time series*

		Constant	$CAPUT_{t-2}$	CTO_{t-2}	R^2
Austria	1961–6	138,759·76	−109·43 (1·05)		0·465
		181,908·22	−98·62 (0·90)	−1·30 (0·81)	0·597
Belgium	1959–66	210,724·49	−88·17 (0·34)		0·137
		307,037·76	−374·72 (1·13)	2·72 (1·30)	0·518
France	1959–66	−768,672·42	1,109·83 (1·03)		0·387
		−220,488·66	97·52 (0·08)	1·65 (1·57)	0·656
Italy	1959–66	−553,326·04	899·63 (0·90)		0·345
		−839,954·37	394·19 (0·69)	8·23 (3·77)	0·878
Japan	1961–6	24,517·88	560·08 (0·91)		0·415
		68,635·52	607·31 (0·86)	−0·41 (0·20)	0·454
Luxemburg	1959–66	597·27	45·18 (0·54)		0·217
		−18,398·94	89·12 (0·96)	−0·68 (1·03)	0·462
Netherlands	1959–66	19,183·52	32·94 (0·33)		0·134
		−323,838·61	328·27 (3·84)	2·39 (4·29)	0·889
Sweden	1961–6	−486,059·48	625·34 (2·49)		0·780
		−285,598·96	303·17 (0·82)	1·47 (1·15)	0·853
United Kingdom	1961–6	−59,481·54	506·83 (0·35)		0·171
		−32,628·53	−1,081·62 (0·81)	5·41 (2·04)	0·771
United States	1959–66	150,985·07	1,524·07 (0·80)		0·310
		2,163,475·26	−4,641·78 (2·33)	2·37 (3·68)	0·870
West Germany	1959–66	572,447·17	−19·37 (0·03)		0·013
		215,948·71	−281·71 (0·62)	1·62 (2·68)	0·768
All countries		−12,488·40	88·40 (0·33)	1·22 (19·33)	0·938

SOURCES: See appendix, pp. 195 ff.

Notes: (i) CAPUT = capacity utilisation index.
CTO = cash throw-off (in $ thousands).
(ii) Numbers in brackets are *t*-ratios.

The individual firm data provide us with an opportunity to test some-what more complex investment functions, because there are more observations in these samples. Owing to the long gestation period involved in steel industry investment and because of our desire to average out some of the cyclical and other effects of only peripheral interest to the present study, we used as our dependent variable total investment by a firm for the four years 1963–6 inclusive divided by total assets in 1962. We then modified the independent and explanatory variables to correspond; that is, we used the sum of cash throw-off

Table 6.8. *Determinants of individual firms' investment, 1963–6*

Constant	SUMCTO (1963–6)	AVKUT (1963–6)	Aggressive-ness score (1962–4)	KLR (1962)	LI (1962)	R^2 Unadjusted	Adjusted
0·24	0·46 (2·98)					0·111	0·099
0·21	0·47 (3·03)	0·032 (0·06)				0·116	0·091
0·21	0·46 (2·84)	0·036 (0·69)	0·0092 (0·47)			0·119	0·081
0·28	0·35 (2·12)	0·073 (1·36)	0·0404 (1·66)	−1·38 (2·07)		0·171	0·122
0·21	0·37 (2·24)	0·057 (1·03)	0·0419 (1·72)	−1·20 (1·75)	0·22 (1·09)	0·186	0·125

SOURCE: NBER estimates.

Notes: (i) The dependent variable SUMI = total investment 1963–6/total assets 1962.
SUMCTO = total 1963–6 (cash throw-off/total assets).
AVKUT = mean 1963–6 (sales/capital employed), where capital employed = capital stock + reserves and long-term provisions + carry forward + long-term debt.
Aggressiveness score as in table 6.5.
KLR = interest payments 1962/wage bill 1962.
LI = wage bill 1962/sales 1962.
(ii) Numbers in brackets are *t*-ratios.

divided by total assets and the average capacity utilisation over those years as explanatory variables. One special aspect of these variables should be noted: since international cross sections were involved, all variables were defined (sometimes at a price in conceptual clarity) to avoid any need to adjust for differences in national currency values.

With the larger sample provided by the individual firm observations we also tested three additional variables:

(a) the aggressiveness score for particular firms as determined by the average value of the first principal component or aggressiveness factor for the years 1962–4;[1]

[1] The reason for concentrating on these years for definition of the aggressiveness score was explained on pp. 173–4 above.

(b) the capital to labour ratio for 1962 for the individual firm, taken (in this context) to be a crude measure of the newness of a firm's capital stock at the beginning of the period;

(c) the labour intensity of the firm in 1962, taken as a measure of the potential profitability or pay-off from further investment or modernisation.

The results obtained from fitting these investment functions to individual firm data are shown in table 6.8. Again there are no particular surprises, in that cash throw-off is clearly the best explanatory variable just as in the previous analyses. Similarly, the capacity utilisation variable has the right sign and makes some small, but not very significant, contribution to the explanation of investment. The capital to labour ratio for 1962 has the expected negative sign and is almost as significant as cash throw-off. The labour intensity variable does not make a substantial contribution to the explanation of individual firm investment but does have the expected positive sign.

The aggressiveness score adds (at least marginally) to the explanation of investment and, as postulated, has a positive sign. Given the rather tenuous and arbitrary way in which the aggressiveness scores were constructed, these results are at least somewhat reassuring. But, in the main, and in keeping with most previous findings about the investment behaviour of the steel industry, fairly conventional and straightforward investment functions, stressing cash throw-off and capacity utilisation, seem to provide reasonably adequate explanations of behaviour in this industry.

EMPIRICAL RESULTS: ADOPTION OF THE BASIC OXYGEN PROCESS

National comparisons

To test our hypotheses, we fitted two different formulations of the diffusion function to the cross-section data for national industries in specific years, using change in oxygen capacity as the dependent variable. Two functions were necessary rather than one all-inclusive model because of the limited size of our national cross-section samples and of collinearity between some of the explanatory variables. The two models varied mainly in their measures of scale. In one, lagged total steel production was included as a measure or control for total scale of the national industry; it was also considered possible that the larger a national steel industry, the larger the expected or average size of production units might be and therefore the more attractive the oxygen process in relative terms. The second model, on the other hand, incorporated a direct measure of the proportion of smaller plants in a

Table 6.9. *Determinants of change in oxygen process capacity, national cross sections, 1962–7*

	Constant	I_{t-1}	SCEXP	$STPROD_{t-2}$	SMPLNS	ELECPR	R^2	
							Unad-justed	Ad-justed
1962	114.20	0.0015 (1.54)					0.457	0.121
	−210.14	0.0025 (4.15)	−0.0328 (4.49)				0.881	0.719
	−212.70	0.0039 (2.38)	−0.0217 (1.84)	−0.027 (1.17)			0.901	0.732
	193.59	0.0026 (3.93)	−0.0356 (3.63)		−594.27 (0.45)		0.884	0.688
	−244.13	0.0024 (3.16)	−0.0343 (3.31)		464.87 (0.22)	−17.04 (0.66)	0.893	0.661
	−925.58		−0.0432 (2.75)	0.032 (2.18)	2,355.27 (1.01)	−45.05 (1.57)	0.836	0.497
1963	−330.30	0.0043 (6.98)					0.919	0.827
	−250.43	0.0041 (6.11)	0.0072 (1.02)				0.928	0.827
	−188.81	0.0014 (1.45)	−0.0090 (1.27)	0.046 (3.16)			0.971	0.919
	−64.90	0.0041 (5.57)	0.0059 (0.61)		−275.85 (0.21)		0.929	0.804
	239.06	0.0042 (5.14)	0.0054 (0.52)		−989.86 (0.48)	11.27 (0.46)	0.931	0.779
	−689.88		−0.0150 (2.05)	0.065 (9.24)	1,419.70 (1.24)	−25.69 (1.84)	0.976	0.922
1964	−313.25	0.0054 (5.71)					0.885	0.760
	−213.21	0.0051 (4.86)	0.0092 (0.80)				0.895	0.750
	17.09	−0.0023 (1.77)	−0.0329 (3.85)	0.124 (6.04)			0.984	0.954
	−135.67	0.0051 (4.39)	0.0087 (0.55)		−114.82 (0.06)		0.895	0.715
	−904.85	0.0052 (4.32)	0.0080 (0.50)		1,561.50 (0.52)	−29.56 (0.81)	0.905	0.699
	−625.71		−0.0230 (2.62)	0.090 (10.69)	1,123.88 (0.83)	−20.75 (1.25)	0.981	0.938
1965	497.74	0.0053 (3.66)					0.774	0.554
	−18.15	0.0068 (4.84)	−0.0502 (2.16)				0.864	0.683
	−367.57	−0.0027 (1.95)	−0.0989 (9.21)	0.199 (7.33)			0.985	0.958

Table 6.9 (*continued*)

	Constant	I_{t-1}	SCEXP	STPROD$_{t-2}$	SMPLNS	ELECPR	R² Unadjusted	R² Adjusted
	614.95	0.0069 (4.43)	−0.0548 (1.74)		−923.97 (0.24)		0.865	0.640
	−1,643.07	0.0073 (4.69)	−0.0589 (1.90)		3,917.71 (0.69)	−95.77 (1.16)	0.891	0.657
	−76.20		−0.0940 (6.00)	0.152 (11.28)	−317.97 (0.12)	−8.88 (0.24)	0.978	0.928
1966	−181.95	0.0062 (14.49)					0.979	0.954
	−328.28	0.0067 (13.52)	−0.0092 (1.51)				0.984	0.960
	−422.86	0.0045 (2.09)	−0.0201 (1.86)	0.041 (1.07)			0.986	0.961
	223.32	0.0068 (12.60)	−0.0180 (1.48)		−801.22 (0.56)		0.985	0.956
	−62.33	0.0068 (11.73)	−0.0181 (1.39)		−164.55 (0.07)	−12.42 (0.37)	0.985	0.950
	661.20		−0.0314 (2.12)	0.119 (10.82)	−2,610.49 (1.03)	46.94 (1.29)	0.982	0.942
1967	1,019.08	0.0030 (1.33)					0.406	0.072
	−428.58	0.0071 (4.09)	−0.1384 (3.97)				0.848	0.648
	−976.44	−0.0030 (0.33)	−0.1564 (4.15)	0.186 (1.14)			0.873	0.661
	2,433.82	0.0075 (4.06)	−0.1600 (3.55)		−4,155.19 (0.79)		0.861	0.631
	−2,181.64	0.0079 (5.13)	−0.1580 (4.26)		5,974.38 (0.91)	−191.57 (2.08)	0.922	0.750
	−2,022.68		−0.1659 (4.23)	0.140 (4.97)	4,503.81 (0.67)	−148.18 (1.58)	0.917	0.736

SOURCES: See appendix, pp. 195 ff.

Notes: (i) I = investment

SCEXP = net scrap exports averaged over period

STPROD = steel production

SMPLNS = percentage of all plants producing under 500,000 tons a year

ELECPR = proportion of total steel output by electric reduction.

(ii) Numbers in brackets are *t*-ratios.

national industry (those with a productive capacity of under 500,000 tons annually); such a variable could also indirectly reflect pure scale effects in the regression. The second model also included a lagged measure of the proportion of a national industry using direct electrical reduction; the hypothesis was that the greater the proportion of total production manufactured by electric processes (in preceding periods), the more such processes were in serious competition with the oxygen process because of favourable electricity and scrap prices. In both models, lagged investment in the steel industry (as a measure of total demand for expansion of steel facilities) and the average net scrap export position of a nation (as a measure of the availability and price of scrap within a national market) were included.

The results are shown in table 6.9. The strongest single positive finding is the influence of the general rate of expansion of the steel industry, as expressed by lagged investment. Lagged output is more often positively than negatively correlated with the rate of expansion of oxygen capacity, thus having the postulated sign. The second size variable, the proportion of plants in a nation with an annual output of less than 500,000 tons, tends more often than not to be of the right sign (negative) but is almost invariably insignificant by any standard statistical test.

The two factor price or technological variables, the mean scrap export rate and the proportion of total output in electric production, perform consistently and are often significant. The scrap variable, in particular, is almost always not only of the right sign but significant by usual tests. The proportion of total output in electrical production is not as significant as the scrap measure but does tend to be of the right sign (negative).

Time-series results from the national aggregates on diffusion of the oxygen process are intrinsically of less interest than those from the cross sections because variables that could be expected to influence the rate of technological diffusion almost certainly display more variance between different national markets than within a given national market over time. Indeed, only two variables of those previously assumed to influence the rate of adoption would seem at all potentially suitable for time-series analysis – the lagged investment rate and the share of total output accounted for by direct electric production. Even these two, particularly the proportion of electric production, might not be expected to display enough change within a nation over a decade to influence the diffusion rate significantly. In general, the empirical findings, as reported in table 6.10, substantiate this scepticism. In essence, the diffusion rate within a country over time does not seem to be very well explained by the two variables tested.

Table 6.10. *Determinants of change in oxygen process capacity, national time series*

		Constant	I_{t-1}	ELECPR	R² Unadjusted	Adjusted
Austria	1961–6	13·99	−0·0004 (3·22)		0·849	0·652
		−56·34	−0·0002 (0·94)	5·03 (1·13)	0·897	0·674
Belgium	1959–66	−1,066·40	0·0121 (0·69)		0·324	−0·119
		2,026·64	−0·0003 (0·02)	−305·67 (1·10)	0·601	−0·065
France	1959–66	252·05	0·0009 (1·13)		0·491	0·051
		4,192·03	−0·0003 (0·30)	−399·81 (1·35)	0·726	0·212
Italy	1960–7	−675·47	0·0049 (2·79)		0·813	0·576
		8,494·23	0·0046 (7·55)	−230·88 (5·58)	0·985	0·950
Japan	1962–7	7,291·19	−0·0027 (0·12)		0·062	−0·245
		47,925·10	0·0023 (0·14)	−2,103·56 (2·11)	0·774	0·331
Luxemburg	1960–7	1,120·11	−0·0192 (2·15)		0·732	0·419
		1,308·36	0·0004 (0·04)	−796·19 (2·44)	0·919	0·740
Netherlands	1960–7	226·81	0·0001 (0·02)		0·008	−0·250
		500·20	0·0009 (0·11)	−37·08 (0·41)	0·228	−0·580
Sweden	1962–7	564·14	−0·0048 (1·34)		0·558	0·139
		3,327·68	−0·0110 (4·21)	−57·49 (3·40)	0·926	0·764
United Kingdom	1962–7	971·43	0·0010 (0·70)		0·329	−0·115
		11,937·17	−0·0077 (2·25)	−672·45 (2·62)	0·854	0·548
United States	1960–7	−389·03	0·0045 (1·37)		0·565	0·149
		−4,301·74	0·0036 (0·42)	488·63 (0·11)	0·567	−0·131
West Germany	1959–66	4,668·50	−0·0045 (0·61)		0·290	−0·145
		−13,853·61	0·0062 (0·69)	1,441·44 (1·66)	0·722	0·202

SOURCES: See appendix, pp. 195ff.
Notes: (i) Variables as defined in table 6.9.
(ii) Numbers in brackets are *t*-ratios.

The negative time-series findings could be consistent with the more mechanistic or automatic time-related diffusion hypotheses, such as 'bandwagon' or contagion effects. That is, it perhaps can be argued that once the innovative process is under way within a particular national market, it is reasonably mechanistic and independent of any objective external factors. The sensitivity of national diffusion rates to varying investment rates, so strongly observed in the cross sections, could then be attributed either to differences in national diffusion targets or simply to differences in the sizes of national industries. If the target difference is the explanation, this would imply that, in the cross sections, investment may be as much a function of the basic oxygen process diffusion rate as vice versa.

To test for this possibility we re-ran the diffusion functions on the annual national cross-section data, including all of the previously reported explanatory variables except lagged investment. The observed results are shown in the last line for each year in table 6.9. Comparing these results with those reported above them in table 6.9 shows that omitting the lagged investment variable does not reduce the effective explanatory power of the diffusion function too substantially provided another scale measure, lagged output, is included. When both lagged output and the investment variable are included (as in the third line for each year in table 6.9) the investment coefficient usually becomes negative or nearly zero, and the multiple correlation is little changed from what it is without one or the other of these variables. This suggests that the two variables measure more or less the same effects. (Their simple correlations vary between 0·843 in 1962 and 0·987 in 1967.) As noted, the lagged output variable's positive coefficient is subject to two interpretations—either as a measure of the relative advantage of the oxygen process for larger plants, or as a measure of general scale or size effects. Accordingly, lagged investment might also be viewed as primarily a measure of scale or size effects in the cross sections, rather than as reflecting the impact of expansion in the steel industry overall.

Nevertheless, for conceptual completeness if nothing else, a possible hypothesis is that investment is a function of the diffusion of the oxygen process rather than (or as well as) vice versa. In that case, the functions should be estimated by simultaneous equation techniques. To that end, we again re-ran the diffusion function with current investment included as an explanatory variable, using two-stage least squares. The results for the annual cross sections are reported in table 6.11. In general. these results seem satisfactory and in agreement with prior hypotheses, The importance of the investment variable is, if anything, greater than when using simple least squares estimation. The scrap variable continues to be next in importance, usually being of the right sign and significant. The electric production variable is also of the right sign but not overwhelmingly significant. The small plant variable, on the other hand, is clearly of diminished importance and more often than not associated with the wrong sign. The total correlation, as represented by the R^2s, remains satisfactory.

Table 6.11. *Determinants of change in oxygen process capacity, national cross sections, 1961–6 (two-stage least squares estimates)*

	Constant	I_t	SCEXP	ELECPR (1961)	SMPLNS	R² Adjusted
1961	716·78	0·0029 (2·92)	0·0113 (0·86)	30·40 (0·94)	−2,330·30 (0·85)	0·562
	−525·98	0·0026 (3·16)	−0·0054 (0·53)	8·84 (0·46)		0·541
1962	−1,237·98	0·0022 (2·15)	−0·0292 (2·36)	−33·63 (1·12)	2,297·27 (0·91)	0·726
	−6·42	0·0026 (3·08)	−0·0351 (3·76)	−12·76 (0·73)		0·740
1963	−1,376·76	0·0042 (4·22)	0·0056 (0·42)	−38·64 (1·30)	2,356·21 (0·96)	0·790
	−72·19	0·0045 (4·60)	−0·0003 (0·02)	−18·92 (0·92)		0·766
1964	−2,292·69	0·0041 (5·25)	−0·0031 (0·20)	−76·75 (2·25)	4,719·85 (1·75)	0·858
	371·29	0·0045 (5·22)	0·0158 (1·01)	−37·64 (1·45)		0·815
1965	−1,444·71	0·0074 (8·10)	−0·0764 (3·72)	−73·97 (1·44)	3,157·44 (1·44)	0·918
	303·47	0·0075 (8·68)	−0·0835 (4·62)	−40·71 (1·25)		0·915
1966	421·32	0·0064 (18·55)	−0·0223 (2·65)	2·65 (0·12)	−1,102·19 (0·71)	0·988
	−188·34	0·0064 (19·37)	−0·0198 (2·70)	−9·21 (0·68)		0·987

SOURCES: See appendix, pp. 195 ff.
Notes: (i) Variables as defined in table 6.9.
(ii) Numbers in brackets are *t*-ratios.

An alternative evaluation of the diffusion hypotheses can be obtained by pooling the national industry cross sections over time into a single sample large enough to permit testing all of the various variables or hypotheses at once. The results so obtained are reported in table 6.12 and, overall, can be regarded as basically confirming the underlying hypotheses and previous findings, except for the small plant or scale effects. Again, the rate of general expansion within a nation's steel industry (that is, an investment variable) does not need to be included

Table 6.12. *Determinants of change in oxygen process capacity, pooled sample of all national data, 1962–7*

Constant	I_{t-1}	SCEXP	ELECPR$_{t-1}$	SMPLNS	STPROD$_{t-2}$	R^2	
						Unadjusted	Adjusted
78·99	0·0044 (7·29)					0·674	0·445
−252·10	0·0054 (8·45)	−0·032 (3·28)				0·730	0·519
−555·15	0·0056 (8·35)	−0·037 (2·95)	−39·30 (1·34)	1,186·13 (0·52)		0·741	0·519
−668·90	0·0003 (0·20)	−0·066 (4·73)	−36·48 (1·34)	1,082·60 (0·52)	0·10 (3·65)	0·794	0·600
−721·21		−0·070 (6·49)	−38·11 (1·69)	1,027·36 (0·59)	0·11 (12·58)	0·817	0·652

SOURCES: See appendix, pp. 195 ff.

Notes: (i) Variables as defined in table 6.9.
(ii) Numbers in brackets are *t*-ratios.
(iii) Bottom line based on data 1961–8.

to achieve a reasonably adequate explanation of national differences in diffusion rates.

Individual firm regressions

The individual firm data provide a means of assessing the diffusion process in somewhat greater detail, particularly the influence of differential investment rates, potential scale-economies and managerial differences. Managerial differences in fact only seem cogent at the individual firm level for which they are defined, rather than at the national level, where a good deal of individual diversity within a national industry may simply average out. We have, therefore, concentrated on explaining the percentage of total capacity in the oxygen process for an individual firm in 1968 (the last year for which we have good data) as a function of the firm's characteristics either over the period 1962–6 or of its initial position in 1962. The investment variable, for example, was average annual investment by a firm between 1962 and 1966 divided by the firm's total assets in 1962. The individual firm diffusion results are reported in table 6.13. It should be noted that some variables, SUMI, PDT, the aggressiveness score, AVOUPT and KLR, are specific to the individual firm, but SCEXP and ELECPR vary only from country to country, since they can be meaningfully defined only in terms of national aggregates.

There are no particular surprises in the individual firm results. In

Table 6.13. *Determinants of individual firms' proportions of oxygen process capacity, 1968*

Constant	SUMI (1962–6)	PDT (1962)	SCEXP (1961)	ELECPR (1961)	Aggressiveness score	AVOUTP (1962–6)	KLR (1962)	R^2	F	DF
Ordinary least squares estimation										
−0·052	1·07 (2·93)							0·108	8·589	71
−0·306	1·09 (3·10)	2·62 (2·68)						0·192	8·245	70
−0·319	1·11 (3·11)	2·30 (1·85)	0·85 (0·41)					0·193	5·489	69
−0·195	1·15 (3·24)	2·43 (1·95)	−0·40 (0·18)	−0·92 (1·30)				0·212	4·580	68
−0·177	1·21 (3·26)	2·42 (1·93)	−1·01 (0·41)	−1·07 (1·42)	−0·046 (0·59)			0·216	3·697	67
−0·140	1·16 (2·96)	2·51 (1·96)	−0·88 (0·35)	−0·99 (1·26)	−0·025 (0·25)		−0·74 (0·37)	0·218	3·065	66
−0·126	1·13 (3·13)	2·61 (2·04)	−0·51 (0·22)	−0·92 (1·29)		−0·0072 (0·49)	1·04 (0·65)	0·220	3·101	66
Two-stage least squares estimation										
−0·245	1·21 (2·88)	2·53 (1·79)	−0·24 (0·09)	−0·69 (0·80)		−0·0090 (0·43)	0·27 (0·12)	0·215	2·459	54
Tobit analysis										
0·88	0·88 (1·53)	5·29 (2·05)	−4·53 (0·91)	−2·88 (1·75)	0·090 (0·46)	0·0188 (0·66)	−5·77 (1·38)			

SOURCES: See appendix, pp. 195ff.

Notes: (i) The dependent variable = oxygen process capacity 1968/AVOUTP 1962–6
AVOUTP = mean output 1962–6 (million tons)
PDT = output 1962/number of employees 1962
SCEXP = mean scrap exports 1961–6/national steel output 1961
ELECPR = proportion of national steel output by electric reduction 1961
Other variables as defined in table 6.8.
(ii) Numbers in brackets are *t*-ratios.

general, they confirm the results of the more aggregated national industry observations. The consistently most important explanatory variable is investment; similarly, scrap exports and electric production have their expected negative effect but are not particularly significant, though electric production is considerably the more influential of the two. Little or no consistency or significance can seemingly be attached to average output or to the capital to labour ratio.

Probably the most interesting results in the individual firm regressions concern the productivity variable as measured in 1962, and the aggressiveness score for individual firms. Productivity is clearly second only to investment in significance. In contrast, the aggressiveness score constructed from the principal components analysis (as explained above) is neither significant nor does it have the expected positive sign. A simple explanation for this would be that the aggressiveness score is dominated by the productivity variable as a measure of managerial vigour or motivation.

Furthermore, as we have already seen when investigating the investment functions, the aggressiveness score was positively and somewhat significantly associated with individual firm investment. Accordingly, much or all of the potential influence of an aggressive management on adoption could have been included in the investment variable itself. At any rate, whatever the explanation, it is quite clear that the aggressiveness score adds nothing to the explanation of the adoption of the process by individual firms beyond that provided by the measures of investment and prior productivity.

In general, the picture that emerges from the individual firm analyses differs from that provided by the national industry aggregates mainly in the relative emphasis placed upon the investment variable. That is, no plausible construction of the individual firm diffusion functions seems to provide an adequate explanation of diffusion without the investment variable being included. In contrast, for the aggregates we could achieve as good an explanation of diffusion without lagged investment.

This suggests that the interaction or feedback between diffusion of the oxygen process and investment rates may be stronger (or certainly more observable) at the level of the individual firm than in the national aggregates. Accordingly, we also estimated the individual firm investment functions by two-stage procedures. The results are shown in the second to bottom line of table 6.13; quite clearly, they do nothing to contradict our earlier conclusion that the investment variable is helpful in explaining individual firm diffusion rates.

Since about half of the firms in the sample had no oxygen process capacity by 1968, it can also be argued that the classical regression model yields biased results because of a concentration of observations at the zero bound and the absence of negative values in the sample. Under such circumstances a linear regression model tends to bias the regression constant upward at the cost of flattening the regression line with respect to the 'true' relationship. The standard correction for this bias is a simple probit analysis, but this would not use the available information effectively.[1] The appropriate estimation technique is an extension of probit analysis developed by Tobin, sometimes called the Tobit model.[2]

Basically, the Tobit model solves a cumulative distribution function for the limited dependent variable given the lower (or upper) limit and a linear combination of the independent variables. A maximum likelihood estimate can then be obtained for the coefficients and their standard deviations. However, the normal equations determining the maximum likelihood estimators are non-linear. They are solved iteratively, usually by Newton's method, until the change in the new estimates of the coefficients with respect to the previous estimates is negligible.

The results of a Tobit analysis applied to our sample are shown in the bottom line of table 6.13. Some differences appear when these results are compared with the regression estimates. Under Tobit, all the variables have the right sign including the aggressiveness score; however, on the basis of its t-value the aggressiveness coefficient continues to be no different from zero at the usual levels of significance. The Tobit function is clearly dominated by the 1962 productivity variable, while the investment variable decreases somewhat in significance. Also important are the 1962 capital to labour ratio and the electric production variable. These results confirm, on the whole, the analysis conducted by linear regression, but stress more the influence of previous efficiency and age of existing equipment on the adoption of the oxygen process.

To summarise, there is nothing in the empirical results at any level of aggregation to refute strongly the basic hypothesis that much, or possibly even most, of the differences in diffusion is capable of explanation in terms of general expansion rates, market structure differences, and factor price differentials. We are, though, left with some residual uncertainties as to whether the rate of expansion also represents to

[1] Probit analysis as developed by J. Cornfield and N. Mantel ('Some new aspects of the application of maximum likelihood to the calculation of the dosage response curve', *Journal of the American Statistical Association*, vol. 45, 1950, pp. 181–210) is of interest in explaining the probability of limit and non-limit responses without regard for the value or size of the latter.

[2] J. Tobin, 'Estimation of relationships for limited dependent variables', *Econometrica*, vol. 26, January 1958, pp. 24–36. For a generalisation of that model to situations in which the dependent variable, over some finite range, is not related to the independent variables, see R. N. Rosett, 'A statistical model of friction in economics', *Econometrica*, vol. 27, April 1959, pp. 263–7.

some extent differences in management motivation, as well as (or in lieu of) measuring the general buoyancy or expansion of a particular steel market, especially when discussing individual firm differences. That is, if the managerial effects are observable (as represented by the investment and earlier productivity variables), these seem to be more of an individual firm or intra-national phenomenon than a national characteristic. Specifically, at the level of national or international aggregates we can construct quite plausible explanations of diffusion without recourse to explanatory variables that can be interpreted as measuring managerial motives or vigour; at the firm level, on the other hand, variables that can be construed as measuring managerial influences do make a contribution.[1]

SUMMARY AND SOME FINAL OBSERVATIONS

We have attempted to explain and understand the international differences in rates of adoption of a new production technology, the basic oxygen process as applied to steelmaking. Our investigation has been dominated by two hypotheses:

(a) that most of the differences between firms, and perhaps to an even greater extent between national industries, can be explained by objective differences in the economic environment within which these firms or industries must operate;

(b) that some of the differences observed between firms or national industries are attributable to such non-economic factors as differences in management styles and motivation.

These two hypotheses are not necessarily mutually exclusive. It is entirely possible that both are correct to some degree and are needed to achieve a reasonably adequate understanding of the diffusion. For example, it is entirely possible that all firms respond eventually in a reasonably rational fashion to objective economic signals, but the rate of response may differ because of managerial or motivational differences. Of course, even these differential rates of response may not be strictly rational in a narrow economic or efficiency sense.

In attempting to assess or test these hypotheses, we initially surveyed the aggregate evidence and the technological history of the process. We concluded that neither gave us any basis on which to do even a preliminary sorting or assignment of relative weights to the two hypotheses. In particular, we specifically rejected simple counting exercises as

---

[1] A further discriminant analysis, which sought to identify linear combinations of variables that best differentiated among groups, tended to confirm the previous regression results.

legitimate tests of these concepts; adequate testing required substantially more detail than could be provided by diffusion curves or similar devices.

More detailed measurement and testing, however, immediately brought forth new problems. In particular, objective measurement of non-economic influences is difficult. Indeed, where one is dealing with an international sample, with all its accompanying difficulties of differences in accounting standards and management procedures and practices, it is hard enough even to establish some reasonably objective measures of the economic features.

A common way out of these difficulties is to measure the influence of all those things that one can measure and then attribute what is left unexplained, the residual (say, in a regression equation), to the unmeasurable influences. Such a residual approach should be reasonably satisfactory as long as the specification and measurement of all the other effects are precise and complete.[1] Unfortunately in our case – because of the limited and heterogeneous character of the international data, and the imprecision in translating theoretical specifications into accounting equivalents – there are many reasons for not believing that our models are reasonably complete or precise.

Accordingly, we attempted to calculate a more direct measure of managerial motives and aspirations. For this purpose we adapted some techniques of factor analysis, as commonly applied to psychological or educational testing. Specifically, we construed certain of the values taken from balance sheets and income statements (those that seemed to be particularly under the control of individual managements) as being 'test scores' indicating possible orientations of the managements involved.

It would be extravagant for us to claim that our attempt to measure motivation was completely successful; it was handicapped by the same difficulties which handicap the measurement of more conventional or straightforward economic effects. However, we did create a measure which seemed reasonably plausible, particularly for the years 1962, 1963 and 1964, when major cyclical or other economic disturbances, largely irrelevant to measuring long-run effects such as motives, were mainly absent. Furthermore, we found that our motivational index correlated reasonably well with investment behaviour.

Our index of management motivation, which we called an 'aggressiveness score', was dominated as an explanation of investment behaviour only by cash flow, which has long been considered basic to the timing and stimulation of steel industry investment. Capacity utilisation,

[1] Jorgensen and Griliches, 'The explanation of productivity change'; Balogh and Streeten, 'The coefficient of ignorance'.

another variable commonly found to be influential, was at best only equal to the aggressiveness score in explaining investment behaviour. In short, the steel companies and national industries in our samples seem particularly sensitive to cash flow, but if other important influences are discernible, these would appear to be capacity utilisation and something akin to managerial aggressiveness.

The focus of our study was, of course, upon the diffusion of the oxygen steel process rather than on investment behaviour as such. However, we postulated that one of the more important objective circumstances that would influence the diffusion was the rate of expansion of available markets. Indeed, when we turned to the study of oxygen steel diffusion, the rate of investment, or some similar proxy measure of market growth, was often dominant in explaining diffusion, particularly intra-national or inter-firm differences.

However, factor prices and market structures were also influential. In particular, while their significance varied widely, variables measuring the availability or attractiveness of direct electric production and the availability of scrap materials as a factor input did seem related fairly systematically and in the expected manner to diffusion. There was less evidence of scale effects upon adoption of the process; we tested several different measures, such as total output and number of small plants, and at the most they showed only a very modest impact upon the rate of adoption, with the signs of the coefficients almost as often contrary to hypothesis as in agreement.

We also tested our aggressiveness index as an explanatory variable for diffusion. Unlike investment, however, we did not discover a discernible influence in almost any plausible formulation of the functions. Not only were the coefficients insignificant, but they also more often than not had a negative sign, thus quite clearly running counter to hypothesis.

We tested our aggressiveness score only with our individual firm data or samples, on the grounds that only at that level did measures of managerial motivation seem reasonably plausible. At this individual firm level, however, the second best (to some investment or market expansion measure), and in some instances the best, explanatory variable of diffusion was a measure of productivity (output per number of employees). Productivity could, of course, be regarded as a proxy for management effectiveness or motivation; this would be particularly appropriate when included (as in our equations) with measures of the age of existing productive capacity. In fact the 1962 productivity measure was significant in explaining the share of oxygen steel in total capacity in 1968, whether or not age or the aggressiveness score were included. The 1962 productivity measure could, of course, also have been a gauge of early adoption, but this is not inconsistent with saying it was a reasonable proxy for management motivation or aggressiveness. In short, we were not able to identify at the firm level any managerial effect attributable to our direct measure of aggressiveness, although 1962 productivity, operating independently, could be construed as an alternative measure of such effects. And since productivity was either the best or the second best of the variables tested in our individual firm regressions, we are not able to reject our second basic hypothesis, that managerial differences or motives may explain some of the differences in diffusion.

Nevertheless, the basic evidence in support of this second hypothesis is rather weaker than that in support of the first, which stresses direct economic effects such as rates of expansion, and factor price and market differentials. Perhaps the best overall summary of our analysis of diffusion of the basic oxygen process would be as follows:

(a) general market expansion seems to be the dominant influence;

(b) factor price effects also seem to be influential;

(c) some impact seems attributable to managerial or motivational differences;

(d) only an insignificant influence seems attributable to scale differentials.

It should be observed, however, that in all of our analyses the unexplained residuals remain quite large. Much of what is unexplained may simply represent a good deal of measurement error and other extraneous influences, but the scale of these inexplained residuals is sufficiently large to suggest a very cautious interpretation of any findings or conclusions.

APPENDIX

Statistical sources

Most financial variables have been extracted from European Coal and Steel Community, *Balance Sheets of the Steel Companies* by C. Goudima and G. Schumacher, Luxemburg, 1967, Part I: *Community Countries*, Part II: *Non-Community Countries* (hereafter called 'High Authority').

The EEC national samples cover 15 firms in Belgium, 3 in Luxemburg, 3 in the Netherlands, 25 in Germany, 19 in France and 16 in Italy. The firms account for 70–100 per cent of the national crude steel production. The period covered extends from 1950 to 1966, with the exception of Germany (1953–66).

The non-EEC countries are represented by 4 firms in Austria (90 per cent of steel output), 14 in the United Kingdom (90 per cent of steel output), 5 in Sweden (35 per cent of steel output), 6 in Japan (75 per cent of steel output) and 33 in the United States (90 per cent of steel output). The period covered extends from 1959 to 1966 with the exception of Sweden (1961–6).

(1) Investment expenditure

United States, 1959–66, from High Authority, Part II, Income Statement, item 18.

For all other countries except Belgium from High Authority, Part I or Part II.

Belgium, 1959–66, from OECD, *The Iron and Steel Industry in Europe* (various years).

(2) Capacity utilisation index

United States, 1956–66, Wharton index,[1] raw data from Federal Reserve Board production index.

Belgium, France, Germany, Italy, Luxemburg, 1956–66, Wharton index, raw data from OECD, *Main Economic Indicators*.

Netherlands, 1956–66, OECD capacity figures divided by UN total output figures.

Austria, 1956–66, Wharton index, raw data from OECD.

Japan, 1956–66, from Japan Iron and Steel Institute – capacity and total output figures.

Sweden, United Kingdom, 1956–66, Wharton index, raw data from OECD.

(3) Cash throw-off from High Authority

(4) Oxygen process capacity

United States, 1959–69, Kaiser Steel Corporation, *Linz-Donawitz Process Newsletter* and UNECE, *Steel-Making Processes*, Geneva, 1962.

Belgium, France, Germany, Luxemburg, Netherlands, 1956–69, European Coal and Steel Community, *Investment in the Community Coalmining and Iron and Steel Industries: summary report on the investment surveys* (various years). Capacity is defined as 'production potential' up to 1965 and 'projected potential' thereafter.

Austria, 1959–69, *Linz-Donawitz Process Newsletter*.

Japan, 1959–66, Japan Iron and Steel Institute, *Handbook*; 1967–9, *Linz-Donawitz Process Newsletter*.

Sweden, 1959–66, data provided by IUI; 1967–9, *Linz-Donawitz Process Newsletter* and UNECE *Steel-Making Processes*.

United Kingdom, 1959–69, *Linz-Donawitz Process Newsletter*.

(5) Steel production

All countries except Sweden from High Authority. The figures are sample totals.

[1] L. R. Klein and R. Summers, *The Wharton Index of Capacity Utilization*, Philadelphia (Pa), University of Pennsylvania, 1966. (All Wharton figures are yearly averages of quarterly indices.)

Sweden, 1959–61, by regressing OECD production figures on High Authority figures and extrapolating backward; 1961–6, from High Authority.

Constructed data

(1) Cash throw-off (CTO)

United States, 1959–61, from High Authority (HA).

CTO = retained earnings and earned surplus + total depreciation.

For 1956–9: 'income reinvested in business + depreciation expense' from American Iron and Steel Institute, *Annual Statistical Report* (AISI) regressed against High Authority totals for 1959–66, then extrapolated backward according to the equation $CTO_{HA} = 14 \cdot 31 + 0 \cdot 99$ (AISI).

Belgium, 1956–66, from High Authority.

After comparison with company reports, it was found that gross profits after taxes were equivalent to HA carry forward + HA profit of the year (both from the balance sheet), while the HA item 'dividends – carry forward' was in fact equivalent to the balance sheet carry forward of the following year, with the dividends paid out still to be deducted.

Therefore, CTO = carry forward + profit of the year + allocation for dividends + depreciation.

France, 1956–66, from High Authority.

After comparison with the company reports, it was found that, for Usinor, HA 'long term provisions' is in fact a reserve for price increases. No carry forward could be identified and some years only a profit entry was presented.

For De Wendel, HA 'stocks' were inventories after depreciation and amortisation. HA 'retained earnings, earned surplus' corresponded to the sum of various reserves. HA 'carry forward' was a carry forward of 'residual income', while HA 'allocation to reserves' was the change in reserves for inventory depreciation. HA 'allocation for dividends' turned out to be the sum of carry forward from last year and various current reserves. This entry could, therefore, be equal to 'some profit before dividends payable', but since no entry for dividends paid out was available on HA statements, CTO was computed as HA allocation for dividends + HA depreciation.

Germany, 1956–66, from High Authority.

As suggested by IFO, we took each flow as equal to the profit of the year + carry forward (in the balance sheet) + depreciation − allocation for dividends. We did not include changes in other reserves or long-term provisions, since such reserves seemed not readily available for investment purposes.

Italy, 1956–66, from High Authority.

CTO was computed as profit of the year + carry forward (in the balance sheet) + depreciation.

No dividends were deducted since it was impossible to identify where they were paid out from.

Luxemburg, 1956–66, from High Authority.

After comparisons with HADIR[1] report, it was found that HA 'allocation for dividends' corresponded to dividends and fringe benefits to directors.

[1] Hauts Fourneaux et Acieries de Differdange – St Ingbert – Rumelange.

Since HA carry forward (in the balance sheet) + profit of the year seemed to be equal to gross profits after taxes, CTO was computed as carry forward + profit of the year − allocation for dividends + depreciation.

Netherlands, 1956–66, from High Authority.

After comparison with Hoogovens report, it was found that HA 'other reserves' was the sum of general reserve, investment reserve and capital paid in excess of common stock. HA 'long term provisions' were for 'tax and other'. HA 'profit of the year' was the 'profit to be distributed'.

CTO was computed as profit of the year + carry forward (in income statement) + depreciation.

Austria, 1959–66, from High Authority.

1959, no allocation for carry forward (in income statement) being available, carry forward (in balance sheet) was chosen as an approximation. CTO was computed as profit of the year + carry forward (in the balance sheet) − dividends + depreciation.

1960–6, following OIW suggestion, CTO was computed as profit of the year + carry forward (in income statement) − dividends + depreciation.

Japan, 1959–66, from High Authority.

After comparison with Yawata report, it was found that HA 'other reserves' corresponded to 'earned surplus', while HA 'long-term provisions' were long-term reserves. Yawata's income before dividends was equal to the sum of HA sales, increase or decrease in stocks, capitalised internal deliveries and performances, miscellaneous income and reserves minus HA purchases of raw materials, wages and salaries, miscellaneous expenditure, depreciation, interest payments and taxes. Subtracting HA dividends from this result, Yawata's 'retained earnings' were found and corresponded to HA 'allocation to reserves' (in income statement), which is also the first difference of HA 'other reserves' (in the balance sheet).

Thus, CTO was computed as the sum of HA allocations to reserves and depreciation, both income statement items.

Sweden, 1961–6, from High Authority.

Following IUI suggestion, CTO was computed as HA carry forward (in income statement) + depreciation.

United Kingdom, 1959–66, from High Authority.

Following NIESR suggestion and after comparison with United Steel Company report, CTO was derived as HA depreciation + allocation to reserves.

(2) Diffusion coefficient (see table 6.1.)

In order to combine in one number both the speed of adoption and the share of a new technique in the total capacity, we used a particular application of the mean inter-individual difference, a measure originally developed by Corrado Gini and specifically applied for computing a coefficient of concentration with respect to the Lorenz curve.

It can be shown that, in a Lorenz chart, the area of the polygon *below* the broken straight lines linking the plotted points is equal to $\frac{1}{2} \sum_{i=1}^{n} r_i(q_i + q_{i-1})$, where r_i is the percentage of families within each income class.

If on a technological diffusion chart for a given country, the percentages of capacity achieved by the new technique are plotted in each year (q_i) from 1955 to 1969 $(i = 15)$, applying the above formula, we can compute a value for the diffusion area, noting that $r_i = 1$ since we are only concerned with one country at a time.

If 100 per cent capacity is the upper limit, the total area of the box is 15 and a country's relative diffusion coefficient will be equal to its diffusion area divided by 14. This will show how well a country has approximated to the optimum coefficient of 15 or, in other words, how that country has scored under the assumption that the absolute best score would be to have had all its capacity installed in the new technique for all the 15 years.

If, on the other hand, we fix a different upper limit for each country, say 80 per cent, the total area becomes $15 \times 0.80 = 12$, and the relative diffusion coefficient, now computed in terms of a lower, upper or optimum limit, will rise.

The first column in table 6.1 gives the relative diffusion coefficient when the optimum coefficient is 15, and the second column gives the relative coefficient when each country is given a different optimum coefficient assumed to be equal to the asymptote of its diffusion curve.

CHAPTER 7

FLOAT GLASS

By G. F. Ray, NIESR

MAKING FLAT GLASS

Apart from the traditional and now outdated system of blown glass, until recently the methods for manufacturing flat glass were the Fourcault process, introduced in Belgium in 1914; the Libbey–Owens process (often called the Libbey–Owens–Ford or LOF process), introduced in the United States in 1915; the Pittsburgh process, introduced in the United States in the 1920s; and the rolling–polishing method, further developed by twin-grinding. The first three are the main methods for manufacturing sheet (window) glass, and are similar in the sense that the sheet is drawn off the melted glass; the two surfaces of the sheet are fire-finished, but they are not perfectly parallel and may contain distortions. The fourth is mainly used for thicker glass; the glass passes through two steel rolls which leave heavy marks in the hot glass, so that the raw plate glass has then to be ground and polished. This requires expensive equipment and is a delicate exercise; the most up-to-date method is twin-grinding (grinding the plate on both sides in one operation), evolved some 30 years ago by Pilkington.

THE FLOAT PROCESS

Float glass was introduced at the end of the 1950s by Pilkington Brothers Limited of St Helens, England, who protect the process by worldwide patents. The basic idea is to draw the liquid glass into a tank full of molten tin, where it floats on the surface of the metal. The heat applied from above melts out any irregularities on the top surface of the glass, whilst the bottom surface retains the finish of the liquid tin. Float glass does not require costly grinding and polishing but is comparable in quality with polished glass, and the two, although made by different methods, are interchangeable. Indeed Pilkington's float process was meant to produce 'polished plate glass', which is the highest quality, in an improved way.

Initially there were limitations on the thickness of float glass; these were gradually overcome and now the float process can produce flat glass of any thickness over two millimetres. Therefore, as from perhaps 1970, there has also been considerable interchangeability between float and sheet glass.[1] As a result of further developments, light and heat rejecting glasses (with a reflective surface), as well as body-tinted glass, are now also being made by the float method.

The float process is very profitable in comparison with conventional production, since it is a continuous process, lending itself to long trouble-free runs, replacing a non-continuous process. Float glass can be produced at three-quarters of the manufacturing cost and two-thirds of the capital investment of the comparable earlier product – lustrous and distortion-free polished glass, from which float glass is indistinguishable.[2]

Chart 7.1. *Two methods of making polished plate glass*

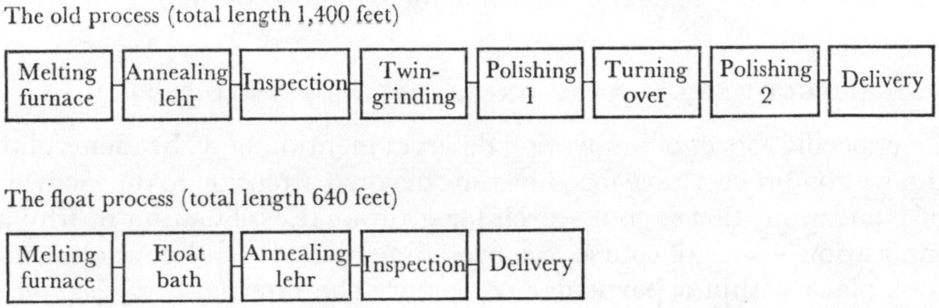

The old process (total length 1,400 feet)

Melting furnace	Annealing lehr	Inspection	Twin-grinding	Polishing 1	Turning over	Polishing 2	Delivery

The float process (total length 640 feet)

Melting furnace	Float bath	Annealing lehr	Inspection	Delivery

Note: Both production lines are based on a tank capacity of 1,200 tons.

To understand these very considerable savings some details of the two processes should be compared as in chart 7.1. In the old system the glass in a molten state passed between rollers into an annealing lehr, in which its cooling was carefully controlled to eliminate internal stresses. After inspection it passed through twin grinders which smoothed the upper and lower surfaces of the continuous glass ribbon simultaneously. After cutting, large sheets of smooth glass were bedded on to continuous tables, which passed under the polishers, finishing one surface at a time. In the float process the molten glass flows from a tank on to a bath of liquid tin metal, on which it floats in a chamber in which the atmosphere is carefully controlled. Through the annealing lehr the glass emerges as the finished product – perfectly flat and clear with a brilliant fire-finished surface.

The first striking difference is in the layout of the two plants. A complete polished plate production line is 1,400 feet long; it is a highly

---

[1] In the United Kingdom sheet (window) glass accounts in square footage for more than half of all glass sold, and float or plate for about 15 per cent (the rest being cast or rolled glass), but, in terms of value, sheet accounts for about 40 per cent and float or plate for rather more. The proportions may, however, vary from country to country.

[2] *EFTA Bulletin*, vol. 9, no. 8, December 1968, p. 13.

integrated and complex system, on which variations in the width of the glass produced cannot be made quickly or cheaply. The float process, by cutting out grinding and polishing, reduces the length of the line by more than half (to 640 feet) and thus reduces the floor area required. This is the origin of the large saving in investment; production costs are reduced through decreased depreciation. The main savings in production costs come, however, from the elimination of twin-grinding, of turning the plate, and of polishing the two surfaces. These are delicate operations, with a very high risk of breakage and loss. Accidental breakage and the scrapping of faulty products were, by the nature of the process, inescapable and 'a loss of 30 per cent was regarded as very near the theoretical minimum for plate glass before plate was largely replaced by float.'[1] The float process reduces these losses to practically nil.

ACCOUNTABILITY: ONE ASPECT OF INNOVATION

One specific aspect of innovation deserves mention here. Students of the innovation process have for some time devoted attention to the incidence of innovation, that is to a search for a rational explanation of why an innovation – and, of course, the preceding research and development – took place within a particular company. The internal organisation of the innovating company, its research and development set-up, and many situational and behavioural conditions have been studied, and the literature on this question is already of respectable size.

It is not intended to go into the details of this interesting problem here, but the study of the float process may throw light on allied questions from one particular angle – the accountability of a company to its shareholders or otherwise. Major innovations require huge spending in the early stages. The innovator of the float process, Pilkington, allocated altogether £7 million to the pursuit of an idea which, many times in the course of its development, would have appeared indefensible at any meeting of shareholders.[2] Pilkington, however, had no outside shareholders; at the time of the development of the float process it was a family-owned private company.[3] Spokesmen for the industry, and for management sciences as well, are inclined to believe that this played a considerable part in the eventual success of the float venture which, in view of the large sums involved, could well have been discouraged within a company accountable to the public.

[1] Monopolies Commission, *Flat Glass: report on the supply of flat glass*, HC 83, London, HMSO, 1968, p. 71.

[2] J. Jewkes, D. Sawers and R. Stillerman, *The Sources of Invention*, 2nd ed., London, Macmillan, 1969, pp. 334–7.

[3] The company went public at the end of 1970.

THE INDUSTRY

The United States output was well above that of the other countries studied. The French and British industries both produced about 550,000–600,000 metric tons of flat glass in the late 1960s, and the German industry 750,000–800,000 metric tons (including mirror glass, a bigger item in Germany than elsewhere). Italian production was around 400,000 metric tons in the mid-1960s, but rising fast to above 500,000, while both Austria and Sweden produced around 50,000 tons. Scandinavian output was doubled at the end of the decade by the coming on stream of new plant in Denmark, in joint Swedish–Danish ownership. These figures are shown in table 7.1.

Table 7.1. *The output of flat glass*

	1962	1964	1966	1968	1969	1970[a]
			(thousand metric tons)			
Austria	46	55	54	52	53	49
France	476	539	575	548	587	560
Italy	275	350	390	400	468	541
Sweden	41	44	45	47	42	105[b]
United Kingdom	470	560	514	560	596	534[c]
West Germany[d]	684	736	746	744	787	850
			(million square feet)			
United States[e]	647	765	879	952	983	971

SOURCE: inquiry.

[a] Estimated.

[b] Includes the jointly owned Swedish–Danish plant at Korsør, Denmark.

[c] Not adjusted for strike effects.

[d] Includes mirror glass which accounted for about 25 per cent of the total tonnage.

[e] Plate, float, rolled and wire glass only; by value these accounted for 55 per cent in 1962–4, 60 per cent in 1965–7, and 64–5 per cent in 1968–9 of all US flat glass production.

In the United Kingdom the four plants which produce flat glass are all owned and controlled by Pilkington Brothers.[1] In the other five European countries covered by this inquiry the position is more complex, and in most of them the industry is not really national. The two French concerns – St Gobain (with their Belgian associates St Roch) and the Boussois Group – and one huge Belgian company – Glaverbel – dominate the making of flat glass in continental Western Europe. Between them they control or have some interest in 17 companies out of 23: in Austria all three, in Germany all eight, in Italy five out of ten, and in Sweden one, with interests also in Spain and Holland. Two other

[1] The exclusive position of Pilkington was investigated by the (British) Monopolies Commission, see *Flat Glass*.

glass companies in Italy are under American control, and the remaining three, which are independent of international ownership, are quite small.

Thus, apart from Britain, France and Belgium, it is meaningless to speak of 'national' industries in the context of decisions to embark on such a large and indivisible investment project as the building of a float plant; such decisions are likely to be taken outside national boundaries. In this respect float glass differs markedly from the other processes considered in this book.

THE INQUIRY

The structure of the flat glass industry affected the course of the inquiry in this area; the dominance of a few large companies excluded certain questions because of the obvious danger of disclosure. Furthermore, in continental Europe, any conclusion would characterise the policy of large international companies rather than national industries.

In these circumstances, the purpose of the inquiry was first to assess the various aspects of the diffusion of the process, and then to study some of the factors which have affected diffusion, although this was restricted by the above limitations. The inquiry covered the whole of the flat glass industries in Austria, Sweden and the United Kingdom, but in the other countries coverage was only partial. Data collected nationally were supplemented by the NIESR, using other national and trade sources. The coverage can therefore be considered satisfactory overall.

DIFFUSION OF THE NEW TECHNIQUE

Diffusion was assessed in the following terms:

  (a) the number of licence agreements at different points of time (taken as proxies for investment decisions, although of course licence agreements would be concluded after the actual management decision, with varying timelags);
  (b) the number of users, as indicated by the actual commissioning of a first float line;
  (c) the spread of the process within firms:
  (d) the share of flat glass output produced by the float process.

The data available permit these different measures of diffusion to be analysed on a worldwide scale, except for the last, which is restricted to selected countries.

Table 7.2. *Licence agreements and float plants in operation, early 1971*[a]

Licence granted	Licensee	Country	Float plant	Start of operations
1962, July	Pittsburgh Plate Glass Industries	USA	Cumberland	1963, December
			Crystal City	1965, December
			Meadville	1968, October
			Meadville	1970, May
1962, December	Glaces de Boussois	France	Boussois	1966, February
1962, December	Glaverbel	Belgium	Moustier	1965, March
1963, April	Compagnie de St Gobain	Italy	Pisa	1965, December
1963, April	Glaceries de St Roch	W. Germany	Porz[b]	1966, February
		Belgium	Auvelais	1970, February
		W. Germany	Herzogenrath	1971, February
1963, April	Libbey–Owens– Ford Company	USA	Lathrop, Cal.	1964, September
			Rossford, N.Y.	1966, September
			East Toledo	1969, June
			Ottawa, Ill.	1970, April
			Rossford, N.Y.	1970, July
1964, March	Asahi Glass Company	Japan	Tsurumi	1966, May
			Amagasaki	1968, October
			Amagasaki	1971 (early)[c]
1964, March	Nippon Sheet Glass Company	Japan	Maizuru	1965, November
1964, June	Cristaleria Española[d]	Spain	Aviles	1967, February
			Arbos	1971 (end)[c]
1964, July	Ford Motor Company	USA	Nashville, Tenn.	1966, March
			Dearborn	1967, March
			Nashville, Tenn.	1968, June
1965, March	Vidrio Plano de Mexico	Mexico	Mexico City	1968, July
1965, October	Pilkington Brothers	Canada	Scarborough, Ontario	{1967, February {1971,[c]
1966, December	Sklo Union	Czechoslovakia	Teplice	1969, October
1967, March	Technopromimport	USSR	Bor. nr. Moscow	1970, August
1968, February	Central Glass	Japan	Matsuzaka	1969, May
1970, May	Combustion Engineering	USA	Floreffe, N.J.	1971 (end)[c]

SOURCE: inquiry and *Financial Times*.

[a] Excluding Pilkington's plants in England.   [c] Expected.
[b] Joint operation with St Gobain.   [d] Controlled by St Gobain.

Table 7.2 shows the licensees (the companies which acquired the float licence from Pilkington), the dates of the licence agreements, the locations of the float plants, and the dates these plants were commissioned.[1] Chart 7.2 indicates the diffusion in terms of licence agreements (as a measure of decisions), starts of the first plant (as a measure

[1] Pilkington operate four float plants in the United Kingdom at their Cowley Hill works, St Helens. The first float plant started production in 1959, the fourth was completed in 1971.

of the number of users), and the total number of float plants in
operation. The difference between 'first' plants and 'total' plants
demonstrates the diffusion within firms in terms of equipment.

Measuring diffusion by output is difficult since most of the data are
estimated. At Pilkington float output increased from small beginnings
in 1959 to 67,000 tons (14 per cent of British flat glass output) in 1962
and 232,000 tons (39 per cent) in 1969. The French figures show a
similar development with a considerable lag (chart 7.3), and the

Chart 7.2. *Measures of diffusion of the float process*

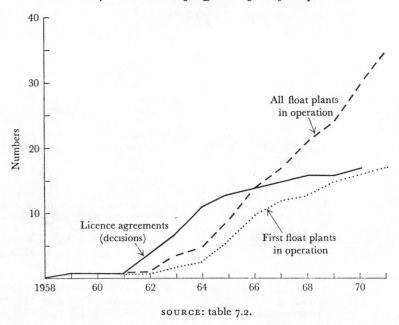

SOURCE: table 7.2.

German data are also likely to have followed a line parallel to the
French. Some 10 per cent of the Italian output was recently produced
by the float process. In both the United States and Japan, with thirteen
and five float plants respectively, diffusion is likely soon to reach the
British level. By now all but one of the large-scale makers of flat glass
in the Western world (the American St Gobain Corporation), and
some in the socialist countries too, are currently making float glass.
Many of them already have several float lines in operation.

It has been suggested that the diffusion of an innovation follows a
biological pattern evolved in epidemiology, usually illustrated by a
logistic curve. It is therefore of some interest to test whether the use of
the float process has been spreading like an epidemic and if so, whether

there is any 'biological' regularity to be detected in the form dissemination has taken. Experiments aimed at testing this suggestion gave inconclusive results. The diffusion of the technique in terms of decisions seemed to follow a logistic curve, but the other two measures – first and all float plants in operation – took a course which was more linear than logistic.

Chart 7.3. *Float glass output*

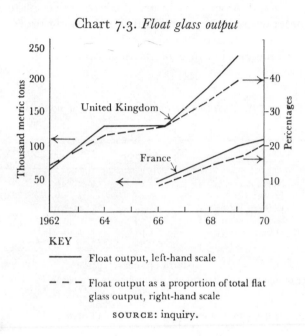

KEY

——— Float output, left-hand scale

– – – Float output as a proportion of total flat glass output, right-hand scale

SOURCE: inquiry.

It is difficult to find definitive evidence that the diffusion of a new technique spreads like an epidemic. Companies will not often admit that the board was convinced or influenced in a decision by an earlier decision of another company, possibly its competitor. The companies in this case are mostly large groups, and it can be assumed that major decisions by their boards would be based on considerably more than the 'infection' of a technique already being used elsewhere.

Another aspect which is important is the wide ranging international interests of the holding groups. Many cases of application of the float process across national frontiers in fact indicate diffusion of the technique within a company or group. Thus, a float plant in Canada may be still part of the Pilkington group, or a plant in Italy and Spain still within the St Gobain group.

The pattern of diffusion of this process may, however, change in future. For a long time following its introduction it was intended primarily to replace the old method of manufacturing polished plate

8

glass with a thickness of five millimetres and over. Adapting the technique to the production of thinner flat glass, basically sheet (mainly window) glass, took a long time. It has only recently reached the critical point of producing flat glass not more than two millimetres thick, that is window glass, with the superior qualities of float and also many of its economic advantages. Thus, earlier it replaced one particular conventional process, twin-grinding of rolled plate glass, but now it competes with all the traditional sheet-making processes as well, so that in future the course of diffusion, whatever measure is considered, will probably change; because of its development, the process now enters new areas.

Table 7.3. *Gestation period[a] for building a float plant*

Months

	Average	Range
North America[b]	17	16–19
Japan	20	15–26
Western Europe[c]	35	28–39
Socialist countries[d]	39	39
Other[e]	40	40

SOURCE: inquiry.

[a] The number of months from the date of the licence agreement to the date of the start of float operation.
[b] United States and Canada.
[c] Includes data for Belgium, France, Italy, Germany and Spain.
[d] USSR and Czechoslovakia.   [e] Mexico only.

An interesting sideline is to compare the dates of licence agreements with those of the start of float operations. This gestation period, based on data in table 7.2, could, of course, be influenced by many factors. It is not necessarily the construction time proper, since it includes time required for obtaining government approval where this is necessary for the building, and for legal and planning preparations. In some cases tax and other commercial considerations might have influenced the date of agreement, whereas the date of commissioning could have been affected by other circumstances at the various plants. Yet, the lengths of this period, as shown in table 7.3 and chart 7.4, indicate that much longer is required for similar large-scale investment projects in Europe than in North America and Japan. Whatever the reason for these differences they are significant, especially when we consider that the averages shown are of observations within a comparatively narrow range.

It is worth noting that the length of the gestation periods shown in chart 7.4 have practically no correlation with time; that is there is no sign of a 'learning' effect, and float plants built towards the end of the period took just as long to erect as those in earlier years – a fact perhaps due to the technological maturity of the process at an early stage.

Chart 7.4. *Gestation period from the licence agreement to commissioning the first float plant*

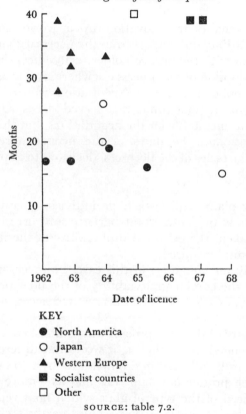

KEY
● North America
○ Japan
▲ Western Europe
▨ Socialist countries
□ Other

SOURCE: table 7.2.

FACTORS INFLUENCING DIFFUSION

Information

In 1959, having started commercial production of float glass at its Cowley Hill factory, Pilkington Brothers publicly announced the invention.[1] In the small world of flat glass makers the announcement

---

[1] The first full-scale plant actually started in 1957 but for 14 months turned out nothing but unsatisfactory glass. The invention was not announced until the quality problems had been overcome.

of an obviously revolutionary innovation got round very quickly. It is inconceivable that any of the large groups did not know of the new process immediately after Pilkington's announcement (perhaps with the exception of enterprises in the socialist countries). It can be taken for granted, therefore, that information concerning the new process reached the world's major flat glass producers at about the same time, very soon after the initial announcement.

Licensing policy

Pilkington protected their innovation by a world licence. Nobody could start a float line, quite apart from the necessary know-how, without an agreement with the licence-holder, whose licensing policy could thus influence adoption of the process elsewhere. As far as one can assess it, this licensing policy was liberal. Negotiations were often lengthy, but were conducted on a 'first come, first served' basis. Understandably, some queuing was inevitable for the negotiations, but this did not cause any major delay and the dates of the licence agreements reflect approximately the order of the licensees' decisions to apply for a licence.

Capital

Building a float plant requires a huge indivisible capital investment. Three factors must play important parts in any investment decision: the risk to be taken, the expected profitability of the investment, and access to the capital required.

Risk is usually unavoidable; in this case, however, it was probably quite low, since the commercial viability of the float process had been proved by the innovator and each licensee had access to its experience and know-how.

The profitability of the float process was established at an early stage and never challenged. Nevertheless, it works out differently in various situations and can be affected in a major way by two factors. The first is the size of the production or of the market—more specifically the quantities required of the type of glass which float replaced initially, polished plate glass. (This is an important, partly technical point to which we return below.) The second is the age of the existing equipment, taking into account its efficiency and also the extent to which it has been written off in the company's books. There are indications that in some countries (France is a case in point), and in some large companies, the construction of a float line was delayed because of existing expensive and relatively new equipment which was using the latest pre-float technology.

The inquiry could not find evidence that any of the potential licensees was hampered by lack of capital. Nevertheless, it is conceivable that availability of capital might in some cases have had an impact, if not on the basic decision at least on the timing of the new plant.

Size

So far all float plants have been built in countries which either have a large market already (Britain, the United States, France, Italy, Germany, Japan, Canada and the USSR), or where, though the domestic market is of moderate size, the export of high-quality glass has for long been traditionally established (Belgium and Czechoslovakia),[1] or where the market is still not large but has a potential future on account of a large population and a relatively fast growth of national income (Spain and Mexico) (table 7.2).

The point to be stressed is that in this case the size of the total market, as distinct from the size of the company or groups of companies, seems to be one of the decisive factors explaining the adoption or rejection of the new technique. This size depends not on national income and population alone, but on local traditions in building and shopfitting. Polished plate glass is a rather special, high-quality product and consumption *per capita* differs quite widely by country.[2] For example, relative consumption in Scandinavia is smaller than in some other European countries with comparable population but markedly lower income *per capita*.

The huge output of even the smallest float plant in comparison with the market size is a highly important factor. One float line alone, if utilised at a rate anywhere near normal capacity, makes more glass than the whole consumption of a country the size of Austria. This is important in relation to the behaviour of firms in smaller markets, or indeed of smaller independent companies.

In continental Western Europe there are 39 companies in eleven countries making flat glass. Four of them are big holding companies, which have controlling or minority interests in another 29 flat glass producers, leaving six independent producers. As table 7.2 indicates, float production was introduced in only a handful of plants in continental Western Europe; all of them controlled by one of the big groups.

None of the independent companies has introduced the float process nor have more than 20 companies controlled by or connected with the big groups. These companies produce flat glass on a moderate or minor scale; if they make polished plate glass at all, their output of this

[1] Czechoslovakia may be a special case; it is possible that several East European countries are supplied with float glass from Czech works in the framework of Comecon. If so the Czechs too have a large market.

[2] It should be recalled that we are covering here the first stage of the development of the float process, the years when it was limited to glass over a certain thickness. Float glass then replaced polished plate glass and virtually nothing else.

product is even smaller. The huge capital requirement of a new float plant may be beyond the financial capabilities of some of them, moreover, the output of such a plant would certainly surpass either the share of the market which they could realistically hope for, or indeed the whole domestic demand in their country. This factor must have been one of the decisive causes of the non-introduction of the float process in the companies controlled by the large French–Belgian groups and located in Austria, the Netherlands, Norway or Portugal. Another reason is likely to have been company or group policy – for example, supplying the Portuguese market from float plants in Spain (the same French group has large shareholding interests in both the Portuguese company and the Spanish float plants), or Dutch requirements from Belgian float plants.

The newest flat glass plant (a non-float plant) built in Europe at the end of the 1960s may explain the background to the decision not to apply the float process. This plant was erected on a greenfield site in Denmark, as a joint Swedish–Danish venture. After commissioning, the Swedish group closed down its glass factory in Sweden. The plant operates basically on the Pittsburgh principle and the decision favouring this technique was supported by the following arguments:

(a) that demand for plate glass in Scandinavia would lag behind the quantity produced by even one float line;
(b) that the float process (at that time) could not produce the thinner sheet glass, for which there was a demand.

The more conventional technique was therefore adopted, despite the admitted advantages of the float process.[1] In other words, a float plant, because its capacity could not have been fully utilised, would have been unprofitable in this particular case.

The dynamic development of the process extended its competitive advantages into thinner glass outside the 'plate grades', so that a wider range of flat glass has recently become 'float-worthy' and accessible to smaller markets and companies. Thus firms which just a few years ago rationally rejected the process may take a different line in the future. At the time of the inquiry (up to the end of 1970), this had not yet happened.

Management
It is reasonable to suppose that some time after the innovation was made public, the management of most glassmaking companies gave serious

[1] This can also be explained on technical grounds. A tank of the same capacity serves one float line or six to eight drawing machines (as, for example, in the Pittsburgh method). One float line gives glass of the same thickness, whereas six to eight machines can provide different

consideration to adopting the float process. This resulted in a decision either to reject or to adopt the new technique.

Rejection might have been a rational decision, as in the Swedish–Danish example above, which was not a unique case. It is known that the float technique was also rejected on similar grounds in Austria and in Australia,[1] and probably in other cases as well. Further, it is quite obvious that, at least during most of the 1960s, the big holding companies' business policy was to concentrate float production in one of their plants, if they controlled several in one market area; for their other plants, they rejected the new idea, at least temporarily.

Furthermore, the conversion of existing production facilities to a float line is not a simple matter. This might have been why the French–Belgian group built an entirely new plant for float glass (and indeed founded a separate company for this purpose) in Germany, instead of associating it with any of the companies existing in that country, of which five out of seven were associated with the same holding group.

The fact that by now all major producers, and none of the minor ones, have adopted the float process seems to support the hypothesis that the smaller producers' management decisions were made on rational grounds, and the outcome was the rejection of this new technique. It is more difficult to explain the delays in adoption among large producers.

The first licence was granted by Pilkington to Pittsburgh in July 1962, three years after the announcement of the innovation. It was significant that the first licensee was Pittsburgh, the owner of the process considered by most experts the most efficient for producing sheet glass in pre-float times. The other two big American companies followed quite quickly, in 1963 and 1964.[2] The lags between the first and the following plants were longer elsewhere: the first two licences to Japanese firms were granted in 1964, a third four years later; the first float plant in Belgium was commissioned in 1965, the second five years later.

The various factors detailed above (such as existing equipment and access to capital) must have played some part in these delays in various companies. Differences in environmental and other circumstances might also have affected the timing of a decision involving a huge capital commitment. Besides, the delays have to be seen in perspective,

grades. The float process is, in this sense, less flexible than the earlier processes, although this can, of course, be overcome if, say, three float lines are in operation, but this requires production on a very large scale.

[1] P. Stubbs, *Innovation and Research*, Melbourne, F. W. Cheshire, 1968, p. 42.

[2] The fourth, Combustion Engineering, was a relative newcomer in the glass industry; it took over a medium-sized glass company in 1968, and then bought the licence soon after, in 1970.

in the light of past reactions in this industry to major innovations.[1] The facts that within about ten years all the major producers of the world have introduced the float process, and that in most large companies significant intra-firm diffusion has also been achieved, indicate that the dissemination of this expensive new technique has been quite fast compared with other similarly expensive new processes.

SUMMARY AND CONCLUSIONS

The float process is a revolutionary new technique for making a product equivalent or superior to high-quality polished plate glass, at considerably lower capital and running costs. Most of the world's important makers of this product have now introduced it and, although the adoption in some cases followed with a timelag, this was shorter than in important earlier innovations in the industry. This is the best illustration of diffusion in an industry which is dominated by big groups, so much so that in continental Western Europe we can hardly speak of national industries.

Since the successful launching of the float process, all new works with a large capacity in 'float-worthy' products have been built on the float principle. Existing, relatively new equipment and access to the large amount of capital required for a float plant have been the main factors influencing the timing of adoption by the large producers. The producers for smaller markets were, however, in a different position. They produced a limited quantity of plate glass only – less than the output of even one float plant. They therefore retained other methods; and indeed some of them built new capacity embodying earlier techniques. Only recently has the float process been developed further, making it possible to reduce the original five millimetre thickness of the float glass to two millimetres, a dynamic development, which is one of several departures from the initial invention and which has opened new areas for future expansion.

[1] A comparison can be made with an earlier successful and important process in the same area, twin-grinding. This was developed in 1935, also by Pilkington, and licensed eventually to most of the world's plate glass manufacturers. The first licence was granted in 1937 to St Gobain, but no further licences were negotiated until after the war, i.e. there was a lag of at least nine years. Continental operators could have bought the licence, as St Gobain did, before the war, and there were no obstacles preventing American companies from introducing this new process during the war (see Monopolies Commission, *Flat Glass*, p. 9).

Further references

L. A. B. Pilkington, ' Float glass ', *Advance*, no. 1, November 1966, pp. 12–19, and ' The development of float glass ', *Glass Industry*, vol. 44, February 1963, pp. 80–1; K. J. B. Earle, ' The development of the float glass process and the future of the glass industry ', *Chemistry and Industry*, 15 July 1967; Patent Specification, London, no. 769,692, 1957; US Patent no. 2,911,759.

CHAPTER 8

THE APPLICATION OF GIBBERELLIC ACID IN MALTING

By G. F. Ray, NIESR

GIBBERELLIC ACID

In 1926 a Japanese scientist, Kurosawa, showed that an extract from the fungus *Gibberella fujikuroi* caused abnormal growth in rice and other plants.[1] The substance gibberellin was, however, first crystallised only in 1938 and shown to have several components; one of them is gibberellic acid, the pure extract of which was identified chemically in early 1950 by Dr P. W. Brian and a team of biologists from Imperial Chemical Industries.[2] In Europe the first report on it from a Swedish investigator, Dr E. Sandegren, was published in 1958 and presented to the European Brewing Convention in 1959.[3] Since then there have been a number of experiments both at pilot and at commercial level, and gibberellic acid has been widely adopted in malting.[4]

Malting is the preliminary stage of brewing, in which the grain – mainly barley – is converted into malt. There are three main steps. First, steeping, when the barley is soaked in water for 48–70 hours. Next comes germination, of which the traditional method was to turn the steeped, drained barley on to the malting floor, but now most plants use more modern (box and drum) methods. Whatever the method, the grain loses weight and changes from a hard mass to the soft texture of the malt over a period of eleven to twelve days at a lower temperature, or seven to eight days if the temperature is higher. Finally, in drying and curing the malt is transferred to the kilns for about 24 hours to remove the excess moisture.

Gibberellic acid is applied at the steeping stage or, more frequently,

[1] E. Kurosawa (article in Japanese on the discovery of the fungus from which gibberellic acid is derived), *Transactions of the Natural History Society of Formosa*, vol. 16, April 1926.

[2] British patents nos. 783,611 and 811,374 of 1959.

[3] E. Sandegren and H. Beling, 'Versuch mit Gibberellinsäure bei der Malzherstellung', *Monatsschrift für Brauerei*, vol. 11, part 12, 1958, p. 231ff.

[4] D. E. Briggs, 'Effects of gibberellic acid on barley germination and its use in malting. A review', *Journal of the Institute of Brewing*, vol. 69, 1963, p. 244ff; R. F. Bawden, R. V. Dahlstrom and M. R. Sfat, 'Effect of growth regulators on barley malt', *American Society of Brewing Chemists. Proceedings of the Annual Meeting 1959*, p. 137ff; W. Kieber, M. Lindemann and P. Schmid, 'Kleinmälzungsversuche mit Gibberellinsäure', *Brauwelt*, vol. 99, nos. 93–4, 1959, p. 1781ff; H. Stadler, H. Kipphahn and S. Siegfried, 'Zur Gibberellinsäureverwendung beim Mälzen', *Brauwelt*, vol. 100, no. 68, 1960, p. 1361ff.

at the beginning of germination; it causes the grain to germinate much more rapidly, the normal period of seven to eight days (depending on temperature) being reduced to five or six, which is a significant saving in time. It also reduces malting loss, increases the yield and quality of the extract[1] and can eliminate dormancy.[2]

Imperial Chemical Industries is one of the world's important producers of gibberellic acid, which is produced under licence from that company in the United States. There are other producers in Belgium, Japan, Poland, Hungary, and the USSR.

THE MALTING INDUSTRY

Malting proper is a relatively minor industry. Most malt is used by brewers, who make a very large proportion of it, but maltsters may also make malt for other uses, such as distilling.

Table 8.1. *Concentration in brewing industries: the ratio of enterprises to plants*[a]

	Ratio
Austria	0·88
France	0·77
Italy	0·74
Sweden	0·43
United Kingdom	0·48
West Germany	0·97

SOURCE: Deutscher Brauer-Bund e.V., *Statistischer Bericht, 1969*, Bad Godesberg, Bonn.

[a] This indicates just one aspect of concentration and omits size or financial associations between enterprises. A ratio of 1 would mean that each enterprise owned only one brewery; the nearer to 0 the ratio, the more plants are (on average) owned by one company and the higher the concentration in this sense.

The industrial concentration varies between the different countries covered by the inquiry; it is highest in the United Kingdom and Sweden, and lowest in Germany. In 1963 there were 142 companies (employing 25 or more) in the United Kingdom engaged in brewing or malting, and 48 of them sold malt; the three largest companies accounted for 31 per cent of total output, and the seven largest for 57 per cent.[3] As a result of mergers and amalgamations this concentration has increased further since 1963. In Sweden nine companies make malt;

[1] Briggs, 'Effects of gibberellic acid on barley germination'.   [2] See p. 229 below.
[3] The number of companies employing over 25 fell from 233 in 1958 to 142 in 1963. In the same period the number of all brewing–malting enterprises (including those employing less than 25) fell from 311 to 196.

four of them belonging to one group of brewer–maltsters produce about 90 per cent of it. In Italy four companies produce more than half of all beer.

One measure of concentration is the ratio of brewing enterprises to breweries (plants). This is shown in table 8.1 for the countries investigated. The importance of the brewing industry varies greatly between countries; beer consumption per head is high in Germany, Austria and the United Kingdom, moderate in France and Sweden, and low in Italy (table 8.2).

Table 8.2. *Output and consumption of beer*

	Output		Consumption	
	1960	1966	1960	1966
	(million hectolitres)		(litres per head)	
Austria	5·3	7·3	75	100
France	17·3	20·2	37	42
Italy	2·5	5·2	5	10
Sweden[a]	2·7	2·9	36	40
United Kingdom	43·4	49·4	87	94
West Germany	53·7	76·0	95	126

SOURCE: national data.

[a] Including light beer (under 1·8 per cent alcohol).

Two factors affect the structure of the industry: first, most countries make their own malt, although Italy is an exception and imports about half of its requirements (mainly from France);[1] secondly, most British brewers maintain a large number of 'tied houses' – retail outlets – which provide a valuable distributive network, and the distribution system in Germany is similar, though not so restricted generally.

INNOVATION AND ADOPTION

We started with a number of straightforward hypotheses, postulating that:

(a) all potential users knew of the innovation;

(b) differences between companies in expected profitability would result in different decisions concerning this innovation;

(c) access to capital and the size of the investment required would influence adoption;

[1] Sweden too exports and imports considerable quantities.

(d) the so-called 'bandwagon' effect (joining the successful) would influence diffusion of the new technique;

(e) different management attitudes were extremely important and would greatly influence diffusion;

(f) the structure of the industry would influence diffusion, for example by means of differences in behaviour between large and small firms.

Clearly these hypotheses overlap and the interactions of the various factors cannot be entirely disentangled; for example, expected profitability affects risk-taking and hence management attitudes, as does the size of the company, or the 'bandwagon' effect may just be a symptom, reflecting the combined outcome of the working of a number of factors more conveniently analysed when testing other hypotheses.

These were the initial hypotheses. Very soon, indeed at the stage of a pilot feasibility study, it became clear that another important factor, namely legislative regulations, influenced the adoption and diffusion of the process quite basically. This had a substantial effect on the organisation of the inquiry. In Germany a survey would have been meaningless as gibberellic acid is not allowed; and only basic information was collected in France, where limited use became legal in May 1966.[1] In Austria, although there is no ban, gibberellic acid is not used by brewers or by maltsters; in Italy, the legal position is unclear.[2]

The first application of gibberellic acid on a commercial scale was in the United Kingdom and Sweden in 1959. At least two companies in the United Kingdom were already using gibberellic acid in 1955 for conditioning the barley, but this was considered experimental. French maltsters started to use gibberellic acid in 1966–7, and it is also used in large quantities in the Irish Republic, Australia, Belgium and Canada, more moderately in Poland, Czechoslovakia and a number of other countries. The United States belongs to this last group (at least until 1969), perhaps due partly to the German-oriented outlook of American brewers and partly to the fact that maltsters initially put a premium on treated barley. Gibberellic acid has become increasingly popular throughout the world, although in a few countries, such as Switzerland, it is illegal as in Germany.

The take-off and the tailing-off periods usually observed in the life-cycle of innovations are shown for the United Kingdom (chart 8.1), The pioneers, in both Britain and Sweden were all larger companies;

---

[1] The maximum is 0.5 grammes per ton of barley, compared with up to 2.0 grammes (depending on conditions) in the United Kingdom and the United States.

[2] An application was filed years ago with the Ministry of Health but no decision had been reached by 1969. Probably gibberellic acid is used on a moderate scale in the Italian industry.

Chart 8.1. *Sample companies in the United Kingdom using gibberellic acid*

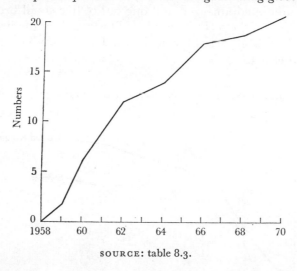

SOURCE: table 8.3.

medium-sized and smaller firms only started using gibberellic acid in about 1962, three years after the introduction by the pioneering companies.

In Sweden, of nine firms producing malt, only three use gibberellic acid, but they account for 94 per cent of malt production. Of the British firms which cooperated in the inquiry, nine out of ten large brewers and

Table 8.3. *The use of gibberellic acid[a]*

	1960	1962	1964	1966	1968	1970
Number of users						
Sweden	1	2	2	2	3	3
United Kingdom	6	11	14	18	19	21
Treated malt			(percentages)			
Sweden						
Large firms	1	55	57	52	49	52
Total	*1*	*50*	*51*	*49*	*48*	*51*
United Kingdom						
Large brewers	20	55	67	79	85	87
Medium brewers	—	8	15	52	53	58
Small brewers	—	1	2	1	1	2
Maltsters	23	44	54	45	57	63
Total	*16*	*46*	*57*	*63*	*70*	*73*

SOURCE: inquiry.

[a] Among responding firms (9 in Sweden, 31 in the United Kingdom), except for total percentages of treated malt, which are estimates of national totals.

six out of seven maltsters were using gibberellic acid, but not more than
four out of nine medium-sized and one out of five small brewers.[1]

The diffusion of the technique is best illustrated by the percentage of
malt treated with gibberellic acid in total malt production, which is
shown in table 8.3.

Chart 8.2. *Shares of malt production treated with gibberellic acid*

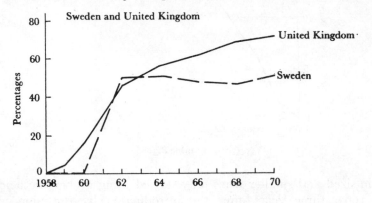

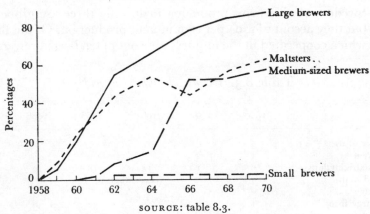

SOURCE: table 8.3.

Note: Large, medium-sized and small brewers defined as in the footnote below.

In Sweden and the United Kingdom the initial breakthrough
occurred between 1959 and 1962 (see chart 8.2), but later there was a
marked difference between the diffusion curves of the two countries. In
Sweden the use of gibberellic acid appears to have reached a plateau in

[1] Large brewers were taken as those with an annual output of over 1 million barrels; small
brewers as those with an annual output of under 100,000 barrels (1 barrel = 36 gallons =
1·64 hectolitres).

1962, whereas in the United Kingdom there was a considerable further increase in diffusion among both large and medium-sized firms; indeed, the use of gibberellic acid by medium-sized British brewers started to spread when it had already levelled off in Sweden, and followed the diffusion path in large brewing companies with a delay of approximately four years.

THE INQUIRY AND ITS FINDINGS

The purpose of the inquiry was to assess the factors which influence the introduction of the new technique and its diffusion, and to try and detect the reasons for any major international differences. As already explained, it was in practice confined to Sweden and the United Kingdom.

Replies from Swedish firms covered 100 per cent of the industry. In the United Kingdom all large and medium-sized maltsters and brewers, and a sample of small brewers, were approached. The replies covered about 80 per cent of all malt in 83 malting plants and are thought to be representative of the whole British industry, although small and medium-sized companies are somewhat under-represented.

Legal regulations

In the case of this process the legal position played a fundamental part. The fact that, in Germany, gibberellic acid is totally prohibited invalidates the assumption on which all such inquiries are based – that the new process is always applicable unless peculiarities of the company's technological conditions exclude it, so that adoption or rejection is a management decision based on rational economic considerations. However, legal prohibition or administrative non-admittance takes precedence. Many food and drink regulations go back a long way in history and it is obviously not easy to alter them; for the purpose of this inquiry they had to be accepted as a fact of life.

A wide variety of edible plants, including barley, maize and beans contain a certain amount of gibberellic acid and allied gibberellins – in some cases significantly more than the amount applied in malting. Furthermore, the natural gibberellic acid content of barley and other plants may vary greatly according to conditions of weather, season, variety and growth; a ten-fold variation is not uncommon.

Toxological tests were first carried out in Japan and the United States. Massive doses were administered to rats (some 25 grammes per kilogramme body weight in one case) without any evidence of toxic or carcinogenic reactions.

The United States Food and Drug Administration, which clears food additives only after the most critical examination, permits gibberellic acid provided the residues in the malt do not exceed 2 grammes per ton, which is incomparably more than the usual residue of something like 0·0015–0·0030 grammes per ton. In France the Ministry of Agriculture has recently (in 1966) approved the use of gibberellic acid, again after a long period of consideration. In the United Kingdom a committee representing the Ministry of Agriculture, the Ministry of Health, the Medical Research Council, the Ministry of Labour and the Home Office, which advises on the safe use of food additives, reported that 'the addition of 0·25 to 2·0 grammes per ton of gibberellic acid should lead to no user or consumer hazard'.

German scientists demonstrated that gibberellic acid was completely destroyed in hot water in $2\frac{1}{2}$ hours, and British investigations showed that malt prepared with 0·2 grammes of gibberellic acid per ton contained a residue of only 0·0015 grammes per ton after kilning, which is significantly less than the amount of natural gibberellic acid known to be present in barley.

On this evidence there seems to be no reason why the use of gibberellic acid in brewing should be regarded as a hazard to health.

Information

Our first hypothesis was that all potential users knew of the new technique. The inquiry among the users did not provide any evidence either for or against this. Among non-users, some admitted that they knew of gibberellic acid early on, but others, especially smaller firms, could not remember or find any record of the innovation, which was first publicly reported more than ten years ago.

This led us to a study, largely conducted in Britain, of the information system within the brewing industry. 'Before information can contribute to the innovation process there must be a suitable channel of communication along which it can flow.'[1] Were there any such channels in the world of brewing, and was information concerning gibberellic acid actually flowing along them?

In the United Kingdom there are two institutions, the Institute of Brewing and the Incorporated Brewers' Guild, whose principal purpose is the dissemination of technological knowledge in the brewing and allied industries. These bodies organise the reading of papers on brewing technology in many centres, with particular emphasis on new developments or discoveries and inventions in the relevant fields. Both publish journals; that of the Guild concentrates on technology, whereas the *Journal of the Institute of Brewing* is regarded as the leading publication on brewing science in the world, each issue containing original papers and also a large quantity of abstracts culled from scientific literature in

[1] L. J. Anthony, 'Introduction' to *Accelerating Innovation*, London, ASLIB, 1970.

Britain and abroad. These widely disseminated journals are not the only specialised publications on brewing in the United Kingdom.

There are no organisations operating on a comparable scale in Sweden, possibly because the Swedish industry is to a large extent dominated by one group of companies, which is likely to have its own internal information system. However, on the international level, the European Brewing Convention has the task of facilitating scientific and technological interchange between countries. This is done principally by means of biennial congresses at which many scientific papers (some 30 or 40) are read. (The 1967 congress in Madrid was attended by some 1,500 brewers and scientists, from practically all European countries.) The European Brewing Convention also organises periodic symposia on special topics. These facilities are available to anyone from within the European industry, and indeed many of the smallest companies are represented.

The properties of gibberellic acid were amply reported in the journals of the brewing world. The first substantial discussion was at the 1959 Convention (although Sandegren's basic report had already been published in 1958 in the leading German scientific journal on brewing). Furthermore, Imperial Chemical Industries and the other producers also did their best to publicise the new technique by advertisements and in other ways. At the time of launching, all maltsters in the United Kingdom were informed of the value of gibberellic acid to them.

Dissemination of new knowledge is also aided by the spirit of co-operation and interchange which is traditional in brewing (at least in the British Isles). It seems that in this industry there are hardly any technological secrets; technical directors and senior staff of the different companies regularly visit each other's breweries to discuss new developments.

According to Thompson, the main barriers to information transfer can be summarised in two phrases: 'don't know' and 'don't want to know'.[1] The first can probably be ruled out (at least in Britain); all brewers were in a position to know of gibberellic acid, and most of them are likely actually to have known of it, shortly after it had become an applicable invention. With a few possible exceptions among the tiniest breweries, there could only be two possibilities – adoption or rejection of the innovation. Lack of information as a third alternative could not have been important and was probably negligible. On the other hand, the lack of desire to change – 'don't want to know' – was apparently widespread, certainly among the smaller companies.

We can therefore conclude that the assumption that all potential

[1] S. K. L. Thompson, 'Barriers to information transfer and technological change' in *Accelerating Innovation*, London, ASLIB, 1970.

users knew of the innovation is substantially correct, so that non-use is likely to have been a deliberate decision. Possible reasons for rejection are further analysed below. Major delay in using gibberellic acid was probably also deliberate.

Profitability

Answers to the inquiry regarding the impact of profitability on diffusion showed that the chief economic advantages of gibberellic acid lay in speeding up the malting process, reducing malting loss and increasing the extract, but such advantages were difficult to quantify, partly because the introduction of gibberellic acid was often connected with other improvements in the works. As a crude approximation, however, a *new* malting plant would produce, according to expert views, some 25 per cent more malt with gibberellic acid than otherwise. This would mean a 20 per cent reduction in capital costs and also in part of the labour costs. Indeed, plants built between 1960 and 1966 (at least in Britain) were in fact designed for the use of gibberellic acid.

In existing plants the savings with gibberellic acid varied. Both Swedish and British users stressed increased production and thereby savings in capital and labour costs. (In no case was additional labour required.) Savings in material costs and improvement in the quality of the malt were also frequently mentioned, although they were less important. A 15 to 25 per cent rise in output and productivity (of the malting plant) was fairly typical of the large brewers in the United Kingdom.

In another group of existing plants the economies worked out differently: germination, the process which gibberellic acid accelerates, is only one part, though an important one, of the whole malting process; the last stage – kilning – is often a bottleneck, especially in small plants, and is expensive to expand. There is not much point, therefore, in using gibberellic acid in a balanced plant unless kilning and all auxiliary parts of the production process can be expanded as well; if only germination is speeded up, costs may actually increase. This is probably the only case where, in general terms, gibberellic acid might be disadvantageous.

Indeed a few small companies seem to have rejected gibberellic acid on this ground; their calculations of expected profitability yielded a negative result. However, such cases were few, so that they are unlikely to be a complete explanation of the startling lack of interest in gibberellic acid by the smaller companies.

There is, of course, no point in introducing a change aimed at increasing capacity when there is no demand for additional output. A few British companies stated that this was the reason for their lack of interest in gibberellic acid, and similar situations may be found elsewhere. Austrian capacity corresponds with demand, and in Italy there appears to be a wide margin of unused capacity.

Investment

Theories which explain the diffusion of new techniques in terms of the size of investment as one of the influencing factors are not applicable to gibberellic acid, since more often than not its application requires no investment at all. Out of 22 companies which gave information, 15 put the capital cost at nil. In five of the other seven cases the capital expenditure could be covered within one to two years by the saving in operating costs resulting from the new process.

However, the introduction of gibberellic acid may require supplementary investment for ' balancing ' the malting plant; in the United Kingdom this can be affected by alternative uses for any available capital. Development of 'tied houses', for example, modernisation or enlargement of existing ones, acquisition or building of new premises, may be more profitable or more necessary than any improvement in production facilities. The situation may therefore arise where retailing is competing with the production side of the same organisation for a limited amount of capital. The inquiry showed that in a number of cases the retail outlets were preferred, and this might be a reason for not introducing this new technique, or for making no change at all in the production process.

The 'bandwagon' effect

This effect is clearly proved in Britain (see chart 8.1). The innovation was first applied commercially in 1959; a year later six companies among the sample firms were using gibberellic acid, by 1962 another five had joined them, and nine years after the initial introduction there were 19 users.

Least squares analysis was applied to the British data to see whether any regular relationships could be detected. The trend of diffusion was measured by:

E_t the number of firms which had adopted gibberellic acid t years after its introduction;

P_t the percentage of all malt treated with gibberellic acid in year t;

P_t^* the percentage of large firms' production of malt treated with gibberellic acid in year t.

It seemed that a logistic curve $A \exp(B/t)$ would provide the best fit,[1]

[1] This was the result that Mansfield arrived at using diffusion data on twelve innovations in four industries in the United States for the period 1890–1958 ('Technical change and the rate of imitation').

and this was calculated on the logarithms of the three variables. The results are shown in table 8.4. They demonstrate with remarkable regularity the 'bandwagon' effect, as well as the logistic diffusion curve both for all companies and for large firms alone.[1] Nevertheless, their interpretation poses difficulties. Strictly speaking the concept implies a philosophy of imitation amongst companies and assumes that firms introduce a new technique mainly or solely because other companies have applied it earlier, presumably with good results. However, this is rather unlikely; possibly the fact of other companies using gibberellic acid induced 'followers' to devote more (and earlier) attention to the question, but beyond this they probably arrived at their decision on the merits of the innovation as applied to their own specific case. Thus, the equations probably demonstrate an effect rather than a cause, and have more descriptive than analytical or explanatory value.

Table 8.4. *Least squares analysis: users and non-users in the United Kingdom*

Dependent variable	Estimates of coefficients		Variance of B	R^2	Standard error
	A	B			
E_t	23·91	−2·60	0·0257	0·970	±0·160
P_t	102·28	−3·62	0·0331	0·990	±0·182
P_t^*	122·28	−3·55	0·0231	0·993	±0·152

SOURCE: NIESR estimates.

Notes: (i) All equations of the form $\log Y = A \exp(B/t)$.
(ii) Dependent variables (Y) as defined on p. 225.
(iii) Results for E_t based on 11 years 1960–70, for P_t and P_t^* on the 6 years for which figures given in table 8.3.

Management attitudes

We have already established that most brewers and maltsters probably knew, and certainly had the means to know, of gibberellic acid almost from the beginning. They also knew that this technique required little or no investment. Hence delayed application and non-application must have been the outcome of a deliberate rejection, or of a lack of desire to change.

Deliberate rejection may be the outcome of thorough discussions, investigations and perhaps even experiments – in other words, some action of the management – and, although the resulting decision was against the new technique, the management's approach might have been just as scientific as the approach by those companies which did introduce gibberellic acid. Some of the many comments obtained in the

[1] Further curve fitting experiments gave less favourable results.

course of the inquiry from firms which rejected gibberellic acid included 'quality might suffer', 'the colour would be darker', and 'not suitable for certain types of beer'. These and similar remarks indicate the great care most brewers take to maintain the quality of their product in every possible respect. Colour may have nothing to do with the quality or flavour of the beer, yet it is considered important. It may be quite correct that a change in the colour or the flavour of beer has an adverse impact on sales, which of course would mean that this innovation could lead to a loss. Nevertheless, such reservations are difficult to reconcile with the experience of those who do treat their malt with gibberellic acid. The reference to 'certain types of beer' meant mainly lager, yet other companies seem to have had no difficulty at all in producing lager from treated malt.

Other typical replies from very small producers of malt were 'customer's refusal' (if the maltster's customer, the brewer, will not accept malt treated with gibberellic acid, obviously it will not be used), 'malt production too small for any innovation', 'no advantage in speeding up germination time' and 'not worth spending on old-fashioned malting plant'. Some of these respondents have correctly recognised the importance of the balance of the plant and therefore rejected gibberellic acid, but the other comments are more dubious.

Comments from brewers who had successfully introduced gibberellic acid included 'the control of fermentation was made more difficult' and 'certain processing problems arose'. These may throw light on difficulties facing small firms in general, and some larger firms in particular situations. The dosage of gibberellic acid demands great care and depends on the condition of the barley and the local requirements of the maltsters; without such care satisfactory results cannot be achieved. There are companies which either do not wish to introduce this additional sophistication or, in the case of smaller firms, cannot afford it. The nature and size of their business does not permit them to employ professional managers or technologists for controlling this more scientific process, or indeed to evaluate the advantages of such new processes.

These replies confirm the importance of management attitudes, in regard to new ideas as well as to risk-taking, as an influence on diffusion. They also point to the deterrent effects of the complications of a new process.

Size of firms

Our last hypothesis concerned the structure of the industry. The inquiry among British firms showed that there were considerable differences in behaviour between smaller firms and medium-sized or larger ones. This was especially striking in the level of diffusion achieved: large companies were the pioneers, medium-sized companies followed with a marked timelag (approximately four years), but small brewers hardly at all.

The same difference is reflected in the answers received concerning future plans of the companies; additional use of gibberellic acid is planned by a number of large companies and also a handful of medium-sized ones (some of them have detailed plans which stipulate the percentage of malt to be treated with gibberellic acid in each year until a maximum is reached). In sharp contrast, small companies convey the same lack of interest for the future as they have shown in the past. No doubt the main reason for this behaviour is the higher degree of professional works management which the process requires and which small firms may not be able to afford.

Another possibility is suggested by the simple concentration comparison presented as an enterprise–plant ratio in table 8.1: gibberellic acid was disseminated rapidly only in two countries, the United Kingdom and Sweden, where concentration – in these terms – was the highest. Low concentration may help to explain the lack of interest in the other countries, and this international comparison supports the view, based on the British inquiry, that larger size favours faster diffusion of this process.

INTRA-FIRM DIFFUSION

Introducing an innovation, such as gibberellic acid, and applying it to the whole of a company's production are two very different things. We therefore analysed the internal diffusion within the using companies, and two factors appeared to be of great importance:

(1) The natural presence of gibberellic acid in barley varies greatly, as already explained. The desirable dosage of gibberellic acid (and in the extreme case, even the initial adoption of the process) varies with this natural content. It is also known that lack of interest in gibberellic acid in Italy is partly because most malt there is made of imported barley, and maltsters prefer to purchase barley naturally rich in gibberellic acid. Maltsters and brewers in other countries using mainly home-produced barley probably have less choice, but this cannot be entirely ruled out as a factor with a limited effect on overall diffusion.

(2) Gibberellic acid is very versatile: within the malting industry it can be used to shorten the period of dormancy, as well as to reduce germination time, and to increase yields and reduce malting losses.[1]

[1] It also increases diastatic power, but this mainly concerns distillers and maltsters producing for distilling, not brewers.

There is a period of dormancy in barley's growth cycle as in that of many plants. During this time the grain is maturing physiologically and until this has occurred it will not germinate even under favourable conditions. Length of dormancy is related to variety and to many other factors, such as environment and drying conditions. Gibberellic acid shortens the length of the dormant period appreciably, although it cannot remove dormancy completely. The question therefore arises, even for companies using gibberellic acid, of whether to tie up working capital by holding larger stocks of mature barley to 'bridge' the dormant period of the new crop, or to apply gibberellic acid to enable the maltster to use the new crop sooner. The answer affects profitability and depends on the particular situation of the company. Any decision is also likely to be influenced by the liquidity position.

Returns from 23 British and Swedish companies contained information which may throw some light on this point, as well as on diffusion within the company. Seven respondents obviously considered gibberellic acid valuable but did not envisage ever applying it to all the malt they produced; they estimated the maximum diffusion within the company as between 50 and 79 per cent. The 'dormancy' question probably explains a considerable part of the shortfall, although there are other reasons too, such as keeping part of their malt free of gibberellic acid to comply with particular requirements of certain buyers, to make special types of beer, or to allow for some barley naturally rich in gibberellic acid.

Another feature is the caution which surrounded the wider use of gibberellic acid even after introduction. Among 14 companies which thought that gibberellic acid would eventually be extended to their total malt output, not more than five had actually reached this stage (100 per cent diffusion) two years after the initial introduction, and in the course of another two years, two more companies joined them. The intra-firm diffusion indicator in the lower ranges has also been moving upwards, but at a fairly moderate pace.

The various possible ways of using gibberellic acid explain the very different course of diffusion in Sweden and Britain.[1] As shown in chart 8.2, usage levelled off at about 50 per cent of all malt production in Sweden, whereas it continued to advance in Britain.[2]

The majority of Swedish companies use gibberellic acid only during

[1] Another significant difference between the Swedish and British companies was that the former reached their own maximum degree of application of the new technique within three years of introduction, whereas in the United Kingdom this took considerably longer.

[2] In Britain in the last two to three years, there have been considerable steps forward in the conversion of barley to malt, involving re-steeping in hot-water. This is yet another new technique in malting, at present still in the development stage; if successfully applied to large-scale production it may eliminate the use of gibberellic acid.

part of the year. The grain is normally harvested there in the early autumn and the new crop is used for malting from the beginning of the following year (January or February). Until then, part of the barley is treated with gibberellic acid mainly in order to shorten the dormancy period, but also to speed up subsequent germination. For the barley used later, in the spring or summer, gibberellic acid is not required. Thus, the major users apply gibberellic acid during some four months only. (Another Swedish producer uses it during most of the year but in various concentrations.) The reason, therefore, for the apparent stagnation in Sweden is that maltsters there do not consider it necessary to use gibberellic acid throughout the year or for the whole malt production. The timing and nature of the crop is different in Britain, and this may explain why the same phenomenon did not arise.

If we could assess a 'technically feasible maximum' for the use of gibberellic acid, taking into account the practices of each company and other relevant factors, the Swedish diffusion rate would be near to 100 per cent; the British rate too would be higher than shown, but still considerably below this maximum.

SUMMARY AND CONCLUSIONS

A number of factors have a significant influence on the diffusion of gibberellic acid in malting; most of them are likely to be relevant to the diffusion of new techniques generally.

(1) Legislation and administrative regulations do not permit the new process in some countries. In view of the international trade in malt, the prohibition of gibberellic acid under German (and Swiss) law may influence its introduction in neighbouring countries as well, even though it is not prohibited there.

(2) Gibberellic acid profitably increases the capacity of one important part of the malting plant; but speeding up output of one section of the whole production line may lead to bottlenecks. If the plant is initially in balance and this cannot be maintained, the introduction of gibberellic acid may not be profitable (it may indeed lead to a loss) and there is no scope for the new technique. Nor is there any point in the adoption of a new process which adds to capacity when in fact this additional capacity is unwanted.

(3) This is one of the very few new techniques which can be adopted without any – or with negligible – capital investment. Nevertheless, it provides an example of the dilemma facing management when allocating a given amount of investment capital. In this case the choice is not between particular techniques or processes

from among competing technologies, but between two different
activities – production or retailing – a situation stemming from
the structure of the British brewing industry.

(4) This technique is complicated and may be too difficult to
introduce at the level of professionalism generally present in the
simpler plants. The dosage of gibberellic acid and the way it is
administered, combined with the changing natural characteristics
of the barley, can be crucial, and without a certain amount of
sophistication satisfactory results cannot be achieved. This may
help to explain its lack of appeal to small producers, who wish
to avoid these complications or cannot afford the professional
staff.

(5) The difference in the attitude to this new technique of the
management of companies of different size was striking. Large
companies were the pioneers, medium-sized firms followed them
with a marked timelag and the small ones hardly at all.

(6) The versatility of gibberellic acid, the fluctuations in the quality
of barley crops, and the particular conditions in individual plants
may affect the expected profitability and thus lead to different
practices among users.

All these factors point to the importance of the situation within
individual companies, which greatly affect technical possibilities as
well as management thinking, and therefore have both direct and indirect implications for the diffusion of any new technique. Apart from
this, however, there still is plenty of scope for bolder and more enter-
prising, as well as very cautious and conservative, management; the
inquiry provided examples of both extremes.

CHAPTER 9

CONTINUOUS CASTING OF STEEL

By W. Schenk, OIW[1]

INTRODUCTION

The aim of this chapter is two-fold – to describe the diffusion of the continuous casting of steel and to show why it has developed in the pattern observed.

Since continuous casting is still in quite an early phase of diffusion, we could not expect to discover functional relationships stable enough to comprise an econometric model; for the same reason it was not possible to test empirically some hypotheses put forward in other earlier research on the diffusion of new technologies. Thus a less ambitious analytical method was necessary – an explorative approach. Hypotheses were formulated and tested against the empirical evidence provided by our inquiry; they led to an analysis based on a model in which the variables explaining diffusion were different, or at least of varying importance, in the different phases of the diffusion process. For the reasons already mentioned this model could not be more than a heuristic approach, offering a reasonable explanation of how continuous casting was spreading in the countries considered and how it might be expected to spread in the future.

Technical factors play a dominant part in the early phases of diffusion of complex new processes such as continuous casting and therefore we must first deal with some technical aspects of this process.

THE CONTINUOUS CASTING OF STEEL

There have been attempts to cast steel continuously since the 1830s, but it was not for more than a hundred years, until after World War II, that continuous casting of steel was developed for commercial application, although continuous casting of non-ferrous metals, mainly developed in Germany and the United States, had become a commercial success in the late 1930s.[2]

Casting is the intermediate operation of the three main stages of primary steelmaking – melting, casting and rolling – which finally

---

[1] This project was directed by Robert Ehrlich in its early stages.

[2] A survey of the technical development of continuous casting is given in UNECE, *Economic Aspects of Continuous Casting of Steel*, New York, 1968, ch. 1.

produce semi-finished rolled sections of steel. Conventional ingot casting methods are characterised by the discontinuity of the casting process and the need for primary rolling of the ingots. From the steelmaking unit (LD-converter, open-hearth or electric furnace) the liquid steel is transferred in a ladle and teemed into ingot moulds, which are either separate or a communicating system. In both methods it is necessary to interrupt casting after each ingot or ingot group to cut off ('trim') sizeable quantities at the top and the bottom of the ingots. This results in a significantly reduced yield of semi-finished steel from a given charge in the ladle. After the metal has solidified and cooled, the ingots are withdrawn from the moulds ('stripped'), reheated in soaking pits and transferred to the blooming mill, where they are rolled into slabs, blooms or billets.

Chart 9.1. *Operations in the production of semi-finished steel*

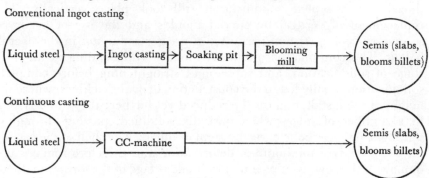

The main purpose of continuous casting is to change the intermittent process of ingot casting into a continuous one, with the liquid metal poured into a mould at the same rate as the solidified metal emerges at the other end. The liquid steel is poured by the teeming ladle into a refractory-lined tundish, from which it flows in an even stream into a reciprocating water-cooled mould. Here the first solidification of the liquid steel takes place; the casting emerges from the mould with a solid outer shell and enters a secondary cooling chamber underneath. During permanent and intensive cooling (preferably by a water-spray), the cast strand, with its core still liquid, is withdrawn continuously by a system of rollers; it passes straightening rollers, solidifies completely and then is cut into pieces of the required length. Thus, the liquid steel is converted into slabs, blooms or other 'semis' for sections. Chart 9.1 shows how continuous casting replaces the soaking pit and blooming mill of conventional ingot casting.

Four main types of continuous casting machines are known. In order of their development they are vertical machines, vertical machines with subsequent bending, curved mould machines, and oval machines.

The pioneering firms, Mannesmann in Germany and Böhler in Austria, originally used vertical machines with straight water-cooled moulds. In these machines not only the casting, but also the subsequent phases – secondary cooling, conveying and cutting – take place vertically. Having been cut to the required length, the 'semis' are tipped over for further horizontal processing in a rolling mill.

Vertical machines are of considerable height (up to 35 metres), which makes them difficult to install in existing plants, so that further development of the machines was desirable. A new design was tested in 1956 at Barrow-in-Furness in the United Kingdom. After being poured and cooled vertically, the cast strand was bent through 90 degrees and, after passing a system of straightening rollers, emerged from the machine horizontally. The overall height of the machine was considerably reduced, but complete solidification still took place vertically. The replacement of vertical by curved moulds and the use of a curved secondary cooling system permitted a greater reduction in the overall height. The combination of curved moulds with bending at an early stage of solidification, and subsequent straightening before complete solidification, finally led to the construction of oval machines, where the height of the installation can be reduced yet further; the strand is bent in a number of stages when partially solidified, passing through a parabolic or hyperbolic curved system of rollers. The shell of the casting undergoes only a minimum of deformation and therefore remains undamaged, thus overcoming a major disadvantage of the former methods of bending and then straightening the strand.

Machines for continuous casting vary in the number of strands which can be cast at the same time. Casting capacity, which is a function of casting speed and section size, can be increased on machines with more than one strand. Machines for slabs generally do not have more than two strands, but machines with up to eight strands are used in producing billets.

HISTORICAL DEVELOPMENT

Austria

After experiments which started in 1947, the commercial introduction of continuous casting began in 1952 at a works mainly producing special steels, with a crude steel output of about 100,000 tons. (The same firm installed a second continuous casting machine in 1967.) In 1954, continuous casting was introduced by a small firm (crude steel output 3,800 tons at that time), which installed a second machine in 1962. In 1958 a third firm, with a crude steel production of 71,000 tons, started continuous casting on a commercial scale, but it shut down the machine in 1966 because of unsatisfactory quality. The first continuous casting machine of the bending type was installed in 1961 at another small steelworks; by 1962 this machine was producing all of the firm's crude steel output of 12,000 tons. In 1965 another small firm started operating a curved continuous casting machine, but the largest Austrian steel producer introduced continuous casting only in 1968. Thus, at the end of 1969, eight continuous casting machines were installed in six companies, but only five firms were actually operating them for commercial production. The final products of continuous casting were mainly hot and cold rolled sheets; one small firm produced light sections and rods, all by continuous casting.

France

Commercial application of continuous casting began about 1960, some eight years after experimental application. Four firms, all producers of special steels, operate five continuous casting lines. Three of the firms are very small and use continuous casting for their total production.

Italy

Continuous casting was first adopted in 1958. The first continuous casting machine, installed by a large state-owned company, remained the only one until 1964, when a relatively small private company started continuous casting with a machine of the progressive bending type. Four other companies followed during the years 1965–7. In 1968 continuous casting was adopted by eight companies and two users installed additional continuous casting machines. There were seven new adopters in 1969 and nine in 1970; in these years, four users installed additional continuous casting machines. By the end of 1970, 30 companies were operating 43 machines. Characteristically, nearly all these companies use electric furnaces and cast billets. Only two continuous casting machines (installed in 1968 and 1970) cast slabs.

Sweden

An experimental continuous casting machine was installed in 1954. Commercial application started in 1963 at a rather small steel company. Three other companies of medium size started to apply continuous casting in the years 1965, 1966 and 1967. Although Sweden is a country with a relatively high production of special steel, all four firms using continuous casting are producing mainly carbon and low-alloy steel for plates and sheets. Another firm installed a continuous casting machine more recently in 1970, and three other companies are planning to introduce continuous casting not later than 1975.

United Kingdom

Experimental continuous casting machines were already installed in 1946 and 1952. Commercial application took place during 1961 and 1962 by companies which were members of the same group. A third firm adopted continuous casting in 1964. Besides these, four other companies installed continuous casting machines for experimental purposes or pilot production only. Thus, by 1968 eleven machines had been installed, but only six of them were operated commercially. One plant uses continuous casting for 100 per cent of production, another for about 95 per cent. Continuously cast finished products are mainly light and heavy sections, and hot rolled flat products.

United States

The first experimental continuous casting machine was installed in 1962. Commercial application started in 1963 and 1964, one of these combining a continuous casting machine with an oxygen furnace for the first time. Nine companies introduced continuous casting in 1965, three in 1966, ten in 1967 and another five in 1968. Thus, by 1968 continuous casting machines were installed in 32 steel companies. Most continuously cast steel is carbon and low-alloy.

West Germany

The commercial application of continuous casting started in about 1950 at one of the plants of a large steel company. Another large and three small firms followed in the years 1958, 1961, 1962 and 1967. In 1967 a continuous casting machine of the curved type with an annual capacity of 1·2 million tons was installed at the pioneer steelworks. A smaller machine of this type had operated there since 1964. Two other large steelmaking firms also introduced continuous casting in 1967, and this can be considered the beginning of the take-off in the diffusion of continuous casting. The largest German steel producer has been using continuous casting since 1969; in the same year it was also introduced by a small firm. In 1970 another large firm installed two continuous casting machines; they are under construction or planned in four further large steel-plants. Continuously cast final products are hot and cold rolled sheets, strips, rods and other light sections of commercial steel, and tubes.

ECONOMIC ASPECTS

The application of continuous casting has to be seen in the light of the general tendency in the steel industry to reduce the effects of heavy investment expenditure and a high proportion of fixed costs. During the last two decades, the level of production considered optimal in integrated steelworks has increased from about two to about ten million tons a year. In order to make full use of the economies of large-scale production, a high rate of utilisation is necessary for the huge plants. This requires continuous operations, or at least the greatest possible batch-size, in melting, as well as in casting, rolling and finishing. However, demand shows a pronounced tendency towards diversification, so that individual orders have to be grouped into identical lots for economic production. Computers have become a necessity for preparing production programmes to achieve the advantages of large-scale production, but, despite all possible rationalisation, there is a point beyond which efforts in this direction begin to yield diminishing returns.

The widening discrepancy between trends in supply and demand explains the emergence and rising importance of so-called 'mini' steelplants. Non-integrated or semi-integrated plants, specialising in a few relatively simple products, have been built in some numbers in recent years; usually they produce 100,000–300,000 tons of steel a year of rather uniform quality. Continuous casting has played a part in this development: as well as reducing capital and space requirements, it removes the need for a blooming mill, which would be uneconomic unless its throughput was at least a million tons a year. Continuous casting machines, on the other hand, can be built for smaller, or indeed for almost any desired level of output, so that they are particularly advantageous in either small steel-plants, or larger plants which want to increase output by smaller steps than the capacity of an additional blooming mill.

Another important feature is the continuity of the casting process, which raises the rate of yield as compared with conventional ingot casting. Firms contacted in our inquiries reported increases in yield (the semi-finished product in relation to the liquid steel tapped from the furnace) ranging from 10 to 25 per cent for different grades of steel; gains are highest for stainless and alloy steels, and modest for rimming carbon steels.

One might therefore conclude that continuous casting is particularly suited to the production of special steels. In fact, most of its early development (especially Austria and the United Kingdom during the 1950s and early 1960s) was intended for application to special steels, because the higher yield was supposed to reduce costs more in this sector than in commercial steels. Also, since the special steel sector – at least in Europe – is dominated by smaller plants, its particular advantages to small plants seemed to reinforce this assumption. But there is an inherent contradiction in the use of continuous casting for special steels. Even small producers are proud of being able to offer a variety of sophisticated steels, each in rather modest quantities. Since any change in the quality of the steel substantially reduces the actual operation time (to allow for cleaning, withdrawing the strands, preparing the machine) the heterogeneous production programme of most special steelmakers does not really permit continuous casting to be used efficiently. Indeed nearly all the non-users in the special steel sector, when asked for their reasons for rejecting continuous casting, answered that the process was unsuitable for their products. Certain problems of quality seem difficult to overcome when special steels are continuously cast, and this, as well as small batch-sizes, has retarded the spread of continuous casting among special steel producers.

As a result of development work, mainly in Germany by Mannesmann and DEMAG, and partly also in Austria by VÖEST, continuous casting of slabs became a reliable and promising technique in the second half of the 1960s, thus opening to it the field of commercial steels and high tonnage plants. The former capacity limitations of continuous casting, probably the main reason why large firms showed little interest in introducing the process,[1] were overcome by constructing large one- or two-strand slab casters with a capacity of up to a million tons a year.

With the introduction of continuous casting on a large scale, reorganisation of the existing melting and rolling operations becomes of crucial importance, although reorganisation problems also occur in small plants. The productivity of continuous casting machines depends to a great extent on actual operation time. To achieve sufficiently high utilisation rates, steel-melting units must provide the necessary charges of liquid steel at regular intervals within rather narrow limits. The combination of continuous casting machines and steelmaking furnaces therefore presupposes regular tapping of the liquid metal, which is difficult with open-hearth furnaces, where heat time is relatively long and liable to fluctuations. The shorter refining time and the possibility of accurately timed metal tapping in the basic oxygen process create favourable conditions for coordinating an LD-converter with continuous casting machines. Empirical evidence from both our inquiry and elsewhere supports this view; the majority of large-scale continuous casting facilities installed or under construction are combined with oxygen converters or related steelmaking units.

THE INQUIRY

Because of the very limited significance of continuous casting as a commercial process, hardly any official statistics on a national level are

---

[1] There is a striking similarity between the spread of continuous casting and that of the basic oxygen process; one of the explanations for the relatively late introduction of the oxygen process by large American steel-plants seems to have been that it took some time to develop LD-converters of sufficient capacity.

available before 1960.[1] Thus it was one of the aims of the inquiry to collect data on the commercial application of continuous casting in the steel industry. Questionnaire surveys were carried out in five Western European countries and the United States. Except for Germany and the United States, the responding firms accounted for all or most of steel production by continuous casting in each country (table 9.1).

Table 9.1. *Coverage of the national samples*

	Number of firms	1966 proportion of national production of:	
		Crude steel	CC steel
		(percentages)	
Austria	6	95	100
Italy	38	10	100
Sweden	23	100	100
United Kingdom	39	58[a]	88
United States	12	40[b]	45[b]
West Germany	14	70	36

SOURCES: inquiry; national data (if not published, provided by the relevant institutes).
    [a] 1965.   [b] 1969.

THE DIFFUSION PATTERN

In the early 1970s continuous casting is playing a gradually increasing role in the steel industries of many industrialised countries and its importance will rise further in the near future. But it should be remembered that it took more than a hundred years to develop it from the basic ideas and experiments for large-scale commercial use. A great deal of experience in the non-ferrous metal industry was necessary to adapt the continuous casting technique to steel; numerous metallurgical and thermo-technical problems prevented successful application until some ten years after World War II.

The first attempt to introduce continuous casting of steel on a commercial scale started independently in several countries in the early 1950s. Except in some small firms, it remained very much of an experimental technique and its diffusion, measured by the proportion of continuously cast steel in total steel output, was almost negligible until 1967.[2] In most of the countries considered, take-off in the diffusion process did not occur until 1967–9.

[1] Data on the output of continuously cast steel in OECD member countries are published in *The Iron and Steel Industry in Europe,* but only since 1964.
[2] Exceptions were companies like Mannesmann in West Germany and McLouth in the United States.

9

The rising importance of continuous casting in the steelmaking industry is clearly shown by table 9.2. Total world capacity for continuously cast steel was only 0·38 million tons in 1955. This increased to 1·65 million tons in 1960, to 9 million tons in 1965, and to 38 million tons in 1968 (about 6½ per cent of the world's total crude steel capacity). Recent world capacity for continuously cast steel has been estimated at 48 million tons per annum in 1969, 58 million tons in 1970, and about 70 million tons in 1971.[1] By 1970 therefore, continuous casting comprised some 8·4 per cent of the world total crude steel capacity of 695 million tons.

Table 9.2. *Continuous casting capacity as a proportion of total crude steel capacity*

Percentages

	1955	1960	1965	1970
Europe	0·25	0·62	2·25	7·52
Japan	—	0·40	0·52	10·68
North America	0·08	0·07	1·43	9·06
USSR	0·06	0·50	1·63	8·42
Other countries	—	0·93	1·43	6·02
World	0·13	0·40	1·70	8·40

sources: UNECE, *Economic Aspects of Continuous Casting of Steel*; Wirtschaftsvereinigung Eisen und Stahlindustrie, *Statistisches Jahrbuch der Eisen und Stahlindustrie*; OECD, *The Iron and Steel Industry in Europe*.

This was accompanied by a constant rise in average capacity per cast strand.[2] The annual average per strand was 17,000 tons in 1965, rising to 30,000 tons in 1960, 39,000 tons in 1965 and 65,000 tons in 1968. There are considerable regional differences in this average: in 1968 it was 65,000 tons worldwide, but about 107,000 tons in the USSR, 80,000 tons in North America, 59,000 tons in Japan, 50,000 tons in Europe and 29,500 tons in other countries.

Total crude steel output in six European countries[3] was 123·4 million tons in 1970, of which 6·2 million tons or, about 5·1 per cent, were continuously cast. The corresponding figures for the United States in 1969 were 128·2 million tons total crude steel production, of which 7·8 million tons, or about 6·1 per cent, was continuously cast. The level of diffusion measured by the percentage shares of continuously cast steel in total crude steel production differs considerably among the countries

[1] *Thirty Three Magazine*, vol. 8, no. 10, October 1970.
[2] Interrupted only in 1965, when many small continuous casting machines, mainly with curved moulds, were installed.
[3] Austria, France, Italy, Sweden, the United Kingdom and West Germany.

Table 9.3. *Output of continuously cast steel as a proportion of total crude steel production*

Percentages

	1960	1962	1964	1965	1966	1967	1968	1969	1970
Austria	0·8	1·9	1·3	1·3	1·4	1·3	2·1	6·0	8·0
France	..	..	0·5	0·6	0·6	0·5	0·6	0·6	0·8
Italy	..	..	0·9	1·2	1·1	1·6	3·3	5·8	8·4
Sweden	—	—	0·1	0·9	2·2	5·6	11·4	12·2	14·1
United Kingdom	—	0·2	0·6	1·4	1·6	1·8	1·7	1·8	1·8
United States	—	0·1	0·3	0·8	1·3	3·2	4·9	6·1	11·5
West Germany	..	..	1·3	2·1	2·4	3·7	5·3	7·3	8·3

SOURCES: OECD, *The Iron and Steel Industry in Europe*; ASSIDER, *Notizario*, no. 19, 1970 (for Italy); OIW estimates, based on *Thirty Three Magazine*, vol. 8, no. 7, July 1970 (for the United States).

studied (table 9.3 and chart 9.2). By 1969, diffusion in Sweden had already reached 12·2 per cent, followed by 7·3 per cent in West Germany, 6 per cent in Austria and the United States, and 5·8 per cent in Italy. Diffusion was below average in the United Kingdom with less

Chart 9.2. *Shares of continuously cast steel in total crude steel production*

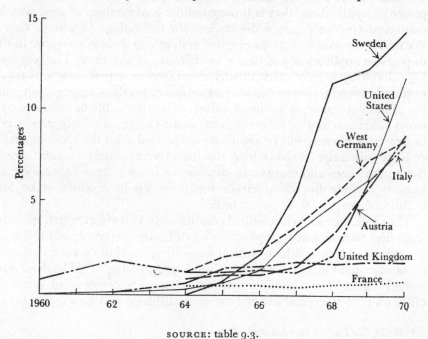

SOURCE: table 9.3.

than 2 per cent and in France with less than 1 per cent. In 1970 diffusion rose in all these countries except the United Kingdom.

The ranking is quite different when the level of diffusion in 1969 is measured by the proportion of steel-plants with continuous casting machines. In Austria this is almost half, in Italy a sixth and in Germany a seventh; but in the United Kingdom it is only about one in ten, and less than this in France and Sweden.[1]

Direct national comparisons such as these implicitly presuppose similar conditions for the application of continuous casting in all countries and all firms. Technical and other conditions may, however, vary, so that the next step is to compare actual diffusion with some 'potential diffusion' defined as a 'technological ceiling'. The level of diffusion is then measured by the share of continuous casting in that sector of crude steel production which is technologically suited to it. This enables us to assess and analyse differences in diffusion abstracted from the effects of differences in composition of the national output.

AN INFORMAL MODEL OF DIFFUSION

The analytical framework

Diffusion of continuous casting depends on the size of the field of potential application, that is those qualities and sections of steel which can be continuously cast in the state of the technology at a given time. We call this variable a 'technological ceiling', to denote an upper limit to possible application and hence to diffusion at any time. The technological ceiling is most conveniently measured as a percentage of total crude steel production or capacity at arbitrary levels of aggregation – in the plant, enterprise, or national industry. It is plausible to assume that, *ceteris paribus*, actual diffusion of continuous casting similarly measured in percentage terms will be positively correlated with the technological ceiling; with a rise in the ceiling, the incentive to introduce continuous casting increases and more firms consider its introduction because it has become technically suited either for their whole production or for additional parts of their programme.

Thus a change in technological conditions has an effect which spreads from firm to firm and an 'epidemic' of diffusion is started; but this will not spread unless, besides technical feasibility, continuous casting shows economic advantages over conventional ingot casting. This leads to our second variable, profitability, which economists consider of decisive effect on both the speed and the extent of diffusion of a new technology.

[1] OECD, *The Iron and Steel Industry in Europe*, 1970.

Profitability is interpreted relatively, that is as the cost *advantages* of a new process over the established processes to be replaced. The hypothesis as formulated by Mansfield, for example, is as follows:

The more profitable this investment is relative to others that are available, the greater is the chance that a firm's estimate of the profitability will be high enough to compensate for whatever risks are involved and that it will seem worthwhile to install the new technique rather than to wait. As the difference between the profitability of this investment and that of others widens, firms tend to note and respond to the difference more quickly.[1]

However, the assessment of the relative cost savings of an innovation is a difficult and complex task. Mansfield himself has to confess in another article that 'because it was impossible to get a direct estimate of the innovation's profitability to each firm, surrogates were obtained where possible.'[2] Our inquiry faced a similar situation. Cost savings of continuous casting over conventional ingot casting depend on so many factors that a general quantification was impossible.[3] Therefore we had to try a modified approach: with only a few companies able or willing to assess the actual cost advantages of continuous casting in quantitative terms, we turned to expected profitability, based on the view each entrepreneur in the steel industry must take of the benefits likely to arise from the adoption of continuous casting in different types of plant.

On this definition, profitability depends largely on the production programme (the qualities and sections cast) and the possibility of coordinating the supply of molten steel with the needs of the continuous casting machine (mainly determined by the kind of furnace used). Types of plant were distinguished by these criteria which are essentially qualitative, for example as users of the oxygen process, special steel producers, or users of electric furnaces. (Both the last two were usually small plants.) The aim was to form roughly homogeneous groups with regard to the profitability of continuous casting.

Differences in profitability between types of plant were assumed to

---

[1] Mansfield, 'Technical change and the rate of imitation', p. 746.

[2] E. Mansfield, 'The speed of response of firms to new techniques', *Quarterly Journal of Economics*, vol. 77, May 1963, pp. 290–311.

[3] See also UNECE, *Economic Aspects of Continuous Casting of Steel*, from which the following quotation is taken:
'Cost data relating to continuous casting for or in a given works can be affected by a great many factors relating peculiarly to that particular works – the location of the works, its layout and the general complex and details of production processes other than the presence or possible introduction of continuous casting, its general production programme and the size of its market, the supplies of operating materials, e.g. refractories, the character of the casting machine installation, particularly its design and construction details, the coordination of machine operations with steel supply on the one hand and with rolling operations on the other, the types of product made, the aptitude and the experience of the works staff in using the process, and even the costing methods adopted.'

explain general trends in the diffusion pattern of continuous casting: for example, application starting with relatively small plants, and large plants following only with considerable delay and mainly in conjunction with the introduction of oxygen converters. Hence differences in the level and speed of diffusion in national steel industries should be seen partly as the result of different plant structures.

Our profitability variable was thus mainly derived from proxies taken from continuous casting technology. Although very simplified, it seemed to be a legitimate procedure, since during the early phases of diffusion uncertainty about the relative cost advantages of a new technology precludes exact profitability calculations. We can define profitability only with reference to *a priori* expectations of profitability, differing according to the types of production and organisation of the potential adopters. What in fact we did (perhaps also what entrepreneurs do when deciding upon investment) was to apply an ordinal ranking of profitability expectations to typical plant structures.

Explanatory variables and their influence

As stated earlier, the range of steel qualities and sections technically suited for continuous casting was assumed to influence its diffusion. Hence national steel industries as well as individual plants may differ in the applicability of continuous casting because of different production structures.

Table 9.4. *National capacities for continuous casting of steel*

Thousand metric tons per annum

	Billets and blooms			Slabs		
	1960	1964	1969	1960	1964	1969
Austria	20	34	49	—	—	250
Italy	105	285	1855	—	—	200
Sweden	—	250	250	—	—	700
United Kingdom	5	300	300	—	200	608
United States	—	356	5206	—	—	7621
West Germany	150	225	727	—	600	4000

SOURCES: inquiry; UNECE, *Economic Aspects of Continuous Casting of Steel*.

Originally only smaller sections (billets or blooms) could be continuously cast; only from 1962 onwards were slabs successfully cast by this method, and not until 1964 did the first large-scale commercial application take place (table 9.4). Thus until 1964 the technological ceiling in regard to section size was generally rather low. Since national data on the proportion of billets produced were unobtainable, the share of rolled products typically produced from billets or smaller blooms (light sections, wire rods, strips, 'semis' and ingots for tubes) was taken as an approximation to this limit. It was still more difficult to quantify the share of steels unsuited for continuous casting because of quality constraints. In the absence of any better information we chose the share of alloy steels as a crude approximation.

Table 9.5. *Technological ceilings: shares of crude steel production technically suited to continuous casting*[a]

Percentages

	National industry		Users of CC	
	1960–4	1965–70	1960–4	1965–70
Austria	20	86	30	90
Italy	35	91	..	..
Sweden	36	76	..	89
United Kingdom	33	93	..	99
United States	23	89	..	..
West Germany	38	91	63	95

SOURCE: OIW estimates.
[a] Average shares over the periods shown.

From these two shares, a technological ceiling was computed for each country (table 9.5). However, the explanatory power of this variable is not very impressive with regard to observed national differences in the diffusion of continuous casting. There is a slight positive correlation between the technological ceiling in the years 1960–4 and the shares of continuously cast steel in total crude steel output in the years 1965–9.[1] The best result is for the year 1966, for which 46 per cent of the national differences in diffusion can be explained by differences in the technological ceiling. As the latter can influence diffusion only with a considerable timelag, we cannot yet expect to find similar relations for values of this variable in the period 1965–70. There is, however, some weak evidence that national differences in the relative change in the technological ceiling (lagged) partly explain differences in the change in shares of continuously cast steel between 1967 and 1969 or 1970.[2]

[1] The correlation coefficients, R^2, are as follows:

1965	1966	1967	1968	1969
0.18	0.46	0.19	0.16	0.06

[2] Using the 1965–70 technological ceiling divided by its value for 1960–4, R^2 is 0.24 for relative changes in shares of continuously cast steel from 1967 to 1969 (all six countries), and 0.67 for relative changes from 1967 to 1970 excluding the United Kingdom and the United States.

Additional support is provided by the technological ceilings for users of continuous casting which, as shown in the last two columns of table 9.5, were generally higher than those for the national industries.

Diffusion of continuous casting within the sector of steel production technically suited to it is shown in table 9.6. A very slight negative correlation ($R^2 = 0.12$) between the 1964 and the 1970 shares of continuously cast steel gives some support to the hypothesis that the countries which pioneered the process at the beginning (for continuous casting of small sections) have lost their relative advantage after its development for larger sections.

Table 9.6. *Output of continuously cast steel as a proportion of crude steel production within the technological ceiling*

Percentages

	1960	1962	1964	1965	1966	1967	1968	1969	1970
Austria	4·6	9·0	5·9	1·6	1·6	1·5	2·4	6·9	9·3
Italy	..	..	2·3	1·4	1·3	1·8	3·6	6·3	9·2
Sweden	—	—	0·4	1·2	3·0	7·1	14·6	15·9	18·5
United Kingdom	—	0·6	2·0	1·5	1·7	1·9	1·8	2·0	2·0
United States	—	0·4	1·3	0·9	1·5	3·6	5·5	6·9	12·9
West Germany	..	..	3·5	2·3	2·6	4·0	5·7	8·0	9·3

SOURCE: inquiry.

The above figures, as well as the curves of actual (unadjusted) diffusion, provide reasons for believing that, although the diffusion of continuous casting of steel is still in quite an early phase, the general sigmoid diffusion curve, which has been proved to be relevant to the diffusion of new processes or new products, is likely to emerge in this case as well.

We now turn to the closely related aspects of types of steelmaking process and plant size, and their impact on the diffusion of continuous casting. Table 9.7 shows the main data; the major results of this approach can be summed up as follows:

(1) Continuous casting machines have usually been coupled either with electric furnaces in relatively small plants, or, from 1966 on, with oxygen converters in larger works.

(2) In 1970, 41 per cent of all continuous casting capacity installed in the six countries considered was supplied by electric furnaces, 53 per cent by oxygen converters and only 6 per cent by open-hearth furnaces.

Table 9.7. *The diffusion of continuous casting by process*

	Capacity for continuous casting		As a proportion of crude steel production by that process		
	1969	1970	1960	1964	1969
	(million tons)		(percentages)		
Austria					
Electric furnace	0·11	0·11	*8·8*	*23·3*	*23·2*
Open-hearth furnace	—	—	—	—	—
Oxygen converter	0·25	0·25	—	—	*9·2*
Open-hearth + oxygen	0·25	0·25	—	—	*7·2*
All processes	0·36	0·36	*1·1*	*3·0*	*9·2*
Italy					
Electric furnace	1·41	2·06	*4·1*	*4·5*	*21·4*
Open-hearth furnace	0·12	0·12	—	—	*2·3*
Oxygen converter	—	0·35	—	—	—
Open-hearth + oxygen	0·12	0·47	—	—	*1·2*
All processes	1·53	2·53	*1·6*	*1·9*	*9·3*
Sweden					
Electric furnace	0·11	0·51	—	*6·0*	*5·0*
Open-hearth furnace	0·18	0·18	—	*2·8*	*13·3*
Oxygen converter	0·70	0·70	—	—	*40·0*
Open-hearth + oxygen	0·88	0·88	—	*1·9*	*28·4*
All processes	0·99	1·39	—	*3·4*	*18·6*
United Kingdom					
Electric furnace	0·05	0·05	*0·3*	*1·8*	*1·1*
Open-hearth furnace	0·25	0·25	—	*1·4*	*1·8*
Oxygen converter	0·41	0·41	—	*6·6*	*5·5*
Open-hearth + oxygen	0·66	0·66	—	*2·1*	*3·0*
All processes	0·71	0·71	—	*1·9*	*2·6*
United States					
Electric furnace	4·66	6·94	—	*3·1*	*25·5*
Open-hearth furnace	0·27	0·27	—	—	*0·5*
Oxygen converter	7·55	8·28	—	—	*13·8*
Open-hearth + oxygen	7·82	8·55	—	—	*7·1*
All processes	12·48	15·49	—	*0·3*	*9·7*
West Germany					
Electric furnace	0·58	0·96	*6·9*	*7·5*	*13·9*
Open-hearth furnace	0·75	0·75	—	*3·6*	*5·5*
Oxygen converter	3·40	4·00	—	—	*16·3*
Open-hearth + oxygen	4·15	4·75	—	*2·7*	*12·1*
All processes	4·73	5·71	*0·4*	*2·2*	*10·4*
All six countries					
Electric furnace	6·92	10·63	..	*4·3*	*18·9*
Open-hearth furnace	1·57	1·57	..	*0·7*	*1·7*
Oxygen converter	12·31	13·99	..	*0·8*	*13·4*
Open-hearth + oxygen	13·88	15·56	..	..	..
All processes	20·80	26·19	..	..	..

SOURCE: inquiry.

Note: Electric furnace data relate to small plants, and open-hearth + oxygen data to large plants, except in Italy where a large plant is using electric furnaces for continuous casting.

(3) By 1969 electric steelmaking was still the sector with the highest
    relative continuous casting capacity, but in recent years diffusion
    has been faster in the oxygen steel sector, which will soon be
    leading in the application of continuous casting.

(4) Since steel-plants using electric furnaces only are practically
    identical with small plants, we can roughly separate diffusion of
    continuous casting within small plants from diffusion within
    larger plants. Within the larger plants (users of open-hearth and

Chart 9.3. *Continuous casting capacity, 1969, and the share of
oxygen steel production, 1964*

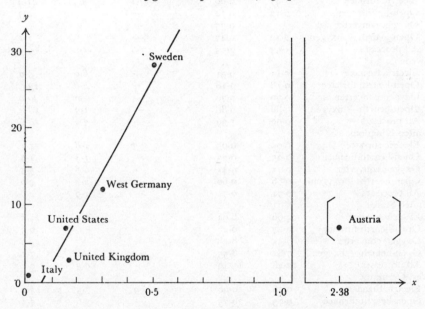

SOURCES: table 9.7; inquiry.

Note: (i) The regression equation is $y = -4.034 + 59.976x$ ($R^2 = 0.891$), where y is relative
          capacity in continuous casting and x is the share of oxygen steel divided by the
          share of open-hearth steel.
        (ii) Based on large plants only.

oxygen furnaces), the diffusion of continuous casting was favoured
by the installation of oxygen converters and retarded by a high
share of open-hearth steel production. From 1964 onwards the
relative importance of oxygen steel production (share of oxygen
steel divided by share of open-hearth steel) gives a fairly good

explanation for the 1969 relative continuous casting capacity in the large plant sector of all countries except Austria (chart 9.3).[1]

INTRA-FIRM DIFFUSION

So far we have tried to analyse the diffusion of continuous casting at the level of national steel industries. Since overall diffusion is the result both of diffusion between firms (more firms using continuous casting) and of diffusion within firms (an increased share of a firm's output being continuously cast), we shall complete our analysis with some empirical findings from the individual plant level.

Table 9.8. *Intra-firm diffusion among users of continuous casting, 1969*

	Output of continuously cast steel as a percentage of:	
	Crude steel output	Technological ceiling
Plant size (crude steel output)		
0–500 thousand tons	93	95
501–1500 thousand tons	41	47
Over 1500 thousand tons	10	11
All plants	19	20

SOURCE: inquiry.

Disregarding the influence of time – the number of years since continuous casting was introduced by a firm – intra-firm diffusion is mainly a function of product programmes and hence of plant types. Small steel-plants using mainly electric furnaces employ continuous casting for a considerably higher share of production than large firms (especially small plants with a rather uniform output, for example the majority of the steel-plants in Italy and 'mini' plants in the United States). Large firms usually introduce continuous casting for additional capacity or for a limited sector of their production programme; it therefore accounts for only a rather small share of their total output.

By using data for 19 steel plants in Austria, Germany, Sweden and United Kingdom which have installed continuous casting, some quantification of intra-firm diffusion is possible (table 9.8). We found also that small firms reached their maximum share of continuously cast steel output quite rapidly, whilst within large firms there seems to have been little attempt substantially to increase the proportion of continuously cast steel before about 1967.

[1] The two large Austrian steel-plants are the pioneers in oxygen steel, but one of them only has been operating a continuous casting line since 1968 and will install a second by 1974.

SUMMARY AND CONCLUSIONS

Starting from a rather limited application in the 1950s, continuous casting has been gradually improved technically, but technological development is still continuing. This has influenced its diffusion pattern considerably. For a number of years diffusion was almost completely confined to small plants, since continuous casting of slabs – the bulk of mass production – was not technically feasible. Thus two phases can be distinguished in the diffusion of continuous casting – within small plants; and within larger plants, starting in the mid-1960s, aided by the increasing use of oxygen converters.

The cost savings of continuous casting over conventional ingot casting depend on so many factors that a general quantification is impossible. The most important advantage for both small and large plants is the increased yield. Reduction in capital and space requirements due to the omission of soaking pits and blooming mills is an additional motive, especially in small plants. Electric furnaces coupled with continuous casting and a fairly uniform output seem to offer a new chance to small steel producers in competing with large firms.

Among large-scale commercial steel producers, the application of continuous casting has become increasingly motivated by the urgent need for a high rate of capacity utilisation, and this requires increased use of continuous operations. Originally, continuous casting machines were installed in large plants mainly for additional capacity, either to overcome possible shortages in primary rolling capacity, or for a limited number of specific products. Now large continuous casting machines coupled with oxygen converters tend to be employed as central production units; they are generally considered to be the best solution when new large-scale crude steel capacity is installed.

Apart from high investment costs, the primary deterrent for most firms is the need for reorganisation if existing melting, casting, and rolling capacities are to be properly coordinated. Technical conditions in oxygen converter shops are considerably better suited for this coordination than those in open-hearth works, which explains why the diffusion of continuous casting has concentrated in the oxygen sector of commercial steel production.

National differences in the diffusion of continuous casting can be partly explained by differences in the potential field of application (as reflected by the technological ceiling) of the new process. However, at this early stage in the diffusion process, the observed development is mainly the result of success or failure in a very few pioneering firms, and objective variables may fail as explanations.

CHAPTER 10

SHUTTLELESS LOOMS

By R. J. Smith, NIESR

THE TECHNOLOGY

The shuttleless loom[1] is a labour-saving technique in comparison with the conventional shuttle loom, and in its most sophisticated form, the Sulzer shuttleless loom, it is both labour-saving and capital-using. The capital cost of air-jet and water-jet looms is about 50 per cent higher than that of a conventional automatic loom, while the Sulzer loom costs up to five times as much. High capital costs make it necessary to minimise the time in which a machine is idle by long production runs and an increase in shift-working to an optimum of three or four shifts ($112\frac{1}{2}$ to 140 hours per week). They also demand mechanical reliability and a highly coordinated production line.

There are three major processes between the fibrous raw cotton and the final woven cotton cloth. First comes spinning, in which the cotton fibres are twisted and bound together, spun successively tighter and drawn out into cotton thread. Then, at the weaving stage, parallel threads are set up lengthwise in the loom to form the warp. In the traditional process, one set of these threads is raised and the remainder lowered as the shuttle carries another thread (the weft) across the loom. Before the shuttle begins its return journey the position of the warp threads is reversed, so that the threads which were formerly raised are now lowered and vice versa. The alternate raising and lowering of the sets of warp threads binds the weft thread deposited by the shuttle into the warp to form woven cloth. Finally, in making-up and finishing the woven cloth is de-sized, printed and cut to the required shape and measurements.

The art of weaving is almost as old as civilisation itself. But it is only since the Industrial Revolution that weaving has assumed its present form, with the invention of Kay's fly shuttle in 1733, and the first practical power loom produced by Cartwright in 1785. It was soon after this that the present mill system began to appear in the British weaving industry. The power loom was, however, slow to be adopted; it is estimated that, by 1815, there were only 2,400 in England. After

[1] This includes all looms which dispense with the shuttle as the means of carrying the weft, the supply of which is instead mounted as a package on the side of the loom – i.e. Sulzer, rapier and air- and water-jet looms.

the Napoleonic Wars numbers rose more rapidly – to 15,000 in 1820 and about 60,000 in 1830 in England and Scotland. Adaptations of various kinds were made to the Cartwright loom all through the nineteenth century, culminating in the development late in the century of the automatic loom, the main advantage of which was a mechanism to change the bobbin automatically without stopping the loom.

The conventional shuttle had obvious disadvantages, particularly for narrow cloth. Frequent replenishment of the bobbin was necessary, at least before the automatic loom; power consumption was high and wasteful; and, since the 1950s, it has become apparent that there are technical limits to the speed of a shuttle loom.

As early as 1836 people were thinking about other methods of inserting the weft; in that year the first English patent was taken out for an automatic shuttleless loom. For the next 30 years there was a flurry of further such patents, but almost all these looms were specifically designed for narrow weaving of tapes and ribbons; virtually all of them operated on the rapier principle with a weaving needle.

Shuttleless looms of the rapier type for weaving broad fabric have been on the market since the 1920s, but it is only since 1950 that a variety of more sophisticated versions have appeared. The term rapier loom covers several different machines. In all of them the weft is carried by a rod into and through the warp shed,[1] but some do this by means of one rapier mounted on the opposite side from the weft package; some by means of two rapiers mounted one on each side of the loom, which enter the warp shed simultaneously, meeting in the middle to transfer the weft from one to the other and finally withdrawing to complete the pick. On both single and double models the rapiers may be rigid or flexible. Some, such as the Draper DSL a double flexible rapier model, are specifically designed for fast weaving and a high rate of output; others, often with single rigid rapiers such as the Spanish Iwer loom, are more suitable for versatile weft mixing, being able to weave up to eight colours in any sequence. The latter variety are, however, often no faster than a conventional multi-colour loom, and usually no costs are saved by their introduction.

A rather different technique of weft insertion was invented by a German, A. Rossmann, who, about 1930, sold his patents to a Swiss financial consortium, Textil-Finanz AG, for whom Sulzer Brothers of Winterthur carried out development. The Sulzer loom, as it has come to be known, uses a miniature shuttle, called a gripper shuttle, to carry the weft across the shed. It is hammered across the loom in much the same way as a conventional shuttle, but draws the weft from a stationary

---

[1] The opening formed by raising one set of warp threads and lowering the other to allow the weft to be inserted.

supply package mounted on the side of the loom instead of carrying the supply with it.

The basis of jet looms is a high-speed jet of air or water coming from a nozzle at one side of the warp and passing between the warp threads carrying with it a single weft. The weft is fed intermittently into the jet from a rotating drum. The air-jet method is employed by the Maxbo loom, the invention of an Estonian, Paabo, living in Sweden. The Czechoslovak Kovo looms (air- and water-jet) and the Japanese Prinz looms (water-jet) operate on the same principle. Jet looms have advantages over other types of shuttleless looms in that floor-space requirements can be appreciably reduced, because the jet virtually frees the weft from the influence of gravity during its passage across the loom, and so the warp can be set up almost vertically; also, they are quieter in operation. On the other hand, they have disadvantages: for example the air-jet method can only weave cloth up to about 45 inches wide and even water-jets have a limit of 60 to 65 inches. There are also constraints on the thickness of the weft. Originally water-jet looms could weave only hydrophobic yarns,[1] which meant in practice that almost all the natural fibres were excluded and they were limited to man-made threads; also the warps could not be treated with the normal soluble sizes. Within the last five years, however, there have been some successful trials of hydraulic weaving of staples (including cotton) specially treated with hydrophobic sizes.

The much smaller and lighter gripper shuttle of the Sulzer loom and air and water jets can transfer the weft much more rapidly: in terms of cycles per minute a narrow Sulzer can work at twice the speed of its conventional counterpart, and air- and water-jet looms, dispensing altogether with solid means of weft transference, can work at up to three times the speed. Consequently shuttleless looms can give considerable savings in labour and energy costs on a standardised production schedule of cloths with relatively simple construction, provided that stops for changes of beam or warp repairs are infrequent. The limitation on construction has recently been overcome with the development by Sulzer Brothers of a sophisticated (and hence expensive) loom capable of weaving Jacquard designs. With this loom, even more than the basic Sulzer, a long production run of each pattern is a *sine qua non*. Jet looms are only capable of single-colour weaving.

The advantages of shuttleless looms are less where a great variety of fabrics is woven and they are used on short runs. Savings in operational costs are largely due to their very high speeds compared with conventional looms, and the Sulzer loom's superiority in this respect increases with the width of the fabric, because the conventional loom's

[1] Yarns which do not absorb water.

rate of insertion falls off steeply when weaving widths greater than 120 inches. The Sulzer is thus eminently more suitable for weaving wide cloths, or two or three (even up to six or seven) widths in parallel, to a maximum total of 213 inches, than it is for weaving single widths of 50 or 60 inches which squander many of its benefits (table 10.1). Whereas on a single, 50- or 60-inch width it can produce perhaps 50 per cent more than a conventional loom of that width, on three-width 130-inch working it can produce approximately as much cloth in the same time as three 40-inch conventional looms; and because the labour and floor-space required for one Sulzer are far less than for three conventional looms, unit costs are much reduced.

Table 10.1. *Potential output of woven cloth on different types of loom*

Indices, conventional automatic = 100

	Width of cloth		
	45–70 in.	130 in.	165 in.
Conventional			
Non-automatic looms	85	85	n.a.
Automatic looms	100	100	100
Shuttleless			
Rapier looms	105	n.a.	n.a.
Jet looms (air or water)	190	n.a.	n.a.
Sulzer looms	150	210	300

SOURCE: NIESR estimates.

One reason for the lower operating costs of shuttleless looms, particularly the Sulzer machine, is their ability, given a good quality warp and weft thread, to work with fewer stoppages, partly due to greater mechanical reliability, but more often to the fact that warp and weft breakages occur less frequently. This is because the warp shed formed on a shuttleless loom, with its miniature weft-carrying vehicle, need only be a fraction the size of that on an automatic loom, where it has to allow for passage of a large, fully laden shuttle. As a by-product of the reduction in warp and weft breakages, also due partly to the lower strain on the threads, the quality of the final cloth produced by a shuttleless machine is often superior to that from a conventional loom. On the other hand, owing to its unusual method of inserting the weft, the shuttleless loom produces an unconventional selvedge, which can sometimes be unacceptable for certain finishing processes; it is obviously less versatile in terms of thickness of the yarn and types of cloth that it can weave; and water-jet looms need a good water supply and effluent system, and facilities for drying the damp newly woven cloth, which require additional investment.

THE INQUIRY

In the six countries, altogether 219 companies in the cotton and cotton-type weaving industries took some part in the investigation (table 10.2),[1] but the main part of the inquiry was limited to 95 firms, which provided details of their motives for adopting or rejecting shuttleless looms, and of their practical experience if they had adopted them. Of these 95 firms, 38 were users of some kind of shuttleless loom and a further five[2] were using one or two only for speciality items, often difficult or expensive to weave on conventional looms. Of the 38, 24 had Sulzer looms, 15 rapiers, and only four (all in the United Kingdom) any kind of jet loom (five firms were using more than one kind of shuttleless loom). The remaining 124 companies, of which 29 were users of shuttleless looms and 95 non-users, answered a simplified questionnaire relating to the kinds of fabric they were weaving and their type of machinery. The data from this simplified survey which are applicable to the main inquiry have been incorporated in the results.

Table 10.2. *Respondents to the inquiry*

	Main inquiry			All inquiries		
	Users	Non-users	Total	Users	Non-users	Total
Austria	3	12	15	3	12	15
Italy	4	13	17	7	41	48
Sweden	3	9	12	3	9	12
United Kingdom	10	8	18	17	30	47
United States	5	6	11	10	19	29
West Germany	13	9	22	27	41	68
Total	38	57	95	67	152	219

SOURCE: inquiry.

It is difficult to assess how representative the country samples are in terms of output, partly owing to the various measures of output volume used in different countries. Nevertheless, the indicators in table 10.3, namely the proportions of total looms in place, of numbers of firms, and of annual cloth output, accounted for by the sample in each of the

[1] Shuttleless looms are also used in other types of weaving (e.g. wool). The present inquiry is, however, confined to cotton and man-made fibres.
[2] Not counted as 'users' in the table.

countries, suggest that coverage was better in Germany and Austria than in Italy, the United States and the United Kingdom. The small Swedish cotton-weaving industry was covered completely, except for some firms mainly weaving man-made fibres. Austria, too, has a relatively small industry and in terms of looms about half of it was covered, although, because of the bias towards larger firms, the number of firms studied was only 33 per cent of the total. For the United States the sample, by concentrating on the very large firms, covered 20 per cent of looms. There, no firm with less than 500 employees took part in the detailed inquiry, although the American industry contains three such firms in five, while nine of the ten respondents came from the 15 per cent of firms in the industry which have over 1,000 employees. The coverage of the United Kingdom and Italian samples was low, not so much because a smaller proportion of firms was sampled (although this was likely since the Italian and United Kingdom industries have the largest number of firms), but because the firms sampled were smaller on average in relation to the national average size than in the other four countries.[1] Partly, this was the result of an attempt to study the behaviour of small firms in some depth in those countries to try to

Table 10.3. *Coverage of the samples*

Percentages

	Main inquiry			All inquiries	
	Looms	Firms[a]	Output	Looms	Firms[a]
Austria	50	33	71	50	33
Italy	12	3	16	32	9
Sweden[b]	100	100	100	100	100
United Kingdom	14	6	18	24	17
United States	20	3	16	37	5
West Germany	27	8	23	47	16

SOURCE: NIESR estimates; inquiry.

[a] Of firms with more than 20 employees in Italy, the United States and West Germany; with more than 25 employees in Austria and the United Kingdom.
[b] Firms engaged mainly in weaving cotton.

illuminate the different reactions of small and large firms faced with similar situations.

In the samples, the ratios of users to non-users of shuttleless looms were substantially higher than the national ratios; this was partly because the policy was explicitly to acquire information about firms'

[1] R. J. Smith, 'The weaving of cotton and allied textiles in Great Britain: an industry survey with special reference to the diffusion of shuttleless looms', *National Institute Economic Review*, no. 53, August 1970, p. 67, fn. 1.

experience with shuttleless looms in operation, and partly because it was found that the users approached were more willing to cooperate in the inquiry than the non-users. Similarly there is a bias in the results towards larger companies. Except for Sweden therefore, the results obtained for each sample should be only cautiously extended to the national cotton-weaving industries.

However, bearing in mind the two directions of bias, towards users and larger firms, for all the countries except the United States the samples may be taken as representative of the national industry, each sample consisting of a wide variety of firms; for the United States the sample results would seem to be extensible at least to the larger corporate sector of the industry.

THE DIFFUSION PATTERN OF SHUTTLELESS LOOMS

Unfortunately there are no historical series from any of the countries considered for the numbers of firms which had adopted shuttleless

Table 10.4. *Adoption of shuttleless looms in the samples*

Numbers at end of year

	1956	1958	1960	1962	1964	1966	1968	1969
Adopting firms								
Austria	—	1	1	1	1	2	3	3
Italy	—	—	1	1	1	1	1	4
Sweden	—	—	—	1	2	2	2	3
United Kingdom[a,b]	1	1	1	1	2	5	11	11
United States[a]	—	2	2	3	3	4	4	5
West Germany	5	7	8	10	10	12	12	13
Total	6	11	13	17	19	26	33	39
Shuttleless looms[c]								
France	..	280	364	728	848	1102	..	..
Italy	..	—	12	48	48	48	48	198
Sweden	..	—	—	42	90	114	130	174
United Kingdom	..	6	42	60	120	192	1385	2089
United States	..	150	250	604	1016	1864	2755	4616
West Germany	..	326	469	635	997	1264	1643	1783
Total (excluding France)	..	482	773	1389	2271	3482	5961	8860
Total (excluding France and United States)	..	332	523	785	1255	1618	3206	4244

SOURCE: inquiry.

[a] Two plants owned by the same company treated as two separate firms.

[b] Includes one firm which did not participate in the remainder of the inquiry.

[c] Austria excluded since figures not available.

looms, or for the total numbers of shuttleless looms installed, for individual years prior to the mid-1960s. For example, it was only in 1967 that the British Textile Council began to record shuttleless looms separately in its quarterly series of looms in operation, and it is still

Chart 10.1. *The time-path of diffusion among the sample firms*

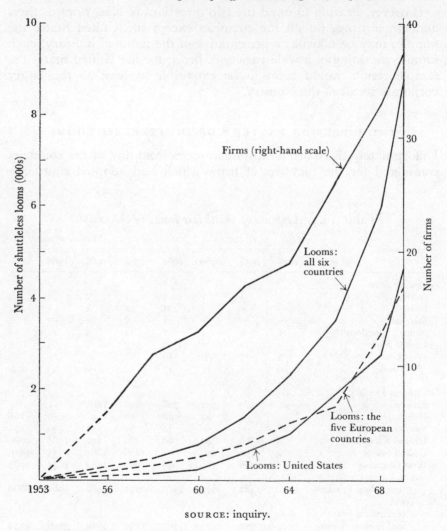

SOURCE: inquiry.

difficult to find precise information on how many firms in the United Kingdom are currently using shuttleless looms. Apart from Sweden, where almost the entire industry was accounted for by our sample, much the same is true for the other countries: there are only isolated (and sometimes mutually conflicting) figures from various sources for the numbers of shuttleless looms installed since about 1965, very little idea of the diffusion of shuttleless looms prior to that date, and no consistent continuous series for subsequent years.

In these circumstances only the diffusion of shuttleless looms among sample firms is examined here. Table 10.4 shows how many firms adopted and how many shuttleless looms were installed by respondent firms in each of the six countries at two-yearly intervals from 1956 to 1969. Charts 10.1 and 10.2 show the series for numbers of looms in total and by country.

Because the national samples are small, no pattern can be detected in the numbers of adopting firms in the individual countries – they are too sensitive to random influences – but the total number of adopters in the six countries, a slightly more regular series, shows a distinct acceleration in the rate of diffusion after 1964. On average, 1·5 firms adopted the process each year before 1964; for the period 1964–9, the corresponding average is almost four.

A pattern is evident too in the numbers of shuttleless looms installed in all six countries, as well as in those countries where there are a substantial number – Germany the United States and the United Kingdom. The series for all six countries, for the United States separately, and for the other five countries together, also show an acceleration after about 1964, although the points of take-off for the separate series do not coincide exactly.[1] From table 10.4 and chart 10.1 it is apparent that diffusion was still accelerating in almost all the individual countries in 1969, more than 15 years after the first commercial introduction of shuttleless looms. In the United Kingdom diffusion lagged behind the other countries in the early years with very few firms showing interest and no sample firms adopting during the six

[1] It is possible to say that these series, as observed to date, conform quite strongly to the lower half of a cumulative normal distribution curve, or to a Gompertz curve tailing off more gradually after the point of inflexion. Both these curves have an acceleration phase in their lower reaches, and both have been frequently found to epitomise the diffusion pattern over time of new techniques which have already reached saturation levels of diffusion. At this stage, however, the point of inflexion not yet having been reached, it is impossible to discern whether the data show a closer approximation to the regular cumulative normal curve, or to the asymmetrical Gompertz.

Despite the two obstacles of a small sample and a short time period, some impressionistic curves of the logistic and Gompertz types were fitted to the observed series to 1969. These suggest that the point of inflexion of the series for looms in the United States and in all countries may be just past, whereas for looms in the United Kingdom it is still some years in the future, implying that the British industry is at an earlier stage of diffusion and substantially further from 'saturation' point (100 per cent of feasible diffusion) than the industries in the other five countries, certainly in the United States. No unequivocal result could be obtained for Germany because that series approximates closely to a straight line (with, however, definite evidence of positive serial correlation), so that the calculated turning point is subject to a very wide margin of error.

Chart 10.2. *The adoption of shuttleless looms in each national sample*

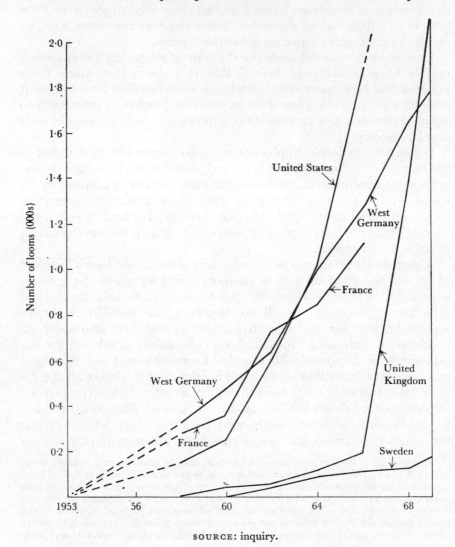

SOURCE: inquiry.

years after the pioneer installation in 1955.[1] The series for adopters in
the United Kingdom took off in 1964, but the majority of installations
were not until 1968 and 1969, when there were two very large con-
versions to shuttleless looms by previously non-adopting companies. In

[1] As in other countries, several firms had individual rapier looms installed long before the
dates of 'first installation' quoted here. But those looms were performing a completely
different function, often weaving yarn that it was impossible, or very difficult and time-
wasting, to weave on conventional looms owing to its weight, thickness or bulked texture.

contrast, the diffusion pattern among the German sample firms has been one of more regular accumulation, so that the series for looms and for adopting companies are very close to straight lines with no strong fluctuation in any period. Even here, however, there has been a tendency for the growth in loom numbers to accelerate in later years. The Swedish diffusion pattern, too, has been one of regular successive increments. The United States series of loom numbers is regular, but conforms more closely to an exponential growth pattern than any of the other sample series.

Table 10.5. *Inter-firm and intra-firm diffusion of shuttleless looms, 1969*[a]

	United Kingdom	United States	West Germany	All countries[b]
Installations				
Adopting firms	11	4	12	30
Subsequent installations				
None	4	—	2	7
One	2	2	2	6
More than one	5	2	8	17
Average number	1.36	2.75	2.42	2.00
Total	26	15	41	90
Shuttleless looms				
First installations	1051	439	511	2103
Subsequent installations	1030	4165	1268	6609
All installations	2081	4604	1779	8712
Ratio subsequent : first	0.98	9.49	2.48	3.14

SOURCE: inquiry.

[a] For firms adopting *prior to* 1969, so figures do not correspond with tables 10.2 and 10.4.
[b] Austria excluded owing to insufficient data; Italy and Sweden included only in figures for 'all countries' due to the small number of adopters prior to 1969 in those samples.

The diffusion process can be divided into two stages: diffusion from firm to firm (inter-firm or primary), and diffusion within firms (intra-firm or internal). In the case of shuttleless looms, our findings indicate that by 1969 intra-firm diffusion had become more important than inter-firm diffusion. Table 10.5 shows the number of firms in each country which had adopted by 1969, and the number of new installations, both in firms which had already adopted and firms which had not.[1] Internal diffusion was of greatest importance among adopters in the United States sample; they tended to start with relatively small numbers of shuttleless looms, possibly for trial purposes, to which they

[1] For this purpose very small installations (five looms or less) have generally been ignored, except where a new set of looms of this size has had a large effect on cloth production.

made regular additions at yearly or two-yearly intervals. The German case was similar, with eight out of the twelve firms which adopted prior to 1969 making at least two additions to their initial batch of shuttleless looms. In the United Kingdom sample, on the other hand, where inter-firm diffusion still predominated at the end of 1969, only five out of eleven firms had made more than one addition to their original installation, and the remaining six were generally smaller firms, which had installed small batches of shuttleless looms in the previous period, but

Table 10.6. *Intra-firm diffusion, 1969*

Percentage shares

	Italy	Sweden	United Kingdom[a]			United States	West Germany
			A	B	C		
All users							
Shuttleless output/total output	23.3	25.7	27.7	31.3	19.9	11.4	48.5
Shuttleless looms/total looms							
Sulzer/total	6.6	6.4	3.0	3.6	1.7	1.3	24.4
Jet or rapier/total	1.2	3.7	11.1	14.4	3.2	8.1	0.6
Total	7.8	10.1	14.1	18.0	4.9	9.4	25.0
Sulzer users[b]							
Sulzer looms/total looms	8.1	25.9	13.4	14.8	8.6	2.9	21.6
Jet or rapier users[b]							
Jet or rapier looms/total looms	5.7	4.9	11.8	14.8	3.9	8.1	10.8
Ratio line (1) : line (4)	*3.0*	*2.5*	*2.0*	*1.7*	*4.1*	*1.2*	*1.9*
Ratio line (5) : line (6)	*1.4*	*5.3*	*1.1*	*1.0*	*2.2*	*0.4*	*2.0*

SOURCE: inquiry.

[a] A = all adopting firms;
  B = firms with 50 or more shuttleless looms;
  C = firms with less than 50 shuttleless looms.
 [b] Figures do not average to those for all shuttleless looms because users of both Sulzer and other shuttleless looms are counted once only in the total.

were then discouraged from further adoptions by liquidity problems. One such firm was, however, intending to install further shuttleless looms later at a similar cost to its earlier investment. In Sweden, inter-firm and intra-firm diffusion were of approximately equal importance at the end of 1969. For all six countries, adopters making no additions to their first installation of shuttleless looms tended, on the whole, to be the smaller firms.

Table 10.6 shows that, in all the countries apart from the United States (where the Draper flexible rapier loom established itself very early as an improved technique for simple, standardised cloths), Sulzer looms diffused faster internally among Sulzer users than did other shuttleless looms among their users. This is mainly attributable to the greater economies of large-scale adoption of Sulzer looms; a number of smaller firms, particularly in the United Kingdom, adopted rapier or jet looms in batches of only eight or sixteen, but such small numbers would hardly be worthwhile in the case of Sulzer looms. It is the German sample which shows the most widespread large-scale adoption of Sulzer looms, and indeed of shuttleless looms as a whole, among the users. Significantly, the rate of internal diffusion among users of rapier and jet looms is higher in Germany than in the United States, despite the large-scale adoption of the Draper loom there. The United Kingdom sample has relatively high internal diffusion levels, especially among the Sulzer adopters, in contrast to low primary rates.

COTTON AND COTTON-TYPE TEXTILE INDUSTRIES IN THE SIX COUNTRIES

The rate of diffusion is affected by certain significant features of, and developments in, the textile industry, and their variations between the six countries. Although in five of the countries the textile industry as a whole was of some importance in the economy, employing in 1969 between 5 and $7\frac{1}{2}$ per cent of all labour in manufacturing industry,[1] in none of the countries was it a major growth industry. During the late 1950s and through the 1960s textile output was declining everywhere relative to the remainder of the manufacturing sector, and in the United Kingdom and Italy it was even in decline in absolute terms. Total demand for textiles rose only slowly; in each country the rise in home demand was modest; the long-term income elasticity of demand for textiles in mature economies was in the region of one.[2] Further, the industry faced import competition of differing degrees of severity throughout the 1950s and 1960s, and this was directed especially to cotton textiles. The share of imports in woven cotton and cotton-type cloth consumption has risen in all the countries (table 10.7). The sources of the imports to most countries have, however, shifted during the 1960s, mainly due to the formation of EEC and EFTA. The United Kingdom has had to face a rapid increase in imports from the Commonwealth countries in South East Asia,[3] while in the United States there

[1] In Sweden employment did not exceed $2\frac{1}{2}$ per cent.

[2] In all OECD countries except Japan, the share of consumer spending on clothing in total consumers' expenditure has remained practically steady over the last decade (OECD, *The Textile Industry in OECD Countries*, 1965/66, appendix table 10, p. 102). For a cross-sectional estimate see also S. J. Prais and H. S. Houthakker, *The Analysis of Family Budgets*, 2nd ed., Cambridge University Press, 1971, pp. 98ff., particularly tables 16 and 20.

[3] There were no tariffs on cotton textiles from the Commonwealth, although fabrics of man-made fibres were subject to a 15 per cent duty. A voluntary quota system was in force throughout the 1960s. This situation ended on 1 January 1972, with the imposition of a 15 per cent tariff on all textiles imported from the Commonwealth in addition to the previous quota arrangements.

Table 10.7. *Import content of consumption of woven cotton and cotton-type cloth*

Percentages

	1960	1966	1968
Austria	40·1	44·1	55·3
Italy	3·4	16·1	22·2
Sweden	51·6	71·3	72·7
United Kingdom	32·2	35·8	45·7
United States	5·4	7·7	6·7
West Germany	13·8	17·3	19·8

SOURCE: national data.

was a large increase in textile imports from Japan, mainly in the field of man-made fibres.

Exports from the United Kingdom and United States continued their long-term decline, so that the external trading position of the weaving industry in those countries deteriorated sharply. Among the other countries, the German and Italian external trading positions also showed some deterioration, while for Austria there was a small improvement.

Table 10.8 shows trends in output in the cotton-type weaving industry in the six countries between 1962 and 1969. Except in Austria output of cotton cloth fell over the period but, apart from the United Kingdom and Italy, the fall was more than offset by large increases in the output of man-made fibre weaves, which in Sweden and the United States more than doubled and in Austria and Germany grew by over 60 per cent. A particular phenomenon was far more important in the United Kingdom than elsewhere – the switch out of weaving into knitting, as a

Table 10.8. *Output in the cotton and cotton-type weaving industry, 1969*

Indices, 1962 = 100

	Austria	Italy	Sweden	United Kingdom	United States	West Germany
Woven cotton and cotton-type cloth						
Cotton cloth	100·4	79·0	70·9	66·9	83·6	85·0
Man-made fibre cloth	162·2	115·2	274·5	106·4	213·0	162·5
Total	120·8	90·4	111·1	81·7	108·4	107·6
All manufacturing industry	133	148	142	126	141	133

SOURCES: national data; OECD, *The Textile Industry in OECD Countries* (various years); United Nations, *Monthly Bulletin of Statistics*.

result of the growing availability of synthetic filament yarns, required particularly for warp-knitting. Knitting is potentially far faster and cheaper than weaving,[1] and its large expansion in the late 1960s in the United Kingdom has certainly caused further uncertainty among weaving management. It must have substantially inhibited the sort of revival in the weaving industry which took place elsewhere with the increasing use of man-made fibres.

Table 10.9. *Labour and loom productivity in the cotton and cotton-type weaving industry*

		Austria	Italy	Sweden	United Kingdom	United States	West Germany
		(indices, 1962 = 100)					
Employment[a]	1968	76·1	65·5	61·7	73·6	97·8	74·6
Output per man	1968	148·7	135·4	168·5	109·0	118·7	136·1
		(thousands at end of year)					
Looms in place	1939	15·9	136·7	11·6	505·0	542·9	200·5[b]
	1962	11·1	90·4	10·0	156·6	302·3	103·1
	1969	6·7	72·1	6·0	82·0	240·6	58·2
Proportions of		(percentages)					
Automatic looms	1953	28	64	87	11	100	60[c]
	1969	92	89	100	50	100	92
Looms in	1958	90	78	95[d]	70	97[e]	..
operation	1969	97	91	95[f]	87	95[g]	87[h]
		(average hours per week)					
Loom-working	1953	67·9	43·9	74·5	37·9	115·2	51·4
	1960	74·6	63·8	76·4	56·4	126·7	70·9
	1969	91·8	72·0	85·0	65·6	116·6	77·8
		(indices, 1962 = 100)					
Output per loom	1969	200·1	113·3	185·2	156·0	136·2	190·6

SOURCES: as table 10·8.

[a] Operatives only. [e] Cotton weaving only.
[b] German Reich. [f] 1967.
[c] 1960. [g] 1968.
[d] 1959. [h] Estimated.

Employment has fallen and labour productivity increased quite fast in all the countries since 1962 (table 10.9). The same is even more true of looms and loom productivity. Three factors have contributed to this: older, slower looms have been increasingly replaced by larger and more

[1] However, some of the qualities of knitted fabrics (texture and comfort, for example) are widely held to be inferior to those of woven spun yarn fabrics.

sophisticated machines; the number of hours the looms are running each week has moved steadily upwards with increased three- and four-shift working; and the proportion of the looms in place that are actually operational at any time has also been rising slowly. Moreover, in the United Kingdom, and to a smaller extent the other countries, the loss of many less productive looms (as well as many jobs) has been the direct result of the closure of uneconomical weaving units that has been taking place at a high rate throughout the 1960s, first in response to the Cotton Industry Act (1959), the object of which was to achieve a greater rationalisation of the cotton-type industry,[1] and later to the effects of import competition.

Despite the 1959 Act and its consequences, however, the British industry, which was far behind the other countries in the average age of its machinery at the beginning of the 1950s, was still lagging noticeably at the end of the 1960s. As table 10.9 shows, the proportions of automatic looms and of looms in place that were in operation, also the number of hours per week the looms were worked, were noticeably lower. This may have been because the machinery, being on average older, was usually fully written off, or else, being largely non-automatic, incurred smaller depreciation costs. Another possible explanation, which, however, is more powerful in Italy than the United Kingdom, is that the low activity rate of looms is due to the relative numbers worked by smaller enterprises, which were not in a good position to organise multi-shift working. Italy has both a relatively short working week and a large proportion of its loom stock inoperative. At the other extreme the United States, Austria and Sweden have the largest proportion of automatic machinery and the longest weekly loom-hours.

Productivity of looms and operatives grew fastest in Austria and Sweden (due partly, no doubt, to the rapid decrease in numbers of looms in those countries), slowest in the United Kingdom, the United States and Italy. The slow growth of loom productivity in Italy must be seen, however, against the background of a slower rundown in loom numbers and a lower rate of capital investment per employee than elsewhere. On the other hand, a fairly high rate of investment in the United Kingdom does not seem to have had any notable effect on productivity in that country; nor, indeed, did the falling relative investment have a retarding effect on productivity in Austria, Germany or Sweden.

[1] The main features of the Cotton Industry Act were its injection of large sums of money into the industry (including financial incentives for the scrapping of obsolete looms and spindles) in order to bring about increased investment in new machinery, and its drive for greater rationalisation, by providing financial support for the closure of the less economic units and the formation of larger conglomerates by means of mergers and take-overs (see C. Miles, *Lancashire Textiles: a case study of industrial change*, Cambridge University Press, 1968).

Finally, the structure of the industry shows strong similarities in the five European countries, the one major exception being Italy, where a vast number of very small enterprises employed between one and twenty people, and accounted for almost four-fifths of the number of firms in the industry. Excluding these, in each of the European countries about three-quarters of the firms employ less than 300 (table 10.10).[1] Italy has 86 per cent of its enterprises employing less than 250;

Table 10.10. *Size distribution of firms in the cotton and cotton-type weaving industry*[a]

Percentages

	Austria 1966	Italy 1961	Sweden 1967	United Kingdom 1963	United States 1963	West Germany 1966
Numbers employed						
Under 100	58	71	30	41	11	32
101–300	14	19	20	40	24	} 46
301–500	9	4	10	10	25	
501–1000	14	3	10	5	25	12
Over 1000	5	2	30	4	15	10
Total firms	*43*	*522*	*10*	*391*	*350*	*283*

SOURCE: national data.

[a] Excluding firms which employed less than 25 in Austria, Sweden and the United Kingdom, and less than 20 in Italy, the United States and West Germany.

Austria, Germany and the United Kingdom all have about 75 per cent in this category and overall have similar size distributions. The structure of the industry in the United States is almost entirely the reverse, with firms employing between 301 and 1,000 accounting for 50 per cent of all the firms in the industry, and 15 per cent of firms having more than 1,000 employees; only 35 per cent of the firms employ less than 300.

FACTORS INFLUENCING INTER-FIRM DIFFUSION

We shall now attempt to identify some of the factors which we might expect to influence the diffusion pattern of shuttleless looms. It will be helpful to consider first the attitudes of the firms in the samples which had not installed any shuttleless looms, and then whether we can learn anything from the experience of those firms which have adopted the technique.

[1] For the purpose of examining the structure of the industry in the various countries, only those firms employing 25 or more persons in Austria, Sweden and the United Kingdom, and 20 or more in Germany, Italy and the United States are taken into consideration.

Attitudes of non-adopters

The non-users in the sample were asked whether they had seriously considered introducing shuttleless looms and, if so, whether a cost comparison, taking into account their individual circumstances, had been made before it was decided to reject shuttleless looms. For those firms which had made cost comparisons, the results were requested and are set out in table 10.11. About 45 per cent of firms had either not considered the introduction of shuttleless looms, or had not troubled to make cost comparisons; a number of them were in a line of production (for instance, fancy goods or Jacquards) for which shuttleless looms would not have been suitable. Among those which had made cost comparisons, rather more than half had found that shuttleless looms would not be profitable if they were installed. The rest, nearly a third of all the non-adopters, had results favourable to shuttleless looms, but had not introduced them for other reasons.

Table 10.11. *Non-users' consideration of shuttleless looms*

	Shuttleless looms		Considered		Costed	
	Considered	Not considered	Costed	Not costed	Favourable	Not favourable
Austria	10	1	7	3	2	5
Italy	6	4	5[a]	1	2	2
Sweden	6	2	..	..	..	..
United Kingdom	4	2	2	2	1	1
United States	5	1	..	..	..	..
West Germany	9	—	6[a]	3	3	2
Total[b]	29	7	20	9	8	10

SOURCE: inquiry.

[a] Including one firm which gave no results for its calculations.
[b] Excluding Sweden and the United States.

The two reasons most frequently cited for non-adoption were the unsuitability of shuttleless looms for the firm's particular product and the high capital cost of re-equipping with a park of shuttleless looms. The unsuitability might be either because the cloth being woven was too heavy, or because it was too fine; gripper shuttles and jet looms are physically unable to cope with heavy yarns, whilst the yarn cost for fine yarns outweighs the labour cost and hence relative savings are far smaller.

Overall, production inflexibilities of all kinds (lines 1–5 in table 10.12) were almost twice as widely quoted as capital problems (lines 6–8). Only in Austria were capital problems cited by the non-users more frequently than production problems. A number of the German firms found the inflexibility of shuttleless looms, mainly the need for rigid production schedules if optimum results were to be attained, a disadvantage, while the reason most commonly cited by United States firms was the unacceptability of the unconventional selvedge. For Swedish firms, the unsuitability of shuttleless looms for the type of cloth being woven was the most common discouragement. Many of the Italian and British firms found the high cost of installing shuttleless looms prohibitive, but the product was generally unsuitable too. Insufficient standardisation of production was a commonly quoted reason

Table 10.12. *Non-users' reasons for not installing shuttleless looms*[a]

	Austria	Italy	Sweden	United Kingdom	United States	West Germany	Total
Production difficulties							
Unsuitable fabric	1	10	7	13	2	7	40
Unstandardised	1	6	—	3	—	7	17
SLs too inflexible	—	2	—	—	2	8	12
Unacceptable selvedge	—	4	—	5	8	2	19
Total	2	22	7	21	12	24	88
Financial problems							
High capital costs	..	11	..	12	—	7	..
Funds unobtainable	..	5	..	4	2	1	..
Total	4	16	2	16	2	8	48
Market uncertainty and low profits	5	4	3	4	5	3	24
Present looms adequate or not written off	1	2	—	6	1	3	13

SOURCE: inquiry.

[a] Some firms gave more than one answer. Other reasons were difficulty in obtaining labour to increase shift-working and lack of space in the weaving shed.

by the German and Italian sample firms, and a substantial number of firms in each country gave market uncertainty and the low profitability of weaving – obviously this was not a problem limited just to one or two countries.

Experience of shuttleless looms in operation

The adopters in the sample were asked how far the shuttleless looms fulfilled in operation all that had been expected of them when they were installed. The Sulzer looms were the most successful on the whole, showing gains over conventional looms on all the points of comparison in chart 10.3, and gains over the other shuttleless looms for all but one of them. Lower weft breakage rates (due to Sulzer looms' destressing of the yarn), higher production from a given floor-space (largely through greater speed of operation), lower labour requirements per unit of output and the improved quality of the output were the four strongest points of the Sulzer looms. The last, however, was frequently qualified by the consideration that the finest quality yarn was needed if the full

Chart 10.3. *The reported advantages and disadvantages of shuttleless looms*

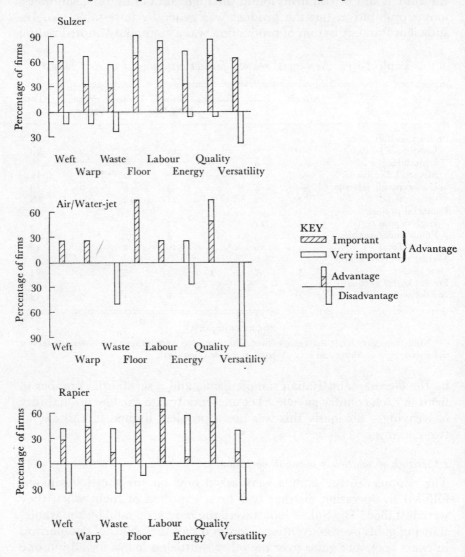

SOURCE: inquiry.

potential gains of the Sulzer loom in other directions were to be achieved, but the general feeling among firms was that the higher price paid for the better quality yarn was negligible compared with the improvements in efficiency and fabric quality that resulted.

Rapier looms were found superior to Sulzer looms only in respect of lower warp breakage rates. On the other points of comparison they had similar advantages to the Sulzer machines over conventional looms, but usually by smaller margins. They fared relatively badly on weft breakage, having no mechanism, as the Sulzer looms do, to dissipate the extra tensions involved in taking weft at high speeds from a stationary bobbin. In addition, a substantial proportion of firms found they increased wastage of yarn. Jet looms too followed a similar pattern, with increased production per unit of floor-space and improved quality of product the special advantages. But on the whole there was no saving in energy costs and, as with rapier looms, yarn waste was increased. A further disadvantage of water-jet looms was the need for a water supply and an effluent system, and air-jet looms were found to bring problems of air compression.

For all types of shuttleless loom the unconventional selvedges were stated to be a disadvantage by about 70 per cent of the adopting firms, with the Sulzer selvedges slightly more acceptable than those produced by the other types of shuttleless loom. (A third of Sulzer users as against only a quarter of rapier and jet loom users regarded the selvedges as adequate for their purposes.) On the other hand, 34 out of 39 firms listing advantages noted the importance of reduced noise levels as a feature of the looms. Overall, therefore, the shuttleless looms were regarded by the firms installing them as quite satisfactory from the operational point of view. Apart from the ancillary construction needed by the air- and water-jet looms, very few firms adopting the other types of shuttleless loom had had to undertake any major reconstruction of their weaving mills.

Relative costs of production

It is clear from the replies of the firms that greater gains can be made weaving some types of cloth than others on shuttleless looms. Shuttleless looms are more productive than conventional looms, either through their higher speeds of operation (in particular higher rates of weft insertion) or, in the case of the wider Sulzer loom, through their ability to weave wide cloths or multi-widths up to 213 inches at a similar rate of weft insertion to that of standard conventional looms 60–70 inches wide.

Table 10.6 provides some evidence of this. For all the countries the proportion of output accounted for by shuttleless looms is higher than

10

the share of shuttleless looms in all looms, and it is notable that the ratio of output to looms increases with the ratio of Sulzer looms to other shuttleless looms. In the United States, for example, where internal diffusion is mainly of the Draper flexible rapier loom, the percentage of output produced on shuttleless looms is only slightly higher than the percentage of all looms that are shuttleless; while, for the United Kingdom small adopters (the group having the highest proportion of Sulzer looms to other shuttleless looms)[1] the proportion of production is over $3\frac{1}{2}$ times as great as the proportion of looms.

Any calculation of costs per unit of output has to take additional factors into account, for example the higher capital costs of shuttleless looms. There will also be differences in the number of hours the looms will, typically, be worked. It is not just a question of one or two factors deciding relative profitability, rather there are a number of more or less mutually dependent considerations. Taking account of these simultaneously by means of conventional cost accounting methods, a single relative cost coefficient was computed for each production schedule and this is a measure of the suitability of the shuttleless loom to the individual firm's production.[2]

The relative cost coefficient, γ, was simply defined as the cost of producing a given length of cloth on a shuttleless loom as a proportion of the cost of producing the length of identical cloth on a conventional loom:

$$\gamma = \frac{g_0}{g_1},$$

where g_0 and g_1 are the operating plus overhead costs per unit of output for shuttleless and conventional looms respectively.[3]

---

[1] Given by the ratio of lines (5):(6) in table 10.6.

[2] No cost comparisons between shuttleless and conventional looms in actual operation were provided by any of the respondent firms, nor were they asked for in the questionnaires. It was felt that consistency could best be achieved, and local differences from plant to plant (with the exception of differences in shift systems and wage systems) best eliminated, by calculating relative costs centrally on a common basis. Many respondents would in any case have been unwilling to provide actual cost comparisons.

[3] It was decided for the sake of simplicity to use only the costings for the Sulzer loom, partly because ample cost data were available for it, but mainly because this is the most capital-intensive and labour-saving type of shuttleless loom, so that differences in costing, item by item, are most accentuated between it and the conventional automatics. This procedure implies that the qualities of the Sulzer machine which would favour or hinder its adoption would also be present, if to a smaller degree, in the jet and rapier looms. Such an assumption appears, upon examination, to be an exaggeration of reality but not a serious one. As with the Sulzer, the greatest cost savings from using the Draper rapier loom, and to a lesser extent jet looms, are only realised on a highly standardised production programme with long runs between fabric changes. Again, like the Sulzer, the jet looms particularly, and the rapiers less markedly, reduce the labour costs per length of cloth produced. One of the marked differences remains, however, the comparatively large capital and depreciation costs

More specifically,

$$g_i = \frac{a_i + A_i + B_i + C_i + d_i}{r_i H_i Y_i}$$

where a_i is the annual fixed labour cost, a function of H_i;

A_i is the variable labour cost, a function of r_i and H_i (the practical distinction between a_i and A_i is that the former refers to labour required for the whole period of operation of the plant regardless of whether the machinery is in operation or idle, whereas A_i covers labour required only in proportion to the actual time the machines are in operation, and is thus more closely linked to the level of output than to anything else).

B_i is the annual power cost;

C_i is the pirn winding cost (relevant to conventional looms only, so that $C_0 = 0$);

d_i is annual depreciation and interest, together with the cost of floor-space;

r_i is the efficiency rate of the machinery in the mills (the average proportion of the total number of hours worked by the plant per month or per year that the looms are in operation). The shortfall is caused by machine stops for repairing breakages of weft and warp, changing beams and fabrics, and even having looms idle through insufficient demand.

H_i is the number of hours worked each year (taken to be the same for each type of loom so that $H_0 = H_1$);

Y_i is hourly output in terms of length.

The percentage cost saving is then computed as $100(1 - \gamma)$, and plainly firms with a lower γ would be likely to adopt shuttleless looms both earlier and in larger numbers.

Other factors

The study of recent developments in the six national textile industries, together with the attitudes of the firms interviewed, suggested that differences in relative profitability are by no means the only reason for differences between firms in rates of diffusion. There is some evidence in the replies to the questionnaire on differences in the market environment and management attitudes, while variations in the size of firms

associated with the Sulzer. Whereas most of the jet and rapier looms are in a similar price-range to sophisticated conventional looms, the Sulzer machines cost on average three times as much (see Textile Council, *Cotton and Allied Textiles: a report on present performance and future prospects*, Manchester, 1969, vol. II, annexe C, p. 93).

may also be significant. A number of factors which might influence the rate of diffusion are examined below.

A major difference in the *market environment* is the degree of competition both from imports and from other home products. Many firms, especially in the United Kingdom, have been forced to alter their output range, others to cut their profit margins to the barest minimum, and a large number to close down altogether as a direct or indirect result of competition, especially from the low-wage developing countries in the Indian subcontinent and the Far East. The problem is exacerbated by the fact that these imports tend to be those fabrics for which the shuttleless loom is best suited where labour costs are relatively high, as in Western Europe and the United States – simple fabrics which can be quickly set up for long production runs on one of the less sophisticated and cheaper kinds of shuttleless loom. This is also true of home-produced warp-knitted fabrics, production of which has recently been increasing quite rapidly. Some firms have been forced out of production of those goods which could earn them the biggest gains if produced on shuttleless machines; others have been constrained to keep their prices at rock bottom, so that cash flows are insufficient for financing investment. It is accepted that shuttleless looms efficiently operated would give many firms a sufficient cost advantage over the imported goods to justify their adoption, and even firms not using shuttleless looms admit that they would be a help in competing with imports, but while cash flows remain at abysmal levels, for the majority of firms this is of academic interest only. Shuttleless looms are likely to appear in firms which can somehow avoid (or beat, although this is rare) import competition – perhaps by some subtle product differentiation.

The best indicators of differences in *managerial attitudes* are growth rates of firms, the degree of vertical integration and the extent of a firm's international interests. We consider them in turn:

(1) A fast growing company might be expected to have a more dynamic management, more ready to try new ideas, than a slow growing one, where often the structure of the firm is not flexible enough to absorb new types of machinery and where management may take a more conservative attitude towards new techniques. The growth rate of a firm can also be taken as a proxy for a firm's expectations about its own future. Sales at some future date will be a function of the growth rate between the present and that date. If we can reasonably postulate that a firm, short of having definite cause to believe the present trends will be reversed at some point in the future, expects the present growth rate to continue, then recent growth will also decide its investment strategy for the next five or ten years.

(2) There are two hypotheses that can be made with respect to the degree of vertical integration (that is whether, besides weaving, the firm is involved also in spinning, converting and making-up the woven cloth, and even, in some larger firms, in marketing the final product). The degree of vertical integration can be regarded as reflecting the firm's adaptability and receptiveness to new ideas, for the traditional structure of the cotton textile industry, both in Great Britain and on the continent, has been one of horizontal integration, with spinners, weavers and converters independent of one another. Vertical integration is the modern pattern and a firm which has taken it up is also more likely to take up other new ideas. But it also serves a second, more direct function: a firm which can dispose of its woven cloth to another company within the same group, or another subdivision within the same firm, for making-up into finished textiles, is more likely to feel that it has a guaranteed outlet for its product (whatever is happening in the retail market) than one which has to sell to an independent converter. A firm which is sheltered in this way from the fluctuations of the market must feel more secure about its future development and growth, and so more certain of reaping the full benefits of any new technology it installs, than a comparable firm with no such protection; to this extent the vertically integrated firm will be the likelier adopter.

(3) A firm which has subsidiaries abroad, or know-how agreements with foreign firms, or is a member of a group of companies, will be likely to obtain information about new techniques in the industry earlier, and subsequently will be more 'exposed' to them, knowing more about their progress, success, and relative efficiency than comparable independent firms.[1] International connections may also have a second role as a proxy for the availability of capital; companies which are members of groups usually have easier access to funds for investment should they need them. On both counts the firm with international involvements is the likelier adopter.

Finally, there is a very large divergence in the *size of firms*, both within countries and between countries, and it may be that this is an indicator of the ability of a firm to use shuttleless looms efficiently. Larger firms have greater opportunities to optimise the ratio of operatives to looms and can more easily achieve longer runs between

[1] However, this is not to accuse all independent firms of introversion. While there are many introspective traditional firms, many also are actively engaged in following market patterns and trends, and the methods of their own competitors, with whom (in the United Kingdom, at least) they have frequent contact.

stops for fabric changes, whereas small firms may not be in a position to organise multi-shift working. Small firms are also likely to be more subject to market fluctuations and, in a very slow growing industry, this may make them less willing to risk a large investment. In addition it may be more difficult for them to raise capital for new investment or a replacement of capacity. A large company with its larger stock of looms will replace looms more frequently than a small firm, even assuming a constant life of capital stock across large and small enterprises.

TESTING THE HYPOTHESES

It is now necessary to check how much confirmation (or contradiction) of the foregoing hypotheses is given by the evidence assembled during the inquiry. First we examine the ranges of the relative cost coefficient, γ.[1]

Relative cost coefficients

The United States sample had a noticeably lower range of γ values than the German and Italian samples, due mainly to the very much longer production runs and greater standardisation in the United States than in Europe (table 10.13).[2] Unit production costs could apparently be cut by over 40 per cent for some production programmes in the United States sample by the installation of shuttleless looms under ideal conditions. The range of values of γ was rather lower generally for users than for non-users, but substantial overlap between the two groups (as in the degree of standardisation)[3] implied that the firms whose output could be produced more economically on shuttleless looms have tended to be those which have actually adopted the process. A point of interpretation arises here, however; in many cases adoption of shuttleless looms must have been accompanied by some change in production schedules and conditions in order that greater benefits could be derived from the new machinery. To this extent (and it is, unfortunately, difficult to estimate how far it is important), some of the lower γ values for users of shuttleless looms must be in part a result, and not a cause, of the changeover to the capital-intensive technology.

From the foregoing it appears that the most important single component in determining γ is the degree of standardisation of the firm, expressed either as the typical length of run (that is, the length of cloth produced between production changes which necessitate shutting down

---

[1] One value of γ was assigned to each firm. Where a firm reported more than one programme which could be costed, an average was taken of the coefficients for each programme. It should be borne in mind that lower values indicate increasing superiority of the shuttleless looms, and vice versa.

[2] Textile Council, *Cotton and Allied Textiles*, vol. I.   [3] See the following paragraph.

the loom park for a number of hours), or in the number of so-called 'standard' products produced by the firm in relation to its total output. In order to quantify the latter concept, an index of standardisation (π) was constructed for each firm according to the formula $\pi = p/\sqrt{q}$, where p is the total volume of output accounted for by all the standard products, and q the number of those standard products. This formula implies that successive standard products have approximately a geometrically declining importance in terms of output volume, which is plausible. The index was then normalised with all firms as base 100.

Table 10.13. *Degree of standardisation of respondent firms*

	Index of standardisation[a]				Typical length of run			
	Geometric mean			Range[b]	Geometric mean			Range[b]
	Users	Non-users	All firms		Users	Non-users	All firms	
	(indices, all firms = 100)				(thousand yards)			
Austria	139	24	30	5–169	2.6	3.2	3.1	1.5–20.0
Italy	165	61	82	22–581	15.3	8.4	9.4	1.0–100.0
Sweden	85	26	42	17–106	12.6	12.2	12.4	5.3–30.0
United Kingdom[c]	..	..	..	..	12.7	6.9	10.1	1.0–75.0
United States	1573	1944	1659	322–6680	..	..	..	100.0–∞[d]
West Germany	160	200	174	35–1084	11.5	10.9	11.2	0.6–500.0
All countries	202	59	100	5–6680	10.4	7.1	8.4	0.6–∞
Inter-quintile range	68–400	21–156			2.0–75.0	3.0–30.0		

SOURCE: inquiry.

[a] See text above for definition.
[b] Full range for users and non-users.
[c] The United Kingdom sample gave insufficient data to calculate standardisation indices.
[d] Based on data for three non-users only.

Table 10.13 summarises the results for each country, apart from the United Kingdom where data on typical numbers of different fabrics woven were not available for the majority of the non-users. The geometric means of the standardisation indices and the typical length of run are shown for users and non-users, together with the ranges of the two statistics. Finally, the inter-quintile ranges of the statistics over the whole sample are given for users and non-users.

As expected, the longest runs and highest values of π are for the

United States; American companies are on average five times larger than their European counterparts, and they sell to a much larger market. Of the European countries, Germany appears to have the most standardised production programmes, with some 10 firms out of 22 having high values of π. Apart from three firms in the Italian sample (two users and one non-user) with high π values, the values for the remaining European firms for which the information was available fell within a narrower range lower down the scale, with users generally showing rather higher values than non-users. Over the whole sample, the range of values for users was higher than for non-users but, as with γ, the substantial overlap shows that the correlation between degree of standardisation and adoption of shuttleless looms at the level of the individual firm is low. There is a still larger overlap between users and non-users for the index measuring length of run, which otherwise shows broadly similar tendencies to the standardisation index; the United States is operating far and away the longest runs if the evidence of three non-using firms is representative. In the remaining countries the run-lengths are of similar order, with only one or two large firms in the German sample operating indefinitely long runs. The range across each of the country samples tends to be very wide, especially in relation to the size of the samples. Users are operating noticeably longer runs only in the United Kingdom and Italy, where the number of small firms in the sample may have strengthened this result.

All in all, it seems that users of shuttleless looms are somewhat more standardised than non-users, but it should be borne in mind once again that at least some rise in the degree of standardisation is likely to have resulted from the adoption of shuttleless looms as production programmes were adapted to the new techniques. The precise direction of the relationship cannot be determined without knowledge of users' standardisation levels before adoption.

Two further components of γ worth commenting upon are the extent of the changeover to (and subsequent use of) man-made fibres as opposed to natural staple yarns, and the extent of shift-working in the sample firms. Both these factors may play an important part in influencing a firm's decision about the adoption of more modern machinery, and may even act as indicators of firms' policies and attitudes to their market.

British sample firms tended to make greater use of man-made fibres than the firms in the other countries, perhaps not surprisingly since the United Kingdom is most affected by competition from cheap cotton imports and at the same time possesses an advanced chemical industry. Elsewhere the use of cotton still heavily outweighs the use of man-made fibres. A comparison of the relative importance of natural staple yarns and synthetic yarns and fibres in 1962 and 1968 shows, however, that it is in the United States sample that plants have moved in the largest numbers towards man-made fibres. The majority of them changed from over 90 per cent cotton weaving in 1962 to about 67 per cent in 1968. Elsewhere the shift towards man-made fibres has taken place in 25 to 30 per cent of sample firms in each country, and in Germany and (especially) Italy significantly more among non-users than users. To what extent a move into man-made fibres has been considered a substitute for adopting shuttleless looms it is difficult to tell. Firms' total use of man-made fibres appears, however, to be positively correlated with adoption of shuttleless looms, particularly in Sweden, where 67 per cent of users work predominantly with man-made fibres, as against 11 per cent of non-users. To a lesser extent this applies in Italy (17 per cent against 5 per cent) and the United States (33 per cent against 20 per cent). In Germany and the United Kingdom the proportions for users and non-users are very similar. Over the whole sample, 29 per cent of users make extensive use of man-made fibres against only 18 per cent of non-users.

Being a more capital-intensive technique, shuttleless looms should show greater benefits in firms where the machinery is in operation for longer hours each week (that is where there is multi-shift working) than in firms on single or one-and-a-half shift systems. Germany and the United States had the highest level of shift-working among the respondent firms (chart 10.4). For the United States, only one out of thirteen firms replying to this question was working less than three shifts, and five firms were working more than 140 hours per week. Again, all 22 of the German respondents to the full questionnaire, both users and non-users, were working three shifts. In Austria, Sweden and Italy the average number of shifts was between two and three. The United Kingdom sample firms had the lowest average, with the majority of the non-users, and as many as two-fifths of all sample plants, on single-shift working.[1,2]

It was in the British sample in fact (that is where there was most single-shift working), that the most marked difference in shifts worked by users and non-users was to be seen. Elsewhere, differences in shift working did not seem to be an important factor influencing the diffusion of shuttleless looms, presumably because differences in the benefits derived from shuttleless looms between two and three shifts are small compared to those between one and two shifts.

[1] See pp. 265–6.
[2] However, this tells only half the story. At the other extreme, a further two-fifths of the British sample, including the majority of those using shuttleless looms, were operating three or more shifts.

Chart 10.4. *Patterns of shift-working*

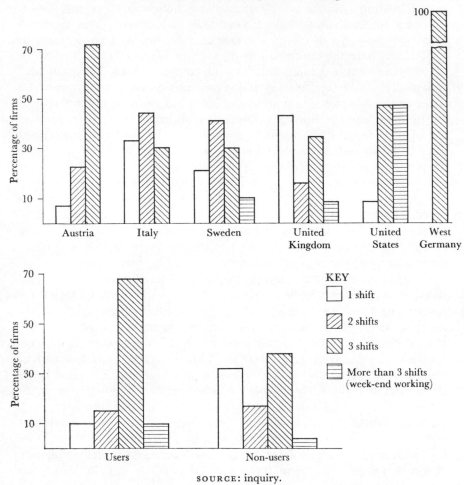

SOURCE: inquiry.

The influence of other factors

The effects of import competition as estimated by the individual firms were ambiguous: the degree of competition by imported fabrics showed similar distributions for users and non-users. A large proportion of the firms which admitted being troubled by import competition (54 out of 81) had either been forced or had chosen to move out of some part of their production, many embarking upon new lines (table 10.14). An equally common reaction (62 firms) was to cut production costs as far as possible and compete, and many firms (38) had done a little on both

Table 10.14. *Competition from imports and warp-knitting, and reactions to it*

	Proportion of firms in each country reporting competition (serious or moderately serious)		Replies mentioning:					
			Take up warp-knitting		Reduce costs or improve quality		Give up some lines	
	Users	Non-users	Users	Non-users	Users	Non-users	Users	Non-users
	(percentages)							
Austria	*100*[a]	*75*	I	I	I	8	I	9
Italy	*57*	*68*	—	I	I	5	2	5
Sweden	*100*[b]	*100*	—	I	2	6	2	6
United Kingdom	*47*	*73*	4	I	6	4	4	3
United States	*90*	*95*	I	—	5	6	2	2
West Germany	*85*	*79*	I	—	12	6	I I	7
All countries	*75*	*78*	7	4	27	35	22	32

SOURCE: main inquiry.

[a] One firm only.   [b] Three firms.

fronts. Users and non-users of shuttleless looms showed the same re-action pattern; how firms combated import competition had little to do with whether they had adopted shuttleless looms or not.

Among the factors illustrating the type of management of the firm, vertical integration seems to be predominant. Chart 10.5 shows this for firms in the sample: among the users there was a predominance of

Chart 10.5. *Vertical integration, users and non-users*

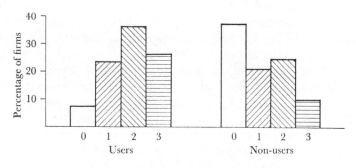

SOURCE: inquiry.

Note: 0 = no vertical association;
 1 = partial vertical association;
 2 = partial vertical association with some involvement in finishing or distribution;
 3 = complete vertical integration.

vertically integrated firms, whereas among the non-users the reverse was the case. Foreign involvement (that is, whether or not a firm has foreign subsidiaries or agreements or other special relationships with foreign companies) appears also to be important.[1] Table 10.15 shows that in all the countries except the United States there is more foreign involvement among users than among non-users.

Table 10.15. *Foreign connections of firms*[a]

	With foreign connections		Without foreign connections	
	Users	Non-users	Users	Non-users
Austria	2	2	–	9
Italy	2	–	2	12
Sweden	1	–	2	9
United Kingdom	4	1	4	7
United States	1	2	3	4
West Germany	7	2	6	8
All countries	17	7	17	49
Total	24		66	

SOURCE: inquiry.

[a] Firms with 'know-how' agreements and foreign subsidiaries, except Sweden where information in respect of foreign subsidiaries was not available.

Firms which expanded output faster over the period 1962–8 appear to have been more likely to adopt shuttleless looms, but this tendency derives almost entirely from a fairly strong correlation between growth of output and adoption in the United States, Italian and German samples. In the United Kingdom and Sweden there was no apparent relationship; a number of declining firms had switched to shuttleless looms and still declined, while a number of the fast growing firms had expanded without the aid of shuttleless looms.

The analysis also suggests that smaller firms were the earliest adopters, so that during the early years they were in the majority; but afterwards many big firms adopted in a short space of time, so that after the earlier years there remained relatively few large firms which had not adopted, but a majority of smaller firms had still not done so. In all the country samples there were some large firms among the non-adopters; it was in the United States and possibly the United Kingdom

[1] This variable overlaps to some extent with vertical integration in what it represents. Indeed a large number of vertically integrated firms in the sample are foreign linked and vice versa, but the correspondence is by no means so nearly one-to-one that the separate consideration of foreign involvement is unnecessary.

samples that they were relatively scarce. The other countries had similar proportions of users and non-users among large and small firms.

Cross-section analysis

A cross-section analysis was carried out using least squares including the variables discussed above, namely the relative cost coefficient, import competition, vertical integration, foreign participation and the growth of the firm's output between 1962 and 1968, together with the size of firm in 1962, as potential explanatory factors for:

(a) whether firms had adopted or not by 1969;
(b) the timing of adoption (inter-firm diffusion);
(c) the extent of intra-firm diffusion, measured first relatively and then by absolute numbers of shuttleless looms installed.

The independent variables were chosen partly with regard to the hypotheses on pages 273–6 and partly to be readily quantifiable. They consisted of the following:

SIZE: the size of the firm in 1962, measured by a weighted average of numbers of looms, numbers of employees, and scale of output, expressed as an index of the value for other firms in the sample from the same country (this neutralised the effect of the wide divergence between the absolute sizes of United States and European firms);

GWTH: the growth of the output of the firm between 1962 and 1968 expressed as an index with 1962 = 100;

GWDM: an integral-valued classification for growth;

IMP: the effect of import competition from overseas (a discrete variable increasing with the number of sources of competition and with the strength of the competition, subjectively assessed by the firm);

VERT: the degree of vertical integration of each firm, increasing from 0 up to 4 with the number of ancillary activities in which the firm or an associate participates, special importance being attached to involvement in converting or distribution;[1]

FORN: the degree of foreign involvement of each firm, measured according to whether the firm has subsidiaries or associate firms abroad, and whether it has know-how agreements with foreign firms;

ABSIZE: the absolute size of the firm measured by 1963 output volume, omitting United States firms;

[1] See p. 275.

PROF: the lowest coefficient of profitability (γ) for each firm calculated as described above;[1]

PROFX: the average coefficient of profitability for each firm.

The dependent variables were:

$Y(0,1)$: a binary variable denoting the absence or presence respectively of shuttleless looms;[2]

YYRI: the timelag in years between 1954 (the first international adoption) and individual firms' adoption (for simplicity non-users were assigned an arbitrary adoption date in the future (1980), except where they had definite plans to adopt for the first time before that date);

YYRN: the timelag in years between the first national adoption and individual firms' adoption (non-users were assigned a date in the same way as for YYRI);

YPC: the percentage of all looms that were shuttleless in 1969;

YSUL: an integral variable representing absolute levels of adoption of Sulzer looms in 1969;

YSRJ: an integral variable representing absolute levels of adoption of all shuttleless looms in 1969.

Austria was excluded from this analysis; for the other countries the sample used was rather smaller than that examined in the last section, some firms having to be rejected owing to missing information.

The first two regressions in table 10.16 show that vertical integration of a firm is the most important explanatory factor of $Y(0,1)$, whether or not shuttleless looms had been adopted by 1969; in addition, foreign connections, the rate of growth and import competition are all significant at the 95 per cent level. These two equations are the ones that perform best in terms of variables showing significant coefficients; only size is not significant and this performs very poorly, implying that actual adoption at a given point in time (1969) is evenly distributed between large and small firms.

In determining the timelag between the innovation (first adoption) of the technique, internationally and nationally, and its adoption by individual sample firms (YYRI and YYRN), vertical integration appears most influential; those firms with higher degrees of integration tending to adopt the new technique earlier. The growth rate of the firm has some influence, with the faster growing firms adopting earlier; firms with foreign connections are also among the early adopters. The degree of import competition and the size of firm are less important.

[1] See pp. 272–3.
[2] Firms having only two or three shuttleless looms were treated as non-users.

For explaining the extent of diffusion by 1969 within firms in relative and absolute terms, YSRJ and YPC, vertical integration and foreign contacts are again more often than not significant at the 90 per cent level, although in explaining diffusion of Sulzer looms, YSUL, foreign contacts

Table 10.16. *Least squares analysis: sample of users and non-users*

	Dependent variable	Constant	SIZE	GWTH or GWDM†	IMP	VERT	FORN	R^2
	$Y(0, 1)$	−0·14	0·0162	0·056†	−0·023	0·027	0·055	0·189
		(0·63)	(0·39)	(2·05)	(2·31)	(2·46)	(2·25)	
*	$Y(0, 1)$	−1·23	0·0229	0·404	−0·108	0·110	0·068	0·191
		(1·26)	(0·40)	(2·50)	(2·36)	(2·49)	(2·31)	
	YYRI	28·97	−0·0028	−0·967†	0·242	−0·378	−1·034	0·132
		(4·04)	(0·25)	(1·55)	(1·00)	(1·39)	(1·72)	
**	YYRI	4·83	*0·1380*	−0·577	0·014	−0·214	−0·041	0·113
		(2·71)	(0·99)	(1·53)	(0·19)	(2·28)	(0·61)	
	YYRN	22·68	−0·0047	−0·719†	0·343	−0·341	−0·936	0·133
		(3·44)	(0·46)	(1·25)	(1·54)	(1·36)	(1·70)	
**	YYRN	4·01	*0·1410*	−0·477	0·083	−0·255	−0·056	0·107
		(1·90)	(0·85)	(1·07)	(0·57)	(2·30)	(0·69)	
	YSUL	−0·76	0·0013	0·107†	−0·008	0·021	0·025	0·121
		(1·12)	(1·19)	(1·83)	(0·34)	(0·81)	(0·44)	
*	YSUL	−3·08	0·2040	1·241†	−0·103	0·106	0·010	0·183
		(2·22)	(1·63)	(2·19)	(0·93)	(1·26)	(0·17)	
	YSRJ	−0·89	0·0034	0·143†	−0·042	0·064	0·181	0·303
		(0·96)	(2·31)	(1·77)	(1·33)	(1·81)	(2·33)	
*	YSRJ	−5·04	0·2870	1·169	−0·247	0·249	0·177	0·285
		(2·16)	(1·57)	(2·37)	(1·54)	(2·03)	(1·99)	
	YPC	−9·93	0·0008	1·787†	−0·374	0·473	0·312	0·094
		(0·88)	(0·05)	(1·83)	(0·99)	(1·11)	(0·33)	
**	YPC	−7·22	*−0·0249*	1·755	−0·624	0·538	0·284	0·213
		(1·64)	(0·07)	(1·89)	(2·06)	(2·33)	(1·69)	

SOURCE: NIESR estimates.

Notes: (i) Unlogged relationships except: * = independent variables logged, and ** = all variables logged.
(ii) For definitions of variables see pp. 283–4.
(iii) Italic coefficients have signs which conflict with the hypotheses.
(iv) Numbers in brackets are *t*-ratios, for which critical values (with 54 degrees of freedom): at 95% 2·00, at 90% 1·67.

perform very weakly. The coefficient for import competition is significant in only one of these four equations. The growth rate of the firm is, however, a strong underlying influence, with the faster growing firms more likely to adopt on a large scale than slower growing or declining firms. The size of firm is important as a positive influence in defining the extent of diffusion in absolute terms (YSRJ and YSUL), but has a negligible effect in the explanation of relative diffusion (YPC), suggesting that smaller adopters have a higher percentage of shuttleless looms than larger ones.

Table 10.17. *Least squares analysis including absolute size of firm: sample of users and non-users from Italy, Sweden, United Kingdom and West Germany*

Dependent variable	Constant	ABSIZE	GWDM	IMP	VERT	FORN	R^2
$Y(0, 1)$	−0·39 (1·73)	0·0061 (1·68)	0·10 (3·54)	−0·031 (3·38)	0·0043 (0·66)	0·036 (2·26)	0·293
YYRI	24·54 (4·77)	−0·1988 (1·86)	−1·71 (2·60)	0·383 (1·52)	0·0375 (0·14)	−1·406 (2·16)	0·247
YYRN	27·33 (4·13)	−0·1939 (1·99)	−1·36 (2·25)	0·480 (2·09)	0·0412 (0·17)	−1·27 (2·13)	0·240
YSUL	−0·97 (1·40)	0·0162 (1·59)	0·13 (2·03)	−0·004 (0·14)	0·0001 (0·00)	0·060 (0·95)	0·150
YSRJ	−1·28 (1·35)	0·0231 (1·65)	0·21 (2·40)	−0·051 (1·55)	0·0415 (1·16)	0·220 (2·58)	0·290
YPC	−17·63 (1·39)	0·1180 (0·63)	2·70 (2·33)	−0·375 (0·85)	0·1700 (0·36)	0·556 (0·49)	0·133

SOURCE: NIESR estimates.

Notes: (i) Unlogged relationships, with heteroscedaticity eliminated from the first equation.
(ii) For definitions of variables see pp. 283–4.
(iii) Numbers in brackets are t-ratios for which critical values (with 47 degrees of freedom): at 95% 2·01, at 90% 1·68.

Table 10.17 shows a further set of regressions, from which data for the United States have been omitted, using absolute size instead of relative size and growth of the firm. Table 10.18 reverts to relative size and is based on only the 38 firms for which the cost variable was computed. Both these sets of equations tend to confirm that the most important influences on the adoption of shuttleless looms were the growth of individual firms between 1962 and 1968, particularly in its integral form, GWDM, and the extent of their foreign associations, FORN. Vertical integration, the size of the firm, degree of foreign import competition, and the suitability of the shuttleless loom technology to the individual firms' production, while generally pervasive influences, rarely took coefficients that were significantly non-zero even at the 90 per cent level. However, nearly all the variables in all the equations took the signs that were consistent with our hypothesis: fast growth, a high degree of vertical integration and of foreign association, and large size were found to be generally conducive to adoption; while a high degree of import competition and a high coefficient of profitability were features associated with non-adoption. In every case too, PROFX, average profitability, performs rather less well than PROF, maximum profitability.

Table 10.18. *Least squares analysis including profitability: sample of users and non-users*

Dependent variable	Constant	SIZE	GWDM	IMP	VERT	FORN	PROF	R²
YYRI	35·52 (2·56)	−0·006 (0·33)	−1·87 (2·09)	0·170 (0·50)	−0·270 (0·69)	−1·319 (1·61)	3·97 (0·55)	0·230
YYRN	25·90 (2·03)	−0·008 (0·51)	−1·37 (1·66)	0·421 (1·34)	−0·241 (0·67)	−1·213 (1·61)	2·57 (0·39)	0·207
** YYRN	6·24 (2·33)	*0·114* (0·54)	−1·76 (1·64)	0·047 (0·21)	−0·313 (1·88)	−0·055 (0·48)	0·81 (0·99)	0·218
* YSUL	−4·27 (2·23)	0·326 (2·17)	1·48 (1·93)	−0·068 (0·44)	0·087 (0·74)	0·027 (0·34)	−0·71 (1·22)	0·307
* YSRJ	−3·82 (1·39)	0·136 (0·63)	1·76 (1·60)	−0·104 (0·46)	0·329 (1·92)	0·168 (1·44)	−1·27 (1·51)	0·335
* YPC	−9·47 (1·85)	*−0·331* (0·82)	4·39 (2·14)	−0·320 (0·77)	0·785 (2·47)	0·262 (1·20)	−1·58 (1·01)	0·349

SOURCE: NIESR estimates.

Notes: (i) Unlogged relationships except: * = independent variables logged, ** = all variables logged.
(ii) For definitions of variables see pp. 283–4.
(iii) Italic coefficients have signs which conflict with the hypotheses.
(iv) Numbers in brackets are *t*-ratios, for which critical values (with 31 degrees of freedom); at 95% 2·04, at 90% 1·70.
(v) If PROFX substituted for PROF, it gave results as follows:

	YYRI	YYRN	** YYRN	* YSUL	* YSRJ	* YPC
Coefficient	1·54	0·66	0·46	−0·50	−1·08	−1·15
t-ratio	(0·23)	(0·11)	(0·56)	(0·85)	(1·28)	(0·73)
R²	0·224	0·204	0·201	0·290	0·322	0·339

Table 10.19 shows the results of the regressions on the sample of users only. Here a number of the variables reverse the direction of their influence; in particular, a high degree of import competition now has a positive effect, and foreign connections a negative one.[1] What is

[1] The signs of these coefficients in the regressions for YYRI are negative and positive respectively because YYRI is itself a negative variable, but they are still reversed from the signs in table 10.16.

surprising is that this does not occur just in one regression, but on both extent and timing of adoption variables with more or less equal force, and in the regression on YPC logged, the perverse influence of FORN is all but significant at the 95 per cent level. The only conclusion we can draw is that, while among the whole sample non-adopters had to face

Table 10.19. *Least squares analysis: sample of users only*

	Dependent variable	Constant	SIZE	GWTH	IMP	VERT	FORN	R²
**	YYRI	2·61	*0·339*	−0·342	*−0·225*	−0·246	*0·094*	0·273
		(1·05)	(1·98)	(0·66)	(1·40)	(1·43)	(0·94)	
	YYRI	12·13	*0·018*	−0·037	*−0·271*	−0·085	*0·048*	0·251
		(2·95)	(2·15)	(1·64)	(1·40)	(0·35)	(0·13)	
*	YSUL	−1·64	0·285	0·262	*0·023*	0·150	−0·171	0·179
		(0·53)	(1·33)	(0·41)	(0·12)	(0·70)	(1·36)	
*	YSRJ	−0·91	0·333	0·276	*0·037*	0·265	−0·037	0·303
		(0·36)	(1·90)	(0·52)	(0·22)	(1·51)	(0·36)	
**	YPC	−1·78	*−0·357*	1·046	*0·027*	0·458	−0·228	0·456
		(0·64)	(1·87)	(1·81)	(0·15)	(2·39)	(2·03)	

SOURCE: NIESR estimates.

Notes: (i) Unlogged relationships except: * = independent variables logged, ** = all variables logged.
(ii) For definitions of variables see pp. 283–4.
(iii) Italic coefficients have signs which conflict with the hypotheses.
(iv) Numbers in brackets are *t*-ratios for which critical values (with 20 degrees of freedom): at 95% 2·09, at 90% 1·72.
(v) If GWDM substituted for GWTH, it gave results as follows:

	** YYRI	YYRI	* YSUL	* YSRJ	** YPC
Coefficient	−0·51	−0·79	0·55	0·20	1·61
t-ratio	(0·49)	(1·28)	(0·42)	(0·19)	(1·35)
R²	0·266	0·214	0·180	0·295	0·420

more import competition than adopters and firms without foreign associations tended to be non-adopters, the majority of the early adopters were smaller firms encountering substantial competition from imports and with little foreign investment. These early adopters tended to invest in both Sulzer and other shuttleless looms to a greater absolute (and hence relative) extent than the larger and foreign-associated firms, many of which adopted a little later on.

There was also marked reversal of sign in the coefficient for size of firms, from almost significantly positive in the logged regressions over the whole sample for the absolute YSUL and YSRJ, to significantly negative in the regressions over the sample of the users alone for YPC. The implication, again, is that, while the larger adopting firms tended to have more shuttleless looms installed than the smaller adopters, the latter had installed more in relation to their total number of looms than the former.

But the fit of all the equations tested leaves much to be desired. Even when all the independent variables are included simultaneously, barely a third of the variance in the diffusion indices is explained by the regression analysis as measured by R^2, and less than one-sixth of the variance in the timelag between first use (1954) and adoption by individual firms. The results thus leave unaccounted for a large residual of as much as two-thirds of the total variation. There are three possible explanations. The first is that one of a number of readily recognisable variables of the firm that were not brought into the equations (such as the age and qualifications of the managing director, or the age of the machinery in use) had a systematic influence on the diffusion, so that their inclusion would have markedly reduced the unexplained residual. This seems unlikely, because one or two further variables would probably not contribute more explanation than all the selected variables already tested taken together, and certainly not up to four times as much.

The second explanation concerns accuracy of measurement in two aspects. First there is the familiar problem of errors in the data, in this case in the answers to the questionnaire, where responses even for objective variables such as size and growth can be no more than approximations. Data on the more qualitative variables, such as vertical integration, are based on different subjective viewpoints, so producing further cumulative errors. Proxy variables, if they fail to reflect accurately the behavioural characteristics they are taken to represent, introduce yet further errors, and this may be relevant to the comparatively poor performance of profitability as measured by the relative cost coefficient.

The final possibility is that there are highly random influences at work: for example, if each entrepreneur is assumed to maximise his profits in the long-term, subject to his own expectations about the future at any given point in time, then vertically integrated firms, orientated towards the adoption of cost-saving techniques and progressive increases in efficiency and productivity levels, and endowed with the necessary managerial and financial resources would regularly install new equipment, reorganise production lines and increase standardisation, at the same time influencing the market to accept more highly standardised articles. At the other end of the scale, traditional small firms would attempt to maintain their profits by reducing costs through minor investments and alterations to their weaving sheds where possible, being almost invariably discouraged from making larger investments by lack of capital and uncertainty about the future; rather than standardise they would be more likely to diversify to reduce the risk of incurring large losses.

In addition to this, there are differences in attitudes among the managers of individual firms. We tried to measure some of these, but a majority of the firms in the inquiry were in the 'small and traditional' group, and here there are almost as many attitudes to the business of weaving as there are weaving managers. Even for two firms in apparently similar circumstances, profit-maximisation may be interpreted completely differently according to the outlook and relative values of management, and, of course, especially among smaller firms, it is rarely the case that managers are in practice working to a profit-maximising formula.

So although each firm may behave 'rationally' in its own circumstances and according to its manager's own interpretation of future prospects, the industry as a whole may appear to act quite irrationally in the long term in deciding for or against a piece of new capital equipment. The multiplicity of ages and types of looms in operation, and the variations in managers' assessment of new machinery (especially in relation to existing machines and their different production schedules), all add to the hazards of trying to establish an empirical link between adoption or non-adoption of the new technology and such characteristics as standardisation, import competition, or the suitability of output to shuttleless looms, even though these factors should be decisive in a theoretical economic context.

CONCLUSIONS

Diffusion of the shuttleless loom was still in progress at the time of our inquiry. Certain methods of analysis that have been used in earlier studies on the diffusion of new technologies were therefore not applicable, or gave open-ended results. It was, however, possible to analyse the early part of the diffusion process and to characterise the early adopters in an informal way, and subsequently to make a more formal differentiation between the adopting and non-adopting firms.

The general picture is one of reluctance to install shuttleless looms until about 1964, that is during the first ten years of their availability, but of relative enthusiasm after that date as the larger firms plunged in. This has been particularly the case in the United Kingdom. No doubt some of the earlier sluggishness was due to the teething troubles with certain types of loom,[1] which were largely overcome by the mid-1960s. Much of the remainder may be ascribed to uncertainty about market prospects, as well as to the failure of large companies to take up the innovation as pioneers in an inspiring way; and, as in the early years of any innovation, there was a lack of first- or even second-hand operational experience of the technique itself.

After some 14 years since the innovation, it seems apparent that, among the six countries under consideration, diffusion of the shuttleless loom has gone ahead faster than average in Germany and perhaps also the United States (although the less representative nature of the United States sample makes this result more tentative), while the British and Italian industries have been slower than the average. This is supported firstly by the series for numbers of shuttleless looms, which by 1969 were further from saturation point for the British and Italian samples than for all the six countries; secondly, by the fact that, in these two samples, internal diffusion was lowest in relation to intra-firm diffusion, while it was highest in Germany and the United States.[2] This 'laggard' tendency in the United Kingdom and Italy is associated with a more heterogeneous weaving industry with a large proportion of small firms, as compared with the highly concentrated American and German industries containing many vertically integrated large firms.

A number of factors that might be expected to influence the rate and pattern of adoption of shuttleless looms were examined. A small sub-group of these factors were found to explain practically the same proportion of the differences as all of them in combination; but there was also a large residual for which some intuitive rationalisation was attempted, but which may equally well result from omitting further variables.

Table 10.20 summarises the effects of the variables considered upon individual firms' adoption or rejection of shuttleless looms for each of the six countries. These results are drawn more from the descriptive inter-firm comparison than from the econometric approach, which used only sub-groups of the national samples because of missing data from some respondent firms, but for size and growth relationships deduced mainly from the least squares analysis are shown.

There are no outstanding inconsistencies between countries in the effects of the various factors.[3] One of the interesting findings is that the

[1] See Ray, 'The diffusion of new technology', p. 64.

[2] This result is tentative for Italy owing to the small number of adopters in that sample. The measures used are those in table 10.5.

[3] Only one factor – the shift towards the use of man-made fibres – was apparently negatively correlated with the adoption of shuttleless looms in one country (Italy) while positively associated with it elsewhere (table 10.20). This is probably a random result.

suitability of the cloth being produced does not seem to be decisive for the adoption or rejection of shuttleless looms. Certainly shuttleless looms are not installed in many situations where a cost comparison would suggest that they would be highly profitable, while in some firms weaving apparently less suitable fabrics they are found in quantity. This suggests two things. First, firms did not generally carry out sophisticated cost

Table 10.20. *Correlations between characteristics of firms and their adoption of shuttleless looms*

	Austria	Italy	Sweden	United Kingdom	United States	West Germany	All countries
Profitability	..	o	+	..	o	o	+
Standardisation	..	+	..	..	..	o	+
Shift-working	+	o	++	+	o	o	++
Size	..	..	o	o	+	o	+
Growth	..	+	o	o	+	+	+
Share of man-made fibres in output	+	−	++	o	+	o	+
Competition from imports and warp-knitting	..	−	o	−	o	−	−
Vertical integration	+	+	o	++	+	o	++
Foreign connections	+	+	o	+	o	++	++
Research and development	o	o	o	+	o	+	o

SOURCE: NIESR estimates.

Notes: (i) The data in this table are impressionistic assessments only based on all the tests used and are not intended to be more precise than the statements in the text.

(ii) + a positive correlation;
++ a strong positive correlation;
− a negative correlation;
o no apparent correlation;
.. no comparison made, often because of the small number of observations.

comparisons. Out of 36 non-adopters who replied to questions about the consideration of shuttleless looms (see table 10.11), 16 either had not considered introducing shuttleless looms or, if they had, had made no cost comparisons. For the other 20 non-users, as well as for all the users (who presumably did some cost calculations), the degree of sophistication, or indeed of accuracy of their comparisons is unknown.

The most universally cogent influences on the rate of diffusion are the degree of vertical integration, the extent of foreign connections and the severity of competition from imported weaves and knitted fabrics, the first two having positive effects in four out of the six countries, and the last being apparently a discouragement in the three countries where imports are most strongly competitive with home production. The use of man-made fibres, size and growth of firms, and the relative advantage of firms' output on shuttleless looms, are less important factors.

Earlier reports on the diffusion of shuttleless looms[1] came to the conclusion that one important obstacle to faster diffusion was the fact that the mass-produced fabrics which were so suitable for weaving on shuttleless looms were precisely those in which the developing countries were specialising. The results of the present study largely confirm this finding. Although it seems that decisions to adopt or reject shuttleless looms by individual firms have been reached largely regardless of the intensity of cheap import competition, many firms which have not yet adopted cite market uncertainty, low profitability, and lack of capital funds among their reasons. At least some part of this uncertainty stems from import competition, especially in the United Kingdom from India, Pakistan and South East Asia. Further reasons for uncertainty are the slow growth of demand for woven fabrics, and competition from giant producers which produce a wide variety of cloths in bulk and at relatively low cost on modern machinery.[2] The market-shares, and even in some cases the absolute outputs, of small and medium-sized weavers (that is, the large majority of firms) have fallen considerably; under these conditions firms which may face the possibility of closing down are unlikely to invest in expensive new machinery before their old machinery is written-off.

[1] Notably Ray, 'The diffusion of new technology'; Smith, 'The weaving of cotton and allied textiles in Great Britain'.

[2] Smith, 'The weaving of cotton and allied textiles', p. 67, fn. 1.

CHAPTER 11

SUMMARY AND CONCLUSIONS

By L. Nabseth, IUI [1]

INTRODUCTION

In the Introduction to this book we stressed the importance of diffusion of new technical processes as a decisive factor in raising efficiency and productivity in industry. Under special circumstances, even if a new process was used only by its innovator in his home country, it might still be of great economic importance. But it is mostly through its diffusion to other companies, both intra-nationally and internationally (including to foreign subsidiaries)[2] that a new process becomes really significant. A free flow of ideas and information between firms and countries is normally essential if a process innovation is to be of economic importance on the international scene. Cultures and societies which suppress such a flow are at a disadvantage in their efforts to increase productivity, and processes developed in secret, for instance in defence work, will probably be diffused much slower than other new technologies. But even in countries like those studied in this book, where information on new technology is fairly freely accessible, there is a real problem of delay in the spread of information on new processes. The theory that such information diffuses very rapidly among companies in different countries was not substantiated in the two cases where we obtained detailed information, numerically controlled machine tools and special presses. We shall take up this point again later.

This book is focused on the diffusion in some countries of a few new

---

[1] This chapter is based primarily on the different chapters of this book. But other results from the investigation have been presented elsewhere, and to some extent they are taken into account. These are: M. Breitenacher, 'Innovation und Imitation fördern den technischen Fortschritt', Wirtschaftskonjunktur (Berichte des IFO-Instituts für Wirtschaftsforschung), vol. 21, no. 3, July 1969; Davies, 'The clay brick industry and the tunnel kiln'; A. Gebhardt, 'Der Tunnelofen in der Ziegelindustrie – Beispeil einer neuen Technologie', IFO-Schnelldienst, vol. 24, no. 27, July 1971; L. Nabseth, 'The diffusion of innovations in Swedish industry', paper given to the International Economic Association conference at St Anton, 1971; G. F. Ray, 'The diffusion of new technology', also 'Ergebnisse von Diffusionsuntersuchungen in Europa' in O. Hatzold (ed.), Innovation in der Wirtschaft, Munich, IFO, 1970 and 'New technology and enterprise decisions' in Z. Román (ed.) Progress and Planning in Industry, Budapest, Akadémiai Kiadó, 1972; H. Schedl, 'Geringe Verbreitung schützenloser Webmaschinen in der Baumwollindustrie', IFO-Schnelldienst, vol. 23, no. 40, October 1970; Smith, 'The weaving of cotton and allied textiles in Great Britain'.

[2] For a discussion of the importance of the multinational firm for the diffusion of new technology see OECD, Gaps in Technology. Analytical Report, Paris, 1970.

processes introduced since World War II. When the project started, we thought it would be easy to find examples of important new technologies and that the only problem would be to choose between the many alternatives. As it turned out, however, it proved quite difficult for engineers in different industries to find examples of new technologies with major effects. For those working close to the production line, technological change seems to go much more in steps than by leaps, or perhaps one could say that it often seems to go by a few leaps and then many small steps. (Float glass is an example in this book.) This general conclusion is based on more material than that presented here, since our attempts to find good examples of new processes were quite extensive. The importance of smooth and continuous progress is also stressed in the introduction to chapter 6, even though basic oxygen steel was considered at first to be one of the clearer cases of a major 'leap forward' in technology.

In the Introduction it was stated that the aims of the investigation were:

(a) to assess the scope and extent of the diffusion of selected new processes in the countries covered, and to establish the international differences in the level and speed of their diffusion;

(b) to study the factors which affect the speed of diffusion;

(c) to make some attempt to account for the differences between countries.

The obvious question to ask in this Summary is: did the group succeed in its intentions?

INTERNATIONAL DIFFERENCES IN THE DIFFUSION OF SELECTED NEW PROCESSES

We were interested only in new processes, or, from the sellers' point of view, new products in the producer-goods industries. New consumer-goods were not considered; one obvious reason being that quite a number of studies of the international diffusion of consumer products, for instance, television sets, cars and man-made fibres, are already available. Studies of new processes, especially in the industrial sector, are fewer and mostly relate to American conditions.[1] Our investigations provided a simple explanation for this: it is more difficult to study producer- than consumer-goods. There are quite good statistics of stocks

[1] Griliches, 'Hybrid corn'; Mansfield, *Industrial Research and Technological Innovation*; J. E. Tilton, *International Diffusion of Technology: the case of semi-conductors*, Washington (DC), The Brookings Institution, 1971.

of the latter, but the same is not true of production equipment, with the one exception of the iron and steel industry among the cases considered here.

For this study, it was decided to obtain information directly from firms, partly because this was thought to improve the possibility of explaining differences in diffusion patterns between countries, partly because it seemed the only way to get the information required, and partly because we were also interested in differences between companies (for instance between firms of different sizes) and in comparisons with other studies.[1] We used some other sources, such as trade associations and individual experts, and found that for our kind of economic research, it was easier to get data from firms in small countries than in large ones.[2] Probably this is because in smaller countries there are fewer companies to contact and it is easier to convince them of the value of the research project. For some big countries, notably Germany, Italy and the United States, the information presented on, for instance, special presses, is so restricted that one must admit the diffusion diagrams are not really representative. This does not, of course, mean that the information is useless. On this point one general conclusion seems to be that producers or licence-holders of the processes can provide as reliable data on diffusion as the firms which use the process (special presses, float glass and shuttleless looms were good cases in point).

One reason for restricting the new techniques considered to processes introduced since the war[3] was that in many countries earlier data were unobtainable. But it meant that in most cases diffusion is still going on, and will continue during the seventies and possibly the eighties as well. In one respect, this represents a limitation on the data and analysis; on the other hand, there is value – certainly novelty value – in studying diffusion at an early stage, as it is for instance in continuous casting. For other processes, such as shuttleless looms and basic oxygen steel, diffusion is well under way or almost complete. In fact the part of the diffusion process analysed for continuous casting is regarded only as a preliminary development stage in basic oxygen steel. This lack of complete data also caused problems in the econometric calculations: for instance, for special presses and shuttleless looms arbitrary introduction dates had to be assigned to non-adopters so that all the available information could be used.

But even if, ideally, one had all the data required, problems would still arise in presenting diffusion patterns for different countries. Total

[1] In Mansfield's studies the only comparisons are between processes and firms.

[2] Some members of our research team think, however, that this is more a question of the technology studied than of the size of country.

[3] The tunnel kiln is an exception; it originated earlier, although its wider application has also been post-war.

output in a country produced by the new process, the increase in capacity that is equipped with the process, the number of firms, plants, or machines using the process, can all be stated, but the data ought to relate to the questions to be answered. From a macro-economic point of view, one might argue that it is the influence of diffusion on total production that is of primary interest – whether a process is used intensively in a few firms or more extensively in many. On the other hand, the decision to introduce new processes must be made by someone, usually managements of firms or plants, so that, to analyse in depth the decision process in relation to new techniques, data from firms or even individual plants are needed. Furthermore, company data are required to understand how the diffusion process might be influenced, for instance speeded up, although, if the object is simply to forecast the diffusion pattern, some type of curve fitting to aggregate data might be sufficient.

The real problem in presenting diffusion diagrams, however, is not the numerator but the choice of a meaningful denominator: what is a reasonable basis of comparison?[1] In studying the diffusion of a new technique, in the paper or steel industry for instance, the data can be related either to the total production of paper or steel, or to the number of firms in the industry. But problems at once arise: either the new technique may never be suitable for certain types of paper or steel, or it may improve over time, so that while it is unsuitable for parts of the production or some types of firms initially, it will be suitable later on. Examples of the first case are special presses, which have never been suitable for some types of paper, and tunnel kilns, which cannot be used for certain grades of clay. The basic oxygen process illustrates the second case, since initially it could not be adapted for big plants, for producing specialised steels, or for processing high-phosphoric ores. A third problem arises with numerically controlled machine tools, which can be used to produce parts of many different products that are, however, not clearly definable, and a fourth (relating both to the numerator and the denominator) is how to fix a starting date for commercial operation of a new process which has been improved over a long period, but initially could be used only in some types of plant. When is it possible to say that the process has really become an innovation in the Schumpeterian sense of the word?

These problems can be solved in different ways, all more or less arbitrary. In the chapters on continuous casting and tunnel kilns, a 'technological ceiling' was assumed for each country, but the problem of defining the ceiling remained. For the diffusion charts to provide a

[1] See also G. F. Ray, 'On defining diffusion of new techniques', *Business Economist*, vol. 4, Summer 1972, pp. 82–8.

definition, either the process must have been in use for a very long time, or some sort of theoretical definition is needed. Another solution is to ignore that part of the production or production equipment which is definitely unsuitable for the new process. This was done for special presses and tunnel kilns, but, of course, here too there is an arbitrary element.

Yet another way of handling the problem is to use Mansfield's method of counting only those firms that have already introduced the new process.[1] Only fairly well established processes can then be studied, and those firms that prefer to retain the old process, possibly because it too has been improved, are not taken into account, thus precluding deeper analysis of the procedure behind the choice of new processes. Examples of competition between a new process and an improved version of the old can be found in tunnel kilns (described in chapter 5), in basic oxygen steel (chapter 6) and in continuous cooking in pulp production.[2]

Even if all the firms that have not introduced the new technique are eliminated from the analysis, the problem remains of how to analyse the case where there is a choice of innovations. This has affected many companies in the computer field, and there are examples of it in the studies of new methods of steel-plate marking and cutting in ship-building.[3]

In general, comparisons of diffusion patterns between processes and between countries require the utmost care. The arbitrary assumptions which are unavoidable mean that conclusions based on casual inspection can easily be quite wrong. In the literature of diffusion, sigmoid curves, representing the development through time of the number of firms using the new technology, or the volume of production or capacity, have been widely used, but two distinct questions remain. The first is simply whether such curves give a good statistical fit to the observed data. (When the diffusion process is manifestly incomplete and the number of observations from the past is small, one may not be able to distinguish with any confidence between the first part of a sigmoid curve, the beginning of an exponential expansion and a straight line.) Secondly, even if one is satisfied that the curve is a good pictorial representation of the facts, how should this particular shape be interpreted? The problem is especially acute when, as in the present context, the measure of diffusion is a ratio for which the appropriate denominator is difficult to find. The analogy from epidemic diseases sometimes used

[1] Mansfield, *Industrial Research and Technological Innovation*.
[2] Nabseth, 'The diffusion of innovations in Swedish industry'.
[3] Ray, 'The diffusion of new technology', pp. 72–6; also briefly mentioned in chapter 2 above.

in consumer expenditure theory did not seem very helpful.[1] Moreover, in some cases presenting the data in this form might be misleading: it could well be that, in the early stages, overriding technical reasons allowed a new process to start rapidly in one country although it remained quite inappropriate in another.

FACTORS AFFECTING THE SPEED OF DIFFUSION

At the beginning of this project, a common theoretical and methodological approach to the problem of diffusion of new technology was sought. It is obvious from the preceding chapters that a strictly 'common' approach was not found. As mentioned in the Introduction, this was less a failure to agree on a standard analysis than a question of differences in the techniques studied and in the empiricial material available. Furthermore, it may very well be that such a standardisation would in fact have hidden important explanatory factors in the diffusion of some processes. New processes are very different – in their relation to old processes, in their own improvement over time, and in other respects – and too much of a common approach might very well conceal these differences. Nevertheless, there are sufficient similarities in the analyses of the different processes to provide a basis for comparisons between them as well as within them.

Of the different stages of diffusion within a firm – first information, awareness, consideration and adoption – it is primarily the adoption stage that has been analysed in this study, although some material on information and awareness is also included. In the adoption stage, a few explanatory variables common to nearly all the processes were found – relative advantage or profitability, other economic variables, institutional circumstances and management attitudes. Before considering their influence, however, the data on 'first information' must be examined.

First information

For the individual firm, information about a new technique is a precondition to adoption. From this point of view, it would seem as relevant to study the diffusion of the information as of the actual adoption. On the other hand, it might be argued that knowledge about new processes spreads fairly rapidly in and between industrialised countries, so that understanding the diffusion of production is not much help in understanding the diffusion of adoption. The bigger and the more important an innovation, the more valid this argument seems to be, but here we must remember what has been said before about the

[1] See Rogers, *Diffusion of Innovations.*

11

difficulty of deciding when an invention has really become an innovation (for instance, in the case of oxygen steel this differed between different types of plant within the industry). Certain information might therefore be very important to some people within an industry, but much less interesting to others. Furthermore, in industries like textiles, paper, bricks and brewing, there are many small firms with limited possibilities of obtaining, let alone making use of, information about new processes. Taking all these things into account, it seems quite probable that the diffusion of information about a new technique is a time-consuming process. Carter and Williams in their study of British industry, conclude that 'the backward firm may not hear of an idea for several years after it is first made known'.[1] Of course, the data presented here are not precise; it is difficult to recall what exactly happened 15 years ago, even if – as in many cases – some of those who introduced the new process are still with the company.

In this study, data on first information were gathered for numerically controlled machine tools and for special presses. Some Swedish data were also obtained for other new processes.[2] These confirm the hypothesis that the diffusion of information about new techniques is quite a slow process. Timelags of about ten years between the first and the last firm are not uncommon. For the majority of firms, however, this is shortened to about five years, which means there are a few firms in each country which lag behind the others. One hypothesis often advanced is that information is diffused more rapidly than adoption.[3] This is not supported by our material, taking into account all the processes studied. The interim report (chapter 2) found that the later a process is introduced in a country, the more rapid the diffusion process will be. This may perhaps be because, during the long time preceding adoption, the process is improved and so spreads more rapidly. A similar hypothesis could be advanced regarding information about new processes, but is is not well supported by the data. Possibly, once started, information diffuses more quickly in small countries, like Austria and Sweden, than in large ones, like Germany and the United Kingdom. This is not so for all the processes studied, but the weakness of the data must be remembered here.

Another interesting question in this connection is whether big firms get information about new processes earlier than small firms. In table 11.1 which covers Germany, Sweden and the United States, this hypothesis gets some support in numerically controlled machine tools and

---

[1] Carter and Williams, *Industry and Technical Progress*, ch. 16. We must, however, bear in mind that this study deals with British conditions. It is uncertain if these results can be extrapolated to the other countries studied.

[2] Nabseth, 'The diffusion of innovations in Swedish industry.'

[3] Rogers, *Diffusion of Innovations*, p. 108.

rather weaker support in special presses. If, however, the American firms (which nearly all have over 1,500 employees, and obtained information in the period 1963–5) are excluded, then the hypothesis gets strong support from German and Swedish data on special presses.

The best sources of information on special presses seem to be the same in the different countries – technical journals, manufacturers and licence-holders of the process. The important question is whether or not

Table 11.1. *Size of firm and date of first information*

	First information obtained		
	Before 1960	1960 or later	Total
NC machine tools			
Employing less than 1000	22	21	43
Employing 1000 or more	30	8	38
Total	52	29	81
Special presses			
Employing less than 1000	10	69	79
Employing 1000 or more	7	28	35
Total	17	97	114
Special presses excluding US firms			
Employing less than 1000	10	69	79
Employing 1000 or more	7	11	18
Total	17	80	97

SOURCE: inquiry.

information on a new technique and its adoption are related (there is some indication that they are, especially in the Swedish material). This could, of course, have important policy implications: improving information channels to firms would then speed up diffusion of the process. On the other hand, obtaining and evaluating information is sometimes costly to a firm, so that the problem of being informed is to some extent a question of management attitudes. If one does not want to be early in introducing new processes, it is otiose to be well-informed about innovations in the field.

Profitability or relative advantage

In all discussions about the diffusion of new technology, the profitability or relative advantage of the new process in relation to the old stands out as an explanatory variable. But it is by no means clear what the causal relationship ought to be. With perfect foresight and perfect capital markets one could say that, as long as the internal rate of return on a new process exceeded a certain level (due regard being taken, of course, of the capital equipment in use), a firm ought to introduce the technique in question as soon as possible. It would then be possible to distinguish only between users and non-users of a process; no theory could be advanced about the order of introduction among firms.

In fact, we know that, since the capital market is imperfect, firms' opportunity costs differ.[1] A high internal rate of return for one firm may very well be considered a rather low rate for another, at least in the short term, so that firms are likely to differ in their speed of application of a new process. A hypothesis about the order of introduction among firms requires that the opportunity costs for different companies be known, but this information could not be obtained.

Secondly, new processes are not introduced with perfect foresight; on the contrary, it is the very essence of new technical processes, especially in the early stages, that the outcome of their introduction is uncertain. Will the process work according to plan or not? From this point of view it seems quite natural that the higher the *ex ante* internal rate of return of a new process the more likely is its introduction, since, *ceteris paribus*, it then offers a high safety margin for uncertainty.[2] The lower the *ex ante* internal rate of return of a process (above a certain level) the longer it may have to wait for introduction, so that the margin of risk is diminished. To a first approximation this type of reasoning lies behind the profitability discussions in the different chapters of this book.

However, one general conclusion seems to be that calculating the profitability of a new process is more difficult than is usually acknowledged in studies on the subject. For some processes, for instance numerically controlled machines and continuous casting, profitability turned out very difficult to calculate *ex post*, and even more difficult *ex ante*. This does not mean that firms do not try to estimate the relative advantage of a new process, but rather that their calculations are very subjective. Of course, new investments always involve uncertainties, but they are probably greater in the introduction of new technologies than, for instance, in straightforward replacement. It follows that profitability calculations for new processes are very much linked with management attitudes, especially when experience of the technology is scarce and perhaps contradictory.

It appears from the technical descriptions in the different chapters that the introduction of a new process is regarded as a unique event by each firm. The very presentation of a profitability calculation therefore

---

[1] This may also be the case even when capital markets are perfect.

[2] Strictly speaking a firm must be assumed to combine the rate of return with some probability distribution for the actual outcome.

involves subjective elements, with some managements stressing the risks and uncertainties, others the benefits that can be gained. An excellent example of this uncertainty problem turned up quite fortuitously in the relationship between continuous casting and the basic oxygen process. Profitability calculations for continuous casting took into account the use of oxygen steel, but very few firms' cost calculations for the oxygen process explicitly considered any extra advantages from combining it with other new processes. This would certainly be very difficult in analysis of the kind presented here, and it could be argued that even the most far-sighted management could not have foreseen, in the early 1960s when many oxygen steel decisions were being made, the drastic changes and improvements in continuous casting that were to occur in the late 1960s. Nevertheless, it is the function of management to foresee the indirect advantages or disadvantages of a certain course of action.

There are many examples given of the difficulties encountered in using a new technology, especially by the first firms. They may be 'leaders' in introducing the process but 'followers' when it comes to its profitability. Of course, a 'follower' in introduction is not necessarily a 'leader' in benefits. On these problems, however, the investigation succeeded in obtaining little empirical evidence.

Another serious difficulty for empirical investigations is that the profitability of a new process for a firm changes over time, not only because processes are improved (old processes as well as new), but also because factor prices change. Tunnel kilns are a good example: they can use either coal or oil, the latter giving a superior technical performance, so that the expected price ratio between oil (or gas) and coal is important; it has been changing over time. In spite of such difficulties, which give the term 'rational behaviour' a rather subtle meaning when it comes to new technology, the profitability aspect has been considered in one way or other in all the chapters. A general conclusion seems to be that profitability is an important factor in explaining the diffusion of new processes, not only in distinguishing between users and non-users, but also in explaining diffusion among firms and within them. This agrees with results obtained elsewhere.[1] But although profitability is a significant variable in most calculations, it is more difficult to say anything about its importance relative to other factors in explaining diffusion of new technology. This is not surprising in view of the calculation difficulties and all the proxies for profitability that have to be used. The most elaborate profitability calculations in this

---

[1] For a discussion of other findings see E. Mansfield, 'Determinants of the speed of application of new technology', paper given to the International Economic Association conference at St Anton, 1971.

study were made for special presses, where profitability explains more of the variation among firms than elsewhere, although some important elements may still have been omitted from the calculations.

When trying to pick out proxies for profitability, it is natural that the various authors should have relied heavily on conventional investment theory. Introducing a new technical process normally involves investment; the application of gibberellic acid in malting is the only process studied which requires negligible capital investment for its introduction.[1] Two relevant variants of investment theory are the accelerator principle and the vintage approach.[2] According to the former it is an increase in demand which calls for investment in new productive capacity. This may also be supposed to lead to more rapid introduction of new processes, since they are very often superior to the old. (However, the accelerator principle may also lead to increased use of outdated capital equipment, which could complicate the econometric analysis.) This principle gets very firm support in our material, notably for oxygen steel and special presses, but to some extent also for tunnel kilns, shuttleless looms and float glass. For instance, in new paper machines special presses are cheaper to introduce than the old type and this, of course, leads to rapid diffusion in firms and countries which are investing heavily in new paper capacity.

The vintage approach implies that, with given demand, new processes will be introduced more rapidly in firms with old than with new capital equipment, simply because replacement of equipment is more urgent for the former. This theory gets some, rather weak, support from our data. For example, the float glass process was probably delayed in France by the expensive new glass capacity that had been installed just before the new process became available.[3] But the vintage theory may be reversed in some new processes. For instance, it is quite clear that special presses are more profitable in newer paper machines. Consequently firms and countries with many old paper machines would be expected to have a slower rate of diffusion than those with newer machines, and this hypothesis was borne out by the data. Another variant of the vintage approach is illustrated by the use of gibberellic acid in malting. As already mentioned, this requires no

---

[1] Lack of *human* capital might be an obstacle to diffusion of this process.

[2] For a more detailed discussion of the accelerator principle see for instance D. J. Smyth, 'Empirical evidence on the accelerator principle', *Review of Economic Studies*, vol. 31, June 1964, pp. 185–202; or R. C. O. Matthews, *The Trade Cycle*, Cambridge University Press, 1958. For a more detailed discussion of vintage models see for instance L. Johansen, *Production Functions*, Amsterdam, North-Holland, 1972, and Salter, *Productivity and Technical Change*.

[3] This particular decision, however, perhaps ought not to be considered in isolation, but in the context of the policy of a multinational company. The same company built their first float glass factory in Italy.

new investment, but the extra capacity it gives at one stage of production would be useless unless the remaining parts of the process were also increased in capacity. Profitability calculations may thus differ between firms according to the situation in stages of the process not directly connected with this innovation.

A major element in profitability calculations are the relative prices different firms have to pay for factors of production. This element differs not only between firms in the different countries, but also between firms in the same country, although the latter was more difficult to take into account. Compared with old processes, new ones may save capital, labour, raw material, or some combination of all three; sometimes they imply increased use of one or more factors of production, for instance capital. Thus differences between firms in relative factor prices have been used in this study to explain varying diffusion rates between different countries. The changes in the factors of production used that the processes would imply are not always clear from the descriptions in the different chapters, but usually it seems fairly plain whether they are positive or negative, and then the profitability variables also seem to contribute to the explanations of different rates of diffusion. In oxygen steel, for instance, differences in scrap prices or availability between countries have a significant explanatory value. The use of coal and the production of fletton bricks in the United Kingdom make tunnel kilns less profitable there than in other countries, and this shows up in the diffusion patterns. Numerically controlled machines and shuttleless looms, which are, apart from their other advantages, very labour-saving, seem to have been adopted more rapidly in firms and countries with a relatively high wage level, such as the United States and Sweden.

In considering the profitability calculations of a new technology, the problem of disposing of increased output is an important factor; one major conclusion from the case studies is that introducing new processes very often increases capacity. For special presses this is a major advantage, and the same is true of shuttleless looms and gibberellic acid; but one production line with the float glass process makes more glass than the whole consumption of Austria. This expansion introduces another element of uncertainty which underlines the previous point concerning the subjectivity of any profitability calculations. With the formula used for special presses, for example, differences between British and Swedish firms seem at first sight rather odd. This process would pay for itself in a year or less in many firms in both countries, but whilst Swedish firms have introduced the process, many British firms have not. A possible explanation is that British firms are less certain they can sell the extra output than Swedish firms, nearly all of which are exporters. In float glass the very large capacity created may often act as a disincentive; when a combined Danish–Swedish plant chose the Pittsburg process instead, the main reason probably was that the expected output of float glass was considered too large to sell easily. Gibberellic acid is of no use to a maltster if the demand for malt is already satisfied. It was found that vertically integrated firms introduced shuttleless looms more rapidly and to a greater extent than non-integrated firms, possibly because the former are more certain of finding outlets for the increased output. Similarly, heavy foreign competition was found to act as an impediment to diffusion, and this could be another factor making for uncertainty in expected demand for the increased output.

In contrast with the accelerator principle, whereby the investment in new plant is decided by an actual or expected change in demand, here new investment *entails* additional capacity, and the question is whether, by price reduction or other means, the firm can dispose profitably of the extra output. This may require gaining market-shares at the expense of others, which raises the question of what constitutes rational behaviour in an uncertain world. If, for instance, Japanese firms started investing heavily in steel capacity while oxygen steel was still in its introductory stage, and, by adapting the process to their special conditions, they obtained a competitive advantage over American firms and invaded the American market, is it still defensible to say (as we tend to as economists) that American firms acted rationally in waiting until the process was well developed and appropriate for their own production facilities before investing in it? Another example is found in continuous casting. Austrian and British firms, which started very early experimenting with this new technology, thought it was best suited to special steel production and followed this line in their development work. Development work started somewhat later by American, German and Swedish firms and directed to application in large-scale production of commercial steels turned out after all to be on the right track, and the 'late comers' gained competitive advantages over the 'pioneers'. Were the pioneers then 'irrational'?

Other economic variables

The introduction of a new process usually involves investment; the financing of that investment suggests itself as a factor explaining differences in diffusion behaviour between firms. Of course, if the internal rate of return on an investment is high, it will pay to borrow money if internal funds are not available. But there are at least two problems. First, capital markets may be imperfect, so that it is not possible to borrow more than a certain amount. Secondly, as mentioned before, the risk factor is important in investment in new technology, especially when experience is scarce. As in investment in research and development, a firm may be reluctant to borrow money for this purpose. The implication is that greater willingness to invest in new processes might be expected if they could be financed out of the firm's own resources. This hypothesis was tested in different ways as shown in the various chapters, but the results were frequently limited by lack of information. They are most clear-cut in oxygen steel, for which it is shown that an increased cash flow leads to higher investment, and this in turn means a more rapid diffusion of the new technology. Special presses give some support to the hypothesis, although it is rather difficult to interpret these results. It is not surprising that the hypothesis is better supported in explaining investment in expensive new equipment, such as that for the basic oxygen process, than in relatively cheap machines, such as special presses. Weavers in Austria, the United Kingdom and Italy often mentioned lack of capital as a major reason for being non-users of shuttleless looms. In Britain, small firms introduced cheaper water and jet looms quite extensively instead of the more expensive Sulzer looms. Capital availability probably also influenced when the float glass process was introduced by some firms.

The importance of international contacts may also indicate the influence of financial resources: firms with close international contacts are to a much larger extent users of shuttleless looms than firms without such contacts, which may, or course, have effects other than purely financial ones on the diffusion of new technology.

It is often said that large firms are more willing to introduce new technology than smaller ones, and this argument has been used to justify the concentration of production. One reason for large firms being more willing to introduce new processes rapidly could lie on the financial side, if, as has been argued, their ability to acquire the necessary finance is greater. Another argument takes account of the risk factor. The failure of a new process in a small company might be a catastrophe; in a large firm, it might be just a small loss to be set off against profits in other fields. A further advantage for large firms may be that they can afford a management qualified to evaluate the advantages of new technology; small firms may have to wait upon the experience of others.

Other investigations indicate that firms must be of a certain size to respond rapidly to new technical processes.[1] This does not mean, however, that they must be very big in any absolute sense; furthermore, the threshold size seems to vary for different technologies. We acquired extensive data on the size of firms, which showed considerable variation,

[1] Mansfield, 'The speed of response of firms to new techniques.'

so that it was possible to compare behaviour as to new technology for different size groups. The results seem largely to support the findings elsewhere. It is by no means inevitable that large firms should be the first to introduce a new process; on the contrary, there are many examples in our material of smaller firms taking the lead, for instance, in oxygen steel and continuous casting, also in shuttleless looms.[1] But we must not interpret this as showing differences in attitude or bureaucratic slowness in the big firms; the technologies of oxygen steel and continuous casting were first developed for smaller firms, larger firms had no particular profitability advantage in the new processes until they had been developed further. Of course, this raised a further question of why these technologies were first developed in smaller firms, which has not been fully answered in this study. Numerically controlled machines are another example of the aspect just mentioned. Here there is no correlation between size of firm and date of introduction, but there is a definite tendency for the number of machines per thousand employees to be higher in smaller than in larger firms. This, however, might very well be because large firms have a different pattern of production, with longer series to which these machines are not as well suited. The only case where we found a definite tendency for larger firms to introduce the process earlier was in special presses, where this was quite significant in the econometric calculations. However, it might equally well have been caused by the profitability of this new technology: larger firms have more paper machines than small firms, which probably means that, on average, each large firm has both more new and more old machines than each small firm. As special presses are more profitable on newer machines, large firms are likely to show an automatic lead over small ones when considering only the date of *first* introduction. Again, many small firms are non-users of shuttleless looms (although, as just mentioned, some small firms were early users); this might be an example of a threshold size effect. Another case is gibberellic acid, where small firms may not have the resources to employ people qualified to handle the new technology.

Institutional circumstances

Quite a few differences between firms in different countries can be explained by institutional differences in the countries concerned, which may take a variety of forms. Some have an effect only for a limited period, whereas others are more fundamental. A very good example of the first is the successive nationalisation and denationalisation of the

---

[1] We must, however, be aware of possible differences in the definition of the term 'commercial application'. A pilot plant in a big American firm would probably be defined as commercial in Austria or Sweden.

British steel industry during the whole post-war period. This led to a climate of uncertainty and relatively low investment for some years and, in turn, influenced British investment in oxygen steel and continuous casting, possibly being one reason for the slow diffusion of these processes in the United Kingdom. A more permanent difference between the countries concerned is found in connection with gibberellic acid. In Germany the process is prohibited, and the legal situation in Italy is unclear, which inevitably influences diffusion, or the lack of it, in these countries.

Another institutional difference between countries lies in the structure of industry. Numerically controlled machines were, to start with, extremely well suited for the aircraft industry. The United States and the United Kingdom had large aircraft industries which clearly contributed to the rapid spread of these machines, whereas in the other countries studied this industry was much smaller or negligible. Countries with a comparatively large number of small firms in an industry seem often to experience slower diffusion of a new process than where the industry is more concentrated. The many small firms in the cotton-type weaving industry in the United Kingdom and in Italy are examples in this study. Another aspect of the same thing is the importance of industrial and research associations in a country; strong associations and high membership ratios might speed up the diffusion rate, as seems to have been the case with special presses in Sweden.

Management attitudes

Although the explanatory variables mentioned so far account for much of the difference in behaviour between firms, it is clear, not least from the econometric calculations, that the unexplained residuals are also quite large. To some extent no doubt, these residuals represent measurement errors, and errors in the variables, which may not measure what was intended, for instance profitability. But another way of looking at the problem is to say that there are differences in management attitudes towards new technology. Other things being equal, some firms are more willing to take risks on new processes than others. This would not be at all surprising, taking into account the difficulties mentioned earlier of making profitability calculations.

It is not too difficult for an aggressive management (in the sense of chapter 6) to present favourable *ex ante* profitability calculations to its board of directors, just as it is not difficult for a less aggressive management to make the calculations less optimistic. Inevitably fundamental problems of management ability (and management luck) enter into all discussions of diffusion of new technology. Rational behaviour in this context is indeed a difficult concept. Other studies also have concluded that differences in attitudes towards new technology affect the rate of diffusion of new processes.[1]

In some chapters of this study we tried to take explicit account of attitudes, although fully aware of the pitfalls in measuring them. These attempts support the hypothesis that management attitudes do differ between firms. The most elaborate analysis is in chapter 6, where it cannot be said to be altogether a success, but at least it suggests one way of attacking the problem and probably could be elaborated. A more direct method in the same chapter, using productivity measures as a gauge of management aggressiveness, gave slightly better results, but of course it is questionable whether productivity differences between firms are really good proxies for differences in attitudes towards new technology.

In chapter 4 it is shown that the same firms tend to be early or late in the introduction of all new processes, not just the one studied, and that this applies to most countries. This result is confirmed in another paper.[2] Some firms seem to want to be among the pioneers, others like to watch their experiences. This theory received further support from discussions with sellers of some of the capital equipment used. Nevertheless the question remains of why certain firms want to be the first; improved measures of aggressiveness might help to answer this question.

Some of the proxies used for profitability or for other economic variables could also be regarded as proxies for management attitudes. Vertically integrated firms, which introduced shuttleless looms earlier and more extensively than non-integrated firms, might have done so as the result of different risk and profitability conditions, but another interpretation could be that under given conditions vertical integration is a sign of progressiveness on the part of management. In that case integration could stand as a proxy for management attitudes.

We also learned that the introduction of new technology often means big changes in structure and administrative practices, changes that some organisations are more willing to accept than others. A good example is numerically controlled machines, the introduction of which is usually accompanied by radical changes in organisation. Big firms have an advantage here in that they can more easily take the risks connected with introducing numerical control, but more research is needed on, for instance, the sources and training of managers, and on organisational structure, to understand what types of firms most easily adapt to new processes.

[1] See for instance Carter and Williams, *Industry and Technical Progress*, especially ch. 10 and ch. 16.

[2] Nabseth, 'The diffusion of innovations in Swedish industry.'

EXPLAINING DIFFUSION DIFFERENCES BETWEEN COUNTRIES

One reason for undertaking this study was to try and explain differences between the participating countries in diffusion patterns of new processes. In the United Kingdom it has often been said that the British are good at basic research and inventing new things, but bad at developing these inventions into innovations and making use of innovations developed initially in other countries. For the NIESR this was one reason for the whole project: they wanted to test this hypothesis. We have tried in one way or another to find factors which can at least partially explain the differences between countries for all the processes considered, but it would be an exaggeration to claim that we succeeded in this task. The analysis is not always up to desirable scientific standards, partly because of the poor quality of the primary data. On the other hand, we have succeeded in finding a number of reasons why diffusion patterns differ between the countries concerned. These may not comprise the full explanation, or even most of it, but we have at least started to account for the differences, and this is more than is yet to be found in the international literature on the subject.

In chapter 2 it was found that, according to the indicators used, no country among those studied had an outstanding general lead in introducing new techniques. In all subsequent chapters we have tried to include American data, which are sometimes rather poor, but if they can be accepted the conclusion of the interim report seems to stand. The United States has not turned out a 'leader' in the sense used in chapter 2. In some cases, for instance numerically controlled machines, diffusion has been much quicker in the United States, whereas in others, oxygen steel, continuous casting and special presses, this is not the case. The implications of 'leading' and 'following' in the introduction of new technology are by no means clear. Simply to count diffusion percentages for firms at different points of time, or to estimate the percentage of output produced by the process in question, does not of itself yield significant results. The diffusion patterns must be adjusted for economic and institutional differences among countries to give more meaningful content to the words 'leader' and 'follower', for example, as indicators of progressive or non-progressive managements. But, as pointed out many times, this is a difficult task when management attitudes and profitability calculations are as intertwined as in decisions on new technology. In comparing the progressiveness of management between industries and countries, it is easier to compare some of the outcomes of behaviour, like profits, profit margins and output growth, than 'inputs' like the use of new technology.

If a government, for some reason, wants to influence diffusion patterns it must, however, know the effects of changes in economic and institutional circumstances on management behaviour. If the uncertainty created by successive nationalisation and denationalisation of the British iron and steel industry had not been engendered, and in consequence the diffusion of oxygen steel and continuous casting had been quicker in that industry than it actually was, then the diffusion patterns for the techniques chosen – in the sense used in the interim report – would have been outstanding in the United Kingdom compared with the other countries. This would imply a denial of the initial hypothesis that British firms lag behind in the use of new technology, but on the other hand, in some instances the data, if they can be accepted at face value, show rather peculiar behaviour by British firms, especially regarding special presses. This is a process that has a very short pay-off period for many companies, yet many British firms have still not introduced the technology.[1] These firms are certainly small by British standards, but not by international standards; nor is there any lack of information about the new process. The data support a hypothesis which needs further research, that, in the United Kingdom after the war, there was room for quite a few small and medium-sized firms that did not maximise profits in a neo-classical sense – competition from abroad was not keen enough to weed them out. In Sweden, with among other things lower tariff barriers, this was not so. Out of a random sample of new processes introduced since the war, Sweden, being a small country, would not be expected to be the innovator of more than a few. But it appears that a new process, once started in another country, spreads quickly in Sweden if experience seems promising; the relatively large foreign trade and heavy foreign competition,[2] together with the close contacts between Swedish firms (in associations and research work, for example) lead to the rapid introduction of new technology. Continuous casting, tunnel kilns and automatic transfer lines in car production are cases in point. Rapid diffusion of such new technologies has been a necessity for firms working in a country paying the highest wages in Europe.

If we consider the various processes in more detail,[3] we find that they differ in the factors which explain the differences in their diffusion

[1] One essential point that has been raised in relation to the pay-off calculations is the proportion of integrated to non-integrated paper production. Some British experts maintain that this is important and that, with due regard to this fact, pay-off values for British firms would be increased. In Sweden, on the other hand, it is maintained that the facts cannot explain differences in behaviour between firms in the two countries.

[2] Notwithstanding what is said on p. 306, above, this means that we do not know with certainty whether heavy foreign competition acts mostly as a stimulus or as a hindrance in the diffusion of new technology.

[3] These remarks apply to six processes only, excluding gibberellic acid and float glass because of their special features.

patterns between countries. Differences in wage levels are considered the most important factor in explaining the lead of the United States and Sweden in the rate of diffusion of numerically controlled machines. Similarly, their slow diffusion in Italy and Austria is thought to be influenced primarily by low wages. This is, of course, a clear profitability consideration. Another important factor has been the size of the aircraft industry in the United States and Great Britain. Early information about this technology might have had some effect both in the United States and in Sweden.

The rapid diffusion of special presses in Sweden is strongly affected by the fact that this was where they were invented and innovated (also independently in the United States), which meant a rapid spread of information about the process. Furthermore, the process seems to have been highly profitable, partly because of investment in new machinery, partly because exports provided a good outlet for the increased capacity created. Such a situation did not prevail in the United Kingdom, where the consumption of paper increased at a much slower rate. Heavy foreign competition and the necessity of buying pulp from abroad may also have held back the process in the United Kingdom, but some differences in management attitudes must probably also be taken into account. In Italy, large investment in new paper machines and a rapid increase in paper consumption explain much of the more rapid diffusion than in Austria and Germany. In Austria a rather old stock of paper machines seems also to have hampered diffusion of the process. The most curious pattern is found in the United States. The process was invented and innovated there too, but still diffusion of both information and adoption was very slow. A slow growth in paper consumption and low investment activity might account for this; furthermore, much recent expansion and investment by American paper companies has taken place in Canada.

The diffusion of shuttleless looms seems to have been most rapid in Germany and the United States. In both countries the large size of firms, their vertical integration, and the possibilities for shift-work probably made this technology profitable from the beginning. Furthermore, import competition has probably not been as severe in Germany as in Sweden, the United Kingdom and, maybe, Italy. In the United Kingdom and Italy the large number of small firms has probably also impeded diffusion; many of them could not afford the expensive investment. In Sweden the large size of firms has probably had a positive influence on the diffusion rate, and the heavy import competition has meant that they have been forced either to invest in new technology or to leave the market.

As to oxygen steel, the main reason why this process diffused much more rapidly in Austria than in any other country seems to have been that the technology was invented and developed there, encouraged by the production structure of the Austrian iron and steel industry and its precarious situation after the war. When the technology had developed sufficiently to be usable in big plants, diffusion started on a more rapid scale in countries like Germany, the United Kingdom and the United States, where plants were big. A faster increase in steel output in Germany than in the United Kingdom gave a more rapid diffusion in the former country. Diffusion in the United States was probably discouraged to some extent by readily available scrap, whereas diffusion in the United Kingdom may have suffered from the uncertainties of nationalisation. In Sweden the relative importance of special steel meant a less rapid diffusion than elsewhere. The Italian position, however, cannot be explained from the data; steel production increased very sharply in that country during the 1960s, but electric production seems to have had more attraction than the basic oxygen process.

The early development of continuous casting of steel started fairly independently in Austria, Germany and the United Kingdom, and rapid and similar diffusion might have been expected in all three countries. However, in Austria and also the United Kingdom, diffusion was delayed in the 1960s by attempts to develop the technology for the production of special steels, which turned out rather a failure. In Sweden and the United States, and later in Germany, development concentrated on its application to large-scale production of ordinary steels, which proved more successful. A fairly uniform output, either produced by small plants with electric furnaces or by larger plants using oxygen converters, offered advantages for the introduction of this technology. From this point of view the plant structure in Austria, Germany and Sweden favoured the process, especially when compared with the British and American structure. In Germany, where the pioneer steelworks are situated, a very rapid diffusion started during the later 1960s.

Brick production has increased most rapidly in Austria and Italy. This ought to have stimulated the diffusion of tunnel kilns in these countries. Brick consumption *per capita* is also much higher in these countries and in the United Kingdom than in Sweden and the United States. In Austria the diffusion of the process has been comparatively rapid, but not in Italy, where the high capital costs of tunnel kilns have meant instead widespread further modification of the Hoffmann kiln. In the United Kingdom, where the first tunnel kiln was built as early as 1902, the use of coal and the unique raw material of fletton bricks have resulted in slow diffusion. Germany and Sweden have both had rather rapid diffusion associated with a decrease in brick production;

keen competition seems to have made it necessary for firms wanting to survive to install the tunnel kiln.

WERE WE STARTING THE PROJECT NOW

In a project like this which has extended over a long period – more than five years – much experience has been gained which may be of help to others entering the same field of research. We can ask ourselves: what would we do differently if we were starting the project now?

In the beginning we discussed whether we should try to get information about diffusion patterns for a large number of new processes, or whether we should confine ourselves to just a few, to be studied in depth. Taking into account all the difficulties described in interpreting diffusion rates, the line we chose of selecting a limited number of processes seems to have been the right one, given the resources available. But the attempt to get most of the data required from individual firms rapidly reached a limit of strongly diminishing returns. In some countries it was just too difficult. If we were to start again, we would probably rely much more on information from other sources, such as producers and sellers of new equipment and licence-holders, and have it confirmed by a few companies. Establishing good contacts with such producers seems to be a better approach, and obviously the more one can rely on published data the better, although when it comes to new processes inevitably such data will be scarce indeed. Another approach would have been to go deeper into a limited number of companies, but then one would probably have had to give up the idea of making any kind of industry-wide or country-wide generalisations.

As to methodology, this study was undertaken in two consecutive stages, a procedure which was dictated by financial considerations. If there had been no such restriction, it would have been better if we could have given more time at the beginning to discussions on how to analyse our material. Then it might have been easier to compare diffusion of the various processes in detail.

Finally, it must be remembered that in this study six different research institutes in six countries were involved. This has stimulated much fruitful discussion and provided each institute with a more rounded appreciation of the complexity of the diffusion process than might otherwise have been possible. But it has also to be said that, despite all its advantages, international cooperation does slow down the progress of the research itself.

LIST OF WORKS CITED

I. BOOKS, ARTICLES AND OTHER SOURCES

ABRAMOVITZ, M. A. 'Resources and output trends in the United States since 1870', *American Economic Association Papers and Proceedings*, vol. 46, May 1956, pp. 5–23.

American Iron and Steel Institute. *Annual Statistical Report.*

ANTHONY, L. J. 'Introduction' to *Accelerating Innovation*, London, ASLIB, 1970.

ASSIDER. *Notizario*, no. 19, 1970.

BALOGH, T. and STREETEN, P. 'The coefficient of ignorance', *Bulletin of the Oxford University Institute of Economics and Statistics*, vol. 25, May 1963, pp. 99–107.

Battelle Memorial Institute. *Final Report on Technical and Economic Analysis of the Impact of Recent Developments in Steelmaking Practices on the Supplying Industries*, Columbus (Ohio), 1964.

BAWDEN, R. F., DAHLSTROM, R. V. and SFAT, M. R. 'Effect of growth regulators on barley malt', *American Society of Brewing Chemists. Proceedings of the Annual Meeting, 1959*, pp. 137ff.

BECKMANN, M. J. and SATO, R. 'Aggregate production functions and types of technical progress: a statistical analysis', *American Economic Review*, vol. 59, March 1969, pp. 88–101.

BOGARDUS, E. S. 'Racial distance changes in the United States during the past thirty years', *Sociology and Social Research*, vol. 43, November 1958, pp. 217–37.

BREITENACHER, M. 'Innovation und Imitation fördern den technischen Fortschritt', *Wirtschaftskonjunktur (Berichte des IFO-Instituts für Wirtschaftsforschung)*, vol. 21, July 1969.

BREITENACHER, M., MENTZEL, W. and RÖTHLINGSHÖFER, K. CH. *The Influence of Research and Development on the Foreign Trade of the Federal Republic of Germany. Statistical analysis and case studies*, Munich, IFO, 1970.

BRIGGS, D. E. 'Effects of gibberellic acid on barley germination and its use in malting. A review', *Journal of the Institute of Brewing*, vol. 69, 1963, pp. 244ff.

BRITTAIN, J. A. *Corporate Dividend Policy*, Washington (DC), The Brookings Institution, 1966.

CARTER, C. F. and WILLIAMS, B. R. *Industry and Technical Progress: factors governing the speed of application of science*, London, Oxford University Press, 1957.

CHOW, G. 'Tests of equality between sets of coefficients in two linear regressions', *Econometrica*, vol. 28, July 1960, pp. 591–605.

CORNFIELD, J. and MANTEL, N. 'Some new aspects of the application of maximum likelihood to the calculation of the dosage response curve', *Journal of the American Statistical Association*, vol. 45, 1950, pp. 181–210.

DAVIES, S. W. 'The clay brick industry and the tunnel kiln', *National Institute Economic Review*, no. 58, November 1971, pp. 54–71.

DENISON, E. F. *The Sources of Economic Growth in the United States and the Alternatives before us*, New York, Committee for Economic Development, 1962.

DENISON, E. F. and POULLIER, J. P. *Why Growth Rates Differ: postwar experience in nine Western countries*, Washington (DC), The Brookings Institution, 1967.

Deutscher Brauer-Bund e.V. *Statistischer Bericht*, Bad Godesberg, Bonn (biennial).

DILLEY, D. R. and McBRIDE, D. 'Oxygen steelmaking – fact vs. folklore', *Iron and Steel Engineer*, vol. 45, October 1967.

DOBROVOLSKY, S. P. *Corporate Income Retention, 1915–1943*, New York, NBER, 1951.

EARLE, K. J. B. 'The development of the float glass process and the future of the glass industry', *Chemistry and Industry*, 15 July 1967.

EDWARDS, A. L. 'On Guttman scale analysis', *Educational Psychological Measurement*, vol. 8, 1948, pp. 313–18.

EILENDER, W. and ROESER, W. 'Metallurgische Untersuchungen über das Arbeiten mit sauerstoffangereichertem Gebläsewind beim Thomasverfahren', *Stahl und Eisen*, vol. 59, September 1939, pp. 1057–67.

GEBHARDT, A. *NC Machine Tools. Handicaps and promotion of their diffusion in the Federal Republic of Germany*, Munich, IFO, 1969.
— 'Der Tunnelofen in der Ziegelindustrie – Beispeil einer neuen Technologie', *IFO-Schnelldienst*, vol. 24, no. 27, July 1971.
GINI, C. *Variabilità e Mutabilità*, Bologna, University of Cagliari, 1912.
GRABOWSKI, H. G. and MUELLER, D. C. 'Managerial and stockholder welfare models of firm expenditures', *Review of Economics and Statistics*, vol. 54, February 1972, pp. 9–24.
GRILICHES, Z. 'Hybrid corn: an exploration in the economics of technical change', *Econometrica*, vol. 25, October 1957, pp. 501–22.
HATZOLD, O. *The Effect of the Introduction of Numerically Controlled Machine Tools on Plant Level Issues in the Federal Republic of Germany. Report on six case studies*, Munich, IFO, 1967.
HATZOLD, O. and SCHWORM, K. *Research and Economic Growth. Diffusion of numerical machine control and effects of the application of synthetics in the Federal Republic of Germany*, Munich, IFO, 1967.
HERREGAT, G. 'Managerial profiles and investment patterns', Ph.D. dissertation, University of Louvain, 1972.
HOGAN, W. P. ' Technical progress and production functions ', *Review of Economics and Statistics*, vol. 40, November 1958, pp. 407–11.
Iron and Steel Institute, *Oxygen in Steelmaking*, London, 1959.
Japan Iron and Steel Institute. *Handbook*, (annual).
JEWKES, J., SAWERS, D. and STILLERMAN, R. *The Sources of Invention*, 2nd ed., London, Macmillan, 1969.
JOHANSEN, L. *Production Functions*, Amsterdam, North-Holland, 1972.
JORGENSON, D. W. and GRILICHES, Z. 'The explanation of productivity change', *Review of Economic Studies*, vol. 34, July 1967, pp. 249–83.
Kaiser Steel Corporation, *Linz-Donawitz Process Newsletter* (monthly).
KALDOR, N. *Essays on Economic Stability and Growth*, London, Duckworth, 1960.
KALDOR, N. and MIRRLEES, J. A. 'A new model of economic growth', *Review of Economic Studies*, vol. 29, June 1962, pp. 174–92.
KENDRICK, J. W. *Productivity Trends in the United States*, Princeton (NJ), University Press, 1961.
KENDRICK, J. W. and SATO, R. 'Factor prices, productivity and growth', *American Economic Review*, vol. 53, December 1963, pp. 974–1003.
KENNEDY, C. and THIRLWALL, A. P. 'Technical progress: a survey', *Economic Journal*, vol. 82, March 1972, pp. 11–72.
KIEBER, W., LINDEMANN, M. and SCHMID, P. 'Kleinmälzungsversuche mit Gibberellinsäure', *Brauwelt*, vol. 99, nos. 93-4, 1959, pp. 1781ff.
KLEIN, L. R. and SUMMERS, R. *The Wharton Index of Capacity Utilization*, Philadelphia (Pa), University of Pennsylvania, 1966.
KRUSKAL, W. H. 'A nonparametric test for the several sample problem', *Annals of Mathematical Statistics*, vol. 23, 1952, pp. 525–40.
KRUSKAL, W. H. and WALLIS, W. A. 'Use of ranks in one-criterion variance analysis', *Journal of the American Statistical Association*, vol. 47, 1952, pp. 583–621.
KUH, E. 'The validity of cross-sectionally estimated behavior equations in time series applications', *Econometrica*, vol. 27, April 1959, pp. 197–214.
KUROSAWA, E. [article in Japanese], *Transactions of the Natural History Society of Formosa*, vol. 16, April 1926, pp. 37–76.
KUZNETS, S. *National Product since 1869*, New York, NBER, 1946.
LINTNER, J. 'Distribution of incomes of corporations among dividends, retained earnings and taxes ', *American Economic Association Papers and Proceedings*, vol. 46, May 1956, pp. 97–113.
MCADAMS, A. K. 'Big steel: invention and innovation reconsidered', *Quarterly Journal of Economics*, vol. 81, August 1967, pp. 457–74.
MADDALA, G. S. and KNIGHT, P. T. 'International diffusion of technical change: a case study of the oxygen steel making process', *Economic Journal*, vol. 77, September 1967, pp. 531–58.
MANSFIELD, E. 'Technical change and the rate of imitation', *Econometrica*, vol. 29, October 1961, pp. 741–66.
— 'The speed of response of firms to new techniques', *Quarterly Journal of Economics*, vol. 77, May 1963, pp. 290–311.

— *Industrial Research and Technological Innovation – an econometric analysis*, New York, Cowles Foundation, 1967.
— *The Economics of Technological Change*, New York, Norton, 1968.
— 'Determinants of the speed of application of new technology', paper given to the International Economic Association conference at St Anton, 1971.
MASSELL, B. F. 'A disaggregated view of technological change', *Journal of Political Economy*, vol. 69, December 1961, pp. 547–57.
— 'Investment, innovation and growth ', *Econometrica*, vol. 30, April 1962, pp. 239–52.
MATTHEWS, R. C. O. *The Trade Cycle*, Cambridge University Press, 1958.
MEYER, J. R. 'An experiment in the measurement of business motivation', *Review of Economics and Statistics*, vol. 49, August 1967, pp. 304–18.
MEYER, J. R. and KUH, E. *The Investment Decision*, Cambridge (Mass.), Harvard University Press, 1957.
MILES, C. *Lancashire Textiles: a case study of industrial change*, Cambridge University Press, 1968.
NABSETH, L. 'The diffusion of innovations in Swedish industry', paper given to the International Economic Association conference at St Anton, 1971.
NELSON, R. 'Aggregate production functions and medium-range growth projections', *American Economic Review*, vol. 54, September 1964, pp. 575–606.
NERLOVE, M. and BALESTRA, P. 'Pooling cross section and time series data in the estimation of a dynamic model: the demand for natural gas', *Econometrica*, vol. 34, July 1966, pp. 585–612.
OPPENLÄNDER, K. H. 'Investitionen und technischer Fortschritt', paper read to the 9th CIRET conference in Madrid, 1969.
PARKER, H. A. and SCHANE, P. (Jr). 'Use of oxygen lances and basic brick in open-hearth furnace roofs', paper prepared for presentation to the American Iron and Steel Institute, 25 May 1969.
PILKINGTON, L. A. B. ' The development of float glass ', *Glass Industry*, vol. 44, February 1963, pp. 80–1.
— ' Float glass ', *Advance*, no. 1, November 1966, pp. 12–19.
PRAIS, S. J. and HOUTHAKKER, H. S. *The Analysis of Family Budgets*, 2nd ed., Cambridge University Press, 1971.
RAY, G. F. 'The diffusion of new technology: a study of ten processes in nine industries', *National Institute Economic Review*, no. 48, May 1969, pp. 40–83 [also as Smatryck Nr. 46, Stockholm, IUI, 1969, and *Die Verbreitung neuer Technologien*, Berlin and Munich, Duncker and Humblot, 1970; *Die Ausbreitung neuer Technologien*, Vienna, OIW, 1969].
— 'Ergebnisse von Diffusionsuntersuchungen in Europa' in O. Hatzold (ed.), *Innovation in der Wirtschaft*, Munich, IFO, 1970.
— 'New technology and enterprise decisions' in Z. Román (ed.), *Progress and Planning in industry*, Budapest, Akadémiai Kiadó, 1972.
— 'On defining diffusion of new techniques', *Business Economist*, vol. 4, Summer 1972, pp. 82–8.
ROGERS, E. M. *Diffusion of Innovations*, 1st ed., New York, Free Press of Glencoe, 1962.
ROSETT, R. N. 'A statistical model of friction in economics', *Econometrica*, vol. 27, April 1959, pp. 263–7.
SALTER, W. E. G. *Productivity and Technical Change*, Cambridge University Press, 1960.
SANDEGREN, E. and BELING, H. 'Versuch mit Gibberellinsäure bei der Malzherstellung', *Monatsschrift für Brauerei*, vol. 11, part 12, 1958, pp. 231ff.
SCHEDL, H. 'Geringe Verbreitung schützenloser Webmaschinen in der Baumwollindustrie', *IFO-Schnelldienst*, vol. 23, no. 40, October 1970.
SCHMOOKLER, J. 'The changing efficiency of the American economy, 1869–1938', *Review of Economics and Statistics*, vol. 34, August 1952, pp. 214–31.
SCHUMPETER, J. A. *Business Cycles*, 1st ed., New York and London, McGraw-Hill, 1939.
SMITH. R. J. 'The weaving of cotton and allied textiles in Great Britain: an industry survey with special reference to the diffusion of shuttleless looms', *National Institute Economic Review*, no. 53, August 1970, pp. 54–69.
SMYTH, D. J. ' Empirical evidence on the accelerator principle ', *Review of Economic Studies*, vol. 31, June 1964, pp. 185–202.

SOLOW, R. M. 'Technical change and the aggregate production function', *Review of Economics and Statistics*, vol. 39, August 1957, pp. 312-20.

STADLER, H., KIPPHAHN, H. and SIEGFRIED, S. 'Zur Gibberellinsäureverwendung beim Mälzen', *Brauwelt*, vol. 100, no. 68, 1960, pp. 1361ff.

STONE, J. K. 'Oxygen in steelmaking', *Scientific American*, vol. 4, April 1968, pp. 24-31.

STUBBS, P. *Innovation and Research*, Melbourne, F. W. Cheshire, 1968.

SUSLOW, B. M. 'Oxygen enriched air in steel making', *Metal Progress*, vol. 26, September 1934, pp. 40-1.

TERBORGH, G. *Dynamic Equipment Policy*, New York, McGraw-Hill, 1949.

Textile Council. *Cotton and Allied Textiles: a report on present performance and future prospects*, Manchester, 1969.

THOMPSON, S. K. L. 'Barriers to information transfer and technological change' in *Accelerating Innovation*, London, ASLIB, 1970.

TILTON, J. E. *International Diffusion of Technology: the case of semi-conductors*, Washington (DC), The Brookings Institution, 1971.

TOBIN, J. 'Estimation of relationships for limited dependent variables', *Econometrica*, vol. 26, January 1958, pp. 24-36.

TSAO, C. S. and DAY, R. H. 'A process analysis model of the US steel industry', *Management Science*, vol. 17, June 1971, pp. B-588-B-608.

United States Steel Corporation. *The Making, Shaping and Treating of Steel*, 8th ed., Pittsburgh, 1964.

Wirtschaftsvereinigung Eisen und Stahlindustrie. *Statistisches Jahrbuch der Eisen und Stahlindustrie* (annual).

WOHLIN, L. *Forest-based Industries: structural change and growth potential*, Stockholm, IUI, 1970.

II. OFFICIAL PUBLICATIONS

(a) *United Kingdom*

Department of the Environment. *Monthly Bulletin of Construction Statistics*, London, HMSO.

Monopolies Commission. *Flat Glass: report on the supply of flat glass*, HC 83, London, HMSO, 1968.

(b) *United States*

United States Bureau of Mines. *The Use of Oxygen or Oxygenated Air in Metallurgical and Allied Processes* by F. W. Davis, Washington (DC), 1923.

(c) *International*

European Coal and Steel Community. *Balance Sheets of the Steel Companies* by C. Goudima and G. Schumacher, Part I: *Community Countries*; Part II: *Non-Community Countries*, Luxemburg, 1967.

— *Investment in the Community Coalmining and Iron and Steel Industries: summary report on the investment surveys*, Luxemburg (quinquennial).

European Free Trade Association, *EFTA Bulletin*, Geneva (monthly).

Organization for Economic Cooperation and Development. *Gaps in Technology. General Report*, Paris, 1968 and *Analytical Report*, Paris, 1970.

— *NC Machine Tools. Their introduction in the engineering industries*, Paris, 1970.

— *The Iron and Steel Industry in Europe*, Paris (annual).

— *The Textile Industry in OECD Countries*, Paris (annual).

— *Main Economic Indicators*, Paris (monthly).

United Nations Economic Commission for Europe. *Some Important Developments during 1953 in Iron and Steel Technology*, Geneva, 1954.

— *Steel-making Processes*, Geneva, 1962.

— *Economic Aspects of Continuous Casting of Steel*, New York, 1968.

— *Annual Bulletin of Housing and Building Statistics for Europe*, Geneva.

United Nations Statistical Office. *Monthly Bulletin of Statistics*, New York.

— *World Energy Supplies*, New York (annual).

INDEX

PUBLICATIONS OF THE
NATIONAL INSTITUTE OF ECONOMIC
AND SOCIAL RESEARCH

published by
THE CAMBRIDGE UNIVERSITY PRESS

Books published for the Institute by the Cambridge University Press are available through the ordinary booksellers. They appear in the five series below:

ECONOMIC & SOCIAL STUDIES

* At present out of print.

OCCASIONAL PAPERS

* At present out of print.

STUDIES IN THE NATIONAL INCOME AND EXPENDITURE OF THE UNITED KINGDOM

Published under the joint auspices of the National Institute and the Department of Applied Economics, Cambridge.

NIESR STUDENTS EDITION

REGIONAL PAPERS

* At present out of print.